LANDSCAPE,
LAND USE
AND
THE LAW

An introduction to
the law relating
to the landscape
and its use

*This book is dedicated
to
Eleanor
and to
John William
and
Duncan James*

LANDSCAPE, LAND USE AND THE LAW

An introduction to
the law relating
to the landscape
and its use

J.D.C. HARTE
MA, Dip Crim (Cantab)

*of Grays Inn and the
North Eastern Circuit,
Barrister*

*Lecturer in Law,
University of Newcastle upon Tyne*

London
E. & F.N. SPON
New York

First published 1985 by
E. & F.N. Spon Ltd
11 New Fetter Lane, London EC4P 4EE
Published in the USA by
E. & F.N. Spon
733 Third Avenue, New York NY 10017

© 1985 J.D.C. Harte

Printed in Great Britain at the
University Press, Cambridge

ISBN 0 419 12510 8 (cased)
ISBN 0 419 12520 5 (paperback)

British Library Cataloguing in Publication Data

Harte, J.D.C.
  Landscape, land use and the law.
  1. Land use—Law and legislation—England
  I. Title
  344.203'256   KD1125

  ISBN 0–419–12510–8
  ISBN 0–419–12520–5 Pbk

Library of Congress Cataloging in Publication Data

Harte, J. D. C. (J. David C.)
  Landscape, land use and the law.

  Bibliography: p.
  Includes index.
  1. Land use—Law and legislation—Great Britain.
  2. Landscape protection—Law and legislation—Great
  Britian. I. Title.
  KD1125.H35 1985   346.4104'5   84–13840
  ISBN 0–419–12510–8   344.10645
  ISBN 0–419–12520–5 (pbk.)

CONTENTS

FOREWORD

In recent years the law has impinged increasingly on all aspects of land use. There have been important developments in the common law and equity; planning law has grown both by statute and judicial interpretation. Now, administrative law, especially judicial review, is evolving faster than any other branch of our jurisprudence. So, non-lawyers in professions concerned with land use need to have ready and convenient access to the general legal principles affecting their field. This book is designed to satisfy that need. In my view it does so admirably. The author has steered a well judged course between writing a detailed text book suitable only for lawyers and writing so general a survey as to be merely of interest rather than of practical use. I am sure that planners, landscape architects, local government officers, other non-legal specialists and students concerned with land use will find this book invaluable. I wish it every success.

THE HONOURABLE MR JUSTICE TAYLOR

PREFACE

The manuscript for this book was completed early in 1984, and it is hoped that it was a correct statement of the law at that time. Meanwhile, inevitably, the legislative processes, and the courts, have been grinding out new law, although, at least in the areas with which this book is concerned, they have been doing so more slowly than they often do. For example, the present government's proposal to abolish Metropolitan Counties (p. 38) received a set back with the refusal of the House of Lords to approve the imposition of nominated in place of elected councillors, so as to ease the destruction of these authorities (*The Times*, 29 June 1984).

Various tax provisions affecting land use are currently passing through Parliament. Notably, Development Land Tax (p. 99) is now to be chargeable only on development value in any one year of over £75 000. In respect of development carried out by an owner for his own use of the land, payment is to be deferred until he actually disposes of it. Stamp duty (p. 250) is now to be payable only on the conveyance of property worth over £30 000. However, value added tax (p. 98) will now generally be payable on alterations to buildings and civil engineering works, although still not on completely new works.

In some areas, substantial changes may well be introduced before long. The Law Commission has in particular produced a major report on Transfer of Land, the law of positive and restrictive covenants. (1984, Law Com. No. 127, H.C. 201). This recommends replacing the present system whereby restrictive covenants may be attached relatively easily to land, whereas the burden of positive ones is generally difficult to attach, with a new concept of *land obligations*. The benefit and the burden of these would run with land, and they could be negative or positive, although their effect would vary depending on whether they were made between neighbours or were designed for the wider benefit of a development scheme.

One significant new piece of legislation affecting responsibility in land use is the Occupiers' Liability Act 1984. This supersedes the changes with regard to trespassers on land made in case law by the House of Lords in *British Railways Board* v. *Herrington* [1972] A.C. 877. (p. 329). The duty has been clarified which is owed by occupiers, to those who are not lawful visitors under the earlier Occupiers' Liability Act 1957 (p. 327). It is now owed to them in respect of any risk of which the occupier is aware, or has reasonable grounds to believe exists, of their suffering injury on the premises by reason of any danger due to the state of the premises or to things done or omitted to be done on them. The duty is owed to those whom the occupier knows or has reasonable grounds to believe are in the vicinity of the danger or may come into its vicinity, provided, 'the risk is one against which, in all circumstances of the case, he may reasonably be expected to offer the other same protection'. The duty requires the occupier, 'to take such care as is reasonable in all the circumstances of the case to see that', the person to whom the duty is owed, 'does not suffer injury on the premises by reason of the danger concerned'. However, it only applies in respect of injury to the person and not to intruding property. The duty may be discharged, 'by taking such steps as are reasonable in all the circumstances of the case to give warning of the danger concerned or to discourage persons from incurring the risk. The Act does not create any new duty to persons using the highway. It also provides that business occupiers are not prevented by the Unfair Contract Terms Act 1977 (p. 308) from excluding or restricting liability to those who come on to their premises for recreational or educational purposes, unless 'granting such access for the purposes concerned falls within the business purposes of the occupier'.

The courts have contributed recently in two particular areas to the development of the law covered in this book. First, in *Pioneer Aggregates (UK) Ltd* v. *Secretary of State for the Environment* [1984] 2 AUER 358, the House of Lords definitively ruled that planning permission can not generally be abandoned so as to cease to be effective (cf. abandonment of established uses p. 113–4). Pioneer Aggregates claimed to be entitled to extract limestone from quarries near the hamlet of Heathcote in the Peak District National Park, under planning permission granted in 1950, although quarrying on the appeal site had ceased in 1966 and the land had been restored to its previous owners. The House of Lords affirmed the decision of the courts below that the quarry could nevertheless be lawfully reopened. The concept of abandonment has derived from private law and could not be introduced into a clear statutory code which provided for planning permission to run with the development site once it had been granted. In such a case local planning authority would be well advised to restrict the duration of planning consent clearly when it was first granted, and to provide that it should terminate once the land had been restored.

A second significant recent amplification of case law was made by the Court of Appeal in *Rimmer* v. *Liverpool City Council* [1984] 2 W.L.R. 426. Mr Rimmer badly cut his left hand in his council flat in Liverpool when he tripped over some of his son's toys and fell through a glass screen which was a standard feature of the block and which he had previously complained was dangerously thin. The Court indicated that a landlord might generally owe no duty in respect of a dangerous feature in premises which it had let. However, Liverpool City Council did owe a duty because it had constructed the flats itself through its direct works department (cf. pp. 330–2). The case is instructive because it recognises that those responsible for making a building or land unsafe may be liable to someone who suffers some physical injury as a result many years later (p. 304). In the words of Stephenson L.J.:

'It might have been the end of this century before anybody put his hand through one of these glass panels. But defects in design and construction are in most cases likely to cause discoverable injury or damage to persons on the property within a reasonable time after the building has been completed, and we do not foresee a spate of actions too late to be tried fairly for builder owners . . .; the expense of replacing all these panels with thicker glass would be very great. But if the flats are dangerous as they are, the money would be well spent in making them safe.'

J.D.C. HARTE

Faculty of Law
The University
Newcastle upon Tyne
2 July 1984

ACKNOWLEDGEMENTS

Although the defects of this book are the fault of its author, if it finds favour with the reader this may be attributed to many who have helped with ideas, comment and criticism in the course of writing and to those who have provided the illustrations and diagrams.

I am grateful to my colleagues in the Faculty of Law at Newcastle University whose views, whether they complement or challenge my own, have been given generously. In particular I would like to thank John Clark, Ian Dawson, Tim Frazer, Tom Gibbons, John Mickleburgh, Derek Morgan, Mike Rowell, Celia Wells, Gail Williams and Ashley Wilton. I am also grateful to members of other departments as diverse as Town and Country Planning, English, and Religious Studies, who have demonstrated the idea of a University by providing a lawyer with a range of extra legal insights and comments however little justice may seem to be done to these in the text. In particular I would like to thank Cameron Blackhall, Tim Shaw, Kelsey Thornton and John Sawyer, and successive years of landscape, planning, surveying and architectural students, many now in practice. Here too I would like to record my thanks to my brother Stephen Harte for his encouragement and professional comments as a practising architect and landscape architect with Hampshire County Council.

Those who provided me with photographs are acknowledged in the text. However I am also extremely grateful to Mr I. Munro, Head of the Graphics Department and Mr J.W. Young, Supervisor of the Still Photography Section of this University. Mr Munro drew the diagrams and line drawings. Mr Young prepared most of the photographs for publication. In obtaining illustrative material I was further helped by John K. Kilner Esq., of Messrs Hay & Kilner, Bryan D.R. Stevens Esq., of Messrs Nicholson and Martin, B.D. Stearn Esq., Chief Planning Officer of Tandridge District Council and Miss Arnold, the Local History Librarian of Northampton Central Library.

My thanks are also particularly due to Rosemary Jewers who continued to talk to me cheerfully whilst typing the bulk of the manuscript whether deciphering my handwriting or listening for hours to my voice on tape. I am also grateful to Christine Markham who helped Rosemary to meet some of the deadlines and to Jill Pearce who adjusted those deadlines and has throughout the gestation of the book provided tolerant help from the publisher's office.

My greatest debt for tolerance and understanding is to my wife who showed interest and encouragement from the beginning and insulated me from the two small boys with whom she shares the dedication.

J.D.C. HARTE
Faculty of Law
The University
Newcastle upon Tyne

INTRODUCTION:
THE IMPORTANCE OF LAW
FOR THE LANDSCAPE
AND SOME LEGAL BEARINGS

Far spread the moorey ground a level scene
Bespread with rush and one eternal green
That never felt the rage of blundering plough
Though centurys wreathed springs blossom on its brow
Still meeting plains that stretched them far away
In uncheckt shadows of green brown and grey
Unbounded freedom ruled the wandering scene
Nor fence of ownership crept in between
To hide the prospect of the following eye
Its only bondage was the circling sky

   . . .

Fence now meets fence in owners little bounds
Of field and meadow large as garden grounds
In little parcels little minds to please
With men and flocks imprisoned ill at ease
John Clare The Mores

The day is come when I again repose
Here, under this dark sycamore, and view
These plots of cottage-ground, these orchard-tufts,
Which at this season, with their unripe fruits,
Are clad in one green hue, and lose themselves
Among the woods and copses, nor disturb
The wild green landscape. Once again I see
These hedgerows, hardly hedgerows, little lines
Of sportive wood run wild; these pastoral farms,
Green to the very door; and wreaths of smoke
Sent up in silence, from among the trees!
William Wordsworth Tintern Abbey

The shifting pattern of the English countryside may be explained as a result of advances in agricultural technique, or of social or economic development. However, a consciously used instrument of both change and conservation has always been the law. Those ancient open fields with their ridges and furrows, complemented by expanses of common grazing, whose passing John Clare mourned, were established and regulated by customary laws administered in local manorial courts. The most complete survival of this old pattern of agriculture in England, at Laxton in Nottinghamshire, illustrates the difficulty of finding suitable legal machinery to preserve pieces of landscape which do not meet the narrow requirements of modern economics (Fig. 1.1). In the early 1960s Laxton was acquired by the Ministry of Agriculture because of its historical interest. In 1980, the government resolved to sell it together with the rest of the Ministry of Agriculture's 13 000 acres. However, it was difficult to find a buyer prepared to observe the covenants which the government agreed were needed to preserve this 'living museum of the rural past from which most of us sprang'.[1] Laxton was eventually acquired by the Crown Estates which administer the ancient private lands of the Sovereign.

The green patchwork of small fields, embroidered with Wordsworth's straggling hedgerows which replaced the open fields, was the creation of statute law, in the form of Enclosure Acts, first used in the late Middle Ages but most extensively in the eighteenth century. Legal arrangements, which might not be apparent to the passer-by, grouped these fields into farms, some run as independently owned units, others let out as parts of great estates. In some areas, today, the enclosure hedgerows around individual fields have been grubbed up, leaving the boundaries between separate owners standing starkly in a utilitarian panorama. In upland and less fertile areas, miles of dry-stone walling, dating back to when the land was first opened up by great monasteries[2] or earlier, still mark off boundaries between the common grazing of neighbouring settlements. Hillsides, darkened by conifer plantations, reveal recent large-scale intervention of the State, in massive planting on Forestry Commission property, and in grants and tax incentives for private landowners.

In urban areas, variations in building styles and aberrations in street lay-out may reveal smaller-scale legal divisions between properties. The similar design of other buildings may recall that when they were developed they were under unified legal control. An underlying uniformity demonstrates the more recent restrictive powers of local planning authorities operating the law of development control, even though it may often be a dull uniformity, the result of unimaginative developers, uninspired architects and uncreative planners.

For the citizen, alert to the quality of townscape and countryside, as for the professional involved in any way with the land, the law is both a safeguard and an obstacle. Those with rights in land may be restricted in exercising

Fig. 0.1 Laxton ancient field system, Nottinghamshire. By permission of Aerofilms Ltd.

them by others with overlapping rights. A person entitled to shooting rights may prevent a wood being built over by its owner.[3] The tenant and the landlord of a building or a piece of woodland may prevent each other from irreparably damaging the structure of the one or the trees in the other. On the other hand they may thwart one another from carrying out renovation or replanting. The law of nuisance restrains many anti-social uses of land which might affect neighbours, for example, the production of noise or smells it can not normally protect a fine view, either by stopping the destruction of what is attractive, or by preventing the introduction of something new and hideous,[4] but, since 1848, the law has enabled private land owners to make covenants restraining their successors from much activity which might be harmful to the amenity of the neighbourhood.[5]

By comparison with the limited restrictions on land imposed by private law, there are now so many constraints by public law that it may be said that a landowner may do whatever he likes with his own land, provided he does nothing different from what he is doing already. The most comprehensive restraints date from the Town and Country Planning Act of 1947. Under this, and a series of Acts which have succeeded it, new development has generally required planning permission. There are many additional or alternative restrictions over all manner of activities, ranging from the extraction of water to the setting up of caravan sites. It is an open question whether today's landscape is more impoverished by poor schemes getting past these restrictions or by the restrictions themselves stifling original new designs.

(a) Law, morality and justice

Lawyers are preoccupied with semantic precision, because the more clearly laws can be expressed, the easier it is to avoid disputes. However, as soon as we try to identify accurately what the law is, we may begin to ask why the rules which make it up are obeyed. The rules recognized by courts are generally accepted as law by ordinary members of society, because it is recognized that the state has some moral authority, or at least wields power which it is dangerous to challenge. The view that the law expresses some underlying objective morality may involve the idea of a *natural law* which is divinely ordained, or which is the natural pattern for harmonious social relations. Alternatively, the moral authority may be seen as a *consensus*, expressed through democratic processes which are intended to represent the real interest and aspirations of the people as a whole. By contrast, some see the law in *positivist* terms, as a self-contained institution standing in its own right with its own coherent rules and system of enforcement. Those who take a *Marxist* approach see it as a structure used by the classes currently in power to impose their will upon the remainder of society.

The concept of Justice, like that of morality, is used to express some underlying ideal law to which the actual law should correspond. Thus, the manner in which the law is interpreted by judges will, to some extent, depend upon the judges' view of the principles of justice which the law is intended to express. English judges have long recognized, as underlying principles, that private rights of property are to be protected by the law, that individual citizens should be treated as equal before the law and that the trial of disputes should be conducted in accordance with certain recognized standards of *natural justice*. However, solutions which the law provides in one generation may change and even be regarded as immoral by the standards of other times. Thus, land law has changed from a system regulating the mutual rights of private landowners to one where various public controls balance private rights with the public interest. To many, if the old system had continued it would have allowed limited natural resources and a rich heritage of buildings and landscape to be destroyed by private greed, through pollution, over-production and third-rate development. Now the statutory controls which have been introduced are increasingly criticized because they fail to give a real say to members of the public themselves.

Even underlying principles may change. Traditionally a statute would not be interpreted as taking away private property rights unless it clearly so stipulated, usually by providing for compensation. However, with increasing state intervention in the use of land, for the public benefit, judges have softened this principle. In *Westminster Bank* v. *Minister of Housing and Local Government*,[6] the bank was refused permission to build a new strong room, because this would hamper an intended road-widening scheme. The bank appealed to the courts, on the ground that there were alternative statutory powers of prescribing a new building line which could have been used to prevent the extension. Under these, the bank would have been entitled to compensation. The House of Lords upheld the refusal to grant planning permission. Lord Reid accepted the principle that 'a statute should not be held to take away private rights of property without compensation unless the intention to do so is expressed in clear and unambiguous terms', but he went on to rule that this intention could be irresistibly inferred from the statute read as a whole. There, the bank had no right to develop without planning permission, and the local authority had legitimate grounds for refusing planning permission.

Even if the appellants' view of the facts is right, the authority had to choose whether to leave the appellants without compensation or to impose a burden on its ratepayers. One may think that it would be most equitable that the burden should be shared. But the Minister of Transport had made it clear in a circular sent to local authorities in 1954 that there would be no grant if a local authority proceeded in such a way that compensation would be payable, and there is nothing to indicate any disapproval of this policy by Parliament and nothing in any of the legislation to indicate that Parliament disapproved of depriving the subject of compensation. I cannot in these circumstances find any abuse of power in the local authority deciding that the appellants and not its ratepayers should bear the burden.

(b) Common law, equity and statute

English law was originally known as *common law*, because (Fig. 1.2), following the Norman conquest in 1066, and particularly from the reign of Henry II (1133–1189), it was developed as a system common to the whole realm and imposed by centralized royal courts. The royal Chancery, the office of the King's chief minister, provided writs for subjects with grievances, commanding the defendant complained of to attend a royal court for the dispute to be resolved. The most frequent and important of such grievances were concerned with disputes over the control of land. Medieval causes of action were developed to fit specific situations, for example where a son was prevented from taking over land on his father's death. However, initiative for dealing with new situations and providing effective remedies ran out. By the end of the fifteenth century, the Lord Chancellor himself had been allowed by the King to settle disputes where the common law courts proved inadequate, by applying the concept of *equity*. As Lord Chancellor Ellesmere explained,

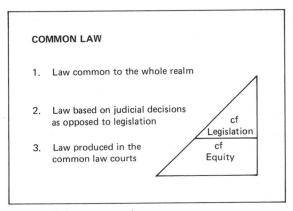

Fig. 0.2 The meaning of the common law.

his office was 'to correct men's consciences for frauds, breaches of trusts, wrongs and oppressions of what nature soever they be, and to soften and mollify the extremity of the law'.[7]

The Lord Chancellor and his deputy, the Master of the Rolls, developed equity into a system of rules parallel with the common law. Notably, they evolved the concept of the trust. By means of this, if property was transferred to anyone so that, in law, he was the owner, but the transfer was on condition that he should hold the property for someone else, Chancery would compel the legal owner to honour this obligation. Similarly, Chancery developed new remedies, notably specific performance and the injunction. The common law courts could sometimes reinstate a person in land from which he had been dispossessed, but generally they were restricted to compensating injured parties by ordering their opponents to pay them damages. Specific performance could be used to compel a person who failed to honour a contract to sell land, actually to transfer it. An injunction could be used to compel a defendant to correct a wrong which he had committed. If he had regularly trespassed on the plaintiff's land, a restrictive injunction would be granted ordering him not to do so again. If he had put up a building on the plaintiff's land, a mandatory injunction could order him to pull it down. By the nineteenth century, equity was as ossified as common law, and the two systems were amalgamated. However, the Chancellor's court has survived as a separate division of the High Court, which was created in 1875. It still specializes in matters such as trusts. Equitable remedies and principles may now be applied by all courts[8] but the concept of equity still survives, for example in a wide discretion of judges in deciding whether to grant injunctions and other equitable remedies.

Although the original common law came to be contrasted with equity, both these bodies of rules were developed, case by case, by judges. By the nineteenth century, it was necessary for major additions and alterations to be made, and Parliament increasingly took the initiative, creating new law in the form of statute. These were supplemented by delegated legislation made under powers, granted in principal Acts, to government ministers or other public officials, such as local councillors. The traditional areas of judge-made law are often termed common-law to contrast with legislation. The United States and Commonwealth countries, influenced by English law, share a common-law tradition. In the United Kingdom the older parts of the law are being progressively codified into statutes and it is the long-term aim of the Law Commission, set up in 1965, to put the entire law into this form. Even then cases decided by judges will continue to provide an important supplementary source of law, filling in the details of legislation and explaining its more general or ambiguous provisions.

(c) Classifications of the law

Legal categories overlap and need to be treated with caution. The law has been likened to a seamless garment. As this book seeks to show, each part relates to many others and can not be looked at in isolation. Many of the classifications used to divide up the law so that it can be studied and taught in a manageable form, result from its historical development. Thus, equity was often treated as a distinct subject for study, although now it is thoroughly entwined with the common law.

The distinction between *public* and *private law* is fundamental to many non-common-law countries. It was found in Roman Law, from which most modern legal systems on the continent of Europe developed. With increasing state intervention, the distinction has been used increasingly in common-law countries. Public law is concerned with the organization of the state and its various accretions, and with the special rules governing the relationships of public bodies with private individuals and organizations. It includes the *constitutional law* governing the various parts of the state, namely the legislature, the executive and the judiciary, and their inter-relation. It also covers the structure and procedure of the legal system, and the legislative and executive functions delegated to local authorities and to public bodies such as statutory undertakers. The significance of various public bodies as sources of law is considered in Chapter 1 of this book. Apart from the rules of *substantive law*, which determine public and private rights and obligations, the rules of *evidence* and *procedure*, which are intended to ensure that issues are resolved fairly, may vitally affect the outcome of a dispute. Modern public law covers many new powers for regulating private activity in the interests of the community as a whole, notably town and country planning restraints on new development, and wide-ranging powers for public bodies compulsorily to purchase private land. The distinction between public and private law cuts across many other categories. Thus there are special rules concerned with

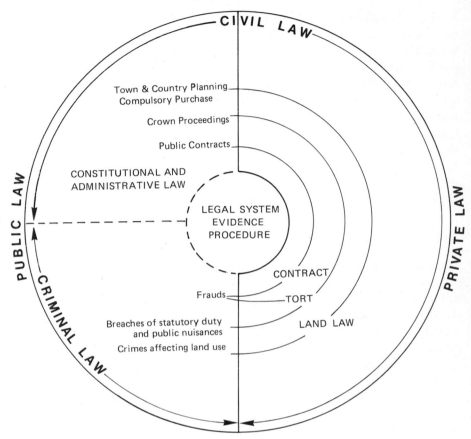

Fig. 0.3 The interrelation of some major legal categories.

publicly owned land, with torts committed by public officials, and with contracts entered into by public bodies. The principles upon which the courts control the exercise of public powers are known as *administrative law* and are outlined in Chapter 8, Sections 8.2 and 8.3 of this book.

The distinction between *civil* and *criminal law* developed in the Middle Ages, when kings were concerned to exert control over the entire country by means of a uniform common law. To maintain order, they punished behaviour which broke the peace, and took the opportunity of gaining revenue by confiscating the goods of offenders or fining them. Today, criminal law is a major part of public law. Crimes are acts or omissions declared by the State to be harmful to the public welfare and which may, therefore, be marked by punishment. They are dealt with in courts which are largely distinct from the Civil Courts. Stricter rules of evidence are applied in criminal cases and different procedures are used. The importance of the criminal law in enforcing responsibility for land is discussed in Chapter 6, Section 6.1.

To swell the royal revenues and to reduce the risk of disorder, by subjects taking the law into their own hands, the royal judges increasingly began to settle ordinary disputes between subjects. Many such disputes were concerned with rights to land, and the King had a particular interest in ensuring that land was held by those who could be relied upon to provide troops in time of war and, later, revenue in the form of taxation. Today *Land Law* is generally treated as dealing with the various legal interests which may be held in land. The art of transferring interests in land, *Conveyancing*, has generally been regarded as a subject for practitioners and has been neglected in academic legal circles. Topics which have been substantially developed by modern legislation are often dealt with separately, such as *Landlord and Tenant*, and *Town and Country Planning*. In this book the public aspects of land law are considered in Chapter 3, traditional private land law in Chapter 4 and the methods of creating and transferring interests in land in Chapter 5. A *tort* is a breach of a legal obligation which was created by the general law rather than by a contract between the parties involved. General aspects of the law of torts are outlined in Chapter 6 and the manner in which this part of the law provides remedies for harm resulting from the use or misuse of land is further discussed in Chapter 7. The law of *contract* provides a framework for agreements made between individuals. In particular it lays down when an agreement will be enforced by the courts and how it will be interpreted. The general principles of the law of contract are briefly reviewed in Chapter 6, Section 6.5.

Classifications for analysing the law are frequently changing. A major English journal concerned with town and country planning law was first published as the *Journal of Planning Law* in the year after the passing of the Town and Country Planning Act 1947 which revolutionized public land control in Britain. It changed its name, in 1954, to the *Journal of Planning and Property Law*, and again, in 1973, to the *Journal of Planning and Environment Law*, so as to extend its scope to the law affecting all aspects of the environment. *Environmental Law* has been chosen in certain law schools to describe courses concerned with public control of land. Elsewhere a different emphasis is reflected in other titles such as *Urban Law*.

In any account of the law it is important to realize that one problem or dispute may involve principles which are dealt with under a number of different headings. There may also be less obvious legal rules which are important. Thus, torts not dealt with here, such as *defamation*, may occasionally have a peripheral bearing upon land use. Defamation consists in publishing material which is likely to expose another person to 'hatred, ridicule or contempt' or which would cause him to be shunned or avoided. If it is in written, or in some other permanent form, defamation constitutes *libel*, and is actionable even if no harm is shown. If it is spoken, it constitutes *slander*. Slander requires proof of harm unless it is of certain blatant types,

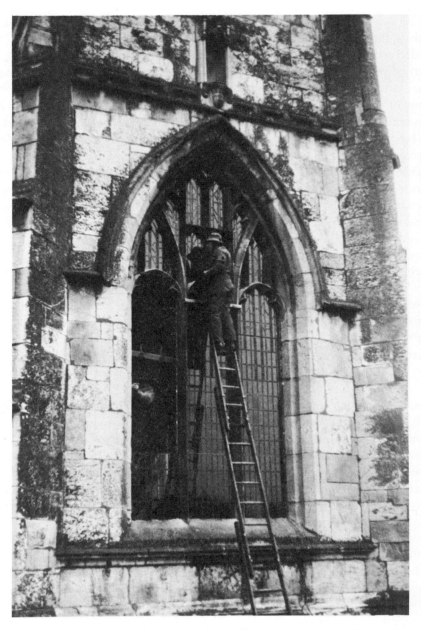

Fig. 0.4 St Augustine's Parish Church, Skirlaugh, Lincolnshire, 'one hundred years on, replacing the glazing which forms part of the 1879 restoration', by kind permission of the Reverend D.W. Perry, Vicar of Skirlaugh and Long Riston.

such as an allegation that the defendant is guilty of a criminal offence, or one which disparages him in respect of his business or profession. In *Botterill* v. *Whytehead*[9] an action was brought by a firm of Weslyan architects, who were restoring South Skirlaugh Parish Church, near Hull, against Whytehead, for writing letters, in which he had abused the firm as incompetent to do the work, because of their Methodist connections (Fig. 0.4). Upholding an award of damages to the firm, Kelly C.B. said:

I am clearly of opinion that to impute to an architect employed in the restoration of an ancient church that he has no experience in the work in which he has been employed is in itself a libel upon the architect in the way of his profession or calling. I think also that the describing him as a Weslyan adds to the injurious character of the letter; and further, that to write of an architect that by his acting in the work in question the masonry of an ancient gem of art will be ignorantly tampered with is in itself libellous and will render an action maintainable.

(d) The importance of law for the land-based professions and for the general public

For the professional concerned with the land, whether as proprietor or developer, private consultant, or public official, the law is a thicket which may all too easily catch the unwary or be used by the knowing to trap others. Anyone concerned with changing the face of the landscape, by building, planting, or excavating, as architect, landscape architect, or engineer, needs to be aware of what the law does and does not allow him to do. Town and country planners structuring the future use of land and controlling its existing use, the surveyor mapping its existing forms and the estate agent concerned with its transfer, all need to recognize the legal framework for the use of land, the legal hurdles to their work and the legal significance of their actions. They must know the duties which the law imposes upon them in their professional capacity, both to clients and to others who may be less obvious.

If a boundary is uncertain, how may it be identified? Would what appears to be a boundary on the ground be recognized by law? If planning consent and other statutory permissions are obtained for building a new housing estate, what private rights may still have to be dealt with before the work can be carried out? If an attractive scheme is created with trees and buildings, how may the law be used to protect it as effectively as possible, and for as long as possible into the future? If a building or a piece of open country is dangerous who is responsible for making it safe? If a person, professing some knowledge of planning law, inaccurately advises a prospective purchaser of land that he will be able to build a hotel on it, and the land is sold to several successive developers on the strength of the advice, what is the legal position of the person giving the advice?

The modern system of development control supposedly operates in the public interest, but it is applied by professional planners, by elected local councillors, and by civil servants acting in the name of the Secretary of State for the Department of the Environment. The views of all of these may be very different from those of the public. Whatever their other skills and experience, these representatives of the public interest may have no training or even belief in aesthetics. If the private citizen is to make any impact on what is done to the landscape he must know something of the relevant law. He himself has very few legal rights as to its enjoyment apart from that of travelling through it as quickly as possible on public routes. However, he may be allowed to express his views on proposed developments which require official permission. If he has some legal interest in a piece of land, whether as the owner of many hectares, or as the tenant of a single terrace house, he may be permitted a greater say. The individual can increase his influence if he acts through pressure groups, such as local amenity or preservation societies, or through national groups, such as the Ramblers' Association or the National Trust. The discovery of a public bridleway by the Ramblers' Association may be a means of stalling the erection of a factory, perhaps forcing the developer to go elsewhere altogether. A treasured piece of land threatened by local authority building may be transferred to the National Trust and made virtually immune from compulsory purchase.

The non-lawyer concerned with land use, whether in a professional capacity or as an ordinary citizen, needs at least to recognize where a legal problem may arise so that he may consult a legal expert. He also needs to understand enough of the law to make use of the advice, which he receives. This book is intended to provide an introduction to those who are aware of these needs.

NOTES: INTRODUCTION

1. Leader, *The Times*, 4 February 1980.
2. Hoskins, W. G. (1955) *The Making of the English Landscape*, Hodder and Stoughton, London, p. 106.
3. *Peech* v. *Best* [1931] 1 K.B. 1. See *post* p. 205.
4. A right to an attractive view cannot even be required as an easement, by long use or otherwise. *Phipps* v. *Pears*]1965] 1 Q.B. 76. See *post* p. 198.
5. *Tulk* v. *Moxhay* [1848] Ph. 774. See *post* p. 215.
6. *Westminster Bank* v. *Minister of Housing and Local Government* [1971] A.C. 508, H.L.
7. *Earl of Oxford's Case* (1615) 1 Rep. in Ch., 1 at p. 6.
8. Supreme Court Act 1981, s. 49.
9. *Botterill* v. *Whytehead* (1879) 41 L.T. 588.

Chapter 1

THE LEGAL BACKGROUND

To reach a conclusion on this matter involved the court in wading through a monstrous legislative morass, staggering from stone to stone and ignoring the marsh gas exhaling from the forest of schedules lining the way on each side. I regarded it at one time, I must confess, as a slough of despond through which the court would never drag its feet, but I have, by leaping from tussock to tussock as best I might, eventually, pale and exhausted, reached the other side where I find myself, I am glad to say, at the same point as that arrived at with more agility by [Lord Denning, M.R.]

Davy v. *Leeds Corporation* [1964] 1 W.L.R. 1218,
Court of Appeal, *per* Harman L.J., at p. 1224

The law which has helped to shape the British landscape consists of rules, recognized at any given time by the established courts as authoritative for regulating human conduct generally, and the control and use of land in particular. The law of England consists of two main sources; first, legislation, that is law made directly by Parliament or by other bodies to which Parliament has delegated its powers, and, secondly, the principles stated in reported cases from the higher courts. The details of legislation are them-selves filled out by case law. *Davy* v. *Leeds Corporation* was concerned with compensation to be paid for property taken in a slum clearance scheme. The three Court of Appeal judges agreed on their conclusion, but, as Harman L.J. showed, they did not reach it for the same reasons. The third judge, Diplock, L.J., likened the relevant legislation to a labyrinth and went on: 'I do not propose to do more by way of introduction than to indicate what I believe to be the sign posts to the right path to the centre of the maze.' The legal answers to many practical problems are equally difficult to find. To some extent this is the fault of those who make the legal rules. However, what may seem to be straightforward to the non-lawyer may be genuinely more complicated. A party to a dispute may fail to realize that a consistent set of rules is sometimes more important than fairness in a particular case. Even if the law is clear it may be difficult to apply it. Courts spend more time deciding the facts of cases than what the law is. For example, if a landowner sues a surveyor for preparing an inaccurate survey, the real dispute may not be concerned with the rules for identifying boundaries, but with conflicting evidence over what the landowner and the surveyor said to each other when they made their contract.

1.1   Parliament and statute

Parliament is the supreme legal authority in the United Kingdom. It can, theoretically, introduce any new law or modify any existing law as it chooses, although in practice it is limited by time and the political pressures on its members, and, as we shall see in Section 1.5 of this chapter, it has transferred some of its powers to the European Community. The British Parliament consists of two Houses, and the Sovereign. It is by their combined authority that Acts of Parliament are enacted. The Sovereign and the original members of the upper House, the House of Lords, are hereditary. Some peers still control large tracts of land, moulded by their ancestors, as country estates or in urban development.[1] From its early days the upper House has included bishops, and from 1876, judges known as Lords of Appeal in Ordinary, appointed for life to deal with final appeals from the court system. Since the Life Peerages Act 1958, other peers have been appointed for life on the nomination of the Prime Minister. Members of the House of Commons are each elected for a local constituency by a straight majority of votes cast by citizens over the age of 18.

1.1.1   Government legislation

Most Acts of Parliament are public and general Acts initiated by the government of the day, which is formed from the political party or parties holding a majority in the House of Commons. Public and general Acts may apply to the whole United Kingdom, although normally there are separate provisions, and often distinct statutes, for Scotland and for Northern Ireland. Thus the Town and Country Planning Act 1971 applies to England and Wales, but there is a separate Town and Country Planning (Scotland) Act 1972.

(a) Parliamentary papers
The detailed form of government legislation is often worked out in the light of public debate on preliminary papers. Although these are not themselves part of the law, they may be published as Parliamentary papers by Her Majesty's Stationery Office. Thus government policy may tentatively be outlined in *green papers*, and more definitely spelled out in *white papers*. Proposals are often published as *command papers* presented to Parliament by formal royal

command. Parliamentary papers also include Bills formally submitted to Parliament as the basis for legislation. A major issue in land use, which illustrates the manner in which government policy becomes legislation, is that of profits resulting from the development of land. Should these be claimed by the community rather than solely benefitting a private developer? During the Second World War the problem was referred by the government to an Expert Committee on Compensation and Betterment, chaired by Lord Justice Uthwatt. His main report was published in 1942 as a command paper (Cmd. 6386). This led to a succession of efforts by Labour Governments to acquire all development profits compulsorily. The latest attempt was outlined in a command white paper entitled *Land* (Cmnd. 5730). This led to both the Community Land Act 1975 and the Development Land Tax Act 1976. The Community Land Act provided a long-term scheme whereby virtually no development was to be carried out except where the relevant land had been acquired by a public authority. The Conservative Government, elected in 1979, promised in its manifesto to repeal the Act. It did so by the Local Government (Planning and Land) Act 1980. Development Land Tax on private developers was intended as a temporary measure until development was finally removed from private hands. The Conservative Government took the view that, by itself, the tax provides a proper balance between public and private interests in developing land. Therefore it has been retained.

(b) Royal Commissions, the Law Commission and similar bodies; consolidating and codifying statutes

If a government wishes a controversial area to be thoroughly investigated, it may set up a Royal Commission, with an independent chairman and members, and a secretariat seconded from the civil service. Such a Royal Commission was set up, under Professor Sir Ivor Jennings, to review the problems of common land. Its report, in 1958 (Cmnd. 462), led eventually to the Commons Registration Act 1965, which provided that many shared rights, for example of grazing and public rights of exercise on open spaces such as village greens, would be extinguished, unless both the land and the rights over it were registered. Independent committees to advise on proposals for law reform may also be appointed by particular government departments. Thus, the Secretary of State for the Environment, in conjunction with the Secretaries of State for Wales and Scotland, set up a committee on planning control over mineral workings chaired by Sir Roger Stevens which reported in 1976. Its proposals were partly implemented in the Town and Country Planning (Minerals) Act 1981. Certain bodies working on law reform are of a more permanent nature. Most significant is the Law Commission, created by Parliament at the instigation of Lord Chancellor Gardiner, in 1965, with full-time commissioners and administrative staff.[2]

These are constantly reviewing the entire law 'with a view to its systematic development and reform', by means of codification. The Commission initiates working papers which are subject to public discussion and lead to final reports which are frequently the basis for legislation. The Law Commission's first programme provided for the codification of important topics concerned with land such as the law of landlord and tenant and the transfer of land. Many of its proposals as to land transfer have now become law, notably in the Law of Property Act 1969 and the Local Land Charges Act 1975. The Law Commission also provides for the consolidation of piecemeal statute law.

(c) Procedure for Government Bills

A government determines its legislative programme in the Future Legislation Committee of the Cabinet. A separate Legislation Committee oversees the drafting of Bills. This is usually carried out by a team of barristers, working in the Civil Service as Parliamentary Counsel. Government Bills may be begun in either House, except that any provision concerned with raising or spending public money is largely kept in the hands of the Commons. In practice, Bills on which the major political parties differ will start in the Commons. Environmental legislation may be controversial and require thorough investigation, but it is not likely to be central to a government's political programme; it may therefore start in the Lords. An example was the Wildlife and Countryside Act 1981, which had major implications for rural conservation, and took three months before it was passed down to the Commons.

Bills begun in the Commons are introduced at a formal *first reading* (Fig. 1.1). The *second reading* consists of a debate on the general principles, followed by a vote. On non-controversial Bills, this debate may take place in a *Second Reading Committee*. The vote is taken in the full House. After the vote on the second reading, the detailed proposals of the Bill are examined at the *committee stage*. In matters of major controversy, the committee is the whole House, but usually it is one of a number of Standing Committees. Generally, political parties are represented on committees in proportion to their numbers in the House as a whole. In committee, amendments may be voted on; this gives private members scope for intervening. The committee stage is followed by a *Report* to the whole House where further amendments may be made by the government or opposition. The *third reading* is usually a formality although there may be a final debate and vote. After the Commons, a Bill passes through a similar procedure in the Lords. Any amendments made in the Lords are reported back to the Commons to accept or reject. The Bill is then transformed into a statute by receiving the *Royal Assent* which is granted automatically. The Parliament Acts 1911–1949 enable a Bill to be sent for the Royal Assent after it has been passed by the Commons but

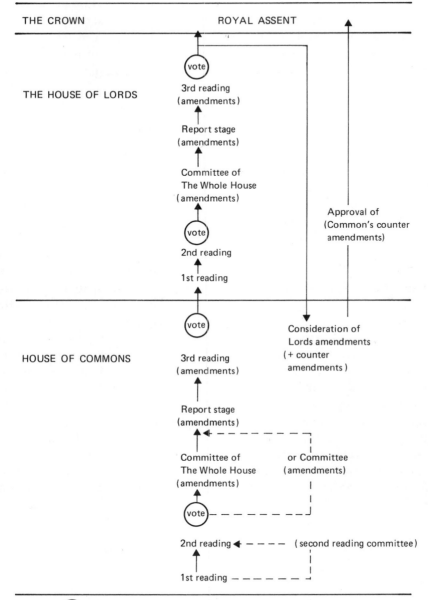

THE CROWN   ROYAL ASSENT

THE HOUSE OF LORDS

(vote)
3rd reading
(amendments)

Report stage
(amendments)

Committee of
The Whole House
(amendments)

(vote)
2nd reading

1st reading

Approval of
(Common's counter
amendments)

(vote)

HOUSE OF COMMONS   3rd reading
(amendments)

Report stage
(amendments)

Committee of
The Whole House
(amendments)

(vote)

2nd reading

1st reading

Consideration of
Lords amendments
(+ counter
amendments)

or Committee
(amendments)

(second reading committee)

N.B. (vote) denotes opportunities for voting on the principle involved in the Bill

Fig. 1.1 Typical procedure for Government Bills beginning in the House of Commons.

rejected by the Lords. First, any Bill which the Lords have failed to pass within one month nevertheless becomes law if it is certified by the Speaker of the Commons as a Money Bill. Secondly, a non-Money Bill may become law without the agreement of the Lords, if it is passed by the Commons, in two consecutive sessions, provided there is an interval of at least one year between the Commons' second reading at the first attempt and third reading at the second attempt. The one situation where the approval of both Houses is always required is where a Bill seeks to extend the maximum duration of a Parliament beyond five years.

(d) Monitoring the operation of government legislation

Even non-controversial statutes require adapting and updating. The operation of an Act may be monitored by the government department which sponsored it. The Law Commission may also review a statute's progress, particularly if it is amended by later Acts, and the combined material needs to be consolidated into a new omnibus statute. The Town and Country Planning Act 1971, and the Highways Act 1980 were consolidating statutes based on work of the Law Commission. Other public bodies are given the task of reporting regularly to Parliament on the operation of statutes which they are responsible for administering. Reports may consist of accounts, such as those produced annually for the ironstone restoration fund under the Mineral Working Acts 1951 and 1971, or they may provide a full review of work for the past year, as do the reports of the Nature Conservancy Council,[3] and of the Ancient Monuments Boards,[4] and Historic Buildings and Monuments Commission[5] for the various parts of the United Kingdom. The standing Royal Commission on Environmental Pollution prepares its own programme and has already reported on industrial pollution, pollution of estuaries and coastal waters, air pollution and the environmental aspects of nuclear power.[6] Its work led to the passing of the Control of Pollution Act 1974, which recast, and considerably extended, previous legislation on pollution. The House of Commons itself monitors the expenditure, administration and policy of government departments by means of twelve select committees set up in 1980 under Standing Order 86A.

1.1.2   Non-government legislation

(a) Private members Bills

Private members of Parliament are allowed limited time by the government to introduce, on their own account, Bills which can become public and general Acts on matters on which the government does not wish to take a lead. Ten Friday afternoons during each Parliamentary session are allotted for this purpose and Bills are selected on a ballot. The government may allow time for a Bill of public interest to be passed right through. If such a Bill involves use of public money, it must be approved by the government. A private member's Bill introduced in the House of Lords is unlikely to be found time in the Commons unless a similar Bill is begun there at the same time.

(b) Local and personal Acts

As Parliament is the ultimate source of law, its authority may be sought for certain purposes by local authorities, statutory undertakers or even private individuals. Such authority may be given in local and personal Acts. Thus the Tyne and Wear Act 1980, replacing the provisions of well over 100 Acts relating to earlier local authorities, grants powers to the metropolitan county of Tyne and Wear ranging from the waterproofing of buildings left exposed when others are demolished, to erecting street kiosks, and to coping with feral pigeons and gulls which cause a nuisance on the highway. In the same year, acts were passed to empower the Eastbourne Harbour Company to construct new harbour works, to reconstitute the Trustees of the Clifton Suspension Bridge in Bristol, and to dispose of the property of the Quaker Meeting House at Reigate and of the burial ground of John Wesley's Chapel at City Road in London.

Local and personal Acts may be initiated in either House, but follow a special procedure. Parliamentary Standing Orders require that local Bills be advertised by their promoters in the locality to which they are to apply and that plans and other details be deposited locally for public inspection. Landowners whose rights may be affected must be individually notified. The second reading deals with any national policy raised by the Bill. The committee stage only takes place if there are objections. It is less like a debate than an inquiry, with arguments presented by Counsel both for the promoters and for the objectors. Unopposed Bills are scrutinized by Parliamentary clerks to ensure that any private rights affected are safeguarded. However, if any such rights are overlooked, a private Act cannot be challenged in the courts any more than can a public one. This was finally made clear by the House of Lords in *Pickin* v. *British Railway Board*.[7] The Railway Board had passed a private Act, the British Railways Act 1968, to ensure that when it closed down any railway line it would retain the land on which the track ran. This involved repealing the effect of over 100 Victorian private Acts obtained by the original railway companies. These had provided that, where lines were closed, the land on which they were built would revert to the neighbouring landowners. Mr Pickin, a railway enthusiast, claimed such rights over a section of the old Bristol and Exeter Railway Company line in Somerset between Clevedon and Yatting. He objected to the courts that British Railways' proposals had not been deposited with Somerset County Council, as Parliamentary Standing Orders required, but the House of Lords held that a private Act could not be impugned in the courts even if the promoters had acted fraudulently.

   Certain Bills are regarded as hybrids. Although basically public Bills, they
may especially affect a particular locality. An example was the Maplin
Development Bill, providing for the implementation of the Maplin scheme
for a third London airport.[8] To protect local rights, after the second reading,
and before the main committee stage of such a Bill, a select committee is
appointed to hear petitions from objectors.

NOTES: SECTION 1.1

1. Newby, H. (1979), *Green and Pleasant Land*, Hutchinson, London.
2. The Law Commissions Act 1965.
3. Nature Conservancy Council Act 1973, sched. 3 para. 17.
4. Ancient Monuments and Archaeological Areas Act 1979, s. 23.
5. National Heritage Act 1983, sched. 3, para. 13.
6. Command Papers (1972) 4894 and 5054; (1976) 6371 and 6618.
7. *Pickin* v. *British Railways Board* [1974] A.C. 765.
8. The Maplin Development Act was passed in 1973 and repealed by the Maplin
   Development Authority (Dissolution) Act 1976.

1.2   The courts and case law

The second major source of English law consists of cases decided by judges in
the higher courts. Many such cases are concerned with land and its use.
England and Wales share a single system of courts, and Scotland and
Northern Ireland have their own systems. In England, following an initial
hearing locally of any disputed matter, there is usually provision for two
successive appeals. The higher appeal courts, namely Divisional Courts, the
Court of Appeal and the House of Lords sit only in London. The legal system
is divided into courts which deal primarily with criminal cases and others
which handle civil proceedings, but there is an overlap, with certain courts
having both a criminal and a civil jurisdiction. Most judges may be called
upon to sit in more than one court and in particular to deal with both civil and
criminal proceedings. The English legal system has itself contributed to the
enrichment of the urban scene by a number of notable buildings (Fig. 1.2).
British courts are no longer entirely self-contained. As we shall see in Section
1.5, matters touching on the law of the European Community, in either the
criminal or the civil field, may be referred to the European Court for its
authoritative ruling.

1.2.1   Customary Law

Many of the rules developed in case law originated in ancient customs
rationalized and applied to the whole country. These include ancient rights of
the public to navigate and to fish in tidal waters. Certain customs in different
parts of the country survived as exceptions to the common law. English Land

Fig. 1.2 The Moot Hall, Newcastle upon Tyne, 1978, by kind permission of the City Engineer's Photographic Department.

Law was overhauled by statute in 1925. At that time, the common law provided that when a person died intestate, his freehold land passed to his eldest son, if he had one. In Nottingham and some other ancient towns, an exception survived, known as *Borough English*, that the youngest son succeeded. In Kent, the custom of *Gavelkind* provided that all sons shared the land. From 1925 the general rule was established that, on intestacy, after provision has been made for any surviving spouse, children share interests in land and personal property equally.[1] Other local customary variations may still be of importance. For example, if standing timber has been sold or if a tenant claims to remove wood not amounting to timber his rights will vary in different parts of the country. At common law, timber consists of sound oak, ash and elm trees with over twenty years of growth.[2] However, by custom, beech trees are included in Gloucestershire, Hampshire, Bedfordshire and Buckinghamshire, but not in Oxfordshire. Birch, willow and even thorn are regarded as timber in certain areas.[3] As we shall see in Chapter 3 Section 3.5 local customs may also provide rights for the benefit of the inhabitants of particular localities, such as rights of way to a church.

1.2.2   Judicial attitudes affecting land use (Fig. 1.3)

The attitudes of prominent judges to matters such as the amenity value of land, may have significant effects upon the law. In the nineteenth century, judges shared the prevalent enthusiasm for industrial expansion and declined to protect even private land owners from the unpleasantness of industrial activity in areas which were suitable for its expansion, unless the industry caused tangible physical harm to neighbouring land. Thus, in 1874, in *Salvin* v. *North Brancepeth Coal Company*,[4] the courts refused to help Mr Salvin when he sued the owners of Littleburn Colliery in County Durham, to stop them operating 254 coke ovens at their coal pit which was 1000 yards from his mansion. In a passage, whose lyricism reads ironically to late twentieth-century ears, James L.J. explained why he would not be prepared to intervene in any such case unless physical harm were shown to the land.

It would have been wrong, as it seems to me, for this Court in the reign of *Henry VI*, to have interfered with the further use of sea coal in *London*, because it had been ascertained to their satisfaction, or predicted to their satisfaction, that by the reign of Queen *Victoria* both white and red roses would have ceased to bloom in the *Temple Gardens*. If some picturesque haven opens its arms to invite the commerce of the world, it is not for this Court to forbid the embrace, although the fruit of it should be the sights, and sounds, and smells of a common seaport and ship-building town, which would drive the Dryads and their masters from their ancient solitudes.

With respect to this particular property before us, I observe that the Defendants have established themselves on a peninsula which extends far into the heart of the ornamental and picturesque grounds of the Plaintiff. If, instead of erecting coke ovens at that spot, they had been minded, as apparently some persons in the neighbourhood on the other side have done, to import ironstone, and to erect smelting furnaces, forges, and mills, and had filled the whole of the peninsula with a mining and manufacturing village, with beershops and pig-styes and dog-kennels, which would have utterly destroyed the beauty and the amenity of the Plaintiff's ground, this Court could not, in my judgment, have interfered. A man to whom Providence has given an estate, under which there are veins of coal worth perhaps hundreds or thousands of

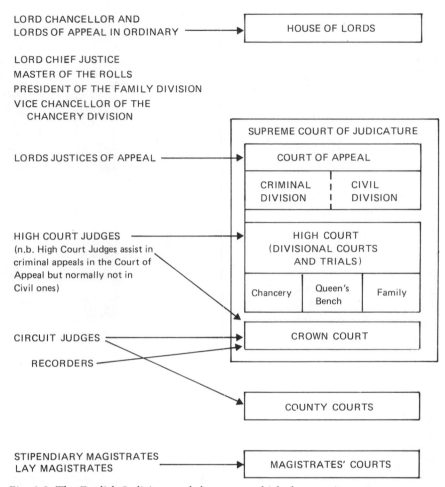

LORD CHANCELLOR AND
LORDS OF APPEAL IN ORDINARY ⟶ HOUSE OF LORDS

LORD CHIEF JUSTICE
MASTER OF THE ROLLS
PRESIDENT OF THE FAMILY DIVISION
VICE CHANCELLOR OF THE
 CHANCERY DIVISION

SUPREME COURT OF JUDICATURE

LORDS JUSTICES OF APPEAL ⟶ COURT OF APPEAL

CRIMINAL | CIVIL
DIVISION | DIVISION

HIGH COURT JUDGES ⟶ HIGH COURT
(n.b. High Court Judges assist in (DIVISIONAL COURTS
criminal appeals in the Court of AND TRIALS)
Appeal but normally not in
Civil ones)

Chancery | Queen's Bench | Family

CIRCUIT JUDGES ⟶ CROWN COURT

RECORDERS

COUNTY COURTS

STIPENDIARY MAGISTRATES
LAY MAGISTRATES ⟶ MAGISTRATES' COURTS

Fig. 1.3 The English Judiciary and the courts which they service.

pounds per acre, must take the gift with the consequences and concomitants of the mineral wealth in which he is a participant.

Nearly ninety years later, in 1962, judges could be equally reluctant to recognize the amenity value of what remained from the industrial revolution. In *Festiniog Railway Company* v. *Central Electricity Generating Board*[5] the railway company was rehabilitating an old slate railway between Blaenau-Ffestiniog and Portmadoc (Figs 1.4 and 1.5). It had already opened the lower section of the line to Tan-y-Bwlch and wished to extend it, but was prevented from doing so by the Central Electricity Generating Board which compulsorily acquired part of the line, including a tunnel which it flooded. The railway company claimed that compensation of £180 000 should be paid to allow for the construction of a diversion. The Lands Tribunal, which was

Fig. 1.4 The track of the Festiniog Railway through the Ystradau Valley in 1954 during the closure period, by kind permission of Mr M Wheeler.

Fig. 1.5 The same scene as in the previous plate, in 1982. The tide in the reservoir is rising to flood the old formation, whilst a train passes on the new deviation line above. The G.E.C.B. power station can be seen in the right centre background, by kind permission of the Festiniog Railway Company.

responsible for assessing compensation, had power to award the reasonable cost of equivalent reinstatement but refused to do so. The Court of Appeal confirmed that the Lands Tribunal had a discretion in making such a decision and had properly exercised it. There was a dispute over whether the railway was run primarily as a commercial venture or as an amenity to benefit visitors and others. In either event, the cost of reinstatement was clearly much greater than the market value of the land. Ormerod L.J. showed sympathy for the aspirations of the company to preserve 'something of historic interest'. He stressed the attractions of the route and the unique form of the rolling stock. Pearson L.J. spoke less enthusiastically of 'the unusual experience of a ride in an ancient carriage drawn by an ancient engine along the ancient narrow-gauge track . . .', Harman L.J. was least appreciative: 'It may amuse a large number of people to go for a trip on this picturesque route drawn by a peculiar engine', but the running of the railway was 'a whim or hobby of some railway enthusiasts, who could not be said to be a class of the public and who might at any time lose their enthusiasm.' The scepticism of Harman L.J. was eventually confounded because the Festiniog Railway Company went on in a later hearing to convince the Lands Tribunal that it was entitled to sub-stantial compensation on the basis that the line was commercially viable, and the line was eventually rebuilt.

1.2.3 Civil and criminal proceedings

Today, many situations can give rise to both criminal and civil proceedings. A vandal who hacks down a tree or defaces a building with graffiti may be prosecuted for criminal damage and also sued by the owner for compensation in a civil court. If there is a protection order on the tree, or the building is listed, the vandal may further be prosecuted for abusing these safeguards. An industrialist who allows contaminated water to pollute a river may be prosecuted for breaking provisions of the Rivers (Prevention of Pollution) Acts 1951–1961 and be sued in the civil courts by those whose fishing rights are harmed or whose banks are affected.

Different procedures apply to criminal and civil proceedings. A person can only be convicted of a criminal offence if the prosecutor establishes the necessary ingredients of the offence so that the court is 'sure' that they existed, or, as is often said, if it is satisfied 'beyond reasonable doubt'.[6] In a civil dispute, the court decides whether the allegation is more probably true than not. Similarly, a person charged with a crime is generally notified of the allegation against him, and, on a serious charge, provided with statements of the evidence, but is not normally obliged to reveal his defence before the trial. In a civil case, both sides must exchange pleadings containing details of facts which they intend to prove, and also any relevant documents and reports from experts, but neither side is obliged to reveal who his other witnesses are or what they will say.

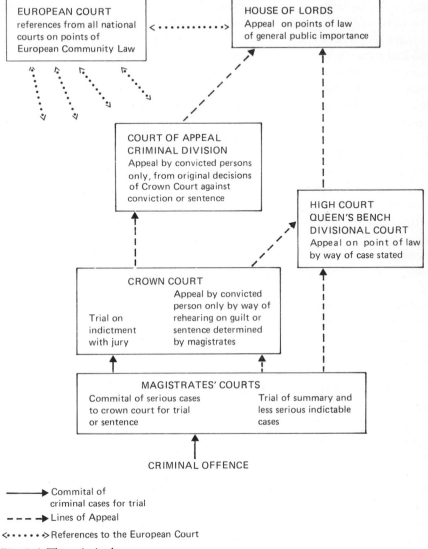

Fig. 1.6 The criminal court system.

(a) The criminal court system (Fig. 1.6)

The foundation of the English criminal court system is the *magistrates' courts*, which have existed in their present form from the nineteenth century. Lay magistrates' courts consist of from two to seven justices who each sit about two days a month. They are advised by a legally qualified clerk, but he does not take part in their decisions. In London and a few provincial centres there are full-time, salaried, stipendiary magistrates who are qualified as barristers or solicitors. Minor, or *summary* offences are tried by magistrates themselves. Serious cases may be committed for trial in the *Crown Court*. The most serious offences of all, such as murder, rape and aggravated burglary, must be committed to the Crown Court for trial. Many offences may be tried in either court, depending on the circumstances.[7] Even for an offence which might have been sent to the Crown Court for trial, magistrates cannot impose more than six months imprisonment and no greater fine than £1000, but in certain circumstances they may send a convicted offender to the Crown Court if they believe he requires a heavier sentence. Offences concerned with the misuse of land which might reach the Crown Court for trial or sentence include arson and serious examples of pollution of land or water with poisonous chemicals.

Trial at the Crown Court is before a legally qualified High Court or Circuit judge or a Recorder. The attraction for an accused person is that if he denies his guilt this is determined by a jury of twelve ordinary men and women selected from most citizens on the electoral register between the ages of 18 and 65.[8] Jury verdicts may in certain circumstances be by a majority but even then if more than two dissent from the majority the case must be retried. The judge is restricted to controlling the proceedings, summarising the facts and directing the jury on the law. Criminal proceedings may generally be brought by any member of the public, but in the Crown Court, they must be prepared by a solicitor, and usually presented by a barrister.

Appeals from trial in a magistrates' court may take two forms. A defendant is always entitled to a re-hearing in the Crown Court as to his conviction or sentence.[9] This is by a judge or Recorder sitting with a new panel of magistrates rather than with a jury. Either the accused, or the prosecution, may appeal to the High Court on a point of law from the original magistrates' court hearing[10] or from the Crown Court after a re-hearing.[11] On the request of the appellant the court *states a case*, setting out its decision and the findings upon which it was made. The appeal is heard by what is known as a *divisional court* of two, or three Queen's Bench Division High Court judges. From a conviction or sentence in the Crown Court, the defendant, but not the prosecution, may appeal to the *Criminal Division of the Court of Appeal*.[12] The prosecution has no power to challenge an acquittal in the Crown Court, but, if it is dissatisfied on the judge's direction, the Attorney General may refer a point of law raised in the case to the Court of Appeal for a ruling.[13] Whatever the ruling is it will not affect the person who has been acquitted. If a divisional court[14] or the Court of Appeal[15] certifies that a case raises a point of law of general public importance, either the defence, or the prosecution, may obtain the leave of that Court, or of the House of Lords, to make a final appeal to the *House of Lords*. There is only a handful of criminal appeals to the House of Lords each year.

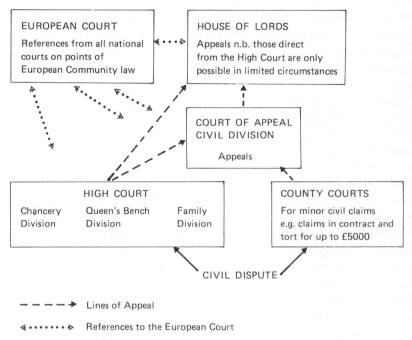

Fig. 1.7 The civil court system.

(b) The civil court system (Fig. 1.7)

Apart from their criminal jurisdiction, magistrates' courts deal with some minor but common civil proceedings, such as those brought to recover rates and taxes and payments for services provided by the nationalized industries. Most civil cases are dealt with in county courts or in the High Court. *County courts* were introduced for small claims in 1846. At present they are largely regulated by the County Courts Act 1959. They have jurisdiction up to £5000 in most civil matters,[16] but in some cases the jurisdiction is more substantial. It includes actions for the recovery of land with a rateable value of up to £1000.[17] Proceedings are heard by circuit judges, or, if less than £500 is involved, may be dealt with by county court registrars.[18] These are responsible for the administration of the county courts. They timetable hearings and oversee the preliminary paper work exchanged between the parties. Registrars also hold preliminary hearings on interlocutory points, such as demands for disclosure of documents by one side to the other, or requests for amplification of written pleadings setting out each party's case.

Major civil matters are dealt with in the *High Court*. This was created in 1875,[19] together with the Court of Appeal, as part of a new Supreme Court, rationalizing a confusion of older courts. The High Court consists of three divisions, in each of which trials are conducted by High Court judges. Cases concerned with the environment are likely to be heard in the Chancery or Queen's Bench Divisions. The third part of the High Court is the more specialized Family Division. The *Chancery Division* is the successor to the Lord Chancellor's Court. It still deals with matter such as trusts and restrictive covenants which were developed in that court, and which may greatly affect the use of land. The Chancery Division has also been entrusted with recently expanded or newly created areas of land law, such as relations between landlord and tenant. A divisional court deals with appeals from county courts on land registration matters.[20] The largest division of the High Court is the *Queen's Bench*. A dispute arising from bad workmanship alleged against an architect or landscape architect, a claim by a person injured whilst visiting premises, or an action brought to control a legal nuisance, would all be dealt with here. The Queen's Bench has an appellate jurisdiction, mainly from magistrates' courts, in summary criminal matters and non-matrimonial civil proceedings. The Queen's Bench divisional Court, of two, or three judges, also has a major supervisory jurisdiction over administrative decisions. This may be exercised under a statutory right of appeal, as from the Secretary of State for the Department of the Environment on a point of law arising on a planning matter, or by virtue of general powers of judicial review of administrative decisions. Both are more fully considered in Chapter 8, Section 8.2. Administrative work of the High Court, including hearings on many interlocutory matters or preliminary points, is handled in London by Masters of the High Court and in the provinces by High Court registrars.

Generally, civil appeals lie as of right to the *Court of Appeal, Civil Division* from the county courts,[21] and from the High Court, both where a case has been tried there by a single judge and after a judicial review.[22] Appeals from the Court of Appeal, Civil Division, lie to the *House of Lords*, even on an issue of fact, provided either court grants leave. To save expense, and to speed up justice, *leap frog* appeals are possible direct from the High Court to the House of Lords, with the consent of the House of Lords. The parties must agree, and the High Court must have certified, that a point of law of general public importance is involved, which it has itself fully considered, and which relates wholly or mainly to the construction of an enactment or of a statutory instrument, or on which there already exists a decision binding the High Court.[23]

1.2.4   The legal profession

The English legal profession consists of two branches. An increasing minority of each are now employed as full-time legal advisers in central or local government, or in businesses. The majority are in private practice. Members of *the Bar* belong to one of four Inns of Court (fig. 1.8), ancient professional societies, resembling university colleges, which act together through a

Fig. 1.8 The walks, Grays Inn, January 1984.

common Senate of the Inns of Court and the Bar. The profession elects a separate Bar Council which deals with matters of professional discipline, payment and conditions of work. Senior barristers are granted the title of *Queen's Counsel* on the recommendation of the Lord Chancellor. They deal only with major cases and are usually assisted by a junior barrister. The *solicitors'* profession has a membership of over 40 000, some ten times that of the Bar. It is organized by the Law Society, which operates under Royal Charter. Most judicial appointments are confined to experienced barristers. However, a solicitor may become a recorder and then be promoted to circuit judge.[24] The right to appear on behalf of a client in the higher courts is confined to barristers, but solicitors may appear as advocates in magistrates' and county courts and to a limited extent in the Crown Court. On the other hand, a layman who wishes to be advised or represented in court by a barrister can only do so through an intermediary solicitor. This restrictive practice is intended to insulate barristers from over-involvement with individual clients and to free them to act as specialists in advocacy. They also act as consultants on difficult points of law, and prepare pleadings and other paper work for court proceedings. Some barristers confine themselves to one speciality such as town and country planning law. In addition to advocacy in the lower courts, solicitors in private practice provide advice and skills over the whole range of legal work. They have a monopoly in carrying out conveyancing of houses and land in general. This reduces the risk of titles, especially of unregistered land, being confused. Legal advice, and, even more, court proceedings, are very costly and the Law Society supervises a state legal aid scheme under which free or subsidized legal advice and representation are provided for those with limited means. Barristers, and probably solicitors, enjoy a limited immunity from claims for negligence in the conduct of any case in court or in preliminary work which is intimately connected with a court hearing.[25]

The head of the Bar is the Attorney-General. He is a member of the government, which he advises on legal matters and represents in major court cases. His deputy holds the office of Solicitor-General. Most criminal prosecutions in England and Wales are handled by solicitors instructed by local police. Usually such solicitors hold full-time appointments. Central control over criminal cases is exercised by the Director of Public Prosecutions, a barrister or solicitor of at least ten years standing, appointed under the Prosecution of Offences Act 1979 by the Home Secretary, and subject to the direction of the Attorney-General. Certain serious, controversial or difficult classes of case, must be reported to the Director of Public Prosecutions, and he may take over the conduct of any prosecution. In England it is still possible for a private person to start a prosecution for most types of offence although this is rare in practice. For a range of statutory offences, however, prosecutions may only be brought by the police or by some other specified public body or with the consent of the central prosecuting authorities.

1.2.5 Peripheral judicial bodies

Many judicial decisions are made by bodies outside the main Court system. Some of these are called courts, and others, tribunals. Similar decisions may be made by administrative bodies such as local planning authorities or the Department of the Environment. These often have a formal system of appeals to the main court structure. The decisions of such bodies are not treated as binding in later cases as are those of the higher central courts, but they are often followed.

(a) The Judicial Committee of the Privy Council

The Judicial Committee of the Privy Council consists of those judges who deal with appeals in the House of Lords, together with distinguished Commonwealth judges. It hears appeals mainly from a number of Commonwealth countries. Although it is strictly outside the British court hierarchies, its rulings are given respect similar to those of the House of Lords. One aspect of the Privy Council jurisdiction is the hearing of appeals from ecclesiastical courts. These are often concerned with the granting of faculties, a special form of control over alterations to Anglican church buildings which takes the place of secular listed building control.

(b) Coroners' courts

The coroner is an official who originated in the twelfth century to supervise the collection of royal revenue. Today, coroners are barristers, solicitors or medical practitioners of at least five years standing, who are appointed by local authorities, generally County Councils,[26] to investigate cases of sudden death. They are also responsible for deciding whether buried gold or silver were hidden by some unknown person in which case they are treasure trove and belong to the Crown. Coroners thus occasionally play an important role in identifying sites of historical importance where burials of gold or silver coins or artefacts are discovered. A coroner may hold a public inquest, sometimes with a jury. As he takes the initiative in calling witnesses, an inquest resembles continental legal proceedings rather than those of a normal English court where the parties choose the evidence and generally frame the issues for the court to determine.

(c) The Lands Tribunal[27]

The Lands Tribunal was created by the Lands Tribunal Act 1949 to deal with land valuation, particularly in disputes over compensation for compulsory purchase. Its jurisdiction also includes discharging or modifying restrictive covenants on land.[28] Its members, who may sit singly or together, are appointed by the Lord Chancellor. The President must be a barrister of at least seven years standing, and other members may be lawyers or persons appointed in consultation with the President of the Royal Institute of Chartered Surveyors as experts in land valuation. The Lands Tribunal operates like a court under procedures laid down in rules prescribed by the Lord Chancellor.[29] Its decisions are given in writing, with reasons, and any aggrieved person may appeal direct to the Court of Appeal by requiring the Tribunal to state a case.[30]

1.2.6   Arbitration

Parties to a dispute may agree to refer it to arbitration instead of using court proceedings. This allows for specialist matters, such as financial accounts, or the quantities and qualities in a building or landscape contract, to be determined by experts in the relevant fields. An arbitration may be heard sooner than a court case and may be dealt with more informally and speedily, although, in practice, payment of the arbitrator, as well as legal representatives, may make such proceedings as costly as those in a court. In practice, most private law arbitrations are provided for in written contracts anticipating a possible dispute, and are regulated by the Arbitration Acts 1950 and 1979. Arbitration is also sometimes imposed under various statutes.[31] These frequently incorporate the provisions of the Arbitration Act.

Normally the parties agree an arbitrator. Sometimes each party appoints one, and if necessary these will choose an umpire to make the final decision.[32] An arbitration decision is expressed in the form of an award.[33] With the consent of the High Court, this may be enforced by the parties as if it were a judgment of that court.[34] Generally this jurisdiction of the court may not be ousted altogether. The court may be needed to appoint an arbitrator if the parties fail to do so.[35] It will also intervene if there is some fundamental irregularity, such as fraud,[36] or if the arbitrator has exceeded his jurisdiction. The court may stay the arbitration, and, if necessary, set aside the award.[37] Under the Arbitration Act 1979, where an arbitration raises some initial point of law, this may be referred to the High Court, before the arbitration, by all the parties, or by any party having the support of the arbitrator, provided this will produce a substantial saving in costs.[38] After the award, an appeal on a point of law may be brought and the court may confirm, vary or set aside the award or remit it to the arbitrator or umpire with the court's ruling.[39] These appeal provisions as to a point of law may be excluded in writing by the parties.[40]

NOTES: SECTION 1.2

1. Administration of Estates Act 1925, s. 46, as amended by Administration of Justice Act 1977.
2. *Honywood* v. *Honywood* (1874) 18 L.R. Eq. 306.
3. An authority discussing a number of the variations is *Dashwood* v. *Magniac* [1891] 3 Ch. 306, C.A.
4. *Salvin* v. *North Brancepeth Coal Company* (1874) 9 Ch. App. Cas. 705, Court of Appeal in Chancery. See further *post* p. 347.
5. *Festiniog Railway Company* v. *Central Electricity Generating Board* (1962) 13 P. & C.R. 248, C.A.
6. *Woolmington* v. *D.P.P.* [1935] A.C. 462, H.L.
7. Magistrates' Courts Act 1980, s. 17.
8. Juries' Act 1974, s. 1.
9. Magistrates' Courts Act 1980, s. 108.
10. Ibid. s. 111.
11. Supreme Court Act 1981, s. 28.
12. Criminal Appeal Act, 1968, s. 1.
13. Criminal Appeal Act 1968, s. 1.
14. Administration of Justice Act 1960, s. 1.
15. Criminal Appeal Act 1968, s. 33.
16. County Courts Act 1959, s. 39, and S.I. 1981 No. 1123.
17. County Courts Act 1959, s. 48 and Administration of Justice Act 1973, s. 6, and Sched. 2.
18. County Court Rules, 1981, Order 21, Rule 5.
19. Judicature Acts 1873–1875. The present Act governing the constitution of the High Court is the Supreme Court Act 1981.
20. Rules of the Supreme Court, Order 93, Rule 10.

21. County Courts Act 1959, Part V as amended by the Supreme Court Act 1981.
22. Supreme Court Act 1981, s. 15.
23. Administration of Justice Act 1969, Part II.
24. Courts Act 1971, ss. 21 and 16 and Administration of Justice Act 1977, s. 12.
25. *Saif Ali* v. *Sydney Mitchell and Co.* [1980] A.C. 198, H.L.
26. Coroners (Amendment) Act 1926, s. 1.
27. See also Agricultural Land Tribunals *post* p. 184 and Rent tribunals *post* p. 185.
28. See *post* p. 258.
29. Lands Tribunal Rules, 1975, S.I. 1975, No. 299.
30. Lands Tribunal Act 1949, s. 3.
31. For example Coast Protection Act 1949.
32. Arbitration Act 1950, s. 8 as amended by Arbitration Act 1979, s. 6.
33. Arbitration Act 1950, s. 13.
34. Ibid. s. 26.
35. Ibid. s. 10 and Arbitration Act 1979, s. 6 (4).
36. Arbitration Act 1950, s. 24.
37. Ibid. s. 23.
38. Arbitration Act 1979, s. 2.
39. Ibid. s. 1.
40. Ibid. s. 3.

1.3   Central and local government: subordinate legal materials

In addition to making legislation itself, Parliament may delegate to public officials in local or central government, power to make subordinate legislation in the form of statutory instruments or byelaws. These have the same authority as statutes, although within narrower limits. As we shall see in Chapter 8, Section 8.2, unlike statutes they are subject to control by the courts. Other decisions made by administrators are applied consistently even though they have no strict legal authority.

1.3.1   Central government

The decisions of Parliament are effectively those of the government of the day. Ministers are in theory merely advisors to the sovereign in whose name they make their decisions. In practice the policy of government is decided by regular meetings of leading ministers making up the *Cabinet*. This has no formal legal powers, and its policies are carried out through individual ministries or on the approval of the *Privy Council* which consists of leading politicians, judges and other national figures. Decisions of the Privy Council are in practice generally made by a small group of current government ministers.

(a)   Government departments

Central government is exercised primarily through large departments, each

with a senior minister called a Secretary of State, who has a place in the
Cabinet, supported by one or two ministers of state and one or more under-
secretaries of state. Ministers are members of one of the Houses of Parliament,
where they may be publicly questioned on relevant topics. Parliament also
exercises control because only it can grant statutory powers to a minister or
his officials and because its approval is required for annual government
expenditure. Each department is staffed by civil servants, who remain in
office whatever the government of the day, with a permanent secretary,
heading an hierarchy which may include deputy, under, and assistant secretaries. Most civil servants are recruited directly into the service, but some,
with special qualifications, for example in law or transport engineering, are
appointed direct to specialist posts in a particular department. Some departments, notably the Department of the Environment, operate in the provinces
through regional offices.

In England, the *Department of the Environment* has the widest ranging
responsibilities for the environment. It was created in 1970 and combines
oversight of local government, housing and land-use planning, with
responsibility for water resources, control of pollution in its various forms,
coast protection and preservation of the amenities of the countryside and of
historic buildings. The *Department of Transport* was separated from the
Department of the Environment in 1976. Its main impact on the landscape is
through its responsibility for road schemes. A particular responsibility for the
rural landscape lies with the *Ministry of Agriculture, Fisheries and Food*. This
ministry, which has never adopted the modern title of department, is consulted over the release of agricultural land for development. It also controls
the financial structure of farming, with profound effects on the ways in which
agricultural land is used. It has particular responsibility for the improvement
and drainage of agricultural land and supervises forestry through the Forestry
Commission. The Departments of Energy and Industry, both dating back to
1974, also have considerable impact on the landscape. The *Department of
Energy* is responsible for co-ordinating energy policies and in particular may
determine the siting of power stations, and pipe and power lines for gas and
electricity and similar activities. The *Department of Trade and Industry* is
responsible for general industrial policy, and affects the siting and form of
industrial development. It has particular responsibility for mineral workings.

(b) Public corporations

Certain functions of central government are given to public corporations
with varying degrees of political independence. Some may be virtually
branches of the civil service, in which case they are limited by government
financial controls, and are subject to detailed supervision by related
government departments. This was the case with the Countryside

Commission which is concerned with enhancing the public amenity of open countryside, until it was reconstituted by the Wildlife and Countryside Act 1981 on a more independent basis with its own staff.[1] Certain industries are *nationalized industries*, theoretically in public ownership, and are run as public corporations under statutory constitutions. Here public control is usually exercised through the powers of a minister to appoint a chairman and board such as the National Coal Board. These are responsible for day-to-day management. Parliament will only question the minister on general matters of policy where he has laid down guidelines. Services such as gas and electricity which need to be planned on a national basis are organized by public corporations known as *statutory undertakers*. For certain functions *regional structures* have been created, such as the ten *Regional Water Authorities* each of which is a public corporation and which control water resources.

In exceptional cases, a body which is quite distinct from government may be given a special status and power to carry out public functions. Thus the *National Trust*, for preservation of places of historic interest or natural beauty, established on a statutory basis in 1907, and its counterpart in Scotland, have special powers to hold land for posterity with special protection from compulsory purchase, and with power to receive heritage property, under arrangements which reduce the tax liability of a donor. The Trust is controlled by its members who may vote at general meetings and appoint a council to carry out its business.

(c) 'Quangos'

Many government decisions are influenced, or are made, by bodies consisting of appointed experts or public figures outside government, who recover expenses, and may receive other remuneration, and are staffed by civil servants. For example, the Historic Buildings and Monuments Commission for England was set up under the National Heritage Act 1983 to manage sites previously looked after by the Department of the Environment, and to advise on the preservation of historic buildings by grants, compulsory purchase or other means. These 'quasi autonomous non-governmental organisations', are often criticized as costly and non-democratic, but they do involve independent experts in government. Many quangos have recently been abolished. For example the National Water Council and the Water Space Amenity Commission which were intended to advise on coherent policies for water resources and their amenity value were abolished by the Water Act 1983.

1.3.2   Local government
Many powers concerned with the environment are vested in local authorities,

created in their present form, as a coherent pattern of public corporations, under the Local Government Act 1972 (Fig. 1.9).

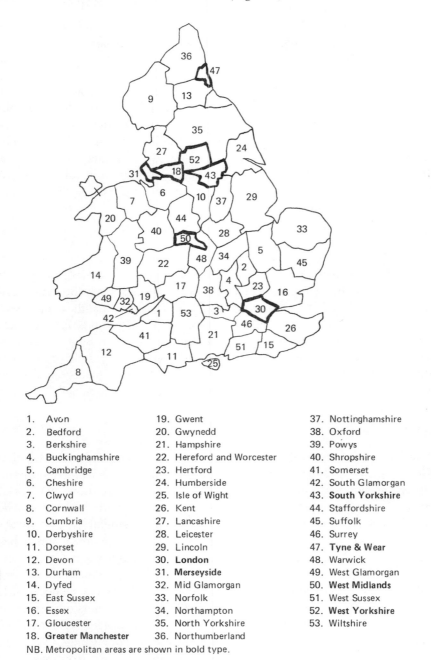

1. Avon	19. Gwent	37. Nottinghamshire
2. Bedford	20. Gwynedd	38. Oxford
3. Berkshire	21. Hampshire	39. Powys
4. Buckinghamshire	22. Hereford and Worcester	40. Shropshire
5. Cambridge	23. Hertford	41. Somerset
6. Cheshire	24. Humberside	42. South Glamorgan
7. Clwyd	25. Isle of Wight	43. **South Yorkshire**
8. Cornwall	26. Kent	44. Staffordshire
9. Cumbria	27. Lancashire	45. Suffolk
10. Derbyshire	28. Leicester	46. Surrey
11. Dorset	29. Lincoln	47. **Tyne & Wear**
12. Devon	30. **London**	48. Warwick
13. Durham	31. **Merseyside**	49. West Glamorgan
14. Dyfed	32. Mid Glamorgan	50. **West Midlands**
15. East Sussex	33. Norfolk	51. West Sussex
16. Essex	34. Northampton	52. **West Yorkshire**
17. Gloucester	35. North Yorkshire	53. Wiltshire
18. **Greater Manchester**	36. Northumberland	

NB. Metropolitan areas are shown in bold type.

Fig. 1.9 County Authorities in England and Wales.

(a) Principal councils

England and Wales are divided into 369 *districts*. These replaced a mass of small local authorities of varying sizes and efficiency. The districts are grouped into *counties*: six are *metropolitan counties* based on the main centres of population outside London. The Conservative Government elected in 1983 is committed to their abolition, and the transfer of their powers to thirty-six metropolitan districts which they contain. A further forty-seven counties largely correspond with ancient English counties and regroup the old Welsh ones into larger units. Counties and districts are known as principal councils. Important functions are divided between the two tiers. Thus counties are responsible for structure plans[2] setting out a general framework of future land use and for detailed control of mineral extraction[3] and highways. District councils are responsible for the details of other development control.[4]

(b) Parishes

The Local Government Act 1972, s. 112 empowers councils to appoint Wales, community councils. These are entirely distinct from the old ecclesiastical parishes of the Church of England. They are mainly a means of consulting local opinion,[5] but also have power to provide certain local facilities such as allotments,[6] parks[7] and graveyards.[8] In England, secular parishes generally exist only in rural areas whereas the whole of Wales is divided into community councils. The electors of a parish meet annually and when they number more than 200 must have an elected council.[9]

(c) London

London retains its own pattern of local government, under the London Government Act 1963. The whole area, including the City of London and thirty-two London boroughs, is represented on the Greater London Council which, however, the government elected in 1983 is committed to abolish. The division of responsibilities relevant to land use is similar to that in the provincial metropolitan areas although the Greater London Council has rather wider planning powers than its provincial counterparts.

The Local Government Act 1972, s. 112 empowers councils to appoint officers. These constitute the equivalent of local civil services. Under s. 101, power to make decisions may be delegated by a council to its officers or to committees. Each council makes its own standing orders regulating the delegation of decision-making and the general conduct of business.[10] Ways in which decision-making is shared and conflicts resolved between different local authorities and central government are discussed in Chapter 3, Section 3.2.

1.3.3 Legal materials produced by public bodies

As government activity has expanded during the twentieth century, it has become increasingly difficult for Parliament to find time for the new detailed legislation which has been needed. Instead it has increasingly delegated power to make subordinate legislation to central and local government. The Interpretation Act 1978, s. 14 provides that power to make delegated legislation usually includes power to revoke it in the same manner.

(a) Special procedure orders

In the nineteenth century the provisional order procedure was developed. Such an order could be made by a local authority or other official body. It was brought before Parliament as a schedule to a single clause bill. Now, the Statutory Orders (Special Procedure) Act 1945, provides that such an order may itself be laid before Parliament, where it may be annulled by a resolution of either House, or challenged by a petition by an interested party. In the latter case it is dealt with rather like a private or hybrid bill, in a joint committee with three members from each House with power to approve, reject or amend it. This procedure is used to provide an extra safeguard on the compulsory purchase of land from local authorities, statutory undertakers or the National Trust.

(b) Statutory instruments

Powers to make subordinate legislation may be delegated with varying degrees of independence. The Statutory Instruments Act 1946 provides for legislation by statutory instrument, where Parliament delegates power, either to the Privy Council to make an Order in Council, or to an individual minister of the Crown. A statute delegating power to make statutory instruments may specify a range of Parliamentary controls. It may require that the instrument be laid before Parliament either in draft, or in its final form. It may require affirmative approval from Parliament before the instrument can come into force, or it may provide for the instrument to be annulled if a prayer to that effect is made and approved in one or other House. On the other hand it may merely be required that the instrument be laid before Parliament for its information. Even if there is no requirement that it be laid at all it will normally at least be published as a statutory instrument by Her Majesty's Stationary Office. This is required in most cases by s. 2 of the 1946 Act.

Where a power is granted to a minister, it can generally be exercised by a competent official within his department. As Lord Green M.R. said in the Court of Appeal, in *Carltona Ltd* v. *Commissioners of Works*,[11] a case concerned with the requisitioning of housing in war time:

The duties imposed upon Ministers and the powers given to Ministers are normally exercised under the authority of the Minister by responsible officials of the department. Public business could not be carried on if that were not the case . . . The whole system of departmental organisation and administration is based on the view that Ministers, being responsible to Parliament, will see that important duties are committed to experienced officials.

Lord Greene made clear that this included the power to make regulations such as those for requisitioning property.

(c) Byelaws

Power to make byelaws may be granted to a minister, or to some public body, such as a local authority, a water authority or the National Trust. Byelaws may provide rules for the management of property or the detailed regulation of an area. For example, under the National Trust Act 1971, s. 24, byelaws may be made to control damage of Trust land by removing turf, soil or plants, lighting fires or depositing refuse, and to exclude the public from parts of such land. The Local Government Act 1972, s. 235, gives district councils and London boroughs a general power to 'make byelaws for the good rule and government of the whole or any part of the district or borough, as the case may be, and for the prevention and suppression of nuisances therein'; s. 236 provides a standard procedure for making byelaws. They require confirmation by a higher authority, which in the case of local government byelaws, as of many others, is the Secretary of State for the Department of the Environment. Although there are standard requirements that byelaws be prominently displayed, and they have the advantage of allowing rules to be tailored to special situations, their variety can lead to confusion. For this reason the Public Health Act 1961, s. 4, provided for the replacement of a mass of local authority building byelaws by standard building regulations in the form of statutory instruments.[12]

(d) Circulars and administrative decisions

Central government control over the use of powers by local government and other public bodies is often exercised by publishing guidance on standard policies, notably in circulars and in decisions such as those made on planning appeals. Circulars are duplicated letters distributed by government departments. Some are widely distributed and have considerable practical importance. The circulars each department issues for a given year form a continuous sequence. Thus, a circular on *Development control – policy and practice*, published in 1980, is referred to as Department of the Environment circular 22/80. Occasionally a circular is used specifically to legislate. Thus, Department of the Environment circular No. 39/81, on the safeguarding of aerodromes, technical sites and explosive storage areas, contains a directive specifying consultations to be made by local planning authorities before they grant planning permission for land forming, or in the neighbourhood of, an aerodrome. The power to make such a directive was contained in the General Development Order 1977 which is a statutory instrument. Especially if a circular has legislative effect, it is important for the public that it should be drafted and published like more formal legislation. In *Patchett* v. *Leathem*,[13] a case on the war-time requisitioning of houses, Streatfield J. condemned the misuse of circulars:

Whereas ordinary legislation, by passing through both Houses of Parliament or, at least, lying on the table of both Houses, is thus twice blessed, this type of so-called legislation is at least four times cursed. First, it has seen neither House of Parliament; secondly it is unpublished and is inaccessible even to those whose valuable rights of property may be affected; thirdly it is a jumble of provisions, legislative, administrative or directive in character, or sometimes difficult to disentangle one from the other; and fourthly, it is expressed not in the precise language of an Act of Parliament or an Order in Council but in the more colloquial language of correspondence, which is not always susceptible of the ordinary canons of construction.

Circulars are often issued to explain the purpose of more formal legislation or to state government policy in implementing legislation. Circular 22/80 sets out criteria for deciding applications for planning decisions. At paragraph 20 it states that designs should only exceptionally be rejected for aesthetic reasons: 'Even where such detailed control is exercised it should not be over-fastidious in such matters as, for example, the precise shade of colour of bricks.' Such guidance has no legally binding effect but it makes clear to local authorities that, if they exercise tight control over the aesthetics of development, their decisions may well be reversed on appeal to the Department. Similarly, decisions of the Department of the Environment on planning appeals are usually followed consistently. Significant examples are summarized regularly in the *Journal of Planning and Environment Law*.

If circulars are acted on over a long period, they may be shown considerable respect by the courts. In *Coleshill and District Investment Co. Ltd* v. *Minister of Housing and Local Government*,[14] Lord Wilberforce discussed the argument that outright demolition of a building was not covered by the statutory definition of development requiring planning permission. He said that the argument derived important support by being stated in a circular[15] which had been issued twenty years earlier: '[T]he circular had no legal status: but it acquired vitality and strength when, through the years, it passed, as it certainly did, into planning practice, and text books, [and] was acted on, as it certainly was, in planning decisions.' This was reinforced by the fact that the definition of development interpreted in the circular was repeated in later legislation.

Like the normal circular, a planning decision is not a true source of law. It is not a binding precedent like a reported case from the higher courts, which must be followed on subsequent occasions. In practice, however, administrative decisions are followed consistently. For example the *Journal of Planning and Environment Law* contains reports of decisions made after planning inquiries and these provide valuable guidance as to the manner in which similar cases will be dealt with.

NOTES: SECTION 1.3

1. Wildlife and Countryside Act 1981, s. 47 and Sched. 13. See Foulkes, D. (1982) *Administrative Law*, Butterworth, London, 5th edn, pp. 16 and 17 and *post* p. 128f.
2. See *post* p. 57f.
3. See *post* p. 140f.
4. See *post* p. 107f.
5. Local Government Act 1972, s. 182 and Sched. 16 para. 20.
6. Small Holdings and Allotments Act 1908, ss. 23, 26 and 42.
7. Public Health Act 1875, s. 164.
8. Open Spaces Act 1906, ss. 9 and 10.
9. Local Government Act 1972, s. 9 (2).
10. Basic procedural rules for local authorities are provided in the Local Government Act 1972, Sched. 12.
11. *Carltona Ltd* v. *Commissioner of Works* [1943] 2 All E.R. 560.
12. Now S.I. 1976, No. 1676.
13. *Patchett* v. *Leathem* (1949) 65 T.L.R. 69 at p. 70.
14. *Coleshill and District Investment Co. Ltd* v. *Minister of Housing and Local Government* [1969] 1 W.L.R. 746, H.L. at p. 765; see *post* p. 42f and p. 111f.
15. No. 67/49.

1.4 The form and interpretation of legal materials

In 1966 Coleshill and District Investment Co. Ltd, the owners of a war-time ammunition dump on the outskirts of the village of Hampton-in-Arden between Birmingham and Coventry, decided to make the old magazine buildings convenient as stores by removing blast walls and vegetation-covered embankments which screened them from view. After they had moved the embankments, the local planning authority was stimulated by local complaints to serve an enforcement notice ordering that these should be restored. The owners appealed to the Minister of Housing and Local Government. They also asked for a ruling as to whether they needed planning permission for the further stage of removing the walls. The Minister ruled that both stages were development requiring planning permission. The owners successfully appealed to the Divisional Court, but the Minister was upheld on further appeals to the Court of Appeal and the House of Lords.[1] The final decision in this case is an important legal authority on the meaning of development for which planning permission is needed. Development control is examined in Chapter 3, Section 3.3. However, the case illustrates the general difficulties of applying legal rules in practical situations. The definition of development which is still found in the present Town and Country Planning Act 1971, includes, 'building, engineering, mining or other operations'. The House of Lords approved the Minister's view that removal of the embankments was an engineering operation and that the removal of the walls and embankments would be a building operation because it would affect the external appearance of the remaining buildings. The House also considered, somewhat inconclusively, the general meaning of 'operations' and in particular whether these included outright demolition of a building. The owners had argued that a traditional rule of interpretation known as *eiusdem generis* applied. Under this rule where a list of related terms which may be regarded as making up a single genus is followed by a general term this is confined to the same genus. Thus the owners argued that 'operations' must be a single genus of which building, engineering and mining operations were examples but demolition was not. The House of Lords retorted that this list was so disparate that it could not constitute a single genus. Building and engineering involved a positive or constructional aspect but this could not be said of mining. Nevertheless Lord Pearson suggested that under the wider principle of *noscitur a sociis*, that is reading the words in their context, 'there are three genera and the other operations must be similar to building operations or to engineering operations or to mining operations'. On this basis also outright demolition would probably not be covered by the definition of development.

The different forms of legal material are handled by lawyers in different ways. How to interpret and apply them is a major part of the lawyer's skills. Legislation, both statutes produced directly by Parliament, and delegated or secondary legislation, is interpreted in accordance with a number of well-established rules. Cases decided by the Courts are applied in later cases in accordance with other rules. However, the rules are flexible and give much scope for judges to come to different conclusions if they choose to do so. This may enable justice to be done in varying circumstances. However, it means that the law is uncertain and it is often difficult to be certain in advance how a court would resolve a particular dispute, even if the facts are clear.

1.4.1 Legislation

(a) The form of statutes

A public and general Act of Parliament will begin with a *long title* explaining its purpose, but it is referred to by its *short title*, which is usually included in a section at the end. The date on which a statute received the Royal Assent and became law is stated immediately after the long title, but to allow for publication and setting up of necessary administrative machinery, it often provides a different *commencement date*, when it will come into force. Frequently, commencement dates are left open, to be made by a minister in a later statutory instrument. Large and complex statutes, such as the Control of Pollution Act 1974, may be brought into effect one or two sections at a time over a large number of years, as administrative arrangements are made to enforce the new law. Since 1850 each statute has been divided into *sections, sub-sections* and *paragraphs*. In a Bill which has not yet been passed, sections are called *clauses*. A key provision to look for in any statute deals with the *extent* of its application. This often specifies that the Act is not to apply in Scotland or Northern Ireland. *Schedules* at the end of an Act are used for such matters as repeals, alterations of earlier legislation, and transitional arrangements. They are sub-divided into *paragraphs* and *sub-paragraphs* or take the form of *tables*.

(b) The form of delegated legislation

Statutory instruments, the typical form of delegated legislation, are cited by their number for a given year rather than by their title which is often cumbersome. Thus the Town and Country Planning (Use Classes) Order 1972 may be cited as S.I. 1972, No. 1385. Statutory instruments specify a date in the future when they will come into operation. They set out the statutory authority under which they are made and are signed in the personal name of the Minister responsible for them. Statutory instruments may be couched as *Orders, Regulations* or *Rules*. They are divided into *articles, regulations* or *rules* respectively. All are sub-divided into *paragraphs* and *sub-paragraphs*. They may contain *schedules* and are generally published with explanatory notes which do not form part of the law.

(c) Interpreting legislation

Judges use a collection of principles for drawing out the meaning of legislation. Their starting point is the *literal rule*, that words are to be given their ordinary and natural meaning.[2] However, if the wording is ambiguous or if it is not clear what is included in certain words, meaning must be found to carry out the underlying purpose of the legislation. Here judges apply a second main principle, the so called *mischief rule*.[3] This involves looking at the pre-existing law and identifying the defect or mischief which the Act was intended to deal with. The underlying purpose is found partly by internal means, looking at the statute as a whole in the light of a number of detailed rules, and to a more limited extent by means of external aids. A third principle known as the *golden rule* starts with the literal approach that 'the grammatical and ordinary sense of the words is to be adhered to', but recognizes that if this leads to 'absurdity, or some repugnance or inconsistency with the rest of the instrument . . . the grammatical and ordinary sense of the words may be modified, so as to avoid that absurdity and inconsistency, but no further'.[4] This principle has been used, for example, to make *or* mean *and*. In *Federal Steam Navigation Co. Ltd* v. *Department of Trade and Industry*[5] the House of Lords upheld convictions of both the owner and the master of a British ship, the *Huntingdon*, for discharging oil into the sea off Nova Scotia, contrary to the Oil in Navigable Waters Act 1955, although this provided that 'the owner *or* master of the ship' should be liable for such discharge.

Certain standard definitions for statutes are provided by the Interpretation Act 1978. Thus, under s. 6, one gender includes the other, words in the singular include the plural, and words in the plural include the singular. In *Annicola Investments Ltd* v. *Minister of Housing and Local Government*,[6] Lawrence J. said that where the Housing Act 1957, s. 42 provided slum clearance powers for houses in an area, this enabled a local authority to make a single house a clearance area. Section 7 of the Interpretation Act provides a further useful general rule that distances are to be 'measured in a straight line on a horizontal plane'. A schedule defines certain common terms. Thus '*land* includes buildings and other structures, land covered with water, and any estate, interest, easement, servitude or right in or over land'. Other more detailed definitions of land are found in particular statutes such as The Law of Property Act 1925, s. 205 (1) (ix). Often legislation contains explicit interpretation provisions. Thus the Town and Country Planning Act 1971, s. 22 provides that 'except where the context otherwise requires' development means either one of the specified forms of operational development or 'any material change in the use of any buildings or other land'. This is a comprehensive definition whereas the definition of land in the Interpretation Act merely gives examples of what are covered by the definition.

The judges have developed a number of detailed principles of statutory interpretation in case law. The basic rule that words of a statute are to be read in their context is expressed in the maxim *noscitur a sociis* which is referred to at the beginning of this section together with the narrower principle of *eiusdem generis*. Although judges will look at a statute in its entirety they will not refer to the long title, headings, marginal notes or punctuation unless these are needed to resolve an ambiguity or uncertainty.[7] Judges also generally refuse to look at the background of a statute even to understand the purpose for which it was made. In particular, Parliamentary debates are not taken into account. A majority vote may reflect various conflicting views expressed in speeches made during the preceeding debates. It has been stressed that if Parliamentary debates could be referred to in the courts, legal proceedings could be excessively prolonged.[8] Judges do refer to official reports which lead to legislation, such as those of the Law Commission, but only to ascertain the previous state of the law and the defects which the legislation was designed to remedy. Other Acts of Parliament may be referred to, but only when they deal with the same subject matter. The supreme example of external aids in the construction of statutes is previous case law. Where statutes have been consolidated or otherwise replaced, old case law is still used to interpret the new legislation if this is not clear. However, Parliament is not necessarily assumed to have endorsed such earlier interpretation and a higher court may feel free to overrule it.[9] Generally, in construing statutes, judges observe certain presumptions. Thus, unless otherwise provided, an Act is presumed to apply to the whole United Kingdom. Also, any new substantive provision, as opposed to a change in rules of procedure or evidence, is presumed to come into effect at the time when the statute comes into force and not to be retrospective.[10] Similarly a statute is deemed not to alter previous law unless it does so expressly.[11]

1.4.2   Case law

A reported case usually begins with key issues set out in italics, followed by a headnote summarizing the facts, and the principles which were decided in the case. The main body of the report contains a statement of facts together with an account of the legal proceedings prior to the hearing dealt with in the report, and then the judgements themselves.

(a) The ratio decidendi and obiter dicta

The key part of any reported case is known as the *ratio decidendi*, that is the reasoning on which the decision is based, including the facts selected by the judges as leading to their decision. The English system of case law depends upon courts consistently following their own previous decisions and those of higher courts. The *ratio decidendi* constitutes the principle or principles in a case, which will be followed on subsequent occasions. In addition judges may include other pronouncements on the law which are known as *obiter dicta*, that is things said incidental to the instant case. They may have no real bearing on it or they may appear to be the principle on which the case is decided but actually go further than is necessary. In Chapter 6, Section 6.2, the leading case on negligence of *Donoghue* v. *Stevenson* is discussed. This could have been regarded as laying down a narrow rule concerned with the duty owed by manufacturers to the consumers of their products. However, its *ratio decidendi* has been treated as establishing a much wider duty of care.

The usual means of avoiding following a previous authoritative decision is to find a convincing means of *distinguishing* it. This may be done by interpreting its *ratio decidendi* in a narrow manner. Sometimes a decision may be reached on several grounds. In particular, where there are several judges they may give different reasons for reaching the same conclusion. In a

Fig. 1.10 Lintz Cricket Ground, County Durham, showing the house of the plaintiffs in *Miller* v. *Jackson* [1977] Q.B. 966, by kind permission of R. Jackson and of Lintz Cricket Club.

later case each reason may be treated as equally authoritative or one may be preferred to another. A preference must be made where the reasons are inconsistent. In *Miller* v. *Jackson*,[12] the Millers moved into a house at the village of Linz in County Durham. They complained to the courts that a neighbouring cricket ground was a legal nuisance because balls were frequently batted into their garden (Fig. 1.10). The trial judge awarded damages for glass broken by balls and granted an injunction forbidding the future playing of cricket. The Court of Appeal quashed the injunction. Lord Denning held that there was no nuisance at all, since the plaintiff had moved next to a cricket ground where there was an existing use which provided a public benefit, and this amounted to a defence. The other two judges held that there was a nuisance, but, whereas Geoffrey Lane L.J. went on to hold that there were no valid grounds for refusing the injunction, Cumming-Bruce L.J. held that it would be contrary to the public interest to grant one. Thus although Cumming-Bruce L.J. differed from the other two judges his decision in effect determined the case.

On appeal a decision may be *reversed* by a higher court. A higher court may also *overrule ratio decidendi* of a lower court in a previous case, although this will not affect the parties in that earlier case.

(b) The hierarchy of the courts

The House of Lords binds all lower courts, and used to regard itself as bound by its own previous decisions. However, in 1966 it declared that it would in future be prepared to overrule these 'when it appears right to do so'.[13] This power is used sparingly, so as to avoid making the law uncertain, but it can involve major changes of direction. There was a well-established rule that although occupiers of premises owed a duty to take care of legitimate visitors to their land, they owed no duty to provide for the safety of trespassers. This was overruled in *British Railways Board* v. *Herrington*;[14] there, a child of 6, playing on Runce's Meadow belonging to the National Trust at Mitcham in Surrey, strayed on to an electric railway line where he was badly burned. The House of Lords held that a duty is owed, even to trespassers, to treat them in accordance with the standard of 'common humanity'. The British Railways Board was held liable because its officials had failed to repair the fence guarding the railway line, although they knew that it was in a bad condition.

The Court of Appeal binds lower courts and it is now established that it must also follow its own previous decisions.[15] There are exceptions, where an earlier case was decided *per incuriam*, that is without taking account of some earlier relevant authority, or is in conflict with another decision, or if there is a House of Lords case with which the Court of Appeal's own earlier decision cannot stand, even though it has not been expressly overruled. The Criminal Division of the Court of Appeal is somewhat more flexible than the Civil Division and may be prepared not to follow one of its earlier decisions where this could 'result in an unjust conviction'.[16] Divisional Courts of the High Court are bound by the House of Lords, the Court of Appeal, their own previous decisions and those of other divisions. Cases decided by single High Court judges bind magistrates and circuit judges sitting in lower courts, but they do not have to be followed by other High Court judges or even by the same one on a later occasion.

In any area where the European Court has jurisdiction it can overrule English authorities and binds English courts for the future although it does not regard itself as bound. The House of Lords is the final Appeal Court for civil cases from Scotland and for cases from Northern Ireland. Decisions in such cases are treated as binding in the English Courts where the House of Lords has regarded the relevant law as the same in England. The most famous example is the case of *Donoghue* v. *Stevenson*, discussed in Chapter 6, Section 6.2 which laid the foundation of the modern law of negligence. Opinions of the judicial committee of the Privy Council are treated as sufficient to overrule previous English decisions in areas where the law is believed to coincide with that of the country from which the appeal is brought. Such key decisions are the two *Wagon Mound* cases which are discussed in Chapters 6 and 7 and which established that a person may be liable in the two torts of negligence and nuisance only for damage of a type which is reasonably foreseeable.

(c) Law and fact

Reported cases are authority for the legal rules upon which they were decided. However, it is important to realize that, in most cases that come before the courts, the real dispute is over matters of fact. On the other hand, cases which go on appeal are more likely to be those where there is some uncertainty over a point of law. Indeed criminal appeals by way of case stated to the Divisional Court are necessarily concerned with whether the lower court had jurisdiction or with some error of law generally.[17] Appeals against conviction on indictment in the Crown Court require the leave of the Court of Appeal except on a ground which involves a question of law alone.[18]

Often even where an issue of law is in dispute this is entangled with questions of fact. Where a court dealing with an appeal from another court on a question of mixed law and fact holds that the lower court wrongly applied the law, it may go on to apply the correct principles to the facts decided below. However, notably on a case stated to the Divisional Court or on a hearing concerned with an administrative decision, if the original decision was based on an error of law, the appeal or review court may be obliged to return the matter to the original court or administrative body which made the decision. For example in *Birmingham Corporation* v. *Minister of Housing and Local Government and Habib Ullah*,[19] Birmingham Corporation had served an enforcement notice[20] on Habib Ullah to stop him letting two houses so that between them they accomodated some eight families or individuals. After receiving the report of an inspector who had held a public inquiry, the Minister ruled that because the premises remained residential there had not been a material change of use and therefore no development had taken place to which the planning authority could object. However, the Queen's Bench Divisional Court ruled that: 'the Minister erred in law in saying that because these houses remained residential or remained dwelling houses in which people dwelt there could not be a material change of use. Whether there had been in any of the cases a material change of use is a matter of degree and fact and therefore one for the Minister.'[21] The court therefore referred the case back to the minister for his further decision.

Habib Ullah's cases illustrates that often questions of fact are not open and shut but involve drawing a line somewhere on a spectrum. By contrast with the mixed question of law and fact posed in that case, there could have been a simple dispute of fact. For example if the Minister had found that Habib Ullah had only shared a house with members of his family this would clearly have ruled out any question of a material change of use. Thus the local planning authority would not have been able to appeal to the courts on the ground that the evidence showed that Habib Ullah shared with seven separate families. On the other hand if the Minister had ruled that although Habib Ullah had shared only with members of his own family, nevertheless because the family was very large this amounted to a material change of use, Habib Ullah could have challenged this by appealling to the courts on a pure issue of law.[22]

NOTES: SECTION 1.4

1. *Coleshill and District Investment Co. Ltd* v. *Minister of Housing and Local Government* [1969] 1 W.L.R. 746, H.L.
2. *Stock* v. *Frank Jones (Tipton) Ltd* [1978] 1 W.L.R. 231, H.L.
3. *Heydon's Case* (1584) 3 Co. Rep. 7a.
4. *Grey* v. *Pearson* (1857) 6 H.L. Cas. 61, *per* Lord Wensleydale at p. 106. But see *Magor and St. Mellons Rural District Council* v. *Newport Corporation* [1952] A.C. 189.
5. *Federal Steam Navigation Co. Ltd* v. *Department of Trade and Industry* [1947] 1 W.L.R. 505, H.L.
6. *Annicola Investments Ltd* v. *Minister of Housing and Local Government* [1968] 1 Q.B. 631.
7. *R.* v. *Schildkamp* [1971] A.C. 1.
8. *Beswick* v. *Beswick* [1968] A.C. 58, *per* Lord Reid at p. 74.
9. *Farrell* v. *Alexander* [1977] A.C. 59, H.L.
10. *Croxford* v. *Universal Insurance Co. Ltd* [1936] 2 K.B. 253, C.A.
11. *Maunsell* v. *Olins* [1975] A.C. 373, H.L., *per* Lord Reid at p. 383.
12. *Miller* v. *Jackson* [1977] Q.B. 966, C.A., see further *post* p. 384, note 26.
13. *Practice Statement (Judicial Precedent)* [1966] 1 W.L.R. 1234.
14. *British Railways Board* v. *Herrington* [1972] A.C. 877, H.L. *post* p. 329.
15. *Young* v. *Bristol Aeroplane Co. Ltd* [1944] K.B. 718, C.A., affirmed in the House of Lords [1946] A.C. 163. See also *Davis* v. *Johnson* [1979] A.C. 264, H.L.
16. *R.* v. *Gould* [1968] 2 Q.B. 65.
17. Magistrates' Courts Act 1980, s. 111 (1) and Supreme Court Act 1981, s. 28 (1).
18. Criminal Appeal Act 1968, s. 1.
19. *Birmingham Corporation* v. *Minister of Housing and Local Government and Habib Ullah* [1964] 1 Q.B. 178. See further *post* Chapter 8, Sections 8.2 and 8.3.
20. See *post* p. 93.
21. At p. 190, *per* Lord Parker C.J.
22. In such a case, today the court would still be obliged to refer the decision back to the Secretary of State. Town and County Planning Act 1971, s. 246(3) and Rules of the Supreme Court, Order 94, Rule 12 (5) and (6).

1.5   The international and European dimensions to environmental law

1.5.1   International law

In the United Kingdom, Parliament has long been regarded as the supreme law-making authority. Where powers to make legislation are delegated to subordinate bodies, Parliament can always revoke their authority and change the subordinate legislation. In reality, however, any British Government will be influenced in certain respects by other nations and regards itself as bound by international law to honour treaties which it makes with them. Treaties may deal with matters such as pollution control. Water contaminated by a factory beside a British river may affect fish in the open sea. Acid in smoke from the same factory may damage crops abroad when it falls as rain. Disputes over such matters may be resolved by special forms of international adjudication, notably the International Court of Justice in the Hague provided for under the charter of the United Nations Organization.

The potential effect of judgements of the International Court in environmental issues is illustrated by a number of cases on boundary and fishing disputes. Thus, in 1951, a major decision over fishing rights between Norway and the United Kingdom came down in favour of a base line for marking out Norwegian territorial waters, using rocks, some of which were far off the shore and only exposed at low tide, rather than the main coast line.[1] This added some 6900 km^2 to Norway's waters.

1.5.2 The European Community

The United Kingdom belongs to the Council of Europe, a wide grouping of European states which has influenced British law through a number of conventions such as the 1979 Convention on the Conservation of European Wildlife and Habitats which was partly put into effect by the Wildlife and Countryside Act, 1981. However the independence of British law itself was breached by the accession of the United Kingdom to the European Community in 1972. The Community grew from a group of economic treaties after the Second World War, signed between France, Germany, Italy, Belgium, Netherlands and Luxembourg. Apart from the United Kingdom, the Community has now swelled to include Denmark, Eire and Greece. Spain and Portugal have applied for membership. The aims of the Community are to establish a free internal Common Market and to develop a shared economic policy to that end. These aims may have considerable impact on land use, for example by initiating changes in agriculture and regulating transport systems and the production of energy.

(a) Administration and legislation of the EEC

The Community is dominated by the Council of Ministers and by the Commission. It also has an elected Assembly, the European Parliament, which must be consulted on legislation and has powers to question the Council and Commission, and to approve the Community budget. Usually is consists of foreign ministers from each Member State, but for specialized purposes it may be constituted by other ministers, for example those responsible for agriculture. Regular work is carried on by a Committee of Permanent Representatives, consisting of civil servants of the status of ambassador from each Member State. The Commission consists of fourteen Commissioners; they are appointed by agreement amongst Member States and there may be no more than two Commissioners from any one member. Once appointed, Commissioners are required to act independently of their national interest and to represent the general interests of the Community. The Commission has a President and five Vice-Presidents appointed for two years each. It maintains a permanent staff divided into Directorates General specializing in areas including Environmental and Consumer Protection, Agriculture, Transport and Development. The Commission initiates Community legislation by laying proposals before the Council. Powers are conferred upon it in certain areas to make detailed legal rules itself which are binding in the Member States.

The powers and operation of the Community and its organs are determined by the treaties under which they were set up, including the accession treaties of later members such as the United Kingdom, and also by annexes and protocols agreed by the Member States. The policies of the Community are enforced on Member States and their citizens in three ways. *Regulations* produced by the Council or on certain matters by the Commission are automatically enforceable in the Member States without the need for any national implementing legislation. *Directives* are binding as to their objectives, but require Member States to implement them through suitable national legislation. Specific orders called *decisions* may be addressed to individual states or persons. Regulations, directives or decisions are invalid unless they give 'the reasons on which they are based' and refer to any formal approvals which they require before they become effective.[2] Regulations enter into force on the twentieth day from their date of publication in the *Official Journal of the Communities*, unless they specify some other date. Directives and decisions are effective from the time that they are notified to those to whom they are addressed. In addition to the formal legislation of the Community, principles for common action may be expressed informally in various forms such as *communiqués* or *resolutions* of various meetings of representatives of the member governments. These may influence national policy and legislation. It has been said that: 'It sometimes appears that the more important the decision, the less formal the procedure and the measure.'[3]

In certain areas, Community legislation may profoundly affect the use of the British landscape.[4] The Common Agricultural Policy, developed since 1960, encourages uniform agricultural practices aimed at higher productivity of foodstuffs and concentrating production in specialized areas. In 1968, the Commission submitted to the Council a Memorandum on the Reform of Agriculture in the Community. This led to a resolution of the Council[5] which in turn was implemented by a number of directives encouraging the modernization of farms and the closing down of uneconomic units.[6] The need for a concerted environmental policy for the Community was recognized at a summit conference of heads of government in Paris in October 1972. A year later, the first of a series of Community Environmental Action Programmes had been produced by the Commission and was adopted by the Council of Ministers.[7] It aimed to reduce pollution and similar nuisances and positively to improve the environment and quality of life within the Community. On a wider front, it aimed at co-ordinating action by member states in international organizations dealing with the environment, for example in controlling pollution at sea and in the atmosphere. This first programme concentrated on reducing pollution. Its approach has been to ensure that the 'polluter pays'. Thus, industrialists are obliged to carry out their procedures in accordance with detailed standards. Community legislation on pollution has largely consisted of directives which require national legislation for their implementation.[8] A major contribution of the Community to environmental control has been the establishment of co-ordinated research into the effects of various activities on the environment.

(b) Courts and the Community

The Community has its own Court of Justice sitting in Luxembourg with judges, appointed by the governments of the Member States for six years at a time.[9] Its procedure is very different from that of an English court. Parties to a case present their detailed arguments in written form. These are considered by one judge, acting as *juge rapporteur*. He may hear evidence himself or arrange for it to be heard by several judges or by a full court. The final stage is an oral hearing where the full court hears a report from the *juge rapporteur*, then arguments from advocates for the parties and finally a submission by one of five Advocates-General attached to the court. These submissions are printed with the final judgments. If new facts of decisive importance are discovered within ten years of an original judgment, interested persons may apply within three months for the judgment to be revised. Judgments against Member States may be enforced by the imposing of sanctions by other members. Other judgments are enforced as judgment debts, by national courts. The jurisdiction of the European Court includes claims against the Community or its organs by individuals, or Member States, and also actions against Member States, either on any matter which members involved agree to submit to the court or over an alleged breach of Community Law. Disputes over alleged breaches by one Member State against another, must first be referred to the Commission, which has three months in which to deliver a reasoned opinion. The Commission may itself initiate proceedings against a Member State for a breach of Community law.

A vital aspect of the work of the European Court is that of giving rulings on

Community law to national courts. Under the *European Communities Act, 1972*, s. 2, law made under the Community Treaties, with the intention that it should apply in Member States, is enforceable in the United Kingdom. Power is given to the government to make statutory instruments for implementing directives. United Kingdom courts are required to take judicial notice of the EEC treaties, the *Official Journal of the European Communities* and any decisions or 'expressions of opinion' by the court.[10] Thus, in interpreting a statutory instrument which is intended to implement an EEC directive, a British court may take note of the underlying purposes of the legislation. More fundamentally, 'any questions as to the meaning or effect of any of the Treaties, or as to the validity, meaning or effect of any Community Instrument', are to be decided in accordance with earlier decisions of the European Court or may have to be referred to the European Court for a ruling. Decisions of the European Court are in much more general terms than those of English courts and the European Court is not itself bound by precedent as English courts may be. Therefore, English judges may be required to adapt their techniques for following previous decisions when dealing with questions of Community law.[11] Under Art. 177 of the Treaty of Rome, where an issue concerning the interpretation of Community law has been raised before a national court, and a determination of the issue is necessary to decide the case, the national court may seek a ruling from the European Court. Where there is no right of appeal from the national court, it must seek a ruling from the European Court. After a ruling the case is sent back to the national court. Any national court or tribunal is entitled to refer a point of European law to the European Court and it is possible that this could include an administrative body in the United Kingdom such as a licensing authority.[12] However, the House of Lords has made clear that, a trial court should normally determine the facts and decide the case leaving it to an appeal court to make any reference needed to the European Court.[13]

1.5.3   The United Kingdom: The law in Scotland

The United Kingdom includes its own international dimension to law by containing distinct legal systems for England and Wales, for Scotland and for Northern Ireland. Thus, although Scotland shares the British Parliament with the remainder of the United Kingdom, often separate legislation is produced for it. There are special legislative arrangements for matters of principle to be dealt with before the second reading in the House of Commons, by the Scottish Grand Committee, mainly consisting of Members of Parliament for Scottish constituencies, and for matters of detail to be debated in the Scottish Standing Committee. The Scottish court system is entirely distinct save for common provisions for references to the European Court and a common final appeal in civil matters to the House of Lords. In Scotland lesser criminal and civil cases are all dealt with in Local Sheriffs' courts. The higher judiciary sit at a number of centres, as Lords Commissioners, with jurys of fifteen, to try serious criminal cases. They sit in panels in the High Court, or the Scottish Court of Criminal Appeals to hear criminal appeals. The same judges deal with major civil cases in the Court of Session. Trials are heard by a judge sitting as Lord Ordinary in the Outer House and appeals are heard in the Inner House.

Central government in Scotland operates through the Scottish office, headed by the Secretary of State for Scotland, with five departments based in Edinburgh. Of these, the Scottish Development Department has oversight of local government, water supplies, public works and conservation, housing and highways. The Scottish Economic Planning Department is responsible for transport, electricity and tourism. There is a separate Department of Agriculture and Fisheries for Scotland. Local government is administered by nine regional councils and fifty-three district councils set up by the Local Government (Scotland) Act 1973. In the three island areas of Orkney, Shetland and the Western Isles there are self-contained island authorities.

It is not possible, within the scope of this book, to make more than passing reference to Scottish law, but its criminal and land law especially, differ in significant respects from those of England. Unless they qualify separately in both countries, lawyers are restricted to practice on one side of the border or the other and may envy the ease with which planners, surveyors and other professionals concerned with land use move to and fro. However, in each jurisdiction the use of land raises similar legal problems even if they may be answered in different ways.

NOTES: SECTION 1.5

1. *North Sea Continental Shelf Case*. Reports of the International Court of Justice, 1951, 116.
2. EEC Treaty, Art. 190.
3. Mathijsen, P.S.R.F. (1980) *A Guide to European Community Law* 3rd edn, Sweet and Maxwell, London, p. 98.
4. Shoard, M. (1981) *The Theft of the Countryside*, Temple Smith, London.
5. *Journal Officiel*, 1971, C52.
6. Directives 72/160 (O.J. 1972, L 332) and 72/161 (O.J. 1972, L 339).
7. Seventh General Report of the Commission (O.J. 1973, C112/1).
8. For example Council Directives 76/464 (O.J. 1976, L 129/23) 80/68 (O.J. 1980, L 20/43). Concerned with water pollution.
9. Treaty of Rome, Arts. 164–188.
10. European Communities Act 1972, s. 3.
11. See *R. v. Henn; R. v. Darby* [1980] 2 All E.R. 166, *per* Lord. Diplock. at p. 196.
12. In *Re. an absence in Ireland* [1977] 1 C.M.L.R. 5.
13. *R. v. Henn; R. v. Darby. supra* note 11.

Chapter 2

THE LAW AND PHYSICAL LAND BOUNDARIES

They do much provoke the wrath of God upon themselves,
which use to grind up the doles and marks, which of ancient
time were laid for the division of meers and balks in the fields to
bring owners to their right. They do wickedly, which do turn up
the ancient terries of the fields, that old men beforetimes with
great pains did tread out, whereby the Lord's records (which be
the tennants' evidences) be perverted and translated sometime
to the disinheriting of the right owner, to the oppression of the
poor fatherless, or the poor widow.

Second Book of Homilies of the reign of Elizabeth I
(1844) 5th edn Oxford University Press, p. 440

2.1 The legal significance of boundaries

Boundaries, the imaginary lines marking off pieces of land from one another
for various purposes, have been a preoccupation of all societies. So important
was it for ancient boundaries to be known that they were often set out with
permanent landmarks. In Anglo-Saxon England these often took the form of
deep ditches with the excavated earth thrown up at the side into banks. Many
such ditches survive today, as sunken roads, and often still serve as
boundaries. Because of their importance, and the risk that they might be
obliterated or moved, church ceremonies were often performed at regular
intervals to keep the memory of the landmarks alive. Some rural parishes
maintain the tradition of beating the bounds on Rogation Sunday, at the
beginning of the harvest period. When religious processions were abolished
in the English reformation, Elizabeth I expressly provided that perambula-
tions around parish boundaries would be continued,[1] and the exhortation set
out above, *for use in walking the bounds*, was included in the *Book of
Homilies* for this purpose.

2.1.1 Public law boundaries

Old ecclesiastical parish boundaries would coincide with those of the manor, the local community controlled by its lord. Today, manorial boundaries are of little significance, but communities are divided into modern administrative units, which may include secular parish boundaries.[2] Both judicial and administrative functions are largely organized locally. However, although local administrative boundaries determine the limits of power and responsibility vested in public bodies, they do not need to be particularly precise. In uncertain cases, provision is usually made for the responsibility to be shared by the authorities on either side of the boundary. Thus, if a civil action is brought in a county court, for pollution of a river, it could be started in the district where a company alleged to have caused the pollution carries on business, the district where the discharge occurred, or the district where the pollution caused harm to the plaintiff's water rights. If a mistake is made, the court has discretion to transfer the case to the correct district.[3] A summary criminal charge should normally be tried by magistrates of the county where the offence was committed, but where an offence has been committed within 500 yards of a boundary, or on any piece of water lying between two counties, it may be tried in either. Similarly if the offence was begun in one county and completed in another, it may be tried in either.[4]

2.1.2 Boundaries in planning law

In planning law boundaries may be important both in the framework provided by plans setting out public policy on future land use and also in the operation of development control.

(a) Development plans

Under the Town and Country Planning Act 1971, Part II, development plans consist of one or more *structure plans* produced by each county council and of *local plans* which are generally the responsibility of district councils.[5] There are provisions for these plans, and subsequent modifications, to be based on research surveys and to take account of relations with other areas. Thus Section 6 requires an initial survey for structure plans, including details as to how physical and economic characteristics, especially land use, communications, transport systems, and traffic do, or in future may, affect neighbouring authorities. In the preparation of a structure plan itself, or in reviewing it, such authorities must be consulted. Also account must be taken of current policies with respect to the economic planning and development of the region as a whole.[6] Structure plans must be approved by the Secretary of State for the Environment before they become operative, and he may take

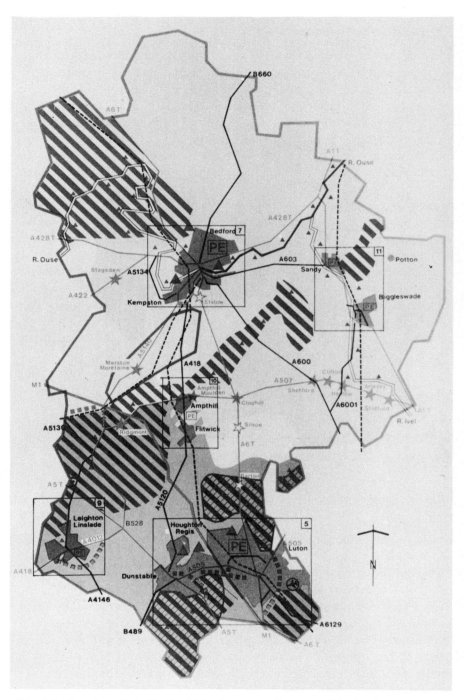

Fig. 2.1 Key plan of the Bedfordshire Structure plan, copied by kind permission of Bedfordshire County Council.

County Key Diagram | 4

Existing Structure

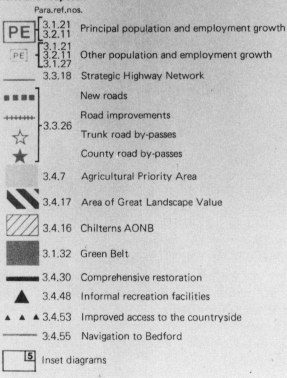

Urban area

Main roads, other than Strategic Network

Passenger railway

River

Luton airport

County boundary

Policies and Proposals

Para.ref.nos.

PE $\begin{bmatrix} 3.1.21 \\ 3.2.11 \end{bmatrix}$ Principal population and employment growth

PE $\begin{bmatrix} 3.1.21 \\ 3.2.11 \\ 3.1.27 \end{bmatrix}$ Other population and employment growth

3.3.18 Strategic Highway Network

New roads

Road improvements

3.3.26 Trunk road by-passes

County road by-passes

3.4.7 Agricultural Priority Area

3.4.17 Area of Great Landscape Value

3.4.16 Chilterns AONB

3.1.32 Green Belt

3.4.30 Comprehensive restoration

3.4.48 Informal recreation facilities

3.4.53 Improved access to the countryside

3.4.55 Navigation to Bedford

5 Inset diagrams

account of what may be strongly conflicting views of adjacent counties. For example, a dispute may have to be resolved as to whether a green belt[7] around a metropolitan area should be in the metropolitan county itself, or in neighbouring rural counties. The Secretary of State may create joint planning boards for two or more authorities, or for parts carved out of their territories, if he regards this as expedient and provided he holds a public inquiry before doing so if a constituent authority objects. Such joint planning boards are particularly appropriate for national parks which span more than one county.[8]

A structure plan is a written statement of a county council's general proposals for development and land use in an area, with the reasons justifying these. It includes a key diagram and appropriate insets, indicating, for example, distribution of population, and proposed development of particular forms, such as new housing and industry. However, these must not be on a map base and so in no way indicate precise boundaries,[9] Fig. 2.1. On the other hand a local plan consists of a map and written statement, which may detail the exact geographical location of proposed land use.[10] Even so, such proposals will be implemented either on the application of private developers within the area or by the local authority or other bodies acquiring land. In either case, precise boundaries will be determined by the normal rules for identifying property boundaries. Thus, problems could arise where development is proposed for land which straddles a local authority boundary. If the neighbouring authorities do not agree, the developer might only be able to proceed on one side of the administrative boundary, and this would have to be located precisely.

(b) Planning units

For planning purposes, boundaries between counties and districts often mark changes of land use. These may be shown on local plans. Within planning districts, areas may be zoned or designated for specific uses such as housing, or industry. Each piece of land occupied by any individual will generally have a particular approved use, perhaps as a farm or as an office building, and this may be the use of most properties in that area. As we shall see in Chapter 3, Section 3.3, anyone wishing to make a material change in the use of land requires planning permission. Within a piece of land with a single occupier, there may be several distinct uses, and the occupier may require planning permission if he wishes to transfer a use to a different part of his property. Any particular use is confined within the boundaries of what is known as the planning unit (Fig. 2.2).

The importance of the planning unit was spelled out by Bridge J., in the Divisional Court decision of *Burdle v. Secretary of State for the Environment*.[11] Mr Burdle purchased a scrap yard in the New Forest where salvaged

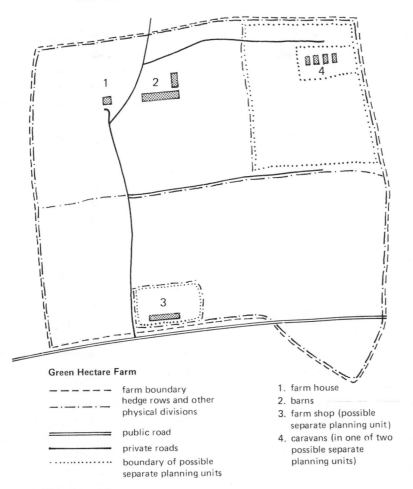

Green Hectare Farm

- – – – – –   farm boundary
- – . — . — . —   hedge rows and other physical divisions
===========   public road
—————   private roads
· · · · · · · · · · · · · ·   boundary of possible separate planning units

1. farm house
2. barns
3. farm shop (possible separate planning unit)
4. caravans (in one of two possible separate planning units)

Fig. 2.2 Planning units.

car parts and some new parts were sold. He reconstructed a lean-to office on the site and used it to sell new parts for cars, together with camping equipment. The local planning authority served an enforcement notice, ordering this to stop. The Secretary of State upheld this notice, but he did so on the basis that the lean-to alone was the proper planning unit to consider, and that its use taken in isolation had been materially changed. He ruled that as the enforcement notice was directed at a shop, as a matter of law, because of the definition of shop in the planning legislation, it must be confined to a building. The Divisional Court accepted that it was possible that

the use of the lean-to annexe for purposes appropriate to a shop had become so predominant and the connection between that use and the scrap yard business carried on from the open parts of curtilage had become so tenuous that the lean-to annexe ought to be regarded as a separate planning unit.

However, the court referred the matter back to the Secretary of State because he had been wrong to ignore the possibility of the premises as a whole forming the planning unit with an existing shop use. Bridge J. sketched out three main possible categories to help identify planning units. First, a piece of land may have one predominant use with secondary related activities. Thus an office building may have a car park attached, or a farm may contain barns for storage.[12] A secondary activity is dependent upon the main use. To start such secondary uses may not require planning permission, provided the main use is lawful and provided no structural alterations take place. However, if the main use is stopped, the secondary use cannot be continued in its own right. Secondly, there may be a variety of activities for which an entire area is used. These activities may be integrated into one composite use, so that if the composite use ceases the activities making it up cannot be continued independently. Thus if a site is used for a research establishment, offices and laboratories may be transferred freely between different parts of the whole site, but the offices could not be kept on without planning permission after the laboratories closed.[13] However, a site may be used for several distinct purposes, none of which are ancillary to any other. These may be moved about on the site, and may be continued even after the others are terminated, provided they are not significantly intensified. Thus where a site used for car breaking and storage of materials came to be used entirely for storage, there was a material change of use, not because the car breaking had stopped, but because the storage area had significantly expanded.[14]

In Burdle's case, Bridge J.'s third category in identifying planning units was 'that within a single unit of occupation two or more physically separate and distinct areas may be occupied for substantially different and unrelated purposes. In such a case each area used for a different main purpose (together with its incidental and ancillary activities) ought to be considered as a separate planning unit.' It is in such cases that internal boundaries may need to be identified within a single unit of occupation. Bridge J. suggested that, however many uses are operated on a piece of land, it 'may be a useful working rule to assume that the unit of occupation is the appropriate unit, unless and until some smaller unit can be recognised as the site of activities which amount in substance to a separate use both physically and functionally'. The unit of occupation is that which is directly controlled by a particular person. It may be part of a larger block of property with a common landlord. In such a case planning permission or proceedings for enforcement would normally relate to the unit occupied by a single tenant.[15] However, a planning application could be made by a landlord, or by a prospective developer with no interest in the land, to develop say a number of separately occupied flats. For such a purpose, the plots would be treated as a single larger planning unit. Similarly, a landlord might develop land which he had let to a number of different tenants, perhaps by erecting an extremely high wall around an entire estate. There, enforcement proceedings would be served on him in respect of the entire estate.[16]

For the purpose of planning decisions, it is usually planning authorities which identify planning units, and as we shall see in Chapter 8.2, they can only be challenged in the courts if they do so in a clearly erroneous manner. In reviewing a decision by another court or by an administrative body, a court will be reluctant to substitute its own view of the facts or policy. However, a developer may be able to influence such decisions by taking care in exactly what he does on the ground. Thus, if he has established rights to operate a camping site and wishes to be flexible in where he puts tents, he may plant trees and construct banks so that the initial site appears to be part of a large area.[17] If a factory owner wishes to let out a car park to the public because he no longer needs it for employees, it may be easier to establish that the new car park is a separate planning unit which may be used independently of the factory unit, if it is laid out so as to appear separate.[18]

Problems over planning units often arise where property in sole occupation is split up, or separate properties are combined. The changes may involve an alteration of use, as where a part of a field is bought as an extension to a storage yard. Probably, even if there is little or no physical change of use, the fact that a planning unit has changed its identity may itself constitute development. Thus, if part of a field is incorporated into the garden of a house, it becomes ancillary to the use of that house and this may constitute development even though the land itself is still left under grass or planted with potatoes just as it was before.[19] However, where there are adjacent properties with the same established uses, there would not seem to be a change of use merely in adjusting the boundaries, or, for example, in throwing into one two or more houses. On the other hand separating existing units of control may amount to development if this involves the use of land becoming more intense or other material changes in quality. Thus if a storage depot were divided into separate plots, this could amount to development if the plots were then used much more intensively than the whole original site.[20] Where a unit is divided up, it would amount to a material change if an old subsidiary use were continued in its own right as a principle use, as, if a barn, once used for farm produce or machinery, were sold off separately as a warehouse.[21]

2.1.3 Property boundaries

It is with the boundaries between separately owned or occupied properties that accuracy is most important. Disputes between neighbours are often particularly acrimonious, and bad blood which has been simmering for years may literally be spilt if a garage or a fence is built a few yards over a disputed line. It is very important to establish the boundaries of a property clearly at the time when it is being sold or let, and there may be little excuse for unclear boundaries where a single property is subdivided. The problems which may result from unclear boundaries are illustrated by the case of *Scarfe* v. *Adams*.[22] On 14 November 1978, the Rake Manor estate Milford, in West Surrey, was auctioned in lots. The estate included 82 acres, two substantial houses and other smaller buildings. Of these, a coach house was sold in two plots. The Adams, who had bought one of the plots then claimed that they were entitled to parts of their neighbour's rooms and gardens, as these fell on their side of a line marked on the plan bound up with the conveyance. This plan was based on a small-scale Ordnance Survey map of 1:2500. The neighbour, Ms Scarfe, sued for a declaration that her boundary lay along the internal wall and extended thence through the gardens. A deputy circuit judge in the county court held that the plan showed the true position. However, the Court of Appeal reversed him, saying that the plan was worse than useless. Because the deed and plan were, 'uncertain, contradictory and ambiguous', extrinsic evidence could be looked at. The architect's plans for the auction clearly showed that the division was intended to run along the internal walls and be continued so as to separate the gardens. Cumming-Bruce L.J. described the case as, 'a cautionary tale to be noted and digested by every conveyancing solicitor and legal executive'.

Boundary disputes may arise between landlords and tenants as well as between neighbouring landowners. A tenant may claim that he has been let a larger piece of land than the landlord accepts. There may also be a dispute over the extent of a right of way. Thus a person entitled to use a private road may be challenged by the owner if he brings large farm vehicles down it which overhang the verges. The owner of the land across which the road runs may wish to build on the land right up to the road or may simply object to any extended use. In some boundary disputes, neighbours may each claim that the other owns land which neither wants, perhaps because it is waste and unusable and is a breeding ground for weeds or vermin which may be expensive to eliminate. Again, it may be important to identify the exact boundary in cases where one landowner claims that trees on neighbouring land have grown over or under it. If trees cause harm across boundaries without actually penetrating beyond them, the tree owner is unlikely to be responsible for the harm.[24] There may also be a dispute where one piece of land is threatened by earth movement from adjacent land.[25] Thus a question might arise as to whether a retaining wall belongs to the lower or the higher property, as this would determine who was responsible for its maintenance.

NOTES: SECTION 2.1

1. Church of England Ordnance, No. 18 of 1559.
2. *Ante* p. 38.
3. County Court Rules, 1981, S.I. 1981, No. 1687, Order 4, Rule 2 and Order 16, Rule 2.

4. Magistrates' Courts Act 1980, s. 3.
5. Town and Country Planning Act 1971, s. 20.
6. Ibid s. 7(4), as amended by Local Government (Miscellaneous Provisions) Act 1982, s. 47, and Sched. 6, Para. 7.
7. See *post* p. 132.
8. Town and Country Planning Act 1971, s. 1 as amended by Local Government Act 1972, s. 182, and Sched. 16, Para. 43. For National Parks. See *post* p. 129.
9. Town and Country Planning Act 1971, s. 7 (1A) and (6) as substituted by Local Government Planning and Land Act 1980, s. 89, and Sched. 14, Para. 2.
10. Town and Country Planning Act 1971, s. 11(3).
11. *Burdle* v. *Secretary of State for the Environment* [1972] 1 W.L.R. 1207, D.C.
12. *G. Percy Trentham Ltd* v. *Gloucestershire County Council* [1966] 1 W.L.R. 506, C.A., see *post* p. 113, note 25.
13. *Re St Winifred's Welcomes Road, Kenley, Surrey* (1969) 20 P. & C.R. 583.
14. *Wipperman* v. *Barking London Borough Council* (1965) 17 P. and C.R. 225 D.C.
15. *Johnston* v. *Secretary of State for the Environment* (1974) 28 P. & C.R. 424.
16. Under the Town and Country Planning Act 1971, s. 87 (5), enforcement notices are served on the owner even if there is a different occupier, who is also to be served.
17. Cf. *Williams-Denton* v. *Watford Rural District Council* (1963) 15 P. & C.R. 11, D.C. This case was concerned with a caravan site. The limits even of well-established caravan sites are now generally settled by the terms of site licences required under the Caravan Sites and Control of Development Act 1960, see *post* p. 146.
18. *Steel Barrow Co. Ltd* v. *Central Land Board* (1953) 4 P. & C.R. 234, L.T.
19. *Sampson's Executors* v. *Nottinghamshire County Council* [1949] 2 K.B. 439, D.C.
20. *East Barnet Urban District Council* v. *British Transport Commission* [1962] 2 Q.B. 484.
21. *G. Percy Trentham* v. *Gloucestershire County Council, supra* note 12.
22. *Scarfe* v. *Adams* [1981] 1 All E.R. 843, C.A.
23. A landowner is obliged to control nuisances arising on his land, and these probably include weeds and vermin. See *post* p. 348.
24. See *post* p. 198 and p. 338.
25. See *post* p. 198f. and p. 348.

2.2 How to identify legal boundaries

A striking aspect of English property boundaries is that their detailed locations are not normally recorded in any authoritative form. As we shall see in Chapter 5 Section 2, increasingly the title to pieces of English land now depends on entries in state land registers. There the locations of relevant pieces of land may be marked out on maps based on the Ordnance Survey, but the boundaries are only general and are not delineated precisely.

2.2.1 Identifying existing boundaries

The exact position of boundaries may sometimes be ascertained from documents, but often, where there is a dispute, what may prove of greater importance are physical features on the ground and the extent to which the claimants have exercised control over the relevant land.

(a) Maps and documents for general purposes

It might be thought that the most obvious public source of information about boundaries would be Ordnance Survey maps. These are still made under powers given in the Ordnance Survey Act 1841,[1] and are now ultimately the responsibility of the Department of the Environment. The Act provided for the fixing of county boundaries 'by the putting down of any posts, blocks, or bolts of wood, metal or stone, or by the affixing of any marks on or against any church, chapel, bridge, house, or other public or private building or post', with appropriate 'distinguishing letters or figures'.[2] The Act stipulated that it was not to affect the position of property boundaries[3]. However, a survey map may help to establish the location of a boundary which is known to be related to any feature such as those mentioned in the Act, or for example a track, particularly where these have changed or ceased to exist since the boundary was originally established.[4] A new boundary may be defined expressly by reference to a survey map. This may vary the normal rules particularly for fixing boundaries on hedges or ditches, since the Ordnance Survey marks boundaries down the middle of such features, whereas normal legal presumptions would place them on one piece of property or another.[5] There are dangers in using Ordnance Survey maps as the basis for a conveyance. In *Blacklocks* v. *J.B. Developments (Godalming) Ltd*[6], part of a farm had been sold off to raise capital for new buildings. The original purchaser re-sold some years later to a property company which sought planning permission to develop the site, including a triangle on which the farm had now built a barn. The triangle was shown on the plan prepared for the original sale as part of the land which had been sold. The parties to the original sale had, however, in fact agreed to put the boundary along a road which was not marked on the Ordnance Survey map upon which the plan was based. This road separated the triangle where the barn had been built from the land which had been sold. On an application by the farmer, the High Court ordered the plan in the Land Registry to be rectified so as to make clear that the triangle and the barn were not part of the developers' land. However, J.B. Developments had been aware of the mistake when they bought their land and realized that they were not entitled to the land on which the barn was built. Had they not known this, the court would not have ordered rectification.

Apart from the Ordnance Survey other public maps and documents may sometimes provide evidence of the location of boundaries. Even Domesday Book could still be used for such a purpose.[7] At common law, public documents, including maps, are generally admissable as evidence of the facts stated in them, provided they have been made by authorized public agents in the course of their official duties and the facts are of public interest or notoriety.[8] In civil disputes, this rule is now given statutory effect by the Civil Evidence Act 1968.[9] Under s. 4(1) of that act, in civil proceedings, a document, generally, may be evidence of the facts stated in it, if direct oral evidence of those facts would have been admissable, and the document is, or forms part of, a record compiled by a person acting under a duty from information supplied by anyone who may reasonably be supposed to have personal knowledge of the relevant matters. If the information is supplied indirectly, it will still be admissable provided the intermediaries had a duty to pass it on. Thus, if a surveyor were employed to make a detailed map, this would probably be good evidence many years later, when the surveyor was no longer available, to show boundaries, provided it appeared that he had identified these, using information from people familiar with the ground who would have known where the boundaries lay. In *Knight* v. *David*,[10] the trustees of the Margam estate in the old county of Glamorgan were battling with the trustees of a charity known as Kenfig Corporation Property over who had the greater legal rights in land known as Kenfig Common. Goulding J. allowed the plaintiffs in the case to put in evidence an early nineteenth-century tithe map, both as a public document and under the Civil Evidence Act s. 4 (1).

(b) Documents of title

The most valuable evidence of boundaries may be the documents of title of the relevant land. However, these are often ambiguous or lacking in detail. They may inaccurately reflect what was intended when the property was split up.[11] Also, the deeds of adjacent properties may conflict or, as we shall see in Chapter 5, Section 5.5, originally clear boundaries may have changed as a result of long use. When the title to land is registered, the Land Registry may be asked to approve fixed boundaries for which an accurate survey will be prepared.[12] However, this is very costly to the appellant and may prompt disputes among neighbours which would not otherwise have arisen. As we shall see in Chapter 5, Section 5.2, the Land Registry will only record a definitive title when it is entirely happy that it is justified,[13] and the Registry takes considerable care to ensure that any disputes with neighbours as to boundaries are taken into account. Even when a title is registered as absolute, because boundaries are normally general, there may be quite considerable uncertainty. It might be thought that when a new building estate is created, the opportunity would be taken to provide for clear fixed boundaries, but because of the expense this is rarely done, and in practice builders may put in boundary fences, or even erect buildings, in different positions from what has been indicated on the maps provided for registration (Fig. 2.3). Thus, in *Lee* v. *Barrey*[14] Mr Barrey had bought one of five building plots at Whetstone in

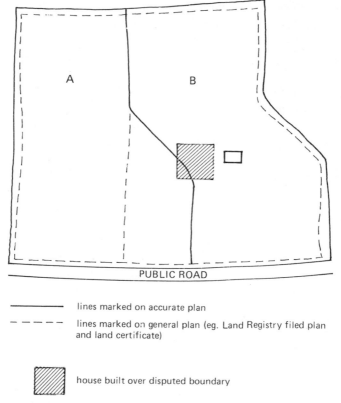

Fig. 2.3 Problems arising from the use of general boundaries in conveyancing (cf. *Lee v. Barrey* [1957] Ch. 251).

Middlesex. The plots together formed a block of land which was essentially rectangular but with a crooked eastern boundary. The vendor had provided the Land Registry with a filed plan of the block marking the internal boundaries between the plots as straight dotted lines. Mr Barrey's land certificate stated that the boundaries were marked from the transfer plan and were subject to revision on survey after the erection of fences. However, his contract showed the precise intention of the vendor which was for the side boundaries to be angled. At its greatest there was a discrepancy of 10 feet in the plans. In the event Mr Barrey built his house following the land certificate and extending on to land claimed by his western neighbour Mr Lee. The courts held that Mr Barrey had committed a trespass. The accurate plan in the Conveyance was correct.

Where land is registered, the land certificate may provide at least as accurate a boundary as any earlier deeds. Nevertheless, these may be used later if a boundary dispute arises. When the land has not been registered, such deeds are likely to be the best evidence of boundaries. Although more recent deeds may be most important in establishing title, if these are ambiguous as to a boundary, older deeds may become crucial. In particular, if a dispute arises over the boundary between two properties which were once jointly owned, the deeds made at the time when they were separated are likely to be vital. Conveyances normally include plans. These may be stated to be only for purposes of identification. Even so, they may still be useful in resolving ambiguity.[15] However, even if such a plan is detailed, it will be subordinate to the written description,[16] and to physical features on the ground to which this may refer.[17] On the other hand, even a plan annexed to a conveyance which does not actually mention it at all may be relied on, provided the two do not conflict.[18] If a deed states that a property is more particularly delineated on a plan, the plan will prevail over any conflicting description in the conveyance.[19] However, the plan may still appear to be inaccurate, for example because it does not correspond with features on the ground which it purports to be based on. One frequent problem with plans purporting to show precise measurements is that these may be unrelated to any feature on the ground at all. Thus measurements may be given from a wall or a hedge but with no indication as to which property owns this. However, plans often indicate ownership of such features by means of T marks. These are drawn with the top part of the T against a feature, and the foot pointing to the land to which the feature belongs (Fig. 2.4).

(c) Presumptions and evidence of use

Because boundaries are so often uncertain, the law of evidence may be crucial

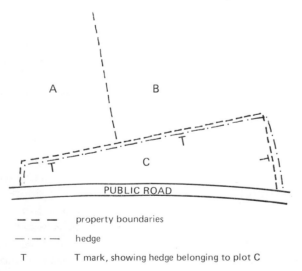

A   B

T

C

PUBLIC ROAD

— — —   property boundaries

— · — · —   hedge

T   T mark, showing hedge belonging to plot C

Fig. 2.4 The use of 'T' marks.

Fig. 2.5 Presumptions drawn from the position of a ditch and bank, as to boundary between property A and property B.

in identifying them. When the deeds do not resolve where a boundary lies this may depend upon certain legal presumptions. Thus, where two pieces of land are separated by a *ditch* and a *bank*, there is a legal presumption that whoever dug the ditch would have thrown the soil onto his own land (Fig. 2.5). Often such a bank is planted with a hedge. The boundary is treated as running along the lip of the ditch furthest from the bank.[20] Even evidence that a ditch has been maintained for a considerable time exclusively by the owner on the side away from the bank, may be insufficient to displace the presumption.[21] Before 1926 *structures on boundaries* in general and *walls* in particular were often owned in common by neighbours. The Law of Property Act 1925, s. 38 had the effect that ownership of such structures built so as to straddle a boundary is divided vertically with mutual rights of support for each part against the other. Each neighbour will be entitled to repair the entire wall, but will not be able to compel the other to participate.[22] In the absence of other evidence, walls, whether of buildings or separating gardens or other open land, may be assumed to be divided in this manner, rather than built exclusively on one of the neighbouring properties.[23] In London, the London Building Acts (Amendment) Act 1939, Part VI includes special rules for party walls in central London. Notably, under s. 46, where there is a party wall with the wall itself straddling a boundary, or where there is a building erected on one side of the boundary but right up to it, the owner of adjoining land is entitled, after giving notice, to carry out works, such as repairs on the wall as a whole.[24] A neighbour who benefits from such work may even be required to contribute to its expense.[25]

Where a *right of way*, whether private or a highway, lies between two properties, the presumption is that these include the soil, or at least, in the case of the highway, the sub-soil, up to the middle. Where a road has wide verges these are likely to be part of the highway. In the distant past adjacent landowners were responsible for maintaining highways if they fenced their land.[26] Thus they tended not to fence. Because roads were so badly surfaced the public would use space along the edges to avoid potholes. Today boundaries on such highways may be difficult to determine, and a highway may not extend right up to a modern boundary fence. Thus in *Hinds and*

Diplock v. *Breconshire County Council*,[27] a Welsh farmer and his
tenant erected a fence along a half-acre piece of land on the road between
Pontneathvaughan and Ystradfeltt. The County Council pulled this down,
claiming that an old fence further back was the boundary of the highway. At
the ensuing trial, Singleton J. held that the Council had committed a trespass.
The old fence had merely been erected in a convenient place for containing
stock and not with any reference to the road. The inference was that the new
fence was within the true boundary. Where a ditch runs beside a road, there is
a presumption that it belongs to the neighbouring land. Thus, Bedfordshire
County Council was treated as a trespasser on land beside a narrow road
between Henlow and Hitchin at Shillington when it filled in an adjacent ditch
after a lorry had slipped into it and broken down the bank.[28] In the case of
highways it is normally the responsibility of adjacent landowners to put up
their own fences. By contrast, the standard requirement under the Railways
Clauses Consolidation Act 1845[29] was that railway authorities were obliged
to fence off the line. Today, fences beside *railways* will still generally belong
with the railway.

Where properties are separated by a *river* or stream, the basic rule is that, as
with highways, they include the bed up to the middle line (Fig. 2.6). Thus

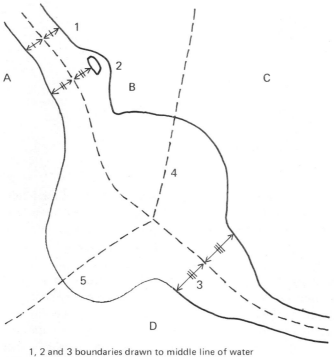

1, 2 and 3 boundaries drawn to middle line of water
4 and 5 extensions of boundaries on land

Fig. 2.6 Water boundaries.

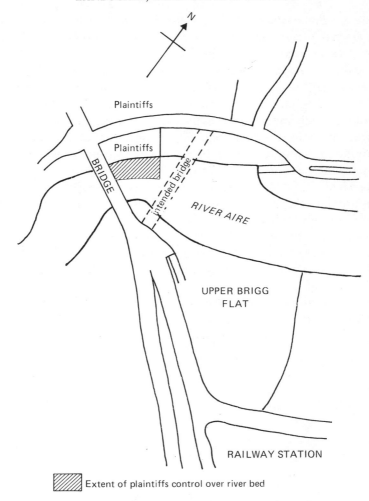

Fig. 2.7 *Micklethwait* v. *Newlay Bridge Co.* (1886) 33 Ch. D. 133.

when the Midland Railway Company bought a plot of land called Upper Brigg Flat beside the River Aire in Leeds to erect a bridge, owners of land on the opposite bank, who had originally sold off Upper Brigg Flat, failed to prevent the construction of the bridge. It would cross part of the river bed between the two properties but only on the Brigg Flat side (Fig. 2.7).[30] If a stream gradually changes course, the boundary moves with it.[31] On the other hand if the course suddenly changes leaving an isolated dry bed, the boundary will remain along the centre of this.[32] Where an island lies on one side of a stream it normally belongs to the nearest bank so that the boundary line runs down the middle of the stream between the island and the further bank.[33] Where a lake is bounded by several properties, there seems to be no clear rule as to how the bed is divided between these, although a likely solution which has been approved in Scotland is to apply the same rule as for streams so as to put boundaries midway between properties on opposite banks. If there are more than two properties, the boundaries may be drawn to a mid point as extensions of those on the land.[34] This may be a delicate exercise for surveyors. Where the shores of a lake gradually shift, as with rivers, the boundaries would seem to move.[35] As artificial water courses or reservoirs are generally constructed on land which clearly belongs to one person or another they are unlikely to be on boundaries. If they are, one side will normally form the boundary. In *tidal areas*, the bed of both tidal rivers and the foreshore, belongs to the Crown or to anyone to whom the Crown has expressly granted it. The foreshore is regarded as the ground below the average tide line, that is midway between spring and neap tides. Thus it is more often covered by water than not.[36]

(d) Above and below ground

Traditionally the owner of the surface of a piece of land owned everything above, up to the heavens, and everything below, down to the bowels of the earth. However, the Law of Property Act 1925,[37] makes clear that land may be divided up horizontally or vertically. Thus the minerals below ground are often separated from ownership of the surface. Where land has been sold, mineral rights may have been reserved by the vendor. Where land has been acquired under statutory powers, for example for a canal or railway, often the subsoil will have been left with the original owner if he retained the adjacent land. A public authority with the legal estate in a highway only requires a thin section of land. Lord Denning once defined this as the top one or two spits.[38] The road only includes as much space above and below the ground as is needed for its effective operation. Therefore, the owners of land across which a road runs may be free to build an office block straddling it.[39] Boundaries within buildings and particularly between floors may be difficult to determine. Thus a building may include cellars under neighbouring land, but only if this is carefully stipulated. In *Grigsby* v. *Melville*[40] a butcher named Fish had owned a building in Knockhundred Row, Midhurst, Sussex. The building was subsequently sold in two parts. Three years after moving into one of the properties, Mrs Grigsby was alarmed by the sound of hammering underneath her drawing-room floor. She discovered that her neighbour, Mr Melville, a veterinary surgeon, was making a ceiling to a cellar reached by steps from his property but lying under hers. Mrs Grigsby successfully sued the Melvilles. The conveyances of the properties had not mentioned the cellar, and were therefore treated as including everything below the ground within the boundaries marked at surface level. By contrast, a building which is separated from adjoining land will normally be treated as including projecting footings and eaves even if the conveyance shows these as being on the adjoining land. In such a case the adjoining land will merely be entitled to the intervening column of air.[41] However, the owner of the building with the projecting footings and eaves will not be entitled to erect an extension into this space or build above the eaves.[42]

Usually, it is easier to ensure proper management of buildings which are divided horizontally, if the freehold of the whole building is kept intact and interests in its parts are granted only for limited periods at a time by means of leases,[43] whether flats are sold freehold, when they are rather alarmingly known as *flying freeholds*, or are let, the boundary between floors may be through the middle of supporting beams so that the properties include their respective floors and ceilings.[44] Each flat will include its exterior wall. Thus in *Sturge* v. *Hackett*,[45] Lt Col Hackett, MC, the tenant of a first floor flat in Henbury Manor, Wimborne, Dorset, accidently burnt the entire house when he tried to smoke out a swallows' nest with a blazing paraffin rag. The Court of Appeal held that the fire was covered by an insurance policy which applied provided fire had started on the colonel's property. The fire actually started from an ornamental cornice which was fixed to the outside wall of the flat and below the floor joints to which the ceiling was attached.

As for air space above a building or open land, statute, now the Civil Aviation Act 1982, s. 76, provides that no action may be brought in nuisance or trespass in respect of the flight of an aeroplane complying with appropriate air controls over land, provided it was flying at a height which was reasonable, 'having regard to the wind, weather and all the circumstances of the case'.[46] However, under the act landowners may recover damages without the need to prove negligence, for any harm caused to person or property by an aeroplane or by any person in it or by any article, animal or person falling out of it. In *Lord Bernstein* v. *Skyviews and General Ltd*,[47] Griffiths J. held that, even apart from the Act, today, the rights of a landowner to air space are restricted 'to such height as is necessary for the ordinary use and enjoyment of his land and the structures upon it . . . [A]bove that height he has no greater rights in the airspace than any other member of the public.'[48] Skyviews took aerial photographs of land to whose owners they offered these for sale. Two such photographs were offered to Lord Bernstein in 1967 and he kept them to hang on the wall of his office. Nevertheless, he wrote objecting to the interference with his privacy, and when more photographs were offered in 1974, he demanded that all prints and negatives be destroyed. A secretary in Skyviews office then tactlessly offered to sell Lord Bernstein the negatives and he sued. Griffiths J. held that taking a run of aerial photographs was not trespass even if it involved flying over someone else's land without their consent. Those of Lord Bernstein's land might, in any event, have been taken from one side. Griffiths J. added that at common law and despite the Civil Aviation Act, proceedings might be brought in nuisance in an extreme case, for example where a house was harrassed by constant aerial surveillance.

2.2.2 Fixing and changing boundaries

Boundaries of registered land may be fixed by the Chief Land Registrar, under the Land Registration Rules, 1925.[49] Owners and occupiers of adjacent land must be notified and the Registrar will adjudicate on any dispute. An appeal lies from his decision to the High Court.[50] The Registrar may himself state a case to the High Court when he is in doubt as to any matter of law or fact bearing upon a title.[51] Generally, if a dispute arises over a boundary to registered land, the Registrar, or the court, may order the register to be rectified under the Land Registration Act 1925, s. 82. A person who is affected by the original inaccurate entry may be entitled to compensation from the Registrar under s. 83. Whether land is registered or not, parties may obtain a ruling from the courts as to the location of a boundary, simply by seeking a declaration or by bringing an action in trespass. Usually boundary disputes will be within the jurisdiction of the county court. In the case of registered land the court may order an appropriate rectification of the register.

The exact location of a boundary may be fixed by neighbours putting in their own marking posts or agreeing on a properly drawn plan. Because such an agreement does not actually involve transferring land it does not strictly have to be expressed in writing. As we will see in Chapter 5, Section 5.3, this is normally necessary under the Law of Property Act 1925, s. 40, for a contract where a transfer of land is involved. Under s. 52, an effective conveyance will require a deed. Where parties agreed to vary a boundary, perhaps straightening it by exchanging pieces of land whose ownership was not in doubt, if the agreement was not expressed in writing it cannot be enforced in the courts unless the parties have acted on it, as by treating the transferred parts as their own, in which case they may rely on the doctrine of part performance.[53] For an effective conveyance there must be a deed. However, as we shall see in Chapter 5, Section 5.5, land may effectively be transferred if it is treated by one person as his own over a long period. This most commonly occurs where a landowner treats land on his neighbour's side of the boundary as if it were his own.

NOTES: SECTION 2.2

1. Interpretation Act 1978, s. 5, and schedule 1.
2. Ordnance Survey Act 1841, s. 6.
3. Ibid, s. 12.
4. *Attorney General* v. *Antrobus* [1905] 2 Ch. 188. Farwell J. *Obiter dicta* at p. 203.
5. *Fisher* v. *Winch* [1939] 1 K.B. 666.
6. *Blacklocks* v. *J.B. Developments (Godalming) Ltd.* [1982] Ch. 183, and see *Scarfe* v. *Adams ante* p. 64.
7. *Duke of Beaufort* v. *John Aird & Co.* (1904) 20 T.L.R. 602 and see *post* p. 235f.

8. Huxley Buzzard, J. *et al.* (1982) *Phipson on Evidence*, 13th edn, Sweet & Maxwell, London, p. 508.
9. Civil Evidence Act 1968, s. 9.
10. *Knight* v. *David* [1971] 1 W.L.R. 1671.
11. As in *Blacklocks* v. *J B Developments (Godalming) Ltd. ante* note 6.
12. *Post*, p. 75.
13. *Post*, p. 238.
14. *Lee* v. *Barrey* [1957] Ch. 251, C.A.
15. *Hopgood* v. *Brown* [1955] 1 W.L.R. 213, C.A.
16. *Manning* v. *Fitzgerald* (1859) 29 L.J. Ex. 24.
17. *Leachman* v. *L. & K. Richardson Ltd.* [1969] 1 W.L.R. 1129.
18. *Eastwood* v. *Ashton* [1915] A.C. 900, H.L.
19. *Stanley* v. *White* (1811) 14 East. 332.
20. *Fisher* v. *Winch, supra* note 5.
21. Compare *Henniker* v. *Howard* (1904) 90 L.T. 157, K.B.D.
22. *Jones* v. *Pritchard* [1908] 1 Ch. 630.
23. *Mason* v. *Fulham Corporation* [1910] 1 K.B. 631 at p. 637.
24. London Building Acts (Amendment) Act 1939, s. 46.
25. Ibid. s. 56.
26. *Steel* v. *Prickett (1818) 2 Stark. 463.*
27. *Hinds and Diplock* v. *Breconshire County Council* [1938] 4 All E.R. 24. Compare *Attorney General* v. *Beynon.* [1970] 1 Ch. 1.
28. *Hanscombe* v. *Bedfordshire County Council* [1938] Ch. 944.
29. Railways Clauses Consolidation Act 1845, s. 68.
30. *Micklethwait* v. *Newlay Bridge Co.* (1886) 33 Ch.D. 133.
31. *Bickett* v. *Morris* (1868) 1 L.R. Sc. & Div. 47, H.L. *Obiter dicta* of Lord Cranworth at p. 58.
32. *Ford* v. *Lacy* (1861) 7 Hurl. & Nor. 151, at p. 156, *per* Martin B.
33. *Great Torrington Commons Conservators* v. *Moore Stevens* [1904] 1 Ch. 347.
34. *Mackenzie* v. *Bankes* (1878) 3 App. Cas. 1324, H.L., *per* Lord Selborne at p. 1338.
35. *Southern Centre of Theosophy Inc.* v. *State of South Australia* [1982] 1 All E.R. 283, P.C.
36. *Mellor* v. *Walmesley* [1905] 2 Ch. 164.
37. Law of Property Act 1925, s. 205 (1) (ix).
38. *Tithe Redemption Commission* v. *Runcorn Urban District Council* [1954] Ch. 383, *per* Denning L.J. at p. 407, C.A.
39. *Hemel Hempstead Development Corporation* v. *Hemel Hempstead Borough Council* [1962] 1 W.L.R. 1158.
40. *Grigsby* v. *Melville* [1974] 1 W.L.R. 80, C.A.
41. *Truckell* v. *Stock* [1957] 1 W.L.R. 161, C.A., and *Williams* v. *Usherwood* (1983) 45 P. & C.R. 235, C.A.
42. *Laybourn* v. *Gridley* [1892] 2 Ch. 53.
43. *Post* p. 182f.
44. *Phelps* v. *Mayor etc. of the City of London* [1916] 2 Ch. 255.
45. *Sturge* v. *Hackett* [1962] 3 All E.R. 166, C.A.
46. Civil Aviation Act 1982, s. 76.
47. *Lord Bernstein* v. *Skyviews and General Ltd* [1978] 1 Q.B. 478.
48. Ibid. p. 488.
49. Statutory Rules and Orders, 1925, No. 1093, Rule 276, made under the Land Registration Act 1925, s. 144.

50. Land Registration Rules, 1925, *supra* note 49, Rule 299.
51. At the request of a party; Land Registration Act 1925, s. 140, or on the initiative of the Registrar; Land Registration Rules, 1925, *supra* note 49, Rule 298.
52. Usually the county court may not grant a declaration of injunction save where they are ancilliary to some other relief, but this restriction does not now apply in claims concerned with rights in land; County Courts Act 1959, s. 51A, added by Administration of Justice Act 1977. See *post* p. 382f. and p. 388.
53. *Penn* v. *Lord Baltimore* [1750] 1 Ves. Sen. 444.

2.3 Fixtures

In 1963, a building preservation order was made to protect Scarisbrick Hall in Lincolnshire, a gothic revival masterpiece by Augustus Pugin and his son Edward (Fig. 2.8). The owners of the Hall sold it to a preparatory school but wanted to dispose separately of many valuable features, including portraits copied from originals at Hampton Court and fifteenth-century carvings. The preservation order specifically included these and also the wrought iron main entrance gates together with their flanking dwarf stone piers and walls. The owners sought to have the preservation order quashed on the grounds that it could not apply to these items as they were not part of a building. Russell L.J. dismissed the application,[1] holding that the relevant items were in law part of the building. Today, the Town and Country Planning Act 1971 provides a listing procedure for the protection of buildings of special architectural and historical interest, and 'any object or structure fixed to a building or forming part of the land and comprised within the curtilage of a building, shall be treated as part of the building'.[2] However, it is still not always easy to tell whether a feature is properly to be regarded as part of a building. Entrance gates or panelling may obviously be included. A chest or set of chairs in a house or garden are unlikely to be, but what for example of statues and ornamental items in the grounds?

2.3.1 The importance of recognizing fixtures

The question of what is and what is not part of a piece of land may be vital in many circumstances. Items which are treated as part of the land are known as fixtures.

(a) The importance of fixtures in the public control of land

As the case of Scarisbrick Hall illustrates, if something in a listed building is a fixture, it may be protected along with the building. The concept of fixtures has also been applied in the more fundamental area of development control. Development, for which planning permission is required, may consist of a material change of use or 'the carrying out of building, engineering, mining or

Fig. 2.8 The King's Room, Scarisbrick Hall, by kind permission of the Principal, Charles A. Oxley Esq.

other operations, in, on, over or under land'.[3] In *Cheshire County Council* v. *Woodward*,[4] a coal merchant brought into his coal yard a hopper and conveyor between 16 and 20 feet high. He had been advised that if it was fixed to the land it would constitute development so he ensured that it had wheels and could be moved around on them, although it was intended for permanent use in the yard. The County Council served an enforcement notice ordering Woodward to remove the hopper, but both the Minister of Housing and Local Government and the Divisional Court treated the order as ineffective. As Lord Parker C.J. stated the law, operational development involves changing the physical characteristics of land, and the question as to what additions have this effect is analagous to the question as to what fixtures pass with land when a freehold is exchanged. Successive planning Acts have defined a building to include any structure or erection and 'the Act is referring to any structure or erection which can be said to form part of the realty, and to change the physical character of the land'.[5] Thus machinery which can be moved around, even although it is extremely large, may not be regarded as part of the land. In many situations, an architect, or landscape architect, may need to establish whether a particular item will constitute a fixture; for example the question may determine whether planning permission is required before realigning a dry stone wall or moving an ornamental feature in a park.

(b) Fixtures and taxation

Whether a feature of a house or a piece of land is a fixture or not may have important tax implications. If a market garden were being sold off, income tax could be payable on plants which were not part of the land, as their sale could be regarded as in the normal course of trade.[6] If fixtures are sold they are more likely to attract capital gains tax,[7] although the person who for example buys buildings so as to demolish them and sell off materials, or who deals in land itself, may be required to pay income tax on such sales.[8]

(c) Fixtures and inheritance

In the Middle Ages it was the policy of English law to keep land holdings, including fixtures, intact by providing that on the death of a landowner all his real property would be inherited by his heir, who would usually be the eldest son if there was one. Today the property of anyone who dies intestate will normally be shared equally between any children. However, provision will first be made for a surviving spouse.[9] This provision includes personal chattels such as furniture. By contrast, the law may require features attached to a house or land to be sold off with the land and the proceeds distributed. If there is a will, this may specifically bequeath a house or land to one person and other property elsewhere. Therefore, disputes may arise between beneficiaries as to what is included with a house or land.

(d) Transfer of fixtures by the living

If land is sold, leased or mortgaged, the original owner will be entitled to take away anything which is a chattel and not part of the land. Thus, in *Moffatt* v. *Kazana*,[10] three years after a bungalow had been sold by the original owner, his executors were entitled to recover a biscuit tin stuffed with £1 notes which had fallen down the chimney where it had been hidden. By contrast, 'buildings erections and fixtures' will pass with land,[11] and a person taking an interest in land may wish to know whether these include, for example, plants and a greenhouse or statues or panelling. Disputes may also arise over the Law of Property Act 1925, s. 40. This provides that no contract to sell or otherwise dispose of land, or of any interest in land, can be enforced in the courts, except where there is a written memorandum or note of the relevant terms, signed by the party who is seeking to evade enforcement or by his authorized agent.[12] A fixture can always be sold off separately from the land to which it is attached, but, so long as it remains a fixture, for there to be a binding contract there must be an appropriate signed document. In *Lavery* v. *Pursell*,[13] Pursell agreed to sell building materials on the demolition of the old London Constitutional Club. The purchaser Lavery was to remove the building within two months. Pursell withdrew from the sale, but Chitty J. dismissed Lavery's action against him because the agreement had not been made with the necessary formalities. Similarly an agreement to sell materials out of the ground such as stone or indeed a slag heap above ground,[14] would not be upheld if it were merely oral. However, the courts may evade the requirement of formalities by treating an item as notionally detached from land even although it has not been removed. In *Marshall* v. *Green*,[15] Marshall agreed orally to sell Green twenty-two standing trees. When Green had cut down six and had already agreed to sell all the tops and stumps to a third party, Marshall wrote revoking the agreement. Green nevertheless removed the remaining trees and Marshall sued him. The old Court of Common Pleas dismissed the claim, holding that the property in the standing trees had passed to Green. It may be sufficient in such a case if there is an oral contract, which provides either for the vendor to detach fixtures such as standing trees or for the purchaser to sever them within a short time. In the interval the ground in effect serves as a warehouse, and its value as a source of nourishment is of no importance. In such a case, if property is sold to one purchaser and then another, the first purchaser will be entitled to it. The second purchaser will have to make do with damages for breach of contract and perhaps for fraud from the double-dealing seller. Nevertheless, in such cases, property will not be transferred immediately, whatever the form of contract, unless this is clearly intended. The Sale of Goods Act 1979, 16 provides that in the absence of express agreement, property in goods which are to be put into a *deliverable state* by the seller will not pass until this has been done. Therefore, although it is generally desirable for a professional person to record in writing any contract which he may enter into, where possible fixtures are concerned, this is essential. For example, the landscape architect whose client tells him that he may keep any top soil which is to be removed from the site should ensure that this is stipulated in writing and signed by the client.

(e) Stolen or lost property

It used to be that a person who wrongfully appropriated the land of another or took away part of the land was only liable in civil law but not in criminal law. Today land itself may still not be stolen. For example it would not be theft to move a boundary fence so as to deprive a neighbour of part of his field. However, the Theft Act 1968 now makes it theft, in most cases, dishonestly to detach and appropriate part of land other than wild plants and foliage.[17] More significantly, where a person has been deprived of his property by theft or otherwise, he will generally be entitled to have it restored to him if he can track it down, but if the property has become fixed to someone else's land he may not be able to recover it. If a contractor were to steal materials or mistakenly took some to which he was not entitled and used them to construct a building or earthworks for a client, or if a landscape gardener were to plant stolen trees or sow stolen grass seed on his client's land, the original owner could not recover the property. As Lindley L.J. once said: 'If I employ a builder to build me a house and he does so with bricks which are not his, I apprehend that they become mine and that the former owner cannot recover them or their value from me.'[18] The original owner would be able to recover damages from the thief or from a person who knowingly allowed stolen materials to be incorporated in his property.

2.3.2   Identifying fixtures

(a) The tests of annexation

There are two tests for deciding whether or not a feature is a fixture. First, *the degree of annexation* must be established. If an object is buried or physically attached to land, by inference, it is a fixture. In *Elwes* v. *Brigg Gas Company,*[19] Elwes leased land for ninety-nine years to the gas company, which began to erect a gas holder. When its workmen discovered a 45 feet wooden boat, 2000 years old, buried over 4 feet deep in the soil close to the river Ancholme, Chitty J. held that Elwes was entitled to the boat as owner of the soil. By contrast if a feature is not physically attached to land it will normally be inferred that it is not a fixture. Thus in *H. E. Dibble* v. *Moore,*[20] Moore was the receiver for a liquidated company which had carried on market gardening at Cottingham near Kingston-upon-Hull. He sold to Dibble various items from the market garden, including two Dutch greenhouses. However, the company had previously sold the land to West and had only remained in occupation under a six-month licence. West objected to

Dibble removing the greenhouses, and they applied to the courts for help. The Court of Appeal ruled that the greenhouses did not belong to the land and therefore Dibble was entitled to remove them. Crucially, the greenhouses were not secured to the ground but stood by their own weight on concrete dollies.

The inference drawn from the fact that an item is attached or unattached to land may be displaced by the second test, *the purpose of annexation*. Thus, even although an item is not physically fixed, it may be treated as part of the land if it is intended to further the use of the land in some manner. For example, a dry stone wall would clearly be regarded as a fixture.[21] A borderline case is that of *D'Eyncourt* v. *Gregory*.[22] John Sherwin Gregory inherited certain property which had previously been subject to a settlement. He was left further property by Gregory Gregory, a previous life tenant, on condition that he renewed the settlement. John Sherwin Gregory declined to renew the settlement, with the effect that he lost the right to any personal property at Harlaxton Manor House in Lincolnshire, which had been the subject of the settlement. Lord Romilly M.R. gave a ruling as to which items at Harlaxton were fixtures. He included carved figures on the stairs, sculptured marble vases in the hall, a pair of marble lions at the head of a flight of garden steps and sixteen stone garden seats, all of which merely rested under their own weight. Lord Romilly likened these to the grinding stone of a flour mill 'which is easily removable, but which is nevertheless a part of the mill itself'. The test of the property at Harlaxton was whether the items 'are part of the architectural design . . . , and put in there as such, as distinguished from mere ornaments to be afterwards added'.[23]

Rather more frequently, items which are physically attached are regarded as not becoming part of the land. In *Webb* v. *Bevis Ltd*,[24] the Court of Appeal took the view that a corrugated iron shed 135 feet by 50 feet should not be regarded as a fixture and could be removed by Bevis. The shed was on waste ground leased from the War Office by Webb, a contractor, who used the rest of the site for storing his materials. Webb had allowed Bevis to erect the shed for the construction of breeze blocks. The court held that the shed was essentially a temporary structure and should be regarded as separate from the 3-inch thick concrete base on which it stood, even though it was bolted to this. Similarly in *Leigh* v. *Taylor*,[25] Madame De Falbe, a life tenant of Luton Hoo house in Bedfordshire, had fixed seven valuable tapestries to walls in the house, with wooden bases screwed to the walls, so that they seemed part of the decoration. Most were completed with moulded surrounds and the walls were repainted to accord with them. Nevertheless, the House of Lords agreed that they had not become part of the house and could be sold separately by Madame De Falbe's executors. On the other hand, in *Re Whaley*,[26] Neville J. held that tapestries and a portrait on wood of Queen Elizabeth I, by Zucchero, should be treated as fixtures. The tapestry was cut to allow a door which it covered to open and 'the ornaments were inserted primarily for the purpose of creating a beautiful room as a whole and not intended for the mere display and enjoyment of the chattels themselves.' Again, in *Re Chesterfield*,[27] Grinling Gibbons carvings, such as decorative panels, overmantles and frames, which were part of the original decoration in the late seventeenth-century Chesterfield mansion of Home Lacy, were treated as fixtures.

(b) Agricultural produce

One class of fixtures which may particularly cause problems is agricultural produce. Here a distinction is traditionally drawn between *fructus industriales*, or annual cash crops which are regarded as distinct from the land, and other plants or trees, which are known as *fructus naturales* and are treated as part of the land. The more a plant depends on the labour and industry of man, rather than on spontaneous natural growth, the more likely it is to be regarded as *fructus industriales*.[28] Where a plant, such as a fruit tree, is treated as part of the land, so are its annual crops. Even if plants are regarded as *fructus naturales* so that any agreement to sell them must be evidenced in writing to comply with the Law of Property Act 1925, s. 40,[29] they may at the same time be treated as goods under the Sale of Goods Act 1979, and so be subject to various implied requirements as to quality. If an agreement is made to sever plants or fruits these may be treated as having notionally ceased to be part of the land.[30]

2.3.3 Rights to remove fixtures

Where an item is regarded as part of land it may sometimes be treated differently from the land itself. In particular, where tenants[31] leave, they have the right to remove three classes of fixtures which they brought onto the land during the tenancy. Before the end of the tenancy, or within a reasonable time thereafter, the tenant may remove *trade fixtures* brought on to enable him to carry out his business, provided their removal will not cause injury to the land. An example is petrol pumps erected at a roadside filling station.[32] Agricultural tenants were not included in this rule but *agricultural fixtures* are now provided for by the Agricultural Holdings Act 1948.[33] This generally allows the tenant of an agricultural holding to remove, within two months after the end of the tenancy, any engine, machinery, fencing or other fixture or any buildings which he has provided on his own account, so long as he has complied with all his obligations to the landlord. However, the tenant must give the landlord one month's notice, expiring before the end of the tenancy, to enable the landlord to purchase any fixtures at a reasonable price. Finally, a tenant may remove *ornamental and domestic fixtures*, such as fireplaces, provided this does not involve irreparable damage to the land to which they are attached[34] and provided they are removed during the tenancy or at least while the tenant remains in possession after it has ended.[35] However, a tenant may not remove substantial structures such as a conservatory which he has built onto a house.[36]

NOTES: SECTION 2.3

1. *Corthorn Land and Timber Co. Ltd* v. *Minister of Housing and Local Government* (1966) 17 P. & C.R. 210.
2. Town and Country Planning Act 1971, s. 54 (9) and see *post* p. 142f.
3. Ibid. s. 22. See *post* p. 110f.
4. *Cheshire County Council* v. *Woodward* [1962] 2 Q.B. 126, D.C.
5. Ibid. at p. 135.
6. Income and Corporation Taxes Act 1970, s. 109, Schedule D., Case 1, and see *post*, p. 98.
7. Capital Gains Tax Act 1979, s. 1 and see *post* p. 98.
8. Compare *Jones* v. *Leeming* [1930] A.C. 415, H.L., and *Snell* v. *Rosser, Thomas & Co. Ltd* [1968] 1 All E.R. 600.
9. Administration of Estates Act 1925.
10. *Moffatt* v. *Kazana* [1969] 2 Q.B. 152.
11. Law of Property Act 1925, s. 62.
12. *Post* p. 246.
13. *Lavery* v. *Pursell* (1888) 39 Ch.D. 508.
14. *Morgan* v. *Russell & Sons* [1909] 1 K.B. 357.
15. *Marshall* v. *Green* (1875) 1 C.P.D. 35.
16. Sale of Goods Act 1979, s. 18, rule 2.
17. Theft Act 1968, s. 4, and see *post* p. 279f.
18. *Gough* v. *Wood & Co.* [1894] 1 Q.B. 713, C.A. at p. 719.
19. *Elwes* v. *Brigg Gas Company* [1886] 33 Ch.D. 562.
20. *H.E. Dibble* v. *Moore* [1970] 2 Q.B. 181, C.A.
21. *Holland* v. *Hodgson* (1872) L.R. 7 C.P. 328, *per* Blackburn J. at p. 335.
22. *D'Eyncourt* v. *Gregory* (1866) 3 L.R. Eq. 382, and see *Monti* v. *Barnes* [1901] 1 Q.B. 205, C.A.
23. *D'Eyncourt* v. *Gregory, supra* note 22 at p. 396.
24. *Webb* v. *Frank Bevis Ltd* [1940] 1 All E.R. 247, C.A.
25. *Leigh* v. *Taylor* [1902] A.C. 157, H.L., affirming the Court of Appeal in *Re. De Falbe* [1901] 1 Ch. 523.
26. *Re Whaley* [1908] 1 Ch. 615.
27. *Re Chesterfield* [1911] 1 Ch. 237.
28. *Marshall* v. *Green, supra* note 15, *per* Lord Coleridge C.J. at p. 40.
29. *Ante* p. 80.
30. *Marshall* v. *Green, supra* note 15.
31. For tenants generally see *post* p. 182.
32. *Smith* v. *City Petroleum Co. Ltd* [1940] 1 All E.R. 260.
33. Agricultural Holdings Act 1948, s. 13.
34. *Spyer* v. *Phillipson* [1931] 2 Ch. 183, C.A., *per* Romer L.J. at p. 209.
35. *Leschallas* v. *Woolf* [1908] 1 Ch. 641, and see *New Zealand Government Property Corpn.* v. *H.M. and S. Ltd.* [1981] 1 W.L.R. 870.
36. *Buckland* v. *Butterfield* (1820), 2 Brod. & B. 54.

Chapter 3

PUBLIC LAW
AND THE CONTROL
OF LAND USE

The law lacks objectivity and neutrality because it is based upon and is available to implement three distinct and competing philosophies or ideologies which dominate or conflict at different points of the system. . . . Firstly, that the law exists and should be used to protect private property and its constitution; this may be called the traditional common law approach to the role of law. Secondly, the law exists and should be used to advance the public interest, if necessary against the interests of private property; this may be called the orthodox public administration and planning approach to the role of law. Thirdly, the law exists to and should be used to advance the cause of public participation against both the orthodox public administration approach to the public interest and the common law approach to the overriding importance of private property; this may be called the radical or populist approach to the role of law.

McAuslan, P. (1980) *The Ideologies of Planning Law*,
Pergamon, Oxford, p. 2

In legal theory, the Crown is the owner of all land in England and Wales. As we shall see in the next chapter, others, whether they are international corporations or private individuals, can own only a legal estate, or some lesser interest in any piece of land. Private land law still provides the framework for the control and exchange of land, but public law controls have become increasingly important. Apart from the theoretical ownership of the soil by the Crown, control over land in the United Kingdom is ultimately vested in the state, because Parliament always has the power to appropriate it or to direct its use. As Professor McAuslan implies, the state is itself merely an organization which gives certain people the power to make decisions because they have been elected or appointed by recognized procedures to some part of the public machine. Land is used by individuals, and the central issue for land law is how the rights which allow control of the land are to be divided and allocated.* Much has been written about who should own the land and who should have the benefit from it, but, whatever philosophy is dominant at a particular time, there is a finite number of ways in which control can actually be exercised, and the law will maintain a balance between control exercised in the name of the public and that left to private individuals or organizations.

3.1   The legal status of public authorities involved in land use

The main public bodies involved in controlling the use of land have already been outlined, in Chapter 1, Section 1.3. Other specialized organizations will be referred to in Section 3.4 below with regard to control over special aspects of land use. In English Law, public bodies are treated as corporate persons, in essentially the same manner as private corporations. Their legal characteristics are discussed at the beginning of the next chapter. However, public bodies do often enjoy a legally privileged position.

3.1.1   Actions against the Crown

Because the Sovereign could not be sued in his own courts, the Crown has always been accorded a unique status in British law. Today the Sovereign is personally immune from any court proceedings. However the Crown, in a wider sense, is used to mean the government, which Lord Diplock has described as a 'term appropriate to embrace both collectively and individually all of the Ministers of the Crown and parliamentary secretaries under whose direction the administrative work of government is carried on by the civil servants employed in the various government departments'.[1]

Before 1947, legal proceedings could only be brought against the Crown, in the wider sense, under a special procedure of *Petition of Right*, for example to recover land or to enforce contracts. The Crown could not be sued in tort. The Crown Proceedings Act 1947 now provides that generally the Crown may be sued as if it were a private individual. Thus, a farmer whose land is flooded by water escaping from government land may sue for damages. If a Crown employee drives a large vehicle onto private land in the course of his work and damages trees or other property, the Crown may be held vicariously liable. However, exceptions remain: the Crown is not bound by any statutory duty unless the relevant statute so provides.[2] Thus, under the Town and Country Planning Act 1971,[3] planning controls apply to any interest in

* Denman, D.C. (1978) *The Place of Property*, Oxford University Press, London.

Crown land which is not actually held on behalf of the Crown. Therefore tenants of Crown land must seek planning permission before they carry out development. However, permission is not needed for development by the Crown itself.[4]

3.1.2 The legal status of public bodies generally

Public bodies, other than the Crown, are normally treated on the same footing as private individuals. They may even be prosecuted for criminal offences.[5] However, public bodies are often given a privileged position by statute. As we shall see in Chapter 6, many statutory powers provide a defence against court actions for their misuse. On the other hand, as Chapter 8, section 8.2 shows, the courts have developed rules of administrative law for regulating decisions made under statutory power. Where public bodies carry out activities which may also be carried out by private individuals or bodies, special procedures are often provided. Thus special arrangements are made by the Town and Country Planning General Regulations 1976,[6] for local planning authorities which wish to carry out development themselves. Such an authority must first pass a resolution to seek permission and then provide publicity similar to that which would be required of a normal applicant. It must consider objections and then, unless the case has been taken over by the Secretary of State, may pass a further resolution to go ahead with the development after which it is deemed to have permission to do so. The Town and Country Planning General Development Order 1977,[7] allows local authorities to carry out certain types of development, such as the erection of lampstands and refuse bins and public shelters, without the need for express planning permission. Other public authorities, in particular statutory undertakers, such as gas and electricity authorities, also have general permission for much of the routine development which they may carry out.[8]

3.1.3 Remedies and procedure

The remedies available against the Crown are generally restricted. Under the Crown Proceedings Act 1947, Part III, judgments may not be exacted by the normal means such as seizing property. Also a court is not able to grant an injunction or make an order of specific performance against the Crown,[9] but may merely make a declaration of the rights of the parties. The Crown is obliged to disclose documents relevant to proceedings,[10] but this is subject to a wide rule that documents dealing with government secrets may not be revealed where this would be contrary to public policy. A related rule protects confidential information of public bodies where there is a danger that the supply of such information would dry up if those who supplied it were named in public.[11] Thus the names of those who alert planning authorities to a breach of planning control may be protected from disclosure. Protection may be claimed in cases where no public body is directly involved. The court may itself take the initiative in excluding such evidence, but normally it will be asked to do so by the public body concerned. The court may look at the document to decide whether the preservation of its confidentiality outweighs its value for justly resolving the case in hand.[12]

NOTES: SECTION 3.1

1. *Town Investments Ltd* v. *Department of the Environment* [1978] A.C. 359 at p. 385, H.L.
2. *Cooper* v. *Hawkins* [1904] 2 K.B. 164, D.C.
3. Town and Country Planning Act 1971, s. 266.
4. *Ministry of Agriculture* v. *Jenkins* [1963] 2 Q.B. 317, C.A. In practice there are standard arrangements whereby the Crown does consult with planning authorities before carrying out development. Department of the Environment Circular 7/77.
5. *Barnet London Borough Council* v. *Eastern Electricity Board* [1973] 1 W.L.R., 430, D.C. See *post* p. 272f.
6. S.I. 1976, No. 1419.
7. S.I. 1977, No. 289, Sched. I, Class XIII.
8. Ibid. Class XVIII.
9. Crown Proceedings Act 1947, s. 2. See *post* p. 382f.
10. Ibid. s. 28.
11. *D.* v. *N.S.P.C.C.* [1978] A.C. 171, H.L.
12. *Conway* v. *Rimmer* [1968] A.C. 910 H.L.

3.2   Methods of public control of land

Public control of land and its use takes two main forms; outright control, and regulation of land left in private hands. In Britain, the need for substantial control by regulation of private land is now taken for granted and even the most ardent opponent of government control of land may accept the need for compulsory powers to acquire particular pieces of land needed for public purposes, such as for schools and libraries.

3.2.1   Direct control

The mechanics of taking land into public ownership are looked at, in Chapter 5, Section 5.1. Land may be acquired, by agreement with existing owners, or by compulsion. It may be acquired permanently or be requisitioned for a temporary period, for example to allow for mineral extraction and then restoration to agriculture. A piece of land may be acquired outright, or some lesser interest, such as a right of access or a right to lay public services may be taken. However, if land is once acquired by a public body, it will normally be retained under public control. For example, local authorities, which have acquired land for public housing, act as landlords through housing departments supervised by elected Councils, although here the Housing Act 1980 has now given Council tenants the rights to buy their homes.[1] The same Conservative Government which produced this Act has encouraged the sale into private hands of other nationalized land, such as agricultural and forestry estates. If a public body retains land in its own hands, it may relinquish day-to-day control by appointing managers, or it may grant a private individual a lease during which he may use the land on his own initiative. An example of how imaginative hybrid schemes may be developed, combining ultimate public control with private rights for a period, is the Land Settlement Association. This manages a number of estates owned by the Ministry of Agriculture which were acquired to resettle unemployed industrial workers in the 1930s, and, later, wartime servicemen with limited means, who wanted to farm. Tenants, who must have had five years practical experience, lease holdings of around 40 acres. They are required to concentrate on intensive horticulture, leaving the association to provide services such as propogation and provision of fertilisers, and to market the produce. However, this association is in the process of being wound up by the government, its tenants being given first offer to buy their holdings.

Where limited resources have been nationalized to ensure their best use, other patterns of control may be used. The boards of nationalized industries are appointed by a minister and are subject to his directions on general matters of policy.[2] Parliamentary Select Committees for the minister's department are also able to keep a check in the public interest on the accounting and general workings of the industry. Otherwise, each board acts basically like a private corporate body. However, their control over the natural resources with which they are entrusted varies. Thus under the *Coal Industry Nationalization Act, 1946*, the National Coal Board owns all coal, and all the plant for excavating it. The Board also controls the excavation and sale of coal. Similarly, oil and natural gas were invested in the Crown by the Petroleum (Production) Act 1934, but by contrast with coal their discovery and extraction have ever since been granted to private companies under franchises. These are now granted by the Department of Energy.[3] They are referred to in the legislation as licences but differ from licences of the normal sort, which permit a landowner to use his own land in a manner which is otherwise prohibited. The British National Oil Corporation, created by the Petroleum and Submarine Pipe Lines Act 1975, has power to supervise the industry and to prospect and win oil itself.

Full state control of land may be essential to initiate major changes in an area, for example clearance of slums or derelict areas in city centres,[4] or the assembly of agricultural units out of scattered or separately owned fields.[5] However, once land has been acquired for such development by a public body, it may be released again entirely into private hands for the development to be carried out, or in its newly developed form. The Labour Government's Community Land Act 1975 was intended to limit almost all new development to land which had been acquired for that purpose by local authorities. It was repealed by the subsequent Conservative Government's Local Government Planning and Land Act 1980. Had the 1975 Act been fully implemented, even it would have allowed land to be returned to private control by the local authority which had taken it for development, although only with the consent of central government.

In furtherance of other powers, public bodies are frequently granted rights of access to private land. These may be a preliminary to finding out whether to acquire the land, or may be needed to carry out a system of regulation. Thus the Town and Country Planning Act 1971,[6] enables the Secretary of State or a local planning authority, to authorize a surveyor to survey land at any reasonable time in anticipation of the compulsory purchase of a listed building which has not been properly maintained or as part of the general system of preparing development plans and exercising development control.

3.2.2   Directions for land use

Rather than take land into its own hands, a public authority may direct a landowner to use it in a particular manner. A major freedom of the private landowner is the choice of his successor to control his land, but it is possible for the state to restrict this right by requiring that the successor must be competent or must employ a competent agent. Under French law, for example, those managing farms may be required to hold agricultural qualifications. By contrast, in England, the Agriculture Act 1947 allowed the Minister of Agriculture to supervise and give directions to farmers who failed to manage their land in accordance with good standards of husbandry. As a last resort he could acquire this land compulsorily. These powers were largely repealed, however, in 1958.

Generally it is easier to control private individuals by preventing them from doing something, rather than by compelling them to act. This has long been recognized by the courts which have always been more reluctant to issue mandatory injunctions than prohibitory ones,[7] and to enforce positive covenants rather than restrictive ones.[8] Positive acts may be more effectively stimulated by grants or other forms of encouragement. When directions are given as to the use of land, these tend to be limited in scope and are often part of a system of restrictive regulation. Thus agriculture is subject to supervision by the Minister of Agriculture, and, under the Weeds Act 1959, he may serve a notice on the occupier of land ordering him to prevent injurious weeds from spreading. The Act specifies five weeds, ragwort, two types of thistle and two of dock. Failure to comply is punishable by a fine and entitles the Minister himself to carry out the necessary work and charge the landowner with the cost. The Agriculture Act 1947, s. 95, provides much more extensive powers for the Minister to make an order for a year at a time, where this appears necessary to him, 'in the interest of the national supply of food or other agricultural products'. The Minister may direct the manner in which land is to be used, and have the work carried out at the owner's expense if the direction is not obeyed, but in practice these draconian powers lie unused. However, other directions are used as steps towards greater, or complete, public control. Thus local authority *abatement notices* under the Public Health Act 1936,[9] may order works needed to remove filth or other statutory nuisances. If an abatement notice is not obeyed, the relevant owner or occupier may be fined by a Magistrates' Court which may also impose a stricter direction in the form of an *abatement order*, authorizing the local authority to do the necessary work itself and to charge the offender. More drastically, a direction by a local authority under the Town and Country Planning Act 1971,[10] for the owner of a listed building to carry out repairs, is a preliminary to the compulsory acquisition of the building if it is left unrepaired, possibly with only nominal compensation.

3.2.3   Control by regulation

The most common form of public control of land use is restriction of private use by regulation. Regulations can be imposed as part of the private law as a means of evening out inequalities between parties. Thus, the Rent Acts provide tenants with protection against the greater bargaining power of landlords.[11] Often, however, regulations are special sets of controls imposed independently of the rules of private law.

(a)   The level of regulation

Certain types of activity are regarded as clearly harmful or undesirable and are subject to a *complete prohibition*. Thus, the Litter Act 1983,[12] makes it a criminal offence to leave litter in a public place in the open air. The Wildlife and Countryside Act 1981 makes it an offence to kill many types of wild bird[13] or animal[14] or to destroy many types of rare wild plant.[15]

   More commonly, activities on private land are prohibited subject to *licence*. Thus development control, which is discussed in the next section, imposes a general prohibition on significant changes of activity on any land unless planning permission has been obtained. Many activities require other forms of licence, whether or not planning permission is also needed. Sometimes an individual prohibition may be imposed. For example it is not generally necessary to obtain permission to cut down trees on domestic property, but under the Town and Country Planning Act 1971, s. 60, an order may be made by a local planning authority to protect individual 'trees, groups of trees or woodlands from cutting down, topping, lopping, uprooting, wilful damage, or wilful destruction' unless a licence has been obtained.[16] Similarly, under ss. 54 and 55, 'buildings of special architectural or historic interest' may be protected, by inclusion on a list maintained by the Department of the Environment, from demolition, alteration or extensions which would affect their character, except under a licence known as 'listed building consent'.[17]

(b) Methods of prohibition[18]

Whether an activity is to be stopped altogether or subjected to licence, the law must clearly identify exactly what is to be controlled. Absolute restrictions tend to be precise and limited. Thus, the wild flowers protected in the Wildlife and Countryside Act 1981 are listed at length, in a schedule, beginning with Small Alison (*Alyssum alyssoides*) and finishing with Greater yellow-rattle (*Rhinathus serotinus*). Such detailed provisions are technical and remote from the ordinary individual who is concerned with the quality of the environment. Licencing provisions tend to use more general concepts, such as that of development, in development control. However, a mass of interpretation can grow up around these. Licencing gives the licencing authority discretion, which may be very considerable, as to whether to grant permission on a particular application, but even in the case of an absolute prohibition the supervisory authority has a discretion whether to deal with a breach of regulations. Such exercises of discretion will usually be open for review by a superior body and ultimately, to a limited extent, by the courts.[19]

Decisions over the enforcement of regulations may be made clearer and more consistent if they are directed at the most suitable stage of an activity. Thus the legislature may control pollution[20] by *specification standards*, specifying suitable equipment. Under the Clean Air Act 1956,[21] furnaces for burning pulverized or solid fuel must be fitted with suitable plant for arresting grit or dust. The Act provides that particular plant is to be approved by a local authority. The legislature may, alternatively, use *emission standards*, forbidding more than a certain level of emission from any works. Thus the Clean Air Acts of 1956 and 1968 prohibit the emission of smoke which is darker than shade 2 on a device known as a Ringlemann chart (Fig. 1.3). Such approaches are more popular on the continent of Europe than in Britain and are likely to be used more widely as a result of pressures from the European Community. The traditional British approach is more flexible. It depends largely on *receptor standards*, restricting activities only when they result in a certain level of harm. Thus, the Public Health Act 1936 uses the concept of statutory nuisance in s. 92, to cover such matters as keeping animals or accumulating materials, or generating dust or effluvia which are prejudicial

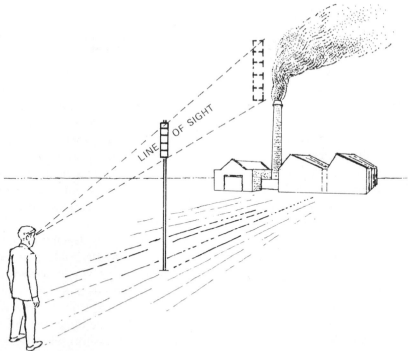

LINE OF SIGHT

Fig. 3.1 The Ringlemann chart (based on an illustration in *British Standard 2742*: 1969).

to health or constitute a common law nuisance.[22] Another favourite British approach is to impose a clear restriction, but to allow a defence where this has been broken, that the *best practicable means* have been taken to control the activity. Thus, the Clean Air Act 1968, provides for detailed regulation of the emmission of grit and dust from furnace chimneys,[23] but also provides a defence when 'the best practicable means' have been used for minimizing the alleged emission.

Regulations also differ in the manner in which they are enforced. Some, such as the Litter Act 1983, and the provisions for protecting animals and plants in the Wildlife and Countryside Act 1981, make forbidden actions criminal offences in their own right. However, development control operates indirectly. Under the Town and Country Planning Act 1971, s. 87, where development has been carried out without permission, an enforcement notice may be served ordering the situation to be remedied. Only if this order is disobeyed will there be a criminal offence. Before obeying, the person served is entitled to appeal to the Secretary of State who may rule that there was no breach after all, or, if there was, may grant planning permission. Such two-stage procedures allow further scope for flexible exercises of discretion, and reduce, though hardly eliminate, the property owner's feelings that he is being arbitrarily restricted.

(c) Forms of licencing

Licences may be used simply as a means of obtaining revenue rather than of control, and generally, where the aim is control, a fee is charged to cover the administrative costs of the licencing system. However, no fee may be demanded unless it has been authorized by Parliament. Thus, in *Liverpool Corpn.* v. *Maiden*,[24] it was held that a local act which allowed for the licencing of advertising hoardings in Liverpool, subject to conditions, did not implicitly authorize the charging of a licencing fee. On the other hand, where they are authorized fees are often payable on an application for a licence whether or not the licence is granted. Thus fees on planning applications were provided for under the Local Government, Planning and Land Act 1980[25]. Apart from fees, other costs, such as legal charges, may make licences expensive to obtain and tend to limit the number sought.

The form taken by a particular type of licence may vary depending on its purpose. It may be intended to ensure that essentially desirable activities are carried out properly. Thus, Building Regulations provide a system for inspecting work so as to ensure that it is carried out to safe and satisfactory standards.[26] They assume that buildings are acceptable in principle, whereas development control is used to prevent unacceptable building and other unacceptable development altogether. The great pressures of differing demands on land and natural resources make licencing an essential tool in rationing activities which compete with one another. Some of these may be regarded as essentially evils, even if to some extent necessary or inevitable. Thus licencing is used to contain the pollution of water, air or the earth which is bound to reduce the amenity of those affected if industry is to operate at all.[27] Activities such as gambling and prostitution may also be regarded as impossible to eliminate but as best controlled by licencing and supervision. Thus, the Local Government (Miscellaneous Provisions) Act, 1982 contains an elaborate schedule to allow for the licencing of sex establishment shops by district councils which resolve to introduce this special control in their areas.

Licences may be attached to a particular piece of land. Thus the Town and Country Planning Act 1971, s. 33 provides that a planning permission shall normally 'ensure the benefit of the land and of all persons for the time being interested therein'. However, it is possible for permission to be restricted to an individual who is regarded as suitable or as reliable enough to carry out the relevant activity. For example, in a rural area, permission to use a building as a dwelling house may be limited to those employed in agriculture,[28] so as to ensure that accommodation which is limited is available to those who need it most. Other licences may be personal, so that closer control may be exercised over some dubious activity. Thus a licence for a sex establishment shop will only be granted to a person who will be operating the relevant premises.

(d) Registration

Registration of individuals for particular purposes may be used to ensure that only suitably qualified people carry out specialized work. Thus, the Architects Registration Act 1938 makes it an offence, now punishable by a £500 fine, to use the title *Architect* without being registered as such with the statutory Architects' Registration Council, after completing approved examination and training. On the other hand, the Act specifically provides that it does not affect people using the designation *Landscape Architect* or *Golf Course Architect*. Nor does it affect the validity of a building contract, so that a person who does not purport to be an architect is not prevented from carrying out work normally done by that profession.

Registers are also used where it is desirable to make public the fact that certain activities are happening and who is responsible for them. In such a case there may be no discretion for any licencing body to refuse registration. Thus the Town and Country Planning Act 1971 requires local planning authorities to keep a register, with planning applications in one part and decisions in a second part. Although there is much discretion as to whether planning permission should be granted, the entry in the register is a mandatory administrative duty. Anyone is entitled to make an application for planning permission to use a piece of land in a particular manner. Thus in 1982, Kirklees Metropolitan Council regarded themselves as bound to consider as a serious application a proposal to turn a listed disused Sunday-school building in Huddersfield into a brothel. The owner was making a protest because he had been refused permission to use the building for student bed-sitting rooms.[29] The requirement of registration in such a case gives members of the public at least some warning of bizarre or undesirable planning proposals.

(e) Giving notice

A further means of control is a requirement to give notice. Thus the Town and Country Planning Act 1971, s. 26, stipulates that applications for planning permission must be notified to owners of any part of the relevant land, including tenants with more than ten years left of a lease, where these are not themselves making the application, and also to any agricultural tenants. A more specialized notice requirement in the same Act obliges any one demolishing a listed building, not only to obtain listed-building consent, but also to give the Royal Commission on Historical Monuments for England or for Wales and Monmouthshire one month in which to record the building for posterity.[30]

(f) The effect of regulation on rights in land use

A system of regulation may affect existing private rights over land in various ways. When an activity is prohibited, or the requirement of a licence is first imposed, landowners will be subjected to new restrictions. However, what they are already doing is likely to be protected. For this reason the Town and Country Planning Act 1947, only required permission for development carried out after 1 July 1948. Even then, enforcement proceedings could only be brought within four years of any unauthorized development. The Town and Country Planning Act 1968 removed the four-year limit on changes of use other than conversions of buildings to use as a single dwelling house. However, no changes already more than four years old were affected. Today, enforcement proceedings can be brought only for breaches of planning control after the end of 1963.[31] Similarly the Water Resources Act 1963 requires a licence to be obtained for most cases of abstracting or impounding water.[32] However, when the Act came into force, anyone who was already using water from a given supply was entitled to a licence to continue doing so as of right.[33] Water authorities have a discretion as to whether or not to grant a licence to new users.[34] Where the granting of a licence is discretionary, the licencing authority must act reasonably within its statutory guidelines. These will usually provide some safeguard both for applicants and for other users who may be affected. In particular, appeals are usually available to disappointed applicants. Others may be able to obtain a judicial review from the courts.[35]

Sometimes statutory controls give neighbours a new right to challenge antisocial development or to obtain damages for harm which it causes to them, because unlicenced behaviour may be regarded as a public nuisance or as a breach of statutory duty designed to protect a particular class of individuals.[36] On the other hand, the grant of certain types of licence may actually override pre-existing rights in others. The system of water abstraction licences under the Water Resources Act 1963[37] requires the water authorities responsible for granting licences to take account of existing lawful uses and, specifically, not to derogate from existing rights of extraction, but, once a licence has been granted, it constitutes a defence to any actions brought by persons with existing licences or other rights to extract water.[38] Instead, these are given a new action for breach of statutory duty against the water authority.[39] By contrast, if someone extracts water without a licence, others who are affected can only seek redress under their common law rights. In *Cargill* v. *Gotts*,[40] Mr Cargill claimed an easement to extract water for his farm at Gimmingham in Norfolk from Mr Gott's millpond (Fig. 3.2). The Court of Appeal held that a valid easement had been established before abstraction licences were introduced. Even though it had become unlawful for Mr Cargill to extract the water without one, it was for the water authority

Fig. 3.2 The Mill Pond at Gimmingham, Norfolk, by kind permission of Mr Cargill and N.C. Raywood Esq. of Messrs Daynes, Chittock and Back, Solicitors, Norwich.

rather than for Mr Gotts to restrain the extraction of water until a licence was obtained. The majority of the court upheld an award of £50 damages against Mr Gotts for forcibly interfering with the extraction.

A further aspect of licencing is that, once a licence has been granted, it may be temporary or it may establish a permanent right, unless it is revoked and the person entitled to it compensated. Normally planning permission which has been acted on gives a permanent right to use the relevant land in a new manner, although it is possible for permission to be given for only a limited period. On the other hand, s. 41 of the Town and Country Planning Act 1971 provides that, unless the permission specifies a different period, if it is not acted on within five years it will expire. Activities which are essentially undesirable are more likely to be licenced for only a limited period. Thus, shops licenced as sex establishments must be relicenced at least annually.[41] On the other hand, certain licences which are designed to share out limited natural resources, are normally granted to remain in force indefinitely, although they may require those benefiting from them to pay a regular charge to the licencing authority. Thus, the Water Act 1973, s. 26 authorizes water authorities to charge for rights which they make available.

3.2.4   Public stimulus of land improvement

Many factors, beside public restrictions, affect the manner in which land is used. Thus the resources available for change are important, such as private capital and public grants. Also crucial, are such matters as availability of spare land to erect new buildings without interfering with those which it is intended to retain. A landowner who wishes to erect attractive and long-lasting buildings will only do so if he can afford to. Otherwise he will make do with something mediocre, or not develop his land at all. However, positive motives can be harnessed by legislation. The developer who is not interested in the appearance of the factories or houses he builds may become interested if he gets a bigger profit by making them more attractive. The farmer who is inclined to destroy the amenity value of his land by uprooting hedgerows and copses, demolishing dry stone walls and erasing footpaths, so as to increase crop yields, is likely to take the initiative in improving and adding to such features if he gets as good a financial return on the amenity value of his farm.

(a) Financial controls

Financial controls, designed to stimulate certain types of development rather than others, may take several forms. Thus outright *grants* or *loans*, may be made for certain types of development, such as agricultural land reclamation, industrial regeneration of derelict inner city areas,[42] or housing renewal.[43] In other cases a landowner may be pressurized into spending money on improving his land. Thus, if certain directions or regulations as to the use of land are disobeyed, the supervising public authority may be able to carry out necessary works itself and charge the landowner or occupier with the cost.[44] In other situations, as with coast protection work,[45] or the maintenance of highways,[46] it is normal for the public authority to do what is necessary to maintain land at a safe level or to conserve its amenity value for the public. Normally the expense of such works is met from local rates, charged on all property owners in the area, from central exchequer grants, or from a combination of the two. Sometimes, however, those landowners directly benefiting will be charged for the service.[47]

Land use is affected by the general taxation system which is mainly provided for in the Finance Acts which are added to year by year. Thus levels of *income tax* may affect the numbers of employees whom a landowner can afford to pay. For example gardeners and painters who may make a considerable contribution to the appearance of land and buildings for a modest proportion of an employer's expenditure may be regarded as too costly. *Value added tax* is now provided for in a consolidated Value Added Tax Act 1983. This tax is payable on services and repairs, but not on new work, and may have the effect of discouraging regular maintenance, but encouraging extensions or inappropriate alterations. Other taxes, notably *capital transfer tax* on gifts and bequests of property and *capital gains tax* on profits made from its disposal, are designed to prevent accumulation of wealth, and therefore tend to break up private land holdings, sometimes destroying viable estates and undermining the communities which live there. Concessions are made to relieve such taxation, for example on stately homes which form part of the national heritage.[48] However, these concessions have their limitations. Thus a great house passed on from one generation to the next may be spared capital transfer tax or be accepted by the state intact in lieu of tax and then handed over to be looked after by a body such as the National Trust.[49] However, the Inland Revenue may refuse to include surrounding land in such an arrangement if it is not part of the landscape setting even though it is indispensable for providing an endowment fund to keep up the buildings. This limitation was highlighted in 1983 in the case of Calke Abbey in Derbyshire which, with its contents, was described in the House of Commons as a perfect time capsule and as quintessentially English. The government acknowledged it to be of considerable architectural and historical interest but refused to use the acceptance in lieu provisions of the Finance Acts so as to provide an endowment fund.[50]

The form of taxation most directly related to the development of land is *development land tax*, which is designed to make those who increase the value of land by carrying out development share their profits with the community, currently to the extent of 60% of sums over £50 000 in any one year.[51] The Development Land Tax Act 1976, provides that this tax is payable on a disposal of land. Therefore it applies to a landowner who obtains permission to build and then sells his land to a developer.[52] The proportion of profit which is left after tax may not deter such sales. However, the tax is also payable by persons with any significant interest in land when they begin any material development on it.[53] Material development is generally development for which planning permission is needed, with exceptions for small works of various sorts.[54] Thus, if a developer envisages carrying out a large-scale integrated development he may be obliged to meet a considerable tax bill long before the scheme is completed and he can obtain his profits on it.

(b) Public covenants

Development land tax is paid to the central government exchequer. However, local authorities may direct development profits to their own ends, by persuading private developers to enter into covenants, which may permanently bind land controlled by the developer, for carrying out public works, as part of a scheme for which the developer is seeking planning consent. Unlike private restrictive covenants which are discussed in Chapters 4 and 5, such covenants may be made with local authorities, including both county and district councils, for the general public benefit, rather than for the benefit of some specific piece of neighbouring land. Under the Town and

Country Planning Act 1971, s. 52, such covenants may be made 'for the purpose of restricting or regulating the development or use of land either permanently or during such period as may be prescribed by the agreement'. Under the Local Government (Miscellaneous Provisions) Act 1982, s. 33, more far-reaching and positive covenants may be made 'for the purpose of carrying out work'. These powers enable local authorities to obtain positive planning gains from development in their areas over and above such public benefit as the development might itself provide. For example, a developer might agree to provide a park or public road on part of the development site, or even on other land. Views differ considerably over the propriety of such agreements,[55] since they may require a developer to do things which would be invalid if contained in a planning condition. However, if a developer who refuses to agree to such a bargain is denied planning permission, he may appeal to the Secretary of State. It is also objected that such agreements lead to permission being given for development which is not in the public interest. However, they cannot bind a local planning authority to give planning permission, if this later seems inappropriate after all.[56] Made under seal, such agreements do not require the consideration, that is mutual benefit, normally needed to make a binding contract.[57]

3.2.5   The complexity of control

Each public control over the use of land usually involves more than one public body. This may help to ensure that sound decisions are reached. On the other hand it may hamper efficient decision-making. From the point of view of the private landowner a greater problem may be the overlap of controls which make it difficult for him safely to do what he wants. For example, he may obtain a justices' licence to open an hotel but may not realize that he also needs planning consent.

(a) Hierarchical control

As we have seen in Chapter 1, Section 1.3, central government generally supervises the powers exercised by subordinate authorities, such as local councils. Thus compulsory purchase orders made by subordinate authorities require confirmation by central government.[58] Similarly, structure plans and any subsequent alterations, which provide the framework for planning in each county, are prepared by county authorities, but, under the Town and Country Planning Act 1971, must be approved by the Secretary of State for the Environment.[59] Where powers are given to a subordinate authority, central government is often able to step in and take them over. Thus planning control is generally the responsibility of district councils, but under s. 35 of the 1971 Act, the Secretary of State may direct that particular categories of application are to be referred directly to him, or he may call in specific cases to be decided by himself. These powers are usually exercised where a local planning authority seems likely to approve development which is a departure from a structure or local plan. The Secretary of State has made a direction attached to his circular 2/81, on development plans, that such anticipated departures must be notified to him. If local objectors or another authority such as the county council alert him, he may decide to call in other cases, provided they are of more than merely local significance. Other ministers may also override planning authorities. Thus under the Town and Country Planning Act 1971[60] if the authority of a government department is required for a particular type of development, where that department grants such permission, ordinary planning consent is not normally needed as well. If the department confirms the purchase of land needed for the development, whether by compulsion or not, or even approves the use of money on the scheme, this is sufficient to authorize the work. For example, the Secretary of State for Energy may override the objections of a local planning authority by authorizing the construction of a generating station,[61] overhead powerlines,[62] or opencast coalmining,[63] although, in each case, if there are objections by the local planning authority, he must hold a public inquiry to air them.

Central government commonly provides supervision over decisions by bodies, such as local authorities, by means of administrative appeals. For example, if planning consent is refused by a local planning authority, a disappointed developer may appeal to the Secretary of State under the Town and Country Planning Act 1971, s. 36. The Secretary of State also has default powers to act in place of a local planning authority, for example where it neglects to stop unlawful development by serving enforcement proceedings.[64] Generally, where an offence has been committed, anyone, including a private citizen, may bring a prosecution, but with a number of environmental offences, permission is needed from the Attorney General or the Director of Public Prosecutions. For example, prosecutions under the Water Resources Act 1963 may only be instituted by a water authority or by or with the consent of the Director of Public Prosecutions. Furthermore the Attorney General has power at his discretion to take over any proceedings and to stop them. Also, injunctions to control public nuisances and other breaches of public rights, or to stop an anticipated crime, may only be obtained by the Attorney General,[65] or, under the Local Government Act 1972, s. 222, by a local authority.[66]

(b) Shared control

In some cases, the public authorities involved in controlling land use share responsibility without a clear-cut hierarchy of powers. Certain public bodies are composed of, or include members of, other authorities. Thus, in a national park, under the Local Government Act 1972,[67] the planning authority is normally a special planning committee of the county council, but includes a minority of members, some of whom are appointed by the Secretary of State and some by district councils within the park. At central government level, it is assumed that any conflicts between Ministers and their departments will be resolved, if necessary, in the Cabinet. Thus it is provided that certain decisions may be made jointly by government departments. Under the Town and Country Planning Act 1971,[68] applications for most development, by statutory undertakers, which reach the Secretary of State for the Environment, will normally be dealt with jointly by him and the Minister responsible for the undertaking, such as the Secretary of State for Energy.

Certain responsibilities are divided clearly. Thus structure plans, which provide the framework for planning policies throughout each county, are the responsibility of county councils. Under the Local Government Act 1972, planning applications which departed from the structure plan were originally referred to the county. However, the Local Government Planning and Land Act 1980, has now amended this,[69] to provide that such departures are to be dealt with by district councils, although these must consult the county and also notify the Secretary of State, who may call in a case for his own decision. On the other hand, certain matters have been firmly put under county control, notably mineral workings,[70] and in England, but not Wales, refuse disposal.[71] County councils may, however, thwart development favoured by a district council because of their powers as highway authorities. District planning authorities may not deal with any application for development which would affect any classified road or the route of any such proposed road which has been adopted and notified to the district, until they have received the views of the county. They must then comply with any directions from the county restricting the proposed development.[72] In the case of major roads which are the responsibility of the Secretary of State for Transport, he must be consulted and has similar powers.[73]

(c) Consultation

Consultation is the main device for giving the public a say in planning the environment, without giving them power over what is actually decided. The same device is used to involve public authorities other than those given the immediate responsibility for the decision which has to be made. In particular, the General Development Order 1977,[74] requires local planning authorities, before granting planning consent, to consult with other relevant authorities, including neighbouring local planning authorities, highway authorities, the National Coal Board, water authorities, the Nature Conservancy Council and the Minister of Agriculture. Under the Local Government Act 1972 parish and community councils may require a district council to notify them of planning applications in their area and county councils are generally entitled to be notified so that they may make representations.[75] In those cases where an authority is required to consult before making a decision it must allow an adequate time for representations. In most cases a local planning authority must allow fourteen days, although where it consults with the county council on departures from a structure plan it must allow twenty-eight days.[76]

If a decision is made without consultation required by statute it may be quashed by the courts.[77] Consultation involves the consulting authority supplying sufficient information to the party being consulted 'to enable them to tender advice, and, on the other hand, a sufficient opportunity must be given . . . to tender that advice'.[78] A consulting party would probably be acting wrongly if it kept up its sleeve and did not mention any matter on which it considered the party being consulted could provide help. Provided consultation is carried out, the deciding authority will not be required to do more than consider the views of those whom it has consulted and will be free to reject them if it wishes. However, the process should at least ensure that the deciding authority is more fully informed on the relevant matters.

(d) Parallel licencing controls

A developer may well feel frustrated by the number of different permits which he may have to obtain to carry out work. Often such consents are independent of one another even though they may have to be sought from the same authority and it does not matter in which order they are applied for. Thus a businessman wishing to turn a shop into a bingo hall may require planning permission and also further local authority approval as to the safety of structural work, under the Building Regulations.[79] He will also need permission from the licencing justices for the sale of alcohol.[80] Unlike the other two permits, building-regulation approval leaves relatively little discretion to the officials concerned. Provided the detailed legislative requirements are complied with, the developer may be confident that he will obtain his licence. Far greater discretion is exercised by the local authority in considering a planning application and by licencing justices. Parallel licencing provisions may operate on different criteria and in different ways. Some licences, such as those for the sale of intoxicating liquor, are granted to named individuals, although they are in respect of particular premises. Permission must be obtained to transfer such licences to anyone else. Also they have to be renewed annually.

There may be a conflict between parallel licencing provisions, particularly where different licencing authorities are prepared to give their consent on different terms. For example, the Licensing Act 1964 allows justices to grant new on-licences for the consumption of alcohol on premises, subject to conditions.[81] In particular these must ensure that the premises are structurally adapted to the class of licence required. However, a local authority asked to grant building regulation consent or planning permission might find the conditions imposed by the licencing justices unsatisfactory for safety or aesthetic reasons. Again, a planning authority might turn down a proposal for licenced premises because of matters on which the licencing justices were satisfied. For example, Emma Hotels Ltd expanded a private hotel on the sea front at Westcliff-on-Sea and obtained a full publican's on-licence to allow the general public into their extended bar area. However Southend-on-Sea Borough Council, the local planning authority, served an enforcement notice to stop what it claimed was a material change of use. The Secretary of State upheld the notice. On appeal to the Divisional Court he was held to have erred in his view that planning permission was needed in the first place. However had permission been required, the planning authorities' reasons for objecting to the change of use were ones on which he would have been entitled to refuse a new use, namely increased custom, traffic, noise and disturbance of the neighbourhood.[82]

The problems of alternative controls may be met by ensuring that one clearly takes priority. Under the Forestry Act 1967[83] a felling licence must generally be obtained from the Forestry Commission to cut down timber trees. This requirement was introduced during the Second World War to conserve timber resources, but it is now usually exercised for the protection of the amenity provided by forests and woodlands.[84] Where trees for which a felling licence is required are also protected by a tree preservation order,[85] if the Commission intends to grant a felling licence, it must notify the local planning authority which made the tree preservation order.[86] Unless the local planning authority agrees, to the felling, the matter is referred to the Secretary of State for the Environment. On the other hand if a local planning authority authorizes development which requires the removal of trees this obviates the need for a felling licence.[87]

A public body may not transfer its responsibilities for controlling development to another body unless it has been expressly authorized to do so by legislation.[88] However, overlapping controls can lead to unsatisfactory development falling between two stools and being approved. Then a developer who has obtained a necessary licence may have it quashed by the courts if a licencing authority has left a key issue which is its responsibility to another authority. In 1972, Stour River Estate sought planning permission to construct a marina at Harwich which would hold 500 30-feet yachts. The Department of the Environment called the application in and granted permission. The main objector to the proposal was the Harwich Harbour Board which feared that increased traffic would cause danger to navigation. This was accepted by the department's inspector at a planning inquiry. The

Secretary of State authorized the scheme against the recommendation of the inspector on the grounds that safety was entirely a matter for the Department of Trade which had already granted a licence under a private act of 1865 and had further powers to control obstruction to navigation under the Coast Protection Act 1949.[89] However, the Court of Appeal approved an order granted to the Harbour Board quashing the grant of planning permission.[90] The powers of the Board of Trade applied only to obstruction from new works themselves and not to any increase in traffic which these might generate.

(e) Cumulative controls

Some licences do not overlap, but are cumulative. Thus anyone who wishes to open a caravan park must first obtain planning permission. Then he must also obtain a site licence under the Caravan Sites and Control of Development Act 1960, usually from the same local authority.[91] The site licence must be granted if planning permission has already been obtained, but it provides an opportunity to impose conditions on the use of the site. In other cases, planning consent could be dependent upon an earlier licence. The Town and Country Planning Act 1971, s. 67 used to require that before planning permission could be granted for new industrial buildings, an industrial-development certificate was required from the Secretary of State stating that the proposal would be carried out 'consistently with the proper distribution of industry'. Under s. 74 there were similar requirements for office development permits for proposed office development. Both these requirements are now in abeyance. A rather different form of cumulative control is illustrated by the Agricultural Land (Removal of Surface Soil) Act 1953,[92] whereby it is an offence to remove surface soil from agricultural land with a view to sale. The offence only applies where this operation amounts to development and therefore provides, for that special type of development, a more immediate form of control than normal enforcement proceedings.

NOTES: SECTION 3.2

1. *Post* p. 185.
2. *Ante* p. 36.
3. S.I. 1970, No. 1537, Art. 2 (2).
4. *Post* p. 132f.
5. *Post* p. 139.
6. Town and Country Planning Act 1971, s. 280.
7. *Post* p. 382.
8. *Post* p. 214f.
9. Public Health Act 1936, s. 92, *post* p. 144.
10. Town and Country Planning Act 1971, s. 115, *post* p. 143.
11. *Post* p. 183.

12. Litter Act 1983, s. 1.
13. Wildlife and Countryside Act 1981, s. 1.
14. Ibid. s. 9.
15. Ibid. s. 13.
16. *Post* p. 141
17. *Post* p. 142f.
18. For a detailed analysis of different forms of regulation see Richardson, G.M. and Ogus, A.I. (1979) The regulatory approach to environmental control. *Urban law and policy*, 2, 337–57.
19. *Post* p. 390f.
20. *Post* p. 144.
21. Clean Air Act 1956, s. 6.
22. *Post* p. 342.
23. Clean Air Act 1956, s. 2.
24. *Liverpool Corpn.* v. *Arthur Maiden Ltd* [1938] 4 All E.R. 200. Croom Johnson J. relied on the authority of the Court of Appeal and the House of Lords in *Attorney General* v. *Wiltshire Dairies* (1922) 127 L.T. 822.
25. Local Government Planning and Land Act 1980, s. 87.
26. S.I. 1976, No. 1676, *post* p. 103.
27. *Post* p. 144.
28. *Fawcett Properties Ltd* v. *Buckinghamshire County Council* [1961] A.C. 636, H.L.
29. *The Times*, 26 August 1982.
30. Town and Country Planning Act 1971, s. 55.
31. Ibid. s. 87 (1).
32. *Post* p. 137.
33. Water Resources Act 1963, s. 33.
34. Ibid. s. 29.
35. *Post* p. 391f.
36. *Post* p. 341f.
37. Water Resources Act 1963, s. 29, *post* p. 137.
38. Ibid. s. 31.
39. Ibid. s. 50.
40. *Cargill* v. *Gotts* [1981] 1 W.L.R. 441 C.A.
41. Local Government (Miscellaneous Provisions) Act 1982, Sched. 3, Para. 9.
42. *Post* p. 133.
43. *Post* p. 134.
44. *Ante* p. 91.
45. Coast Protections Act 1949.
46. Highways Act 1980, Part IV.
47. Ibid. ss. 57 and 59.
48. For example, Finance Act 1976, ss. 76 and 77 with regard to capital transfer tax.
49. Ibid. sched. 4 para 17.
50. *The Times* 8 December 1983.
51. Finance Act 1979, s. 24 (1)(a) and Capital Gains Tax Act 1979, s. 24 (2).
52. Development Land Tax 1976, s. 1.
53. Ibid. s. 2.
54. Ibid. s. 7. and Sched. 4, Part II.
55. See for example the discussion in Grant, M. (1982) *Urban Planning Law*, Sweet & Maxwell, London, pp. 359–77.
56. *Stringer* v. *Minister of Housing and Local Government* [1970] 1 W.L.R. 1281, *post* p. 117.

57. *Post* p. 317.
58. *Post* p. 223.
59. Town and Country Planning Act 1971, ss. 9 and 10.
60. Ibid. s. 40.
61. Electricity Lighting (Clauses) Act 1899.
62. Electricity (Supply) Act 1919.
63. Open Cast Coal Act 1958.
64. Town and Country Planning Act 1971, s. 276.
65. *Gouriet* v. *Union of Post Office Workers* [1978] A.C. 435, H.L.
66. *Kent County Council* v. *Batchelor* (No. 2) [1979] 1. W.L.R. 213, D.C. See *post* p. 382.
67. Local Government Act 1972, Sched. 17.
68. Town and Country Planning Act 1971, s. 225.
69. Local Government Planning and Land Act 1980, s. 86.
70. Local Government Act 1972, Sched. 16 Para. 32 and Town and Country Planning (Minerals) Act 1981, s. 2.
71. Town and Country Planning (Prescription of County Matters) Regulations 1980. S.I. 1980, No. 2010.
72. General Development Order 1977. S.I. 1977, No. 289, Art. 12.
73. Ibid. Art. 11.
74. *Ante* note 72, Art. 15.
75. Local Government Act 1972, Sched. 16, Paras. 20 and 19.
76. General Development Order *ante* note 72, Art. 15 (5) and 15A., inserted by S.I. 1980, No. 1946.
77. *Agricultural, Horticultural and Forestry Industry Training Board* v. *Aylesbury Mushrooms* [1972] 1 W.L.R. 190, *post* p. 393.
78. *Rollo* v. *Minister of Town and Country Planning* [1948] 1 All E.R. 13, *per* Bucknill L.J. at p. 17.
79. S.I. 1976, No. 1676.
80. Licensing Act 1964.
81. Ibid. s. 4.
82. *Emma Hotels Ltd* v. *Secretary of State* [1980] 41 P. & C.R. 255 D.C.
83. Forestry Act 1967, s. 9.
84. Forestry Commission (1980) *Private Forestry, Consultative Paper on the Administration of Felling Control and Grant Aid*. Edinburgh.
85. *Post* p. 141f.
86. Forestry Act 1967, s. 15.
87. Ibid. s. 9 (4) (d).
88. *Lavender* v. *Ministry of Housing and Local Government* [1970] 1 W.L.R. 1231, *post* p. 118.
89. Coast Protection Act 1949, s. 34.
90. *Harwich Harbour Conservancy Board* v. *Secretary of State* [1975] 1 Lloyd's Rep. 334, C.A.
91. *Post* p. 146.
92. *Post* p. 139.

3.3   Development control (Fig. 3.3)

The most far-reaching restrictions on private land use were introduced in 1947 and are now stated baldly in the Town and Country Planning Act 1971,

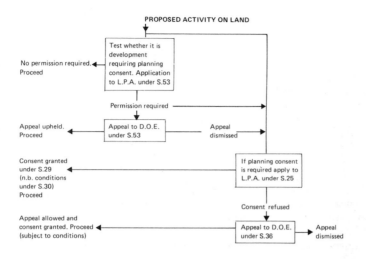

PROPOSED ACTIVITY ON LAND

Test whether it is development requiring planning consent. Application to L.P.A. under S.53

No permission required. Proceed

Permission required

Appeal upheld. Proceed

Appeal to D.O.E. under S.53

Appeal dismissed

Consent granted under S.29 (n.b. conditions under S.30) Proceed

If planning consent is required apply to L.P.A. under S.25

Consent refused

Appeal allowed and consent granted. Proceed (subject to conditions)

Appeal to D.O.E. under S.36

Appeal dismissed

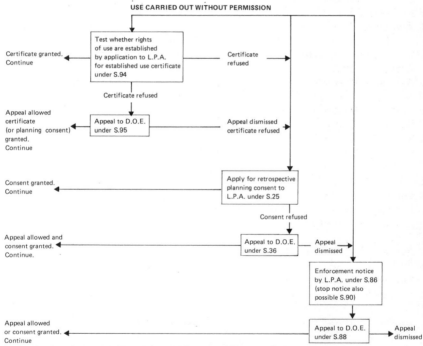

USE CARRIED OUT WITHOUT PERMISSION

Test whether rights of use are established by application to L.P.A. for established use certificate under S.94

Certificate granted. Continue

Certificate refused

Certificate refused

Appeal allowed certificate (or planning consent) granted. Continue

Appeal to D.O.E. under S.95

Appeal dismissed certificate refused

Consent granted. Continue

Apply for retrospective planning consent to L.P.A. under S.25

Consent refused

Appeal allowed and consent granted. Continue.

Appeal to D.O.E. under S.36

Appeal dismissed

Enforcement notice by L.P.A. under S.86 (stop notice also possible S.90)

Appeal allowed or consent granted. Continue

Appeal to D.O.E. under S.88

Appeal dismissed

This flow-chart illustrates the main decisions which may be taken to control development. Section numbers are those of the most significant sections for each decision, in the Town and Country Planning Act 1971.

Abbreviations: L.P.A. = Local Planning Authority   D.O.E. = Department of the Environment

Fig. 3.3 Planning decisions concerned with development.

s. 23 (1). 'Subject to the provisions of this section, planning permission is required for the carrying out of any development of land.' Permission must be obtained from a local planning authority or the Department of the Environment, although certain types of development are given blanket consent by the Department of the Environment, under General Development Orders.[1] Section 45 of the 1971 Act allows a planning authority to *revoke* or *modify* permission which has already been given, and s. 51 provides for *discontinuance orders* to stop even long-established uses or to remove buildings or works. However, these powers which take away existing rights of landowners involve the payment of compensation and are used sparingly. Where development is carried out without planning permission, a local planning authority may order it to stop by serving an enforcement notice, under s. 87 of the 1971 Act.[2] It is an offence not to comply with such a notice, but time is always given for complying, and this may be extended if the landowner appeals to the Secretary of State against the notice. However, under s. 90, a *stop notice* may be served to stop most activities complained of within as little as three days until the dispute is resolved. If the enforcement notice is successfully challenged a person who suffers loss as a result of a stop notice will be entitled to compensation.[3]

Generally an initial planning decision will be made by the district council which is the local planning authority, and a disappointed party may appeal to the Secretary of State for the Department of the Environment. Such an appeal is dealt with more formally, frequently by an inspector appointed to hold a public inquiry. From this second administrative decision, it may be possible for the original appellant or the local planning authority to appeal further to the courts. Sometimes the Secretary of State requires initial planning issues to be referred directly to him and here too an appeal to the courts is possible from his decision. However, as we shall see in Chapter 8, Sections 8.2. and 8.3, the jurisdiction of the courts on such occasions is limited. In particular a court will generally not upset a finding of fact or a policy decision. Thus it is largely left to the local and central planning authorities to decide whether a particular activity amounts to development and if so whether it should be permitted.

3.3.1 The meaning of development

Section 22 of the Town and Country Planning Act 1971 provides that, generally, development occurs whenever there is an alteration to the physical state of land by 'the carrying out of building, engineering, mining or other operations, in, on, over or under land', or whenever there is 'any material change in the use of buildings or other land'. Certain matters are then expressly identified as development or excluded from the definition. The distinction between *operational development* and *material change of use* is central to s. 22. It is couched slightly differently with regard to revocation and discontinuance orders, but has been treated by the courts as applying there too.[4]

An important practical distinction between operational development and material change of use is that enforcement proceedings served by a planning authority to stop unauthorized development must be brought within four years if the development is operational. Where a material change of use has occurred without permission, or in a manner contrary to conditions relating to the carrying out of such operations, and subject to which consent was granted, there is no such immunity, except where the change consists in using a building as a single dwelling house.[5] Thus, creating a new golf course would involve operations in constructing the course. Using the course would involve a material change of use. After the recontouring and other operations had finished the local planning authority would only have four years in which to require the site to be restored to its former state. However, they could at any time prevent it being used as a golf course.

(a) Operational development

The three forms of operational development singled out in the 1971 Act are, building, engineering and mining. They have in common that they all appear to involve a physical change in land itself,[6] but whereas building and engineering imply some addition to what is naturally on the land, mining involves removing part of its physical substance. Therefore, it is difficult to identify a wide genus of operations, and operational development seems to be confined to works of the three specified types, and to operations very similar to one or other of them.[7] Demolition of a building, for example, has generally not been regarded as development because it is essentially different from creative building.[8] However, sometimes it may amount to an engineering operation. If part of the building is left, the demolition may be seen as a building alteration, or, if it is the preliminary to new building, it may be seen as part of an over-all building operation. Nevertheless it remains an anomaly that demolition as such is not regarded as development. In a special report published by HMSO as long ago as 1974, George Dobry Q.C. recommended that it should be treated as a special form of development in its own right but this has yet to be implemented.

Building operations include rebuilding operations, structural alterations of or additions to buildings, and other operations normally undertaken by a person carrying on business as a builder. A *building* includes any structure or erection, and any part of a building, as so defined, but does not include plant or machinery comprised in a building. Clearly the erection of new houses, factories or other architect-designed structures is covered, as is their adaptation. Certain work such as the laying out of a paved square or tarmacking a forecourt might be included as work normally undertaken by a builder, even if it does not involve a structure or erection. Erecting or altering large machinery in the open is included, but only, it appears from decided cases, where the machinery amounts to a fixture.[9] Thus, erecting an 89-foot crane running on fixed tracks has been treated as development,[10] but in another case introducing a huge coal hopper 16 to 20 feet high, which ran on wheels, was not.[11] Erecting small permanent structures such as flagposts or a model village,[12] has been treated as a building operation. Temporary structures such as inflatable pavilions, or modern statuary, which may significantly change the appearance of a site are not operational development, although they may require permission as a material change in the use of land.

Maintenance, improvement or other alterations affecting the exterior of a building are not classed as development, provided they do not do so materially. This may be relevant to landscape features such as walls. Repointing in the original manner would clearly be permissible, but changing the method of pointing could be regarded as development. On the other hand, removing a redundant chimney pot from an ordinary terrace house or a piece of statuary or balustrading from a park or garden, would probably not. To replace a building which has been entirely or substantially destroyed would require planning permission even if it were restored exactly in its original condition.[13]

Engineering operations are not defined in the 1971 act, save that they are said to include 'the formation or laying out of means of access to highways'. They seem likely to cover much that would also be regarded as building work, such as erecting a bridge or laying out a site with stone-faced embankments. However, they would include alterations to the appearance of land, not involving a structure or erection, or mining operations, and which would not be regarded as the normal work of a builder. Much large-scale landscape work would be treated as engineering, such as laying out a golf course[14] or recontouring land by constructing banks, or filling or creating ponds. Thus, in 1957, proposals to fill in a Georgian haha, designed to keep George III's merino sheep in the old deer park at Richmond, were regarded by the Minister of Housing and Local Government as development.[15] Trees could hardly be regarded as structures or erections, so it is not likely that even moving them in full grown conditions to or from a site would be a building operation, but it might be classified as an engineering operation. It could certainly significantly alter the appearance of a site.

To amount to engineering, it does seem necessary for an operation to be on a significant scale. Widening an access by a few inches,[16] or digging out a small boundary bank by hand would not seem to be enough. Even if a mechanical digger were involved, it might not be. In *Coleshill and District Investment Co. Ltd* v. *Minister of Housing and Local Government*,[17] in the Divisional Court, Widgery J. said of the removal of substantial earth embankments, 'this little job of shifting a few cubic yards of soil with a digger and a lorry, is not, in my judgment, an operation of a kind which would ever be dignified with the title of an engineering operation'. The House of Lords held that what had been done was more considerable than this description suggested, but Lord Pearson said that, had he agreed with the description, he would have accepted that there was no engineering operation. Certain common works of highway authorities and of statutory undertakers are expressly excluded from the definition of development.[18]

Mining Operations are not defined in the 1971 Act, but minerals are stated to 'include all minerals and substances in or under land of a kind ordinarily worked for removal by underground or surface working, except that they do not include peat cut for purposes other than sale'. Minerals would therefore include top soil, gravel, sand, clay and stone and any material excavated for building or industrial purposes, including mineral ores. Mining operations are, by implication, fairly substantial activities for the removal of such materials. It is now clear that they include excavations from old tip and slag heaps and also from old railway embankments.[19]

(b) Material change of use

Land use is in a constant state of change. Part of a vegetable garden is made over to flowers. A car is parked for the first time in a back yard. A factory which used to make one type of fertilizer develops another and starts using smelly new processes. Planning permission is only needed where a change is *material*, but this term has never been clearly defined either by legislation or case law. However, the 1971 Act does state,[20] that in three particular situations there is a material change of use. First, development occurs if any building is used as two or more separate dwelling houses. Therefore it is development to split a family house into two flats. Secondly, permission is needed to deposit refuse or waste materials on land already in use for that purpose, if more of the surface area is to be covered, or if the height of the deposit is to be raised above the level of the land adjoining the site. Derelict pits used for waste disposal may be filled up, but extra waste may not be added to allow for more active recontouring, without permission. Thirdly, it is development to display advertisements on any external part of a building which is not normally used for that purpose.

Generally, however, what is a *material* change is a question of fact and degree to be decided by the planning authorities, and it has at least three possible meanings.[21] It could mean a physical change in the use of land, or a significant alteration in the quantity or quality of existing activities, or it could mean a change which is relevant from a planning viewpoint. Where a planning authority is deciding whether to grant permission for a proposed development, it must take into account all material considerations, and that means considerations relevant from a planning viewpoint.[22] Normally, if there is no significant physical change, no development is regarded as occurring. If a builder's yard is used for storing the builder's own materials, it would probably not amount to development should the builder continue storing the same sort of materials there, but sold them off to other builders rather than using them himself.[23] However, it appears that even where there is no physical change in the use of land, planning consent is required if planning considerations are affected by a change in its use in relation to other land. As we have seen in Chapter 2, Section 2.1, change in the boundaries of a planning unit could constitute development, as where a field is detached from a farm to form part of a neighbouring garden.[24]

The relationship of uses in a single planning unit is important where one is ancillary to another. If a particular use is a normal part of the principal activity on the site it cannot be detached and continued independently of the main use without permission. Thus a barn on a farm cannot be sold or let off for storage unconnected with the farm without planning consent.[25] Similarly, if permission is obtained to use a building as a sales area for a garage or factory, it may not be permissible to use the area for selling quite separate products from a different source.[26]

If any use is intensified significantly, this can amount to a material change. For example, land or a house may be divided amongst an increased number of independent occupants,[27] or one or more primary uses may be expanded to replace one which has been phased out. Thus a builder with a yard which he uses both for storing materials and training apprentices could need permission if he expanded the training activities to the exclusion of storage. However, if land is only used for part of the year, it is permissible to expand the use for a greater part of the year or to the whole year. Thus a piece of waste land which had been regularly used by travelling fairs for up to 9 weeks in a year, could be used as an amusement arcade for 150 days or even for the whole year.[28] If changes are slight, they may be regarded as immaterial, on the basis that they are of no planning significance, and whether or not a change is slight may depend on the size of the planning unit. On a large farm with established rights for camping during part of the summer, an increase of six tents to twelve might not be material, whereas it might be material if the planning unit were a small paddock.

(c) Destruction and resumption of uses

The mere abandonment of a use does not require planning permission. Planning legislation can not be used to compel a farmer to work his land or a householder to cultivate his garden. However, once a use is abandoned, permission may be required to resume it.[29] It may therefore be important for a landowner to ensure that a use which is not being actively pursued is merely suspended. It is a question of fact where a use has been abandoned, and both the physical history of the land, and the subjective intention of those controlling it may be relevant. If a caravan site is cleared, but later the same or other caravans are put back on it, the length of the interval before they are put back, and whether the owner always intended to put them back, or initially meant to change the land to some other use, will be relevant.[30] If an existing activity is stopped because the landowner wishes to sell his property or to obtain permission for some other use, he will probably be free to revert to the original activity, provided he does not wait too long. Thus, where owners of a timber yard terminated their tenants' lease, intending to have the land available with vacant possession for light industrial purposes, but planning permission for this development was refused, and the land was compulsorily acquired, compensation was payable on the basis that the land could still be used as a timber yard.[31] Provided during the interval after an activity stops the land is put to no other use, resumption may be allowed after as long a period as seven years.[32]

If land is changed by operational development, this may extinguish the previous uses of the planning unit. Certainly, where a new building is erected, permission will be needed to revive uses previously carried out on that part of the site. Thus after an office block had been constructed on the site of a market it was not permissible to resume the market in an open area underneath the new building.[33]

3.3.2   Exceptions to development, and permitted development

So as to avoid land being sterilized when some existing use stops, the 1971 Act sometimes allows the revival of earlier lawful uses without the need for new planning permission, for example when temporary permission for an existing use expires,[34] or when an unlawful use is stopped by the service of enforcement proceedings.[35] However, some circumstances are expressly defined in the planning legislation as not amounting to development, or are permitted by blanket planning permission granted by the Secretary of State in a General Development Order.

(a)   Exceptions from the definition of development

Section 22 of the 1971 Act stipulates that a number of situations do not amount to development. They include building operations, if these are only interior or do not materially effect the exterior appearance of a building. Similarly, it is not development to use buildings or land within the curtilage of a dwelling house for any purpose incidental to the enjoyment of the dwelling house as such. Thus pets may be kept in a garden, or a car or caravan parked there, without permission, and a householder may use a room as an office for his work. However, if such activities become too prominent, as where commercial vehicles are parked regularly beside a house, they may no longer be regarded as incidental to the primary use of the dwelling house and will require permission. More sweepingly, development is not involved in the use of land for the purposes of agriculture or forestry (including afforestation), or in the use for any of these purposes of any building occupied together with land so used. Again, normally, no development takes place where there is a change from one use to another within classes specified by the Secretary of State, although a planning permission may restrict this normal freedom to change to another use in the same class.[36] There are eighteen of these classes specified in the Use Classes Order 1972.[37] Thus, under Class I, normally no permission is required to change a shop to a different sort of shop, other than one with certain specified potentially anti-social products, namely hot food, tripe, pets or birds, cats' meat or motor vehicles. Under Class II, an office may be altered to a different sort of office. Industrial uses of various sorts are interchangeable, and there are classes of warehouses, hotels and similar buildings. Homes for children, the aged and the disabled are interchangeable. Medical premises of one sort may be changed to another sort. Art galleries are listed with museums and libraries. Theatres are listed with concert halls, and dance halls with skating rinks, Turkish baths and gymnasia!

Express permission is not required for normal ancillary uses even though they are listed in another class. Thus no permission is needed to change buildings in a factory to storage or administrative offices. An important aspect of the Use Classes Order is that it allows an existing use classified in the order to be intensified without any need for planning permission. Thus where a site with existing use rights for making concrete blocks was used to produce four times as many blocks this did not amount to development.[38]

(b) Permitted development

Blanket planning permission for many sorts of development is granted by the Secretary of State in the General Development Order 1977:[39] this contains twenty-three premitted classes.[40] These include minor external alterations to dwelling houses, and other minor operations, such as the construction of modest external walls and other enclosures; temporary buildings and other works needed in construction work, where operational development is being lawfully carried out; substantial alterations, to agricultural buildings other than dwellings, and to industrial buildings and other structures; and much development by statutory undertakers. The Secretary of State, or a local planning authority acting with his approval, may withdraw the benefit of the General Development Order in a particular area or in respect of a particular proposal for development.[41]

Arcitects and landscape architects need to be aware of the details of the classes of permitted development, especially on small schemes. Where there is uncertainty as to whether the classes apply, the local planning authority may be requested to give a ruling under s. 53 of the 1971 Act. For example, Class II authorizes the erection of means of enclosure up to 2 metres in height, but only 1 metre where they abut a highway used by vehicular traffic. If an enclosure is set back from such a highway, or if the highway has a substantial verge, can the enclosure be said to abut the highway? Does an enclosure include a hedge of trees so that this will need planning permission? As the planting of a tree would not normally be described as erecting it, the answer is probably, no. As complying with the details of the permitted classes may require careful survey work, surveyors may also need to be familiar with them. The classes permitting additions to various buildings specify tight limits which vary as between housing, agriculture and industrial buildings and are tighter in areas such as national parks and conservation areas.[42]

3.3.3   Material considerations for planning permission

A person wishing to obtain planning permission must apply to his local planning authority.[43] If permission is refused, or if the application is ignored, the applicant may appeal to the Secretary of State.[44] In the case of the proposed erection of buildings *outline planning permission* may be granted, leaving details of design to be approved later.[45] Thus a developer may establish, in principle, whether he will be allowed to carry out building work, without going to the expense of drawing up detailed plans. Section 53 of the 1971 Act provides a special procedure whereby anyone proposing to do something new on land may obtain from the planning authorities a *determination as to whether planning permission is required*. Again s. 94 provides for *Established use certificates*, obtainable by anyone with an interest in land, from a planning authority, as conclusive evidence that there is an established right to use land for a particular purpose.

   Although a landowner has no right to change the use of his land until he obtains planning permission, the planning authorities must give proper consideration to any application which he makes for planning permission. Section 29 of the 1971 Act provides that the planning authority must have regard 'to the provisions of the development plan, so far as material to the application, and to any other material considerations'. This means that a decision is likely to be invalid and may be quashed by the courts,[46] if it takes into account improper considerations or fails to take into account all relevant matters. Provided all relevant matters are considered it will usually be permissable to discount any of them in favour of others.

(a) Development plans

As we have seen in Chapter 2, Section 2.1, a development plan will include a structure plan with its wide ranging policy statements.[47] Details may be filled out in local plans and these may stipulate future uses of land, including the development site, in clearly mapped-out geographical areas.[48] If the planning authority were to refuse permission for new housing in an area where the structure plan set out a policy to extend housing, it could be challenged if it had ignored the plan. However, an exception may be made to a development plan for good planning reasons. For example, permission could be refused for housing in an area, even if it was earmarked for this purpose in a local plan, if it was premature, or if the proposed development would stand on an exposed ridge which should properly have been excluded from the plan, since building there could spoil the appearance of the whole neighbourhood.[49] Conversely, if proposals for development are inconsistent with any development plan, the planning authorities are not to adhere slavishly to the plan, but must still consider whether an exception should be made. British planning law is very flexible in the discretion which it gives to planning authorities. Even if a development plan provides for a green belt,[50] where there is to be no new building other than for agricultural purposes, exceptions may be made.[51] By comparison, in many other jurisdictions, particularly in Europe, North America, and Australia, more rigid zoning policies are applied, restricting building in certain areas to clearly defined types, and giving no general discretion to planning authorities to make exceptions.

(b) Other policies

In addition to development plans, central or local government may lay down general policies on development. Planning authorities must take account of these.[52] Again, however, they must take account of any arguments that an exception should be made, even if they reject them. In *Stringer* v. *Minister of Housing and Local Government*,[53] Mr Stringer was refused permission by Congleton Rural District Council to build twenty-three houses in Brereton Heath, Cheshire. His appeal to the Minister was dismissed on the recommendation of an inspector after a public inquiry. The key reason on which the refusal was upheld was that the development would pose a serious danger to the working of the Jodrell Bank radio telescope (Fig. 3.4) which was run by a department of Manchester University, directed by Professor Sir Bernard Lovell FRS. Mr Stringer's further appeal to the High Court was dismissed by Cooke J. The Judge accepted that the initial decision by the local planning authority was a nullity. It had acted upon an agreement drawn up by Cheshire County Council between the various local authorities in the area and Manchester University, that in return for the University relaxing its

Fig. 3.4 The Jodrell Bank Radio Telescope, by kind permission of the University of Manchester.

opposition to other development, the local authorities would 'discourage development within the limits of their powers', until at least 1970, in areas in front of the telescope, including Brereton Heath. This agreement was void, because it involved the local planning authorities tying themselves in advance to reject development in the prescribed area. However, the Minister was not a party to this agreement and his decision was made properly, even though he took account of a general policy of discouraging development which would interfere with the efficient working of the telescope. As Cooke J. said:

a Minister charged with the duty of making individual administrative decisions in a fair and impartial manner may nevertheless have a general policy in regard to matters which are relevant to those decisions, provided that the existence of that general policy does not preclude him from fairly judging all the issues which are relevant to each individual case as it comes up for decision.[54]

In *Lavender and Sons Ltd* v. *Minister of Housing and Local Government,*[55] the Minister himself improperly restricted his discretion by applying a policy which was in any case really that of another Ministry. Lavenders were refused permission to excavate gravel from 42 acres on Rivernook Farm near Weybridge. The Minister upheld the refusal. The sole ground for the refusal, in the words of the final decision, was that, 'it is the Minister's present policy that [good agricultural land identified in the Water's Report on sand and gravel as worthy for protection] should not be released for mineral working unless the Minister of Agriculture is not opposed to working'. On appeal to the High Court, Willis J. quashed the Minister's decision on the grounds that he had effectively 'inhibited himself from exercising a proper discretion'. It was quite wrong to apply a policy which eliminated all material considerations but one, and effectively to delegate the decision whether to make an exception to the policy to another Minister.

(c) Other planning considerations

The material considerations which may be the basis of general policies, and which a planning authority must take into account when dealing with an application for planning consent must be related to the planning implications of the proposed development. Proper planning considerations certainly include the impact which the development is likely to have on the physical amenity of the area. Some judges have even implied that this is the only legitimate consideration.[56] However planning clearly takes account of wider social and economic factors. As Cooke J. said in *Stringer* v. *Minister of Housing and Local Government*: 'In principle, it seems to me that any consideration which relates to the use and development of land is capable of being a planning consideration.'[57] The regulations for preparing development plans used to list matters on which these plans may lay down policies,[58] namely, (a) distribution of population and employment, (b) housing, (c) industry and commerce, (d) transportation, (e) shopping, (f) education, (g) other social and community services, (h) recreation and leisure (i) conservation, townscape and landscape, and (j) utility services. The list concluded at (k) with, 'any other matters'. A planning authority may usually be able to demonstrate that any reason for refusing planning permission is of some planning relevance. However, the considerations chosen must be related to the proposed development itself. The need for shopping facilities in an area is a typical planning consideration. However, it could be improper to refuse permission for a shop on the sole grounds that there were surplus shops elsewhere in the relevant district, whilst admitting that there was a shortage in the immediate area.

One matter which may sometimes be irrelevant for planning purposes is the *cost* of a proposed scheme. In *J. Murphy and Sons* v. *Secretary of State*,[59] Murphys applied to have quashed a planning consent granted to Camden Borough Council for a housing scheme on a disused railway depot. Murphys wanted the site to expand their own Kentish Town depot for vehicles and equipment. They contended that residential development would be inordinately expensive, particularly because of the high construction costs to protect against noise from Highgate Road. Ackner J. dismissed Murphys' application, saying, 'what the planning authority is concerned with is, how

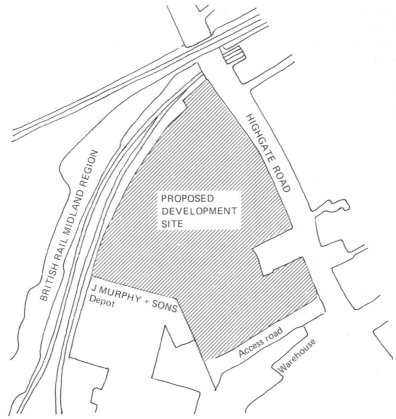

Fig. 3.5 The proposed development site in *J. Murphy and Sons* v. *Secretary of State* [1975] 1 W.L.R. 560.

the land is to be used, and not whether the development proposed is going to be a wise commercial venture. The planning authority exercises no paternalistic or avuncular jurisdiction over would-be developers to safeguard them from their financial follies.'[60] Following this case Murphys in fact obtained the tender for carrying out the very local authority scheme which they opposed. This successfully contained noise and was built without any excessive expense (figs 3.5 and 3.6). Nevertheless, later cases show that the economics of a proposed development may be relevant. For example, a planning authority may be at fault if it declines to take account of the fact that a site may be too expensive to use unless a scheme is carried out which may otherwise conflict with its policies. Thus it may be wrong to refuse permission to use a building for offices without taking account of the fact that the alternative of using it for housing may be too expensive.[61] It would doubtless be a good ground for refusing permission for an uneconomic development if the scheme was likely to be left half finished, so sterilizing the site and perhaps the neighbourhood.

Fig. 3.6 Grafton 3A, Highgate, by kind permission of Ron Simpson Esq., Associate of YRM, Architects and Planners.

Factors which are certainly relevant and must be taken into account, are the *previous planning history* of the site, for example if there is an existing planning permission for some use other than that currently carried out,[62] and the *likely impact on the surrounding area.*[63] Thus if an application were made to replace houses with offices, it would be necessary to consider both whether the offices would themselves be desirable, and also whether the loss to the area of the existing houses was acceptable. It is also necessary to consider whether a particular proposal may lead to a change in the character of the area, for example by encouraging applications for similar changes of other premises nearby. Thus, the Queen's Bench Divisional Court held that it was permissible to refuse permission for converting a warehouse to allow for the retail of electrical goods on the grounds that this might lead to a proliferation of demands for similar development.[64] However in making out a case for a particular type of development, there is no obligation on an applicant to demonstrate that there are no *better alternative sites* available, except where some specific alternative has been suggested by an opponent to his scheme. Thus an applicant wishing to construct a golf course or a park or a hotel,[65] may be required to show that his proposal is needed in the area, but if the site he suggests is otherwise suitable, he need not normally show that it is the only site where this need could be met.

(d) Failure to take considerations properly into account

Not only must a planning authority take account of material considerations, and only material considerations, in determining a planning application, it must also act reasonably in the manner in which it takes account of them. Although the courts are generally loath to overrule an administrative decision, if they regard one as completely outrageous they will be prepared to hold as a matter of law that it could not reasonably have been made.[66] Thus the courts might quash a decision to refuse planning permission for a housing scheme, where the refusal was made on the grounds that the scheme would result in excessive density, whereas, in fact the density would be considerably less than already existed in the area, including the actual site. Where the courts do intervene, by quashing a planning decision, they will not always greatly assist a developer.[67] The application will be referred back to the relevant authority. If, for example, the application had been rejected on several grounds, and only one had been held invalid, it may still be refused on the others.

3.3.4 Planning conditions

A planning authority has wide scope, where it does permit new development, to control the form it takes by imposing conditions. Section 29 (1)(a) of the 1971 Act allows permission to be given subject to such conditions as the planning authority thinks fit. Under s. 36 a developer who objects to a condition may appeal against it to the Secretary of State; although he then runs the risk that the Secretary of State may refuse permission altogether or impose more onerous conditions.

(a) Conditions attached to land controlled by the applicant

Section 30 (1) (a) of the 1971 Act provides, without prejudice to the generality of the wide powers under the previous sections, for conditions to be imposed on the grant of planning permission for regulating the use of any land under the control of the applicant (whether or not it is the land in respect of which the application was made) or requiring the carrying out of works on any such land, so far as appears to the local planning authority to be expedient for the purposes of, or in connection with the development authorized by the permission. A planning application may be made to develop land by someone with no legal interest in the land, but the wording of s. 30 (1) (a) suggests that conditions may only be imposed where the applicant does control the development site or other land to which conditions are applied. Thus if a condition for building a house required access to be provided across a neighbouring field, for the condition to be valid the applicant would need to own the field. However, in practice, if a developer seeks to ignore such a condition, probably he may be prevented from carrying out the development.[68]

(b) Conditions for reinstatement

Sections 30 (1) (b) and 30 (2) of the 1971 Act allow for planning permission granted for a limited period, to include conditions for the subsequent removal of the buildings or works which have been authorized, or for the discontinuance of any temporarily authorized use. Such a condition may require the demolition of an existing building after it has been used for a new temporary use, provided the circumstances of the temporary use justify this,[69] for example because it is liable to leave the building as a health risk. Again, conditions may require the reinstatement of land. In practice it is particularly difficult to ensure that such reinstatement is properly carried out. A site may be levelled and even restored to its original contours, but the soil may be left sour and much attention may be needed before it can bear crops or before grass and trees are established, making it pleasant again. In the case of mineral operations, elaborate provisions have been made for special conditions under the Town and Country Planning (Minerals) Act 1981.[70]

(c) Time conditions

Conditions are usually imposed on every planning consent to ensure that any work is carried out and that any changes of use are implemented, within a reasonable time. Unless an alternative time is specified, the consent lapses if development is not begun within five years of it being granted.[71] However, once development is begun there is no obligation to complete it within any set time,[72] unless the planning authority serves a *completion notice*. This must allow at least a further twelve months to finish the development.[73]

(d)   Other conditions

Just as the matters to be taken into account by a local planning authority in dealing with a planning application must be proper planning considerations, conditions may only be imposed for valid planning reasons and they must be reasonable. Thus, conditions may validly restrict a developer from continuing something which he was doing previously. A factory extension may be allowed on condition that activities in the original factory are restricted, if this is necessary to keep the total noise and traffic activity at the factory to an acceptable level.[74] However, a condition will be invalid if it is vague or is imposed for purposes which are immaterial from a planning point of view. Thus, in 1974, the Queen's Bench Divisional Court quashed an outline planning permission granted by Hillingdon London Borough Council for seven blocks of three-storey flats at Ickenham in Middlesex, because the permission was subject to conditions which would have confined the use of much of the development to council house tenants and were 'the equivalent of requiring the applicants to take on at their own expense a significant part of the duty of the council as housing authority'. This was held to be an unreasonable use of conditions.[75] Nevertheless, where a condition might be treated as unreasonable, planning authorities may obtain what they want by only granting consent for development after entering into an agreement with the developer under special statutory covenants. These may be made under the Town and Country Planning Act 1971, s. 52 or the Local Government (Miscellaneous Provisions) Act 1982, s. 33 and are commonly known as Section 52 agreements.[76]

(e)   The effects of an invalid condition

The courts may not impose their own views in a planning case, and so can only quash or declare invalid a legally defective decision. However, where there is an invalid condition, it is not always clear whether a court may quash the condition by itself, leaving the developer free to act on the planning consent untrammelled, or whether it must quash the whole of the original decision. The possibilities were discussed, *obiter dicta*, by the House of Lords, in *Kingsway Investments (Kent) Ltd* v. *Kent County Council*.[77] However, the judges differed in their conclusions. The stronger view seems to be that, at any rate if a quashed condition is merely minor and incidental, it is likely that the planning permission will survive.[78] This might be the case if permission were given for the construction of a city golf course on condition that the city chief executive should always be able to use it free of charge. Lord Reid went further in holding that if any condition, 'has nothing whatever to do with planning considerations but is only calculated to achieve some ulterior object', it should be severed and the planning permission left to stand. However, on this basis, if the planning authority would clearly not have given permission at all without the invalid condition, the whole permission will fail.[79]

NOTES: SECTION 3.3

1. See post p. 115.
2. As substituted by the Local Government and Planning (Amendment) Act 1981, s. 1 and Sched., Para. 1.
3. Town and Country Planning Act 1971, s. 177.
4. *Parkes* v. *Secretary of State* [1978] 1 W.L.R. 1308.
5. Town and Country Planning Act 1971, s. 87 (3) and Local Government and Planning (Amendment) Act 1981, Sched., Para. 1.
6. *Cheshire County Council* v. *Woodward* [1962] 2 Q.B. 126, per Lord Parker C.J. at p. 133.
7. *Coleshill and District Investments Co.* v. *Minister of Housing and Local Government* [1969] 1 W.L.R. 746, H.L., *ante* p. 42f.
8. *L.C.C.* v. *Marks and Spencer* [1953] A.C. 535, H.L., cf. *Iddenden* v. *Secretary of State* [1972] 1 W.L.R. 1433. This interpretation was regarded as correct in an earlier Ministerial Circular, No. 67/49.
9. See *ante* p. 77f. The use of the traditional land law concept of fixtures for determining what amounts to development has been criticized, e.g. by Alder, J. (1979) *Development Control*, Sweet & Maxwell, London, p. 43.
10. *Barvis* v. *Secretary of State* (1971) 22 P. & C.R. 710.
11. *Cheshire County Council* v. *Woodward, supra* note 6.
12. *Buckinghamshire County Council* v. *Callingham* [1952] 2 Q.B. 515.
13. *Street* v. *Essex County Council* (1965) 193 E.G. 537.
14. Ministerial decision [1970] J.P.L. 713.
15. Ibid. [1957] J.P.L. 452.
16. Ibid. [1970] J.P.L. 542.
17. *Supra* note 7 at p. 770.
18. Town and Country Planning Act 1971, s. 22 (2)(b) and (c).
19. Ibid. s. 290 (1) and Town and Country Planning (Minerals) Act 1981, s. 1 (1).
20. Town and Country Planning Act 1971, s. 22.
21. Alder, J. (1979), *supra* note 9, p. 51.
22. *Post* p. 116f.
23. *Snook* v. *Secretary of State* (1977) 33 P. & C.R. 1.
24. *Sampson's Executors* v. *Nottinghamshire County Council* [1949] 2 K.B. 439, D.C., *ante* p. 63 and note 19.
25. *G. Percy Trentham Ltd* v. *Gloucestershire County Council* [1966] 1 W.L.R. 506, C.A.
26. *Kwik Save Discount Ltd* v. *Secretary of State for Wales* (1978) 37 P. & C.R. 170.
27. *Birmingham Corporation* v. *Minister of Housing and Local Government ex parte*

Habib Ullah [1964] 1 Q.B. 178. See *ante* p. 49f.

28. *Washington Urban District Council* v. *Gray* (1959) 10 P. & C.R. 264.
29. *Hartley* v. *Minister of Housing and Local Government* [1970] 1 Q.B. 413, C.A.
30. *Klein* v. *Whitstable Urban District Council* (1958) 10 P. & C.R. 6.
31. *Graver's Executors* v. *Rickmansworth Urban District Council* (1959) P. & C.R. 417.
32. *Fyson* v. *Buckinghamshire County Council* [1958] 1 W.L.R. 634.
33. *Petticoat Lane Rentals Ltd* v. *Secretary of State* [1971] 1 W.L.R. 1112. cf. *Jennings Motors Ltd* v. *Secretary of State* [1982] 1 All E.R. 471, C.A. See too *Aston* v. *Secretary of State* (1982) 43 P. & C.R. 331, D.C.
34. Town and Country Planning Act 1971, s. 23 (5).
35. Ibid. s. 23 (9) but note *Young* v. *Secretary of State* 1983, *The Times*, 8 February.
36. *City of London Corporation* v. *Secretary of State* (1971) 23 P. & C.R. 169.
37. S.I. 1972, No. 1385.
38. *Brooks & Burton Ltd* v. *Secretary of State* [1977] 1 W.L.R. 1294.
39. S.I. 1977, No. 289. as amended by S.I. 1981, No. 245.
40. Ibid. sched. 1.
41. Ibid. art. 4.
42. S.I. 1981, No. 246, *post* pp. 129 and 131.
43. Town and Country Planning Act 1981, s. 25.
44. Ibid. ss. 36 and 37.
45. General Development Order, 1977, S.I. 1977 No. 289, Art. 5.
46. *Post* p. 395.
47. *Ante* p. 57.
48. *Ante* p. 60.
49. *Provincial Properties (London) Ltd* v. *Caterham & Warlingham Urban District Council* [1972] 1 Q.B. 453, *post* p. 232.
50. *Post* p. 132.
51. *Enfield London Borough Council* v. *Secretary of State* [1975] J.P.L. 155.
52. *J.A. Pye (Oxford) Estates* v. *West Oxfordshire District Council.* [1982] J.P.L. 537.
53. *Stringer* v. *Minister of Housing and Local Government* [1970] 1 W.L.R. 1281.
54. Ibid. at p. 1298.
55. *Lavender and Son Ltd* v. *Minister of Housing and Local Government* [1970] 1 W.L.R. 1231.
56. In *Copeland Borough Council* v. *Secretary of State* (1976) 31 P. & C.R. 403, Lord Widgery C.J. said at p. 407 'the purpose of all town and country planning is to preserve amenities and the sensible and attractive layout of properties'.
57. *Supra* note 53 at p. 1294.
58. Town and Country Planning (Structure and Local Plans) Regulations, 1974. S.I. 1974, No. 1486. Schedules 1 and 2, revoked S.I. 1982, No. 555.
59. *J. Murphy and Sons* v. *Secretary of State* [1973] 1 W.L.R. 560.
60. Ibid. at p. 565.
61. *Niarchos (London)* v. *Secretary of State* (1979) 76. L.G.R. 480.
62. *Spackman* v. *Wiltshire County Council* [1971] 1 All E.R. 257.
63. *Clyde & Co.* v. *Secretary of State* [1977] 1 W.L.R. 926.
64. *Collis Radio Ltd* v. *Secretary of State* (1975) 29 P. & C.R. 390.
65. *Rhodes* v. *Minister of Housing and Local Government* [1963] 1 W.L.R. 208.
66. *Post* p. 396.
67. *Post* p. 395.
68. *Augier* v. *Secretary of State* (1979) 38 P. & C.R. 219. See *post* p. 124, the effect of invalid conditions.

69. But see *Newbury District Council* v. *Secretary of State* [1981] A.C. 578. H.L.
70. *Post* p. 140f.
71. Town and Country Planning Act 1971, s. 41 (2).
72. *Salisbury District Council* v. *Secretary of State and Gillian E. Parnwell* [1982] J.P.L. 702.
73. Town and Country Planning Act 1971, s. 44.
74. *Penwith District Council* v. *Secretary of State* (1977) 34 P. & C.R. 269.
75. *R.* v. *Hillingdon London Borough Council ex parte Royco Homes Ltd* [1974] 1 Q.B. 720, *per* Lord Widgery C.J. at p. 732. See also *Hall & Co Ltd* v. *Shoreham-by-Sea Urban District Council* [1964] 1 W.L.R. 240.
76. *Ante* p. 99f.
77. *Kingsway Investments (Kent) Ltd* v. *Kent County Council* [1971] A.C. 72, H.L.
78. Ibid., Lords Morris and Donovan, c.f. Lord Guest.
79. *Pyx Granite Co Ltd* v. *Minister of Housing and Local Government* [1958] 1 Q.B. 554. See Hodson L.J. at p. 578, and note. *R.* v. *Hillingdon London Borough Council, supra* note 75.

3.4   Legal control of special aspects of land use

The Department of the Environment and local planning authorities are often responsible for the control of special aspects of land use. In certain areas, other public bodies take priority. Some of these, such as the Countryside Commission, are primarily concerned with protecting the amenity of the landscape. Others, such as water authorities, were set up to conserve and develop resources for general use. These authorities too may be required to take account of the amenity aspects of what they are dealing with.[1] There is no absolute separation between rural and urban planning, but controls differ significantly in practice between town and country. For example agricultural activity is largely free from normal planning restrictions.[2] Natural resources such as water and minerals tend to be obtained from open land, whereas the majority of buildings which are protected are obviously in built-up areas. In the city trees are protected solely as an amenity, whereas in the countryside they are often regarded as essentially a commercial asset.[3]

3.4.1   Special areas of land (Fig. 3.7)

In various places, pieces of land have been designated either to enhance their amenity value, or to encourage development. The normal approach in areas thought to deserve protection is to empower appropriate bodies to make agreements with their owners to control land use, and if appropriate to allow for public access. If necessary, special statutory restrictions may be put on what owners may do with their land in such areas, but land will normally only be acquired compulsorily as a last resort. By contrast, where an area demands new development, it is more likely that it will be acquired outright by a public body, although, here too, the alternative method may be used of encouraging private development.

Fig. 3.7 National parks and areas of outstanding natural beauty 30 November 1983, copied by kind permission of the Countryside Commission.

(a) Conservation in the countryside

Apart from development control, the present legal foundation for protecting the amenity of the countryside is the National Parks and Access to the Countryside Act 1949, which provided a special regime for areas designated as national parks, supervised by a National Parks Commission. By the Countryside Act 1968,[4] this was reconstituted as the *Countryside Commission.* Under the Wildlife and Countryside Act 1981,[5] it now operates as a body corporate, distinct from the Crown, owning its own property and without any special legal immunity or privileges. However, it is funded by the Department of the Environment, to which it makes annual reports. The Secretary of State for the Environment appoints its chairman and must approve its chief officer. Also the Secretary of State and the Minister for the Civil Service must approve the numbers of its other staff. The Commission designates national parks and other special areas. Under the 1949 Act,[6] it advises generally on matters affecting the countryside, particularly where any development is likely to prejudice the natural beauty of any area or place. The commission also provides an information service to the public.

The *Nature Conservancy Council* was constituted in its present form by the Nature Conservancy Council Act 1973.[7] It is an independent body appointed and funded by the Department of the Environment, to manage nature reserves and provide advice to the government, together with a general public information service. The council also channels grants for nature conservation under the Wildlife and Countryside Act 1981.[8]

National parks are defined in the National Parks and Access to the Countryside Act 1949[9] as extensive tracts of country in England and Wales, designated for their natural beauty and the opportunities which they offer for public open-air recreation, 'having regard both to their character and to their position in relation to centres of population'. These parks differ from those in countries such as the United States, where pieces of wild landscape made into national parks, remain remote and uninhabited. The British national parks remain largely in many private hands. The public interest is ensured mainly by strict planning controls and by access arrangements. Thus new building which would normally be permitted under the blanket provisions of the General Development Order, 1971,[10] is much more strictly limited in national parks particularly with regard to height and volumes.[11] There are ten national parks in England and Wales. The first was the Peak District, designated in 1950, and the latest the Brecon Beacons, designated in 1955. In most national parks, development control is the responsibility of special committees of the relevant county councils. However, because of the way they straddled county boundaries, the Lake District and the Peak District were provided with their own joint planning boards. Since the reorganization of local government, under the Local Government Act 1972, the Peak District retains its own joint planning board, with responsibility for structure plans. The Lake District now has a special planning board. In each national park, the relevant committee or board was required to produce a national park plan for the management of its park. It must renew this every five years.[12]

Outside national parks, *areas of outstanding natural beauty* may be designated by the Countryside Commission and confirmed by the Secretary of State, under the 1949 Act.[13] Some of these areas are substantial, such as 2538 square kilometres of the Chilterns and North Wessex Downs, on the

Berkshire Ridgeway, and 1507 square kilometres of the Cotswolds. Some are much smaller, such as 71 square kilometres of Dedham Vale, made famous by its associations with the painter Constable. These areas are protected like national parks and conservation areas by restrictions on development,[14] which would normally be permitted under the General Development Order,[15] and by the requirement that the Countryside Commission must be consulted in the preparation of development plans.[16] Joint consultation between the planning authorities concerned is encouraged, as are management agreements to control farming methods. Under the Wildlife and Countryside Act 1981,[17] planning policies are expected to keep major development out of areas of outstanding natural beauty. However, the value of designating an area of outstanding beauty is questionable. Much friction is caused with the farming community which feels discriminated against by comparison with farmers generally. Local authorities are frequently unenthusiastic about taking positive action, and where areas straddle their boundaries neighbouring authorities each tend to leave it to the other to act.

The 1949 Act further provided for *sites of special scientific interest*. These have been given much greater prominence by the Wildlife and Countryside Act 1981, although their effectiveness may in fact have been increased very little. The 1981 Act makes it the responsibility of the Nature Conservancy Council to identify such sites and to notify the local planning authority, the Secretary of State and the owner and occupier of the land.[18] A site may be of special interest by reason of flora, fauna, or geological or physiographical features. The notification will list any operations which appear likely to damage the special features of the site, and it is then an offence, save in an emergency, for an owner or occupier to carry out such operations without giving three months notice to the council. However, a delay of three months may serve as little more than an irritant to the farmer concerned. Furthermore if the operation requires planning permission, the granting of such permission is sufficient authority for the operation to be carried out immediately. The 1981 Act does give the Secretary of State power to make orders forbidding specified operations on sites of special scientific interest, so as to secure the survival of any kind of plant or animal, to comply with international obligations, or to conserve what is of national importance.[19] The Nature Conservancy Council must be consulted before such an order is made and the land owner must be paid compensation. Where a court convicts a person of breaking such an order it may order him to restore the land.[20] However, the provision for compensation means that protection by this method will be rare because of the cost to overpressed public funds.

The 1981 Act does significantly supplement ordinary planning control in respect of one type of scenery, by empowering the Nature Conservancy Council or the Countryside Commission to notify local planning authorities of areas of limestone known as limestone pavements, where the surface of the ground has been fissured by natural erosion, resulting in features of special interest. The Secretary of State may protect these by *Limestone Pavement Orders*, prohibiting the removal or disturbance of limestone.[21]

The 1981 Act,[22] enables the Nature Conservancy Council to apply to the Secretary of State for areas of foreshore or sea bed to be designated as *marine nature reserves*, to be managed by the Council for the purposes of conservation or research. Generally, under the 1949 Act,[23] the Council may make agreements with land owners to protect any land which it wishes to treat as a nature reserve, for the purposes of conservation or research. If this power proves inadequate, the Council may compulsorily acquire land with the consent of the Secretary of State and on the payment of compensation.[24] Nature reserves, supervised by the Council are known as *national nature reserves*.[25] Local authorities have similar powers to set up *local nature reserves*.[26]

Designation of certain other special sites is possible, under the Ancient Monuments and Archaeological Areas Act 1979, part II. However here the purpose is to provide time for recording information before it is irretrievably lost rather than to conserve an amenity. The Department of the Environment may designate *areas of archaeological importance*, where anyone carrying out operations which disturb the ground, flooding or tipping, must notify the district council, or in the case of disturbance by such a council, must notify the Department so as to allow time for emergency archaeological digs. The authority concerned has four weeks in which to decide whether to excavate, and a further four months and two weeks to carry out the excavations.

(b) Conservation in towns

Areas designated for conservation in the countryside may contain buildings. National parks in particular may include villages. Areas may be designated in what are actually urban areas. For example the Peak District runs in to the west of the city of Sheffield. Many country parks are actually in towns. Conversely, conservation areas may be made in rural areas, although they are essentially designed to protect the townscape. *Conservation areas* were introduced in the Civic Amenities Act 1967, and are now provided for in the Town and Country Planning Act 1971.[27] They may be designated by local planning authorities or by county councils, even when these are not local planning authorities, or by the Secretary of State, as 'areas of special architectural or historic interest the character or appearance of which it is desirable to preserve or enhance'. Permission must be obtained before demolishing buildings in a conservation area and notice must be given of any work to be carried out on trees. Local planning authorities are required to produce proposals for the active preservation and enhancement of such areas.[28] As with National Parks and areas of outstanding natural beauty there are restrictions on development which would normally be permitted under the blanket provisions of the General Development Order, 1977.[29]

One special device for protecting the amenity of urban areas, which is normally not statutory, but is provided for in development plans, is the *green belt*. The prototype was set up around London and is still maintained, under the Green Belt (London and Home Counties) Act 1938. In Circular 42/50, other local authorities were encouraged by the Ministry of Housing and Local Government to make similar provisions, 'for checking the unrestricted sprawl of the built up areas, and of safeguarding the surrounding countryside against further encroachment'. Green belts are particularly designed to prevent built-up areas expanding and merging into each other or to preserve the special character of towns. The circular recommended that they be several miles wide and that they should be sacrosant from new building and from alterations of existing buildings unless these were for purposes of agriculture or, sport, for cemeteries or for institutions standing in extensive grounds.

(c) Facilities for public amenity

In the various areas protected by special orders, the relevant public bodies have powers to set up facilities for the public. Local authorities have further powers under the Countryside Act 1968 to create *country parks*, on their own or private land as pleasure grounds, especially near connurbations. If necessary, they may acquire land compulsorily for this purpose.[30] Local authorities may provide public amenities on common land to which the public have rights of access for purposes of open air recreation,[31] and they are given special powers to encourage water recreation.[32] Water authorities themselves[33] have an express responsibility 'to take steps to secure the use of water and land associated with water for the purposes of recreation'.[34]

(d) Areas designated to stimulate development, redevelopment or improvement

Areas may be selected for development or redevelopment rather than for conservation. As part of the much-expanded public control of land use following the Second World War, statutory provision was made for the creation of *new towns*, complete with homes, industries, and all appropriate services. Between 1946 and 1970, starting with Stevenage, twenty-three new towns were designated. They include Milton Keynes, which is a network of new communities rather than a single new town.

The tendency now is for the revitalization of old built-up areas rather than the creation of new ones. However, the powers to create new towns have been consolidated in the New Towns Act 1981. The Secretary of State for the Environment may designate land which may include any existing built up area, as a new town. He will appoint a *development corporation* for each new town to carry out development, using grants from the Treasury, and loans subject to strict central government control. Proposals for development are submitted direct by the corporation to the Secretary of State although he must consult with the district planning authority before giving planning permission. The development corporations have wide powers to acquire land with the approval of the Secretary of State. Compulsory purchase will normally be made without any right for objectors to insist on a public inquiry. The New Towns Act 1981[35] empowers development corporations to dispose of their land, in particular to secure development. However, there is a general requirement that they must obtain the consent of the Secretary of State before transferring any freehold or granting a lease for more than ninety-nine years, although if they do grant a larger estate to anyone, this will not be invalid, so that those acquiring land in a new town do not have to enquire whether the consent has been obtained. Under Parts II and III of the 1981 Act, development corporations may transfer their land to an independent corporation, the *Commission for the New Towns*. Schemes may be set up to transfer dwellings and associated property to district councils. Other appropriate property may be transferred to local authorities or statutory undertakers.

To stimulate redevelopment in existing urban areas, the Local Planning and Land Act 1980 has provided for *urban development areas*[36] and for *enterprise zones*.[37] The Secretary of State may create urban development areas each with its own urban development corporation with the object of securing regeneration, in particular, 'by bringing land and buildings into effective use, encouraging the development of existing and new industry and commerce, creating an attractive environment and ensuring that housing and social facilities are available to encourage people to live and work in the area'.[38] *Urban development corporations* have similar powers to new town development corporations but may also be given further powers which are normally vested in local authorities such as those over development control. When their work is completed it is intended that urban development corporations should transfer their property to local authorities and statutory undertakers and be wound up.[39] District councils, London borough councils or new town or urban development corporations may be asked by the Secretary of State to prepare schemes for enterprise zones. Such a scheme may be adopted by the body preparing it. The Secretary of State may then designate the area as an enterprise zone where planning controls will be relaxed and important tax concessions made available, notably exemption from development land tax and industrial and commercial rating.

The initiative in redeveloping derelict areas is commonly taken by local authorities. Various statutory powers enable them to make grants and loans, and otherwise to assist in the redevelopment of depressed industrial and business areas. Notably, under the Inner Urban Areas Act 1978, the Secretary of State may designate an urban district as one with special social need, where the underlying conditions may be improved by the powers provided in the Act.[40] The district authority may then create *improvement areas* where it may make loans or grants for landscaping and otherwise improving the land.[41] More substantial relief may be provided in *special areas*, where the Secretary of State enters into *partnership agreements* with appropriate local authorities and other bodies or individuals.[42] Local authorities may also stimulate development by their general powers to act in the interests of the local inhabitants,[43] or, for example, by creating independent development companies.

So far as decaying residential areas are concerned, a number of Housing Acts provide a range of powers. Thus, under the Housing Act 1957, Part III, a district council may pass a resolution declaring a *clearance area*, where demolition is the most satisfactory method of dealing with houses in an area, which are 'unfit for human habitation, or are by reason of their bad arrangement, or the narrowness or bad arrangement of the streets, dangerous or injurious to the health of the inhabitants'.[44] With these houses other buildings may be included, if they suffer from similar defects. The authority must be satisfied that alternative accommodation can be provided for those who are likely to be displaced. Originally one method of dealing with a clearance area was to require owners to demolish their own buildings. However, since the Housing Act 1974, district councils are obliged to act by themselves purchasing the land, if necessary under compulsory powers, confirmed by the Secretary of State, after a public inquiry. Additional land may be acquired if it is surrounded by the clearance area and 'is reasonably necessary for the purpose of securing a cleared area of convenient shape and dimensions', or if it is adjacent and 'reasonably necessary for the satisfactory development or use of the cleared area'.

A less drastic approach to slum clearance is that of revitalizing run-down residential areas. Thus, the Housing Act 1974, Part IV, authorizes district councils or London boroughs to make resolutions with respect to areas consisting primarily of housing accommodation, declaring *housing action areas*,[45] where this is the most effective means of dealing with unsatisfactory living conditions within five years, so as to improve the accommodation and the well-being of residents and secure proper and effective management and use of the existing accommodation. The authority must have regard to the physical state of existing housing accommodation in the area as a whole and to social conditions there. It must notify the Secretary of State and he may cancel the declaration or reduce the area to which it applies.[46] The designation lasts for five years, but may then be renewed for two years at a time.[47] Subject to the authorization of the Secretary of State, a local authority may compulsorily acquire land in a *housing action area*,[48] so as to carry out improvements.[49] Alternatively it may leave the buildings in private ownership and make grants to help with their improvement, or provide materials or actually agree to execute work.[50] Under the Housing Act 1969, Part II, the same local authorities may resolve to declare *general improvement areas*, in predominantly residential areas, where they may stimulate improvement by acquiring land by agreement or may assist occupants by making grants or loans or otherwise. Here the approval of the Secretary of State is not required, although he may contribute towards the cost of improvement.

3.4.2   Conservation of natural resources

The law provides special protection for natural resources which are in limited supply. These may be permanent and recyclable like water. They may, like agricultural land, be reuseable but liable to destruction if they are given over to new uses; or, like mineral resources, they may by their nature be exhausted by use.

(a) Water resources

Overall responsibility for water resources is given by the Water Act 1973, s. 1 to the Secretary of State for the Department of the Environment, acting jointly with the Minister of Agriculture, Fisheries and Food. The former has the duty of overseeing the conservation and supply of water, sewage, inland navigation and amenity; the latter is responsible for drainage and fisheries. Under s. 22,[51] the ministers must exercise their functions so as to further the conservation and enhancement of natural beauty and the conservation of flora, fauna and geological or physiographical features of special interest. The Nature Conservancy Council has a duty to notify a water authority where it is of the opinion that the authority's operation may harm any such features which are of special interest. After such notification the authority must consult with the council before carrying out those operations.

When local government was reorganized into larger units in 1972 it was decided to keep water resources largely separate. The 1973 Act replaced some twenty-nine boards with nine English *water authorities* and the Welsh National Water Development Authority. By contrast, in Scotland, where local government is organized in larger regional units,[52] water resources are essentially under the control of local government. The English and Welsh water authorities are based upon a natural water-shed (Fig. 3.8) system. This rational plan for dealing with water is not related to concentrations of population and does not fit into the political structures of local government. Until 1983 local authorities were able to appoint members of the authorities, but, under the Water Act 1983 this power is now confined to the government ministers concerned. Local government boundaries are ignored to the extent that the Severn–Trent water authority extends into part of North Wales and

1   North West   6   Southern
2   Northumbrian   7   Wessex
3   Yorkshire   8   South West
4   Anglia   9   Severn-Trent
5. Thames   10 Welsh National Development

Fig. 3.8 Water authorities in England and Wales.

the Welsh National water development authority extends into parts of
Western England. However, although mains sewage is handled by water
authorities, arrangements are generally made for local sewage collection to be
dealt with by district councils. Much local distribution remains in the hands
of private *statutory water companies.*

Land drainage is regulated under the Land Drainage Act 1976 by a
separate hierarchy of committees. Rivers identified by the Ministry of
Agriculture as main rivers are the direct responsibility of water authorities.
There are also *regional land drainage committees* for each water authority
which may propose local land drainage schemes to be administered by *local
land drainage committees.* These two tiers have members appointed by the
Minister, the water authority and by such county councils as are within or
partly within the relevant areas. Where appropriate, appointments are made

by London borough councils and the Greater London Council. Drainage may be directly supervised by *internal drainage boards* consisting of elected representatives of landowners within the area affected.

Public control of water resources significantly affects private land rights, but the relationship is not clearly spelled out and can be difficult to resolve in particular cases.[53] The three main aims of control are to ensure fair distribution of limited resources, to preserve the purity of water supplies and to prevent flooding or other harm caused from accumulation or poor drainage of water. The Water Resources Act 1963, Part IV, generally restricts abstraction in any form, of more than 1000 gallons of water in any one or a series of operations, to those who have been granted a licence by a water authority and to limited classes set out in s. 24. Thus a licence is not required where water is taken from underground strata for domestic purposes of an individual household or is taken from any water course or a lake or similar source of supply above the ground for domestic or agricultural purposes other than spray irrigation, on the land where it is abstracted. Further, no licence is required for abstraction in the course of or resulting from any operations for purposes of land drainage, or so far as is necessary to prevent interference with any mining, quarrying, engineering, building or other operations (whether underground or on the surface) or to prevent damage to works resulting from any such operation.[54]

Those who had established rights to extract water when the 1963 Act came into force, were entitled to a licence as of right: even they are charged an annual fee. A licence is attached to land and will be transferred to any new occupier.[55] However, the licence lapses unless the new occupier notifies the water authority of the change within one month. Once a licence has been granted, it provides a defence against any action brought by someone else whose supply has been affected, unless the person relying on the licence has been negligent or is in breach of contract.[56] However, in granting a licence, a water authority is required not to derogate from any rights protected by an existing licence or exercised under one of the exceptions where no licence is required.[57] If an authority breaks this duty, its licences are still valid but it may be ordered to pay damages to persons affected unless it can show that the interference with their protected rights was wholly or mainly attributable to exceptional shortage of rain or to an accident or other unforeseen act or event outside its control.[58] The authority has power to revoke or modify a licence on payment of compensation and may thus take back an improperly granted licence.

Most new users of water will rely on public supplies. The Water Act 1945, Sched. 3, lays down standard arrangements for water undertakers, including obligations to supply water for domestic and non-domestic purposes subject to appropriate demand and availability.

The legislation on water resources adds statutory control to the common law duties to protect neighbouring land from flooding.[59] Thus the 1963 Act, s. 36, requires a licence for any impounding works such as dams and weirs. The Reservoirs Act 1975 provides that county councils must register and supervise reservoirs holding more than 25 000 cubic metres of water raised above the adjacent land level. The Land Drainage Act 1976 provides powers for drainage authorities to supervise drainage and this helps to restrict flooding. Drainage authorities themselves have powers to maintain existing water courses and drainage channels.[60] Where they have introduced drainage schemes they may be under a duty to maintain them.[61] A drainage authority may require a person responsible for any water course where the flow is impeded to remedy this. If necessary the authority may then carry out the work itself and send the bill to the person responsible who may also be summarily convicted.[62] Obstruction of a water course may be treated as a statutory nuisance and punished.[63]

A land owner or occupier may apply to the Agricultural Land Tribunal for an order to make a neighbour clear any of his ditches which are in such a condition as to cause injury to his land or to prevent the improvement of its drainage.[64] Again, a land owner may be authorized to do work himself on neighbouring land in furtherance of good drainage.[65] The costs of work done by drainage authorities are defrayed under elaborate provisions set out in Part IV of the 1976 Act partly through local authority rates, and partly by charges allocated to land owners in accordance with the size of their holdings. Protection against flooding from the sea is provided by the Coast Protection Act 1949. It is largely the responsibility of county councils subject to the control of the Department of the Environment.

The Control of Pollution Act 1974 is designed to protect all sources of water from pollution, but it has not yet been fully implemented. Control is at present provided by the Rivers (Prevention of Pollution) Acts 1951–1961. Under the 1951 Act, s. 2, it is an offence to cause or knowingly permit poisonous, noxious or polluting matter to enter any stream. The Water Resources Act 1963, s. 72 makes it an offence to pollute water or underground strata. At common law riparian land owners may still have much additional control over new uses of streams. In 1887 the tenants of the Banknock Colliery near Stirling pumped hard water out of their workings into the Doups Burn. This interfered with the Bankier distillery downstream which required soft water. The House of Lords held that the distillery company was entitled to an interdict preventing the change in the quality of the water even though this remained entirely pure.[66]

(b) Agricultural land

The agricultural industry enjoys remarkable freedom from planning control. Under the Town and Country Planning Act 1971, s. 22 (2)(e), the use of land for agriculture or forestry is not classed as development and so never requires planning permission. The General Development Order 1977, Sched. 1, Classes VI and VII, gives blanket permission for substantial buildings and other works required for agricultural or forestry purposes. However, control may be imposed for example by management agreements made with farmers under the Wildlife and Countryside Act 1981.[67] Generally the law encourages farming by revenue concessions, notably immunity from rates for agricultural land and buildings under the General Rate Act 1967.[68] The availability of grants, many made in accordance with European Community policy, may significantly affect the appearance of the landscape and may conflict with other policies designed to protect amenities. Thus marshland such as the Somerset Levels may either be treated as deserving protection as a site of special scientific interest, or on the contrary as appropriate for drainage grants so as to increase available farmland. The witholding of grants to preserve existing land use in areas such as national parks may be a more potent form of control than positive restriction on development.

As an economic asset, agricultural land is threatened by the expansion of built up areas and other development. This may be ameliorated by powers of the Minister of Agriculture to acquire land, if need be compulsorily, so as to restore it to agriculture, for example, under the Agriculture Act 1947, s. 84, where a piece of agricultural land is no longer viable by itself because it has been severed from a larger area which has been taken under other statutory powers, or under the Mineral Workings Act 1951, s. 23, to restore derelict ironstone workings. Agricultural land is protected from destruction by other development through the policies determined in development plans. Where there is a likelihood of development which is not approved in such plans, consultation must be carried out with the Ministry of Agriculture,[69] which provides a system of grading so that the land which is of greatest value for agricultural purposes is readily identifiable.[70] Under the Agricultural Land (Removal of Surface Soil) Act 1953, unauthorized removal of agricultural top soil for sale is a form of development treated as a crime.[71]

The Agriculture Act 1947, Part II, allowed for supervision orders to be made under which the Minister of Agriculture could direct, or in the last resort dispossess, farmers practising bad estate management or husbandry. This power was repealed in 1958, but s. 95 remains and this would allow the Minister to make directions as to the use of agricultural land, in particular pasture, for up to a year, 'in the interests of the national supply of food or other agricultural products'. The Weeds Act 1959 contains powers for the Minister to order occupiers of land to prevent the spread of spear or field thistles, curled or broad leaved docks or ragwort. If necessary he may have the work carried out himself and recover the cost from the occupier or owner.

Under the Forestry Act 1967, control of forestry is exercised by the Forestry Commission, first set up in 1919, and now charged under the 1967

Act 'with the general duty of promoting the interests of forestry, the development of afforestation and the production and supply of timber and other forest products in Great Britain'.[72] It is specifically concerned to promote the establishment and maintenance of adequate reserves of growing trees and to control timber pests and diseases. The Commission owns large tracts of forest land itself but also operates extensively through forestry dedication covenants and agreements with private land owners.[73] A licence is required from the Commission for the felling of other timber trees.[74] The Commission also has powers, which it has never used, to make felling directions, ordering trees to be felled in order to prevent timber deteriorating or to improve the growth of neighbouring trees.[75]

(c) Mineral extraction

Mineral extraction frequently involves the destruction of good agricultural land, and minerals which are in limited supply are particularly jealously guarded. Gold and silver deposits have always been treated as Crown Property. The property in all coal and coal mines was acquired by the State under the Coal Act 1938 and is now vested in the National Coal Board by the Coal Industry Nationalization Act 1946. Petroleum, including natural gas, was vested in the Crown by the Petroleum (Production) Act 1934 and licences to seek and extract oil may be granted to private undertakings.[76]

New mineral workings to remove deposits of any substance from the earth, whether clay, limestone or gravel, require planning permission, and unauthorized development consisting of the removal within a three-month period of more than 5 cubic yards of surface soil from agricultural land is itself a summary offence.[77] However, once permission is granted, mineral workings are likely to be continued for a considerable period. Many, already established at the time of the Town and Country Planning Act 1947, including some in areas of scenic beauty such as the Peak District, are still being carried out and expanded. Mineral workings are the main form of development controlled by counties rather than district councils.[78] The Town and Country Planning (Minerals) Act 1981 introduced the formal title *mineral planning authority* and added important provisions for mineral control to the Town and Country Planning Act 1971. Thus there is now a duty to make periodic reviews of mineral workings.[79] The standard period for carrying out new mineral workings is now 60 years.[80] Orders may be made to prohibit the resumption of mineral workings and to require the removal of equipment and the restoration of sites where operations have not been carried out for two years and appear unlikely to resume.[81] Supervision orders may be made to protect land where workings have been suspended temporarily.[82] Where new mineral development is permitted, as well as conditions for the restoration of land, detailed aftercare conditions may be made,[83] usually in accordance with an aftercare scheme, to ensure that the land is restored to use for agriculture, forestry or amenity purposes. Usually five years will be provided for the aftercare work to be satisfactorily completed. Aftercare conditions may also be included with a prohibition order.[84] Agreements for planning gain under s. 52 of the 1971 Act are frequently required before the grant of consent for mineral development.

The special position of minerals has resulted in a number of provisions to ensure that the high costs to amenity and sometimes to private property are appropriately spread. The Coal Mining Subsidence Act 1957 provides a scheme to avoid the need for nuisance proceedings whereby the National Coal Board may rectify or pay compensation for subsidence damage. An earlier scheme to cope with subsidence resulting from the extraction of salt is still to be found in the Brine Pumping (Compensation for Subsidence) Act 1891, whereby brine extractors in a particular area may be required to contribute to a fund to compensate those affected by subsidence. Where there is more than one extractor the scheme avoids the difficulty of identifying exactly which caused particular harm. An analogous arrangement is made by the Mineral Working Acts 1951 and 1971 for ironstone operators in Northamptonshire and neighbouring counties to contribute to a restoration fund which then makes payments back to operators when they are restoring their workings so that the variable expenses of restoration are evened out. A further special feature of mineral legislation is, that under the Mines (Working Facilities and Support) Acts 1966 and 1974, subject to the support of the Department of Trade and Industry, even private mineral operators may obtain orders from the High Court enabling them to override the private-property rights of others, for example by letting down land or to obtain access, where this is necessary to extract minerals and the order is in the national interest.

3.4.3   Conservation of amenity

There are a number of special systems for controlling land use so as to protect amenity. These in particular illustrate the variety of the forms which public control of land may take.

(a) Trees

The Town and Country Planning Act 1971, s. 60, empowers local planning authorities to make *tree preservation orders* on individual trees, groups of trees or woodlands in the interests of amenity, to prohibit cutting down, topping, lopping, uprooting, wilful damage or wilful destruction, unless the authority has granted its consent. Such an order may be used to control the agricultural practice of coppicing, still prevalent in Kent and elsewhere.[85] The

Local Government Planning and Land Act 1980 now provides that an order has to be confirmed by the local planning authority which made it, allowing at least twenty-eight days for those affected to make representations. However, when the order is made, the authority may direct that the tree is to be provisionally protected for six months pending confirmation.[86] In conservation areas local planning authorities must be notified of any proposed work on trees,[87] and this gives them an opportunity to serve a preservation order. Breach of a provisional, or final tree preservation order, is a criminal offence which may be dealt with summarily, or in serious cases, on indictment.[88] No consent is needed to do work on a protected tree which is dying or dead or has become dangerous, or in compliance with any statutory duty or so far as may be necessary for the prevention or abatement of a nuisance.[89] This arrangement sits uneasily with private land law, since, as a tree which overhangs a boundary is technically a nuisance, it would seem that it may be disfigured with impunity by its owner or by the neighbour over whose land it projects.

Under the Local Government Planning and Land Act 1980, s. 62, where a tree which is protected otherwise than as part of a woodland dies or becomes dangerous, then the owner is normally obliged to plant a replacement of appropriate size and species. Under s. 59, when local planning authorities grant planning permission they are required to ensure, whenever it is appropriate, that existing trees are protected by s. 60 orders and that conditions are imposed for preserving and planting trees. Detailed procedures for making tree preservation orders are set out in the Town and Country Planning (Tree Preservation Order) Regulations, 1969.[90] These allow that if a tree owner is later refused consent to remove or do work on a protected tree he may appeal to the Secretary of State.

(b) Buildings and monuments

Buildings of special architectural or historic interest are protected by being included on a list kept by the Secretary of State under s. 54 of the Town and Country Planning Act 1971. For buildings on this list, *listed building consent* is required from the local planning authority under s. 55 for demolition or any alteration or extension of the building in a manner which would affect its character as a building of special architectural or historic interest. Where demolition is proposed it must not be carried out until the Royal Commission for Historical Monuments has had opportunity to record the building for at least one month after a grant of listed building consent. Under s. 53, a district planning authority may serve a *building preservation notice* giving protection to an unlisted building for six months whilst the Department of the Environment decides whether to add it to its list.

On an application for listed building consent an appeal may be made from the local planning authority to the Secretary of State. However, there is no provision for challenging original listing decisions. In 1973, Amalgamated Investment and Property Company Ltd agreed to buy for £1 710 000 a site for development in Commercial Road, London, belonging to John Walker and Son, including a bonded warehouse. The purchaser expressly confirmed with the vendor that the property was not listed. Just after the contract had been signed the building was put on the list in a way that was later described, by the Court of Appeal, as startling, because the decision was made by a clerk who claimed no professional judgment in such matters. The effect of listing was to reduce the value of the site by as much as £1 500 000 unless listed building consent could be obtained. However, in an action between the parties, the Court of Appeal held that the contract was still binding.[91] To reduce the danger of such injustices, a new section, 54A, was added to the Town and Country Planning Act 1971, by the Local Government Planning and Land Act 1980. This enables a developer seeking planning consent for any development involving the alteration, extension or demolition of a building to seek from the Secretary of State a certificate that he does not intend to list the building. Once such a certificate has been issued the building may not be listed or be protected by a building preservation notice for five years.

The restrictions imposed on listed buildings are backed up under s. 101 by powers for local authorities or the Secretary of State to carry out urgent works of preservation on any unoccupied listed building after seven days notice to the owner. The owner may be required to pay the costs of such work. More drastically, the Secretary of State may authorize the compulsory purchase of a listed building to ensure its proper preservation.[92] First the owner must be served with a repairs notice, allowing him at least two months to do the necessary works himself. After receiving notice of the compulsory purchase order, anyone having an interest in the building has twenty-eight days to take reasonable steps to ensure its proper preservation, and if he does so may obtain an order from a magistrates' court staying the compulsory purchase. If the compulsory purchase goes through, compensation may be reduced to a minimum if it is shown that the building was deliberately allowed to fall into disrepair for the purpose of justifying its demolition to allow for new development.

Under the Ancient Monuments and Archaeological Areas Act 1979, the Secretary of State maintains a schedule of monuments where it is an offence to carry out works which may be damaging, without *scheduled monument consent*. This must be obtained from the Department of the Environment itself. As with the listing of buildings there is no opportunity to challenge inclusion on the schedule. The Secretary of State has powers to repair or compulsorily purchase monuments where necessary. Buildings may be listed as monuments if they are unoccupied save by any caretaker, and control of the monument takes priority over protection by listing under the Town and Country Planning Act 1971. Monuments may include things which are not buildings such as caves, and sites containing the remains of buildings or even vehicles or aircraft. The Secretary of State or a local authority may accept the *guardianship* of an ancient monument with full responsibility for managing it on the basis that private rights remain intact and may be resumed by a private occupier bringing the guardianship to an end.

(c) Control of pollution

Pollution of the environment has long been recognized as a health hazard. Under the Public Health Act 1936, a nuisance such as premises in a state prejudicial to health, or industrial dust or effluvia, may be controlled by a district authority serving an *abatement notice* on the person responsible, requiring him to execute such works and to take such steps as are necessary to deal with it.[94] If the notice is not obeyed, a magistrates' court may fine the offender and make a *nuisance order*, again requiring him to deal with the nuisance.[95] Further fines may be imposed for each day that the nuisance order is contravened, and the local authority is empowered to take necessary steps itself to remedy the nuisance and to recover the cost of doing so from the person responsible.[96] An aggrieved member of the public may apply directly to magistrates for a nuisance order, even against a local authority.[97] As a last resort a local authority may seek abatement proceedings in the High Court under express powers in the act,[98] or under its general powers in the Local Government Act 1972, s. 222.

Environmental pollution may take many forms. The Control of Pollution Act 1974 generally makes it an offence to deposit waste other than agricultural or quarry refuse on any land without a licence.[99] Where the deposit requires planning permission, that must be obtained first. The 1974 Act was intended eventually to control water pollution. However, the relevant parts have not yet been brought into force and water pollution is at present still dealt with by the Rivers (Prevention of Pollution) Act 1951–1962. Nevertheless the 1974 Act has now replaced and strengthened the earlier statutory control over noise. District councils are empowered to serve *noise abatement notices* prohibiting noise or requiring work to be done so as to reduce it.[100] Breach of such a notice is an offence. A member of the public aggrieved by noise may seek from a magistrates' court a *noise abatement order* which has similar effect.[101] District authorities may exercise closer control by creating *noise abatement zones* with set maximum noise levels. They may enforce these by serving on anyone making an excessive noise a *noise restriction notice* which it is an offence to disobey.[102]

Atmospheric pollution may be dealt with as a statutory nuisance under the Public Health Act 1936, but tighter controls are contained in other legislation. Supervision of industrial premises which may emit specific noxious or offensive gases is provided under the Alkali etc. Works Regulation Act 1906, by the Health and Safety at Work executive and inspectorate, set up under the Health and Safety at Work Act 1974.[103] The Clean Air Acts 1956 and 1968 make criminally liable occupiers of premises from which dark smoke is emitted.[104] They impose specification standards on boilers which emit ordinary smoke and on filtering apparatuses to control grit, dust and fumes from furnaces,[105] and empower district councils to create *smoke control areas* where it is generally an offence to burn non-smokeless fuel.[106]

(d) Waste land

Under the Town and Country Planning Act 1971, district councils and London borough councils have powers to require the owners and occupiers of 'any garden, vacant site, or other open site in their area', the condition of which is seriously injuring its surroundings, to take specific steps to remedy the problem.[107] The order may be challenged by appeal to a magistrates court.[108] Otherwise, if it is not complied with, the owner or occupier may be fined,[109] and the local authority may carry out necessary work itself, charging the cost to the owner. He may recover any expenses which he incurs from anyone else who is responsible for the condition of the land.[110] More positively, under the National Parks and Access to the Countryside Act 1949,[111] local planning authorities have powers to plant trees on land in their areas, 'for the purpose of preserving or enhancing the natural beauty thereof'. Also local authorities are empowered to carry out reclamation work on land which is 'derelict, neglected or unsightly', or which, through collapse of the surface as a result of underground mining other than for coal, is likely to become so. The Derelict Land Act 1982 authorizes the Secretary of State to make grants for such reclamation. When land is already derelict, such grants may be made to any appropriate person and where it is likely to become so, to a local authority.

(e) Special forms of control

The special forms of control over land are numerous. Some are primarily concerned with health and safety, or even with public morals. However, unhealthy or immoral activities, for example gambling and the sale of alcohol or pornography, may affect the amenity of an area by attracting undesirable people and by generally causing offence. Certain specialized controls are more clearly concerned with amenity. For example the Town and Country Planning Act 1971, s. 109 restricts the display of *advertisements*. Detailed regulations made under the act,[112] provide for advertisements to be licenced by local planning authorities, solely, 'in the interests of amenity and public safety'. Detailed exceptions are made where permission is not needed, for example for modestly sized noticed for identifying land, or buildings, or businesses or other activities taking place there, and for notices giving warning of any hazard.

The special provisions for licencing *caravan sites*, under the Caravan Sites and Control of Development Act, 1960,[113] assume that a grant of planning permission has already been made. These provisions are largely designed to ensure that such sites are fit for habitation. However, licences may include conditions which the local planning authority considers necessary or desirable 'in the interests of persons dwelling thereon in caravans, or of any other class of persons, or of the public at large'.[114] Such conditions may, for example, restrict the numbers and size of caravans and their position, and make provision for fire, safety and sanitary facilities, but they may also provide for 'the taking of any steps for preserving or enhancing the amenity of the land, including the planting and replanting thereof with trees and bushes'. On the other hand conditions may not control the materials used in the construction of caravans.

NOTES: SECTION 3.4

1. E.g. Water Act 1973, s. 22, *post* p. 135.
2. *Post* p. 138f.
3. *Post* p. 139f.
4. Countryside Act 1968, s. 1.
5. Wildlife and Countryside Act 1981, s. 47 and Sched. 13.
6. National Parks and Access to the Countryside Act 1949, ss. 85 and 86.
7. Nature Conservancy Council Act 1973, s. 1.
8. Wildlife and Countryside Act 1981, s. 38.
9. National Parks and Access to the Countryside Act 1949, s. 5.
10. S.I. 1971, No. 289, *ante* p. 115f.
11. S.I. 1981, No. 246.
12. Local Government Act 1972, s. 184 and Sched. 17. For structure plans see *ante* p. 57.
13. National Parks and Access to the Countryside Act 1949, s. 87.
14. S.I. 1981, No. 246.
15. *Supra* note 10.
16. National Parks and Access to the Countryside Act 1949, s. 88 (1).
17. Wildlife and Countryside Act 1981, s. 39.
18. Ibid. s. 28.
19. Ibid. s. 29.
20. Ibid. s. 31.
21. Ibid. s. 34.
22. Ibid. s. 36.
23. National Parks and Countryside Act 1949, s. 21.
24. Ibid. ss. 17, 18 and 103.
25. Wildlife and Countryside Act 1981, s. 35.
26. National Parks and Access to the Countryside Act 1949, s. 21.
27. Town and Country Planning Act 1971, s. 277.

28. Ibid. s. 277B, inserted by Town and Country Amenities Act 1974.
29. *Supra* note 11.
30. Countryside Act 1968, s. 7.
31. Ibid. s. 9.
32. Ibid. s. 8.
33. *Post* p. 135f.
34. Water Act 1973, s. 20 (1).
35. New Towns Act 1981, s. 17.
36. Local Government, Planning and Land Act 1980, Part XVI.
37. Ibid. Part XVIII and Sched. 32.
38. Ibid. s. 136 (2).
39. Ibid. ss. 165 and 166.
40. Inner Urban Areas Act 1971, s. 1.
41. Ibid. ss. 4–6, as amended by Local Government Planning and Land Act 1980, s. 191.
42. Ibid. ss. 7–11.
43. For example Local Government Act 1972, s. 137.
44. Housing Act 1957, s. 42.
45. Housing Act 1974, s. 36.
46. Ibid. s. 37.
47. Ibid. s. 39.
48. Ibid. s. 43.
49. Ibid. s. 44
50. Ibid. s. 45.
51. As substituted by the Wildlife and Countryside Act 1981, s. 48.
52. *Ante* p. 55.
53. For example *Cargill* v. *Gotts* [1980] 1 W.L.R. 521. Decision varied on appeal [1981] 1 W.L.R. 441 C.A., *ante* p. 96 and *post* p. 200.
54. For the practical importance of this see *Langbrook Properties Ltd* v. *Surrey County Council* [1970] 1 W.L.R. 161, *post* p. 199 note 28 and p. 348.
55. Water Resources Act 1963, s. 32.
56. Ibid. s. 31.
57. Ibid. s. 29 (2).
58. Ibid. s. 50.
59. See *post* p. 344 and p. 348.
60. Land Drainage Act 1976, s. 17.
61. *Rippingale Farms Ltd* v. *Black Sluice Internal Drainage Board* [1963] 3 All E.R. 726, C.A.
62. Land Drainage Act 1976, s. 18.
63. Ibid. s. 28.
64. Ibid. s. 40.
65. Ibid. s. 41.
66. *Young* v. *Bankier Distillery Co. Ltd* [1893] A.C. 691, H.L.
67. Wildlife and Countryside Act 1981, s. 39.
68. General Rate Act 1967, s. 26 (3).
69. General Development Order 1977. S. I. 1977, No. 289, Art. 15 (1)(i).
70. Department of the Environment Circular 75/76.
71. *Ante* p. 105.
72. Forestry Act 1967, s. 1.
73. Ibid. s. 5.
74. Ibid. s. 9.

75. Ibid. s. 18.
76. Petroleum (Production) Act 1934, s. 2, *ante* p. 89.
77. Agricultural Land (Removal of Surface Soil) Act 1953, *ante* p. 139.
78. Local Government Act 1972, Sched. 16, Para. 32 as amended by Local Government Planning and Land Act 1980, Sched. 14.
79. Town and Country Planning Act 1971, s. 264A as inserted by Town and Country Planning (Minerals) Act 1981.
80. Ibid. s. 44A.
81. Ibid. s. 51A.
82. Ibid. s. 51B.
83. Ibid. s. 30A.
84. Ibid. s. 51A.
85. *Bullock* v. *Secretary of State for the Environment* (1980) 40 P. & C.R. 246.
86. Town and Country Planning Act 1971, s. 61.
87. Ibid. s. 61A (added by Town and Country Amenities Act 1974), *ante* p. 131.
88. Ibid. s. 103.
89. Ibid. s. 60 (6).
90. S.I. 1969, No. 17.
91. *Amalgamated Investment Property Co* v. *John Walker & Sons* [1976] 3 All E.R. 509.
92. Town and Country Planning Act 1971, ss. 114–117.
93. Ancient Monuments and Archaeological Sites Act 1979, s. 12.
94. Public Health Act 1936, s. 93.
95. Ibid. s. 94.
96. Ibid. s. 95.
97. Ibid. s. 99.
98. Ibid. s. 100.
99. Control of Pollution Act 1974, s. 3.
100. Ibid. s. 58.
101. Ibid. s. 59.
102. Ibid. s. 63.
103. *Post* p. 293
104. *Ante* p. 92.
105. Clean Air Act 1956, s. 6.
106. Ibid. s. 11.
107. Town and Country Planning Act 1971, s. 65.
108. Ibid. s. 105.
109. Ibid. s. 104.
110. Ibid. s. 107.
111. National Parks and Access to the Countryside Act 1949, s. 87.
112. S.I. 1969, No. 1532.
113. *Ante* p. 105.
114. Caravan Sites and Control of Development Act 1960, s. 5.

3.5   Rights of the ordinary citizen in the landscape and its use

English land law is still based on a structure of private rights in land which are now modified by centralized controls imposed by government in the name of the public. However, the rights of individual members of the public are mainly given in the form of entitlement to money payments. These are made under the system of social security benefits developed after the Second World War as a foundation of the Welfare State and now provided for in the Social Security Act 1975, and other legislation. The public have minimal rights over the land where they live, work or go for recreation. Nevertheless, district councils, as local housing authorities, have powers to provide council houses, and, under the National Assistance Act 1948, s. 21 and the Housing (Homeless Persons) Act 1977, have duties to provide accommodation for those who would otherwise have nowhere to live. These limited provisions may be enforced in the courts by the public dependent upon them. Members of the public in general have other limited rights to get about the country and to participate in planning the use of land.

3.5.1. Public rights to travel and recreation

The Crown has always given the ordinary citizen the freedom to navigate and fish tidal waters and to travel the Queen's Highway. Highways range from motorways to footpaths. They may coincide with private rights of way so that if one or the other is extinguished the other survives.[1]

(a) The highway

Public rights over the highway are restricted to using it for passing to and fro or reasonably incidental purposes such as pausing to do up a shoe lace.[2] Thus a racing tout called Maisey who walked up and down a fifteen yard stretch of highway across private land on the Wiltshire Downs, spying on the form of race horses, was successfully sued in trespass.[3] It is believed not to be possible for the public to acquire a right of access to land at common law simply for purposes of recreation. Thus in 1905 Farewell J. rejected a claim by the Attorney General that there was a public right of access to Stonehenge.[4] The then owner had allowed the public to visit the monument but was now entitled to shut it off with fences so as to protect it from erosion (Fig. 3.9). The same judge's view that there cannot be a private easement of recreation has now been rejected,[5] but the courts are unlikely to recognize public rights to recreation as well unless they are created by statute. However, Farewell J. did recognize that there could be a public right to use a cul-de-sac provided it had been clearly created.

(b) The foreshore

The public have the right to use water covering the foreshore for fishing and navigation, and, when the tide is down, may be entitled to cross the foreshore to reach the sea for these purposes.[6] However, no public right can be enforced

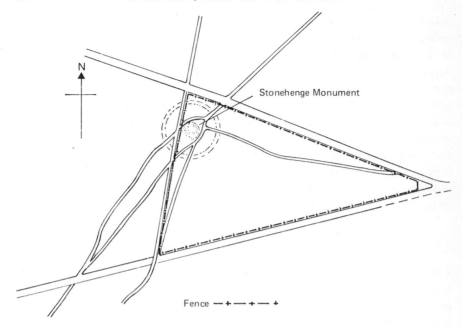

Fig. 3.9 Public access to Stonehenge (*Attorney General* v. *Antrobus* [1905] 2 Ch. 188).

to use the foreshore for other activities such as bathing,[7] or preaching sermons.[8] In *Alfred F. Beckett Ltd* v. *Lyons*,[9] Easington Rural District Council successfully obtained judgment from the Court of Appeal to stop the removal of coal from a nine-mile stretch of beach in County Durham between Seaham and Hartlepool. Sea coal washed up from submarine outcrops had been gathered since before Tudor times and its collection had increased as a result of the dumping of colliery waste in the sea. However, collection was merely tolerated by the Crown and by those like the council to whom the Crown had granted rights over the foreshore.

(c) Statutory rights

Today, new highways are generally created under Statutory Powers, particularly in the Highways Act 1980. Under the Wildlife and Countryside Act 1981, Part III, county councils and London borough councils are required to keep definitive maps and supporting statements showing public rights of way whether in the form of byeways open to all traffic, bridleways or footpaths. These maps provide conclusive evidence of any right of way which they mark. The public may establish extended or new rights, and the mapping authority is required to keep its maps under continuous review and to up-date them. The 1981 Act, s. 59, introduced new safeguards for the public using footpaths, by making it an offence to keep on land, crossed by a public right of way, bulls which are more than ten months old, unless they are of a non-dairy breed, left at large with cows or heifers. There are restrictions in the Highways Act 1980, Part X against interfering with rights of way, notably by ploughing.[10] The National Parks and Access to the Countryside Act 1949, Part IV makes special provisions for the Countryside Commission to create long distance recreational routes such as the Pennine Way. Part V of this act also contains major provisions for public access to open country, consisting 'wholly or predominantly of mountain, moor, heath, down, cliff or foreshore (including any banks, barriers, dune, beach, flat or other land adjacent to the foreshore)'. The Countryside Act 1968, s. 16 extends these provisions to rivers and canals and expanses of water through which these run and to adjacent land sufficient for access on foot, using boats, and picnicking. Local planning authorities may provide for access by acquiring land themselves, by access agreements with land owners or by compulsory access orders. Under s. 60 of the 1949 Act both agreements and orders have the effect of permitting the public to enter the land concerned. However, under s. 66(2), a landowner is not responsible to the public using such rights of access to the same extent as he would be to other authorized visitors.[11] Also, the public becomes trespassers if they abuse these rights, for example by breaking or damaging walls, fences, hedges or gates, or by carrying out any of a long list of activities set out in Schedule 2 such as driving vehicles, lighting fires, harming livestock, wild animals or plants, depositing rubbish, holding political meetings, or generally annoying other people. Under s. 78 local authorities are required to keep up to date maps showing land in their area open for public access.

(d) Commons and customary rights

Common land, as we shall see in Chapter 4, Section 4.4, was essentially land over which a number of people shared rights, for such purposes as grazing cattle or sheep. Commons were generally land shared for such purposes by those with holdings in an ancient village. Often all the inhabitants of such a community used a town or village green for recreational purposes. When other common land was enclosed these were often retained for recreational use. The Commons Registration Act 1965 required all commons to be registered and failure to register a common meant that any rights over it were extinguished. The Act similarly required the registration of town and village greens even when these were not subject to rights of common. Under the Law of Property Act 1925, s. 193 the general public were granted rights to air and exercise over any land which is a London metropolitan common or a manorial waste or a common wholly or partly situated within any other urban area.

Rights of recreation acquired by a community were important examples of customary rights. These are rights vested in fluctuating bodies. They must be clear and reasonable and have been exercised continuously as far back as anyone can remember. The beginning of legal memory is regarded as 1189, the accession of Richard I. A customary right will not be recognized if it could not have been in existence continuously since then. On the other hand the nature of a custom may change. Thus in *Mercer* v. *Denne*[12] Farewell J. said that the right to play cricket on a village green may be recognized even though cricket was not invented until more recent times and indeed would have been unlawful between the reigns of Edward IV and Henry VII when statute compelled villagers to concentrate on archery in their spare time. In *Mercer* v. *Denne* two fishermen of Walmer successfully brought an action to stop building on shingle where they claimed a customary right to dry their nets. Farewell J. ruled that the custom was valid even though the shingle to which it applied must have shifted over the centuries by gradual accretion and even though fishing techniques had changed since 1189.

Customary rights fall between public rights and private easements; they may overlap. In 1895 a Mr Brocklebank bought Irton Hall in Cumberland. He was involved in a dispute with Bootle District Council over a number of alleged public rights of ways through the park. In 1899 the parties settled an action on terms which declared, *inter alia*, that a path to the village church passing some 70 yards in front of the hall was not a public right of way. Mr Irton had claimed that it was only a customary church way. When he later tried to shut it off altogether, Mr Thompson a local farmer, insisted on using it to go to church. In *Brocklebank* v. *Thompson*,[13] Joyce J. held that the path was a church way for the benefit of all the inhabitants of the parish and could be used by Thompson.

A fluctuating group may not acquire a customary right to take produce from land equivalent to a profit, but a similar effect may be achieved by other means, for example a local authority has been treated as a charitable trustee of an oyster fishing bed for certain local inhabitants.[14]

3.5.2 Public participation

It might be expected that modern statutory controls over land use in the interests of the community would have allowed individual members of the public a much greater say in the changing use and enjoyment of the landscape. In practice, however, such controls are largely exercised by administrators in what they perceive as the public interest, sometimes taking relatively little account of what the public really want.[15] Where members of the public express views different from those of the administration they may be written off as uninformed or unrepresentative. Thus a petition supporting development which a local planning authority dislikes or opposing development which it favours may be discounted however many signatures the petition contains, because it merely states a general view and not a reasoned argument and because there are other people affected by the proposal who have not signed. On the other hand where members of the public support the official view they may be invoked to support the decision on the basis that they have taken the trouble to really investigate the issues and, even though few, they must represent many others who are less vocal.

(a) Availability of information

Effective public participation in controlling land use requires availability of relevant information and particularly advance warning of plans and of applications for planning permission so that these can effectively be challenged in time.

The general public are entitled to a certain amount of such information. Perhaps surprisingly they have no right to discover who actually owns land even where its title is registered,[16] but information about land subject to public rights of way and access may be obtained from the statutory maps kept under the Wildlife and Countryside Act 1981, s. 57 (5) and the National Parks and Access to the Countryside Act 1949, s. 78 (2). Similarly the public may refer to the published development plans which we have considered in Chapter 2 Section 2.1, and may discover other details concerned with planning, notably from registers of planning applications and decisions, which planning authorities are required to keep under the Town and Country Planning Act 1971, s. 34. In the production of both structure and local plans, or alterations to these, Part II of the act requires that local planning authorities should take such steps as will, in their opinion, secure adequate *publicity*, and that persons who wish to, may make representation. The methods of publicity vary considerably. Some local authorities try to notify all residents of alternative proposals and sometimes notify them again as to how these have been reshaped in the light of public response. Other authorities are content with much more general publicity in newspapers.

(b) Participation in development planning

Structure plans and their alteration require approval by the Secretary of State who will normally provide for an *examination in public* to consider them.[17] Typically this is chaired by a Queen's Counsel with two planning experts as assessors. The public may attend the hearing but only representatives of public authorities and selected interest groups are allowed to speak. Only selected major or controversial issues are covered. The Secretary of State is required to publish any modification which he proposes to make to structure-plan proposals and to take any objections to these into account in the final plan which he authorizes.

The examination in public was introduced for structure plans in 1972 to replace conventional public inquiries which were regarded as too time consuming and costly to deal with the extremely complex but rather theoretical issues contained in structure plans. The change was particularly attributable to the length of a non-statutory inquiry which had been held on the Greater London Development Plan. This had taken over two years. It was believed that the general nature of structure plans made it unnecessary for private individuals to be given rights to present their cases at any public hearing. The examination in public was intended to clarify the crucial issues so that the Secretary of State could make a more informed decision. Members of the public and pressure groups could make written representations of their views. However, in practice, the nature of modern development plans means that general policy decisions which are likely to affect private property rights are often made long before those who will be affected realize their implications. Thus residents of a village who object to proposals by a developer, or indeed by a local authority, for extensive building on their doorstep may find that, although the structure plan does not earmark the site, its policies will make planning permission for such development almost inevitable.

For local plans the local planning authority must normally arrange a conventional local planning inquiry held by the Department of the Environment inspector. The authority must consider his report, notify objectors of any alterations which it then proposes to make and take representations into account. The Secretary of State is only involved in the details of a local plan if he calls it in to deal with himself.[18] Here property owners at any rate may have a clearer idea of how the proposals are likely to affect them and may make themselves heard. Amenity societies and other groups more generally representative of the community may also be able to contribute to the form of the plan.

(c) Development control

Individual property owners and the public in general are likely to be most concerned with planning matters where an application is made for permission to carry out particular development. As we shall see in Chapter 8, Section 8.3, developers have procedural rights to ensure that their applications are carefully considered. However, if a planning authority is inclined to approve a proposal, objectors have very little protection. Apart from the register of applications, under s. 28 of the Town and Country Planning Act 1971 special publicity must be given by notices on site and in the press, where conservation areas or listed buildings are likely to be affected. Under s. 26 and the General Development Order, 1977, Art. 8, publicity is required where anti-social developments are proposed, such as public conveniences, scrap yards, sewage works, buildings over 20 metres high, slaughter houses, turkish baths, zoos and cemeteries. Even in these cases, objectors have no statutory right to a hearing, although many local planning authorities do hold public meetings of their development control committees where objectors may be heard briefly. If there is an appeal by a developer after an application is refused, objectors may be heard at the discretion of the person appointed to hold a public inquiry. As we shall see in Chapter 8, Section 8.2, the tendency now is for the courts to treat objectors as persons aggrieved, with a right to appeal to them from a decision by the Secretary of State on a point of law under s. 245 of the 1971 act.

(d) Control over public development

It often appears that the more powerful a private developer, the more ready the planning authorities will be to approve his schemes. They may in particular hope to do a deal by means of statutory covenants, under the Town and Country Planning Act 1971, s. 52 or the Local Government (Miscellaneous Provisions) Act 1982, s. 33, whereby the developer will provide some public facility such as a park in return for getting planning permission.[19] Even more obviously, the public are at a disadvantage when development is proposed by a local authority itself or by some other public body.

Local planning authorities may in effect grant themselves planning permission. However, this must be done in two stages; by a resolution to seek permission and a subsequent resolution actually to grant permission. This is designed to allow time for publicity and for objections by the public.[20] Other public bodies which are equated with the Crown,[21] do not require planning permission at all,[22] although in practice they will often carry out consultations with interested parties, and if they require to compulsorily purchase land will normally be subject to formal statutory procedures including a public inquiry.[23]

Controversial proposals for development by public bodies which do require planning consent will generally be called in by the Secretary of State to deal with directly. In such a case a large-scale local public inquiry is often held and may be conducted by a panel of three or five members rather than by an individual inspector. Such inquiries may go on for many months. Thus the Sizewell B inquiry into a proposed pressurized water reactor nuclear power station in Suffolk which would initiate a new stage in the production of atomic power began in January 1983 and at the beginning of 1984 was set to continue well into that year. The very thoroughness of such inquiries makes it difficult for the public, large pressure groups, or even local authorities, to fully present their cases. It is difficult for them to obtain the technical information needed to refute the claims of the public body initiating the development, and the cost of employing lawyers throughout the hearing is prohibitive. Often the procedure seems to be stacked against the objectors, although the inquiry may make concessions. Thus Sir Frank Layfield, Chairman in the Sizewell B inquiry, at first ruled that, whereas the evidence given by the Central Electricity Generating Board could be read aloud, that of objectors would merely be distributed in written form. However, after argument that this would give unfair publicity to the Electricity Board's case Sir Frank allowed the objectors to present their evidence orally after all.[24] Sir Frank also authorized the appointment of a Queen's Counsel, Henry Brooke, to act as Counsel for the inquiry and in particular to co-ordinate the evidence and arguments put forward by objectors.[25] On the other hand, despite efforts by Sir Frank, objectors have claimed extreme difficulty in prising information from the board, for example about the crucial safety aspects of the scheme.

A major defect in certain large public inquiries has been that their terms of reference have excluded fundamental questions of whether the development was desirable at all and have concentrated only on the suitability of particular sites. Thus in the case of the Windscale inquiry dealing with an application for outline planning permission to construct a reprocessing plant for nuclear fuel on the Cumbrian coast, the inspector, the High Court judge, Sir Robert Parker, did not consider it his function to decide on conflicting forecasts of future energy needs for the country.[26] However, the more recent tendency is to provide wider terms of reference and to compare alternative sites at the same time. Thus the application from the National Coal Board for permission to mine in the Vale of Belvoir in Leicestershire was called in by the Secretary of State in 1979 and referred to a three-man public inquiry, chaired by Michael Mann QC, to consider a number of sites in the Vale and to take account of such fundamental issues as future national energy requirements.[27] Public inquiries do provide an opportunity for the public to express their views on controversial proposals for public development and sometimes these views are taken into account. However, many regard them more as a safety valve for exhausting opposition than as an effective means of public participation in decision-making.

NOTES: SECTION 3.5

1. *Attorney General* v. *Shonleigh Nominees* [1974] 1 W.L.R. 305 H.L., and see *post* p. 202.
2. *Earl of Iveagh* v. *Martin* [1961] 1 Q.B. 232, *per* Paull J. at p. 273.
3. *Hickman* v. *Maisey* [1900] 1 Q.B. 752. Also see *post* p. 338.
4. *Attorney General* v. *Antrobus* [1905] 2 Ch. 188.
5. See *post* p. 195.
6. *Williams-Ellis* v. *Cobb* [1934] 1 K.B. 310 C.A., *per* Lord Wright at p. 21.
7. *Brinckman* v. *Matley* [1904] 2 Ch. 313.
8. *Llandudno Urban District Council* v. *Woods* [1899] 2 Ch. 705, *post* p. 383.
9. *Alfred F. Beckett Ltd* v. *Lyons* [1967] Ch. 449.
10. Amended by Wildlife and Countryside Act 1981, s. 61.

11. See *post* p. 330.
12. *Mercer* v. *Denne* [1904] 2 Ch. 534.
13. *Brocklebank* v. *Thompson* [1903] 2 Ch. 344.
14. *Goodman* v. *Mayor of Saltash* (1882) 7 App. Cas. 633, H.L.
15. See generally McAuslan, P. (1980) *The Ideologies of Planning Law*, Pergamon, Oxford.
16. *Post* p. 238.
17. Town and Country Planning Act, 1971, s. 9, as amended by Town and Country Planning (Amendment) Act 1972, s. 3. Detailed regulations for the production of structure and local plans are to be found in S.I. 1982, No. 555.
18. Town and Country Planning Act 1971, s. 14 (3).
19. *Ante* p. 99f.
20. Town and Country Planning Act 1971, s. 270 and Town and Country Planning General Regulations 1976 (No. 1419).
21. *Ante* p. 86.
22. *Ministry of Agriculture etc.* v. *Jenkins* [1963] 2 Q.B. 317, C.A.
23. *Post* p. 223.
24. *The Times*, 23 March 1983.
25. *Journal of Planning and Environment Law* (1983) p. 510.
26. See McAuslan, P. (1980) *The Ideologies of Planning Law*, Pergamon, Oxford, p. 228f. Similar difficulties have also arisen in the case of road schemes. See *Bushell* v. *Secretary of State* [1981] A.C. 75, H.L., *post* p. 405.
27. *Journal of Planning and Environment Law* (1979) p. 139.

Chapter 4

PRIVATE LAW AND THE CONTROL OF LAND USE

It beggars credulity that the existence and use of property power over land is so little recognised and understood in planning circles. Much blame lies at the door of the legislators. In Britain, for instance, the Town and Country Planning Act 1968 [now 1971] required local authorities to initiate surveys and examine the matters which may be expected to affect development; but the more detailed specification of what was expected and deemed relevant made no mention of the incidence and range of property rights.

Denman, D.R. (1978) *The Place of Property*,
Geographical Publications, Great Britain, p. 84

Ideally, a survey of all factors affecting or likely to affect development of land should . . . cover the proprietary structure of the land as displayed in the pattern of its proprietary land units and a record systematically prepared of the land assets and motives of the holders of the proprietary land units.

Ibid. p. 85

Despite the framework provided by the state and the considerable restrictions imposed by public law, in the United Kingdom the control of individual pieces of land is largely governed by private law. Control may take various forms, but it must be vested in a person recognized by the law.

4.1 Legal capacity and personality

4.1.1 Legally incompetent individuals

Certain individuals are not regarded as competent to manage their own affairs. Land in which they have an interest may be held for their benefit by trustees.

(a) Minors

A minor is a person under 18 years of age.[1] He or she is responsible for any torts which he may commit, although some allowances may be made if he acts in a manner which would not be unreasonable for someone of his age.[2] A minor who damaged plants in the course of trespassing would be liable although he might well have no money to pay damages. Parents, teachers or others who fail to keep a young child under proper control, could also be liable for any harm which he causes.

A minor can not be bound by a contract except in limited circumstances, notably where he has agreed to buy necessaries,[3] such as food or clothing, or where a contract of service is substantially for his benefit.[4] Thus a landscape gardener who takes on an apprentice with a condition that without his consent the apprentice shall not work in the area for two or three years after leaving the apprenticeship could probably enforce this condition even if the apprentice left before he came of age. Despite these exceptions a minor is usually not bound by a contract, even if he ratifies it after coming of age.[5] However, if he contracts to acquire an interest in some property which is subject to continuing obligations he will be bound unless he repudiates the contract within a reasonable time of coming of age.[6] Thus an ex-minor will be bound by a lease which he fails to repudiate. Even where a minor is not himself bound by an agreement, he may be able to enforce it against another party. For example, if he agreed to pay for lessons on arboriculture from a tree surgeon who failed to provide them, the minor could obtain damages for breach of contract.

A minor can own personal property but he cannot own any legal estate in land. However, if anyone tries to transfer a legal estate, including a lease, to a minor, this will create a trust for him until he comes of age.[7] Either the transferor will be trustee, or, if the property is transferred to the minor jointly with someone else, that other person will be trustee of the minor's share. Although a minor cannot dispose of land himself, because he cannot own the necessary legal estate, he may occupy and use land. However, if he gives instructions for professional work to be done on the land, such as building or landscape work, he may not be compelled to pay for this unless his trustees approve. An infant in occupation will be responsible for the safety of visitors. Like any other occupier he must be notified if steps are to be taken to compulsorily purchase the land. As anyone may apply for planning permission to develop land, a minor with a beneficial interest could apply on his own initiative for permission to develop a site.

(b) The mentally disordered

A mentally disordered person will probably be liable for most torts which he commits. However, parties to a contract are assumed to have reached an agreement freely. Where, because of some mental incapacity, a person was not 'capable of understanding what he was about', he may later have the agreement made void by a court, unless it was for necessaries,[8] and provided he can show that the other party involved had realized the true position.[9] If a person becomes incapable of administering any property which he controls, including land, his power over it may be taken from him by the Chancery Division of the High Court until he regains his sanity or dies. A judge has wide powers to deal with the property of anyone whom he is satisfied, after considering medical evidence, 'is incapable, by reason of mental disorder, of managing and administering his property and affairs'.[10]

4.1.2   Corporate personality

Individual landowners have contributed greatly to the beauty of the modern landscape. Some great landed proprietors largely designed their own houses or parks. Others acted as discriminating patrons for professional architects and landscape designers. On a smaller scale, gentry and others with sufficient money employed local builders to adorn innumerable more modest properties. Some landowners had complete control over vast acres together with great capital resources which enabled them to carry out the most ambitious schemes, but usually great estates, and many smaller ones, were tied up by settlements or trusts in successive legal interests which restricted what the current occupier could do. The systems of land settlements and trusts outlined in the next section were designed to protect the family as a continuous entity. Land could be regarded as a commercial asset but more often it was a permanent symbol of the family itself, to be preserved and beautified for the family's prestige and enjoyment. Men have always formed groups apart from the family, to further their trades or professions, or to carry on such activities as government and the spread of learning. These groups include town corporations, universities and schools, trade guilds, such as the livery companies of London and other great cities, and the legal profession itself. All these have been great patrons of the arts and have frequently embellished their buildings and land to provide pleasure for the neighbourhood and the public at large. They have been able to do so because the law has recognized them as having legal personality similar to that of an individual human being. Today, corporate personality, and in particular the modern company, is used by families and by individuals as a device for controlling land more effectively than if it were owned directly by one or more individuals. It may be used in place of or in conjunction with the device of the trust.

(a) Forms of corporate personality

A corporate person is usually a *corporation aggregate*, that is, it consists of a group of individuals. There are also *corporations sole*, where an office, such as that of a bishop or minister of the crown, is treated as a legal person irrespective of who holds the office at any time. Thus, if a bishop dies or retires, property which he holds as bishop will automatically pass to his successor. Today, British corporations may be created either by a royal charter or under a statute. Foreign corporations validly created under other legal systems are also recognized. Parliament may create a corporation directly, as it did, for example, with the British Railways Board, the British Waterways Board and the National Coal Board,[11] and also with the present hierarchy of local authorities set up by the Local Government Act 1972.[12] Individual local corporations may be set up by Private Act of Parliament. Particularly in the nineteenth century, various authorities, such as railway companies and port authorities, were created in this manner. Such local Acts are still used. Thus the Felixstowe Dock and Railway Act 1981, gave extra powers to the Felixstowe Dock and Railway Company set up by an Act of 1875. Parliament may delegate the power to create corporations. Thus the Secretary of State for the Environment may create joint planning boards,[13] and district councils may create new parish councils.[14]

Parliament also provides a system for the creation of companies, by registration under the Companies Acts 1948 and 1981.[15] A company registered under the 1948 act is governed by two documents. Its *memorandum of association* sets out its external constitution, including its objects and the powers which it may exercise. These will often include ownership of land. The company's *articles of association* contain internal rules, such as provision for the appointment and powers of directors to run the company, and in particular of a managing director, who may have authority for day-to-day business. The powers of shareholders and the circumstances where these may override decisions of the directors will also be contained in the articles. The Companies Acts allow for *public* or *private limited companies*, the liability of shareholders of either being limited to the value of the shares which they hold. To conform with the European Community requirements, a public limited company whose shares are exchangeable openly on the stock exchange must have the letters *plc* at the end of its name.[16] The title of a private company ends with the letters *Ltd* as did that of every limited company before 1980. Private companies are less rigorously controlled. They may not have more than fifty members but unlike public companies they may have less than seven members. The Department of Trade may waive the use of the letters *Ltd* for a private company which is formed for the charitable purposes of 'promoting are, science, religion, charity or any other useful object', and which uses its income for these purposes instead of paying a dividend.[17]

Usually such companies are registered as companies limited by guarantee rather than by shares.[18] Members guarantee the debts of the company up to a specified sum.

(b) The significance of corporate personality

A corporation is treated in law very like an individual. It must have a name by which it is identified and a seal to be fixed to documents made on its authority. As it cannot die, special arrangements are provided for its extinction by surrender of its charter or by winding up under the Companies Act 1948, Part V. Its constitution will provide for officers who are empowered to carry out its affairs and will stipulate the powers which it may exercise, such as owning property. If these powers are exceeded the corporation is said to have acted *ultra vires* and may be challenged in the courts. A corporation is distinct from its members but it is controlled by them. It is one means of enabling a large number of people to share property efficiently. For example, a farm or a factory owned in the name of a company is owned by a single legal person. If the company sells land or is involved in any other transaction, other parties do not need to concern themselves with the individuals who may have shares in the company. They can simply deal with its authorized officers. If a company is involved in legal proceedings, the identity of its members will usually be irrelevant. Since companies have legal personality, they may own shares and so control other companies. In this way, businesses may be organized in groups of companies, with subsidiaries carrying on different functions or operating in different localities under one or more holding companies. If land is held by a company, shares can be exchanged or adjusted without the need legally to convey the land each time. Individuals who use a company to control land can thus conveniently sell their interest, or hand it over to other members of their family. Day-to-day control of a company will be vested in directors. These will be elected by the shareholders, usually from amongst themselves. In a small private company all the shareholders may be directors.

Although an essential characteristic of a limited company is that shareholders are only liable to the extent of the value of their shares, the law does sometimes take account of who owns the shares. In *Jones* v. *Lipman*,[19] Lipman agreed to sell his home to Jones, but changed his mind. To avoid being compelled to transfer the house to Jones under a court order for specific performance, Lipman transferred it to a private company, which he had acquired simply for this purpose. Russell J. in the Chancery Division ordered Lipman and the company, together, to transfer the house to Jones, even though there was no agreement between the company and Jones: 'the defendant company is the creature of the first defendant, a device and a sham, a mask which he holds before his face in an attempt to avoid recognition by the eye of equity.' Again, statute makes special provision to prevent companies being used as a means of tax avoidance. For example development land tax is not payable on development value of land accruing to any person in any one financial year unless it exceeds £50 000, but tax must still be paid if an estate is split up between a number of companies in a group so that each company obtains less than £50 000 development value.[20]

4.1.3 Unincorporated groups

Individuals often act together without forming a corporation with its own legal identity. Such individuals may be jointly or vicariously responsible for each other's acts on the principles considered in Chapter 6, Section 6.4. Certain relationships which do not create a separate corporate personality are given some measure of legal recognition. Others, including many clubs and similar associations are not formally recognized. However, all the members may be represented in court proceedings by some of their numbers.

(a) Partnership

Partnerships may be created under the Partnership Act 1890 where two or more individuals practice together any trade, occupation or profession, with a view to profit. There must normally be no more than twenty partners, but this restriction has been waived for a number of professions, notably solicitors, consulting engineers, building designers, surveyors, auctioneers, valuers, estate agents, land agents and estate managers.[21] Certain professions, notably the Bar, require that members act as individuals and forbid them forming partnerships. Other professions may or may not allow mixed partnerships. Thus a firm of solicitors may not include estate agents, but a firm of architects could include a landscape architect and also a quantity surveyor. Different partners may contribute different assets, for example one may put up money but play no active role in the business. Another may not provide any capital but may contribute a skill.[22] Partnerships may be created for limited purposes, for example to make profits from renting a shared piece of land, or as the basis under which the partners practice their profession together. An essential characteristic of a partnership in regard to outsiders is that its members may sue or be sued under a firm name, usually the partners' names followed by the term *and Co.* The partners are regarded in law as agents for one another so that they bind each other by any actions done in the name of the partnership. Thus, if one partner makes a contract on behalf of the partnership or injures an outsider in the course of partnership business, the outsider may recover any sum due to him from any member of the partnership.[23] Thus, if a landscape architect were to misdesign an earth work so that it collapsed on a labourer or a visitor to the site, each of his partners would be as liable as he even though they had never been involved on that job, or, if a member of a firm of architects caused a building to be erected over the boundary with his client's neighbour, the other partners would be equally liable for this trespass. However, if the partner in charge of the job was involved in a fight with the offended neighbour, his actions would be outside the scope of the ordinary course of business of the partnership. His fellow partners would only share liability if they previously consented to such actions or afterwards concurred in them.[24] Partners are protected from liability for certain actions of their fellows. For example a partner does not normally have implied authority to execute deeds on behalf of his firm,[25] so land belonging to the partnership cannot normally be conveyed by one partner without the knowledge of the others.

(b) Agents

An agent is a person who is empowered by another, his principal, to create legal relations between the principal and third parties. Partners are agents for each other. Often an employee or a prospective employee is the agent of his employer. Thus, someone appointed as a local authority officer whether or not he has yet taken up his post, may be the agent of the local authority in negotiating the sale of equipment to the local authority.[26] An agent's authority may be expressly given to him or it may be implied. An expressly authorized agent may be given additional authority by implication.[27] Even if authority cannot be implied, provided a person purports to act for someone else, who would have been his principal had there been a proper grant of authority, that person can subsequently become responsible by clearly ratifying the act. Provided the supposed principal learns all the material facts, he may be regarded as ratifying the act by acquiescence, even if he does nothing positive, but simply fails to challenge the act made on his behalf. Thus, where one of several owners of land failed to object to a contract, of which he was aware, being made for the sale of the land by the other owners, he was regarded as ratifying the agreement to sell.[28]

An agent cannot execute a deed on behalf of his principal unless he has been authorized in a deed.[29] Therefore, he cannot convey his principal's land unless he has been authorized to do so by deed. On the other hand, he may bind his principal to convey the land if he makes a contract in writing, even if he was only orally authorized. Conversely, if an agent buys land in the name of his principal he can be compelled to transfer it to the principal even though he was only orally authorized to purchase it.[30]

An agent owes a duty to his principal to take proper care in acting as agent. If he fails to do so he may be sued by the principal in contract or tort. On the other hand, normally an agent is not personally liable to a third party with whom he makes a contract on behalf of his principal. However, if he makes his principal liable in tort, usually he will also be liable himself to the injured party. Thus a landscape gardener employed as a contractor to raise banks on the edge of a property could be liable in trespass and make his employer liable in trespass if he piled earth against a neighbour's wall.

(c) Representative actions and test cases

Individuals who do not have any formal legal association, such as members of a private unincorporated club, may nevertheless have a common interest in some legal dispute. In such a case, one, or usually two or three, may be permitted to bring or defend legal proceedings as representatives of all those with a similar interest.[31] In an appropriate case, a court may nominate suitable persons as representative defendants, and add them to proceedings which have already begun. Representative actions save time and money by avoiding numerous proceedings or a large number of parties. All those represented will be bound by the court's decision although judgment may not be enforced against any of them without the leave of the court. This gives the opportunity for any individual to raise facts or matters peculiar to himself which would entitle him to be exempted from liability. Also any individual who claims for damage peculiar to himself must sue in his own name.

Where a dispute arises between members of an informal body such as a club, it is important that those with conflicting interests should be represented separately. For example the club house and other property may be

Fig. 4.1 The Town Moor, Newcastle upon Tyne, January 1984.

owned by a small number of trustees, perhaps the current committee, on behalf of the remaining members. Obviously in a dispute over this property the members as a whole could not always be represented by the trustees. The use of representative proceedings to protect land is typified by *Walker* v. *Murphy*.[32] There a committee of freemen claiming rights to pasture on Newcastle-upon-Tyne Town Moor (Fig. 4.1) were permitted to sue on behalf of all the freemen, and those who had rented pasture rights from them, for an injunction to prevent the use of the moor during an annual fair, by round-abouts and other machines which injured the ground. The committee also recovered damages for harm to the ground. Representative parties may act in circumstances where there is not even a regular relationship such as that between members of a club. Thus they may be used in proceedings brought to modify or override a restrictive covenant benefiting a number of people.[33]

Even where individuals do not have sufficient common interest for a representative action,[34] where there are several similar claims, one may be treated as a test case and the courts will be careful to lay down a clear solution which will avoid any parallel actions being tried. If these have already begun they may be adjourned for a clear decision in the test case.

NOTES: SECTION 4.1

1. Family Law Reform Act 1969, s. 12.
2. *Yachuk* v. *Oliver Blais and Co. Ltd* [1949] A.C. 386, P.C., from the Supreme Court of Canada.
3. Sale of Goods Act 1979, s. 2.
4. *Chaplin* v. *Leslie Frewin (Publishers) Ltd* [1966] Ch. 71, C.A.
5. Infants Relief Act 1974, s. 2. This rule was intended to prevent money lenders pressurizing young debtors who had just come of age to agree to repay large debts incurred when they were minors in return for some small additional advance.
6. *Davies* v. *Beynon-Harris* (1931) 47 T.L.R. 424.
7. Law of Property Act 1925, s. 19 (1). The minor's interest constitutes an estate contract which needs to be registered under the Land Charges Act 1972 if it is to bind a purchaser in good faith for value to whom the land is later sold. See *post* p. 240f.
8. *In re Rhodes* (1980) 44 Ch. D. 94.
9. *Imperial Loan Co.* v. *Stone Ltd* [1892] 1 Q.B. 599.
10. Mental Health Act 1959, s. 101.
11. Transport Act 1962, and Coal Industry Nationalization Act 1946.
12. *Ante* p. 36f.
13. Local Government Act 1972, s. 182 (1), *ante* p. 60.
14. Ibid. ss. 9 (2) and 14 (2), *ante* p. 38.
15. Special forms of association may be registered under other acts, such as the Building Society Act 1962, the Industrial and Provident Societies Act 1965, and the Trade Union and Labour Relations Act 1974. Some companies remain registered under companies legislation prior to 1948.
16. Companies Act 1980, ss. 2 (2) and 178 (3)(b).
17. Companies Act 1948, s. 19, and see *post* p. 188f.

18. Ibid. s. 21.
19. *Jones* v. *Lipman* [1962] 1 W.L.R. 832.
20. Development Land Tax Act 1976, s. 12, and see *ante* p. 99.
21. Companies Act 1967, s. 120, and Partnerships (Unrestricted Size) Regulations. S.I. 1968, No. 1222, and S.I. 1970, Nos. 835, 992, 1319.
22. *Moore* v. *Davis* (1879) 11 Ch.D. 261.
23. Partnership Act 1980, ss. 10 and 12.
24. *Petrie* v. *Lamont and Others* (1841) 1 Carr. & M. 93.
25. *Marchant* v. *Morton, Down and Co.* [1901] 2 K.B. 829, and see *post* p. 249.
26. *Ashford Shire Council* v. *Dependable Motor Pty Ltd* ₅1961] A.C. 336. P.C., from Australia.
27. *Freeman and Lockyer (a firm)* v. *Buckhurst Park Properties (Mangal) Ltd* [1964] 2 Q.B. 480.
28. *Berkely* v. *Hardy* (1826) 5 Barn. & Cress. 355.
29. *Fothergill* v. *Phillips* (1871) 6 L.R. Ch. App. 770, *obiter dicta* of Lord Hatherley L.C. at p. 778.
30. *Cave* v. *Mckenzie* (1877) 46 L.J. Ch. 564.
31. Rules of the Supreme Court, 1965, Order 15, Rule 12. County Court Rules, 1981, Order 5, Rule 5.
32. *Walker* v. *Murphy* [1914] 2 Ch. 293, upheld on appeal [1915] 1 Ch. 71, C.A.
33. *Guardians of Tendrig Union* v. *Downton* (1890) 45 Ch. D. 583.
34. *Smith* v. *Cardiff Corporation* [1954] 1 Q.B. 210, C.A.

4.2   The general pattern of legal control of land

Because it is immovable, land was early recognized as a unique sort of property. Anyone who was dispossessed from land to which he was entitled could use a *real action* by which the courts enabled him to recover the land itself rather than simply awarding him damages to compensate him for his loss. English land law is still often known as the law of *real property*.

Legal machinery for the control of land reflects changes in the society which has lived on it and used it in the past. Forms of land holding devised for one social purpose may be developed to serve very different ends. Thus, the ancient feudal concept of tenure depended on the Sovereign being lord paramount and ultimate owner of all the land in England. The Crown still technically owns all the land in England and this may be seen as a theoretical justification for modern public involvement in the control of private land. The lease was originally devised with the decay of the medieval feudal system as a means of using land to obtain a money rent on capital. It enabled profits to be made by letting land without the need for the land owner to manage the land itself. However, the lease has also always been a means of enabling a large proprietor to share the control and the benefit of land with tenants under an efficient scheme of management which is in their mutual interest and on terms which they can tailor to themselves rather than have dictated by any public body. Modern statutory controls can support the best of such private arrangements whilst ensuring that they take some account of the wider public interest.

Certain aims of land law changed considerably over the centuries. The concern of feudalism to maximize royal control gave way to a preoccupation with the protection of private property rights which were seen as a guarantee for individual liberty and a stimulus to economic growth. The emergence of the modern welfare state has led to greater protection of the security of those, such as tenants, with more modest property rights.

Other principles have remained more constant. Thus, successive reforms have been introduced to ensure that land may be used more efficiently, first by reducing the number of people who may have a say in the manner in which it is to be used, rather than merely a share in the money which it may produce, and secondly by restricting the extent to which those who control land at any one time may determine what is to be done with it in the future.

4.2.1.   Tenure (Fig. 4.2)

From the eleventh century, after the establishment of Norman society in Britain, the primary social use of land was to maintain central control by means of the legal concept of land holding or, *Tenure*. The King distributed land in blocks to his principal lords who subdivided it amongst their followers. It could in theory be subdivided any number of times. This was the Feudal System, a ladder of control answerable to the King at the top. Each tenant owed duties to those above him in the ladder. Originally the most significant of these were obligations to provide the troops which built up the national army of the period. However, religious houses for example could hold land, under a tenure called *Francalmoign*, in return for saying regular prayers. Other feudal services were in kind, such as the provision of quantities of fire wood, ale or days of ploughing. Most services were commuted to money payments and with gradual inflation became no longer worth collecting.

At the bottom of the feudal ladder tenants in possession of the land, known as *tenants in demesne*, had their own unfree tenants who were not protected by the royal courts but by the baronial courts of the local lord himself. If an unfree tenant transferred his rights over a piece of land to someone else this was copied in the records of the lord's court. His tenure was therefore known as *copyhold*.

The ancient concept of Tenure has now been cut down to an irreducible minimum. In England, since as early as 1290, the statute of *Quia Emptores* had prevented the creation of new feudal subtenants by providing that any attempt at this had the effect of transferring the whole existing tenure. Surviving feudal obligations were largely eliminated in 1660 when nearly all free tenures were reduced to the standard freehold tenure of *socage*. From 1926, the Law of Property Act 1922 upgraded copyhold tenure to socage.

Today, all land is therefore held in freehold under socage tenure, although some symbolic incidents survive such as the obligation of the Duke of

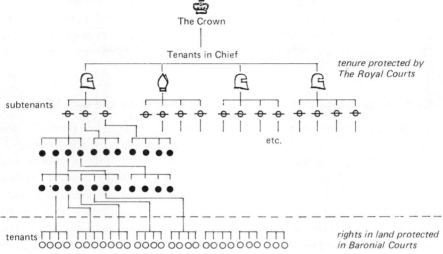

A   THE FEUDAL PATTERN

The Crown

Tenants in Chief

tenure protected by The Royal Courts

subtenants

etc.

rights in land protected in Baronial Courts

tenants

B   MODERN LEASEHOLD TENURE

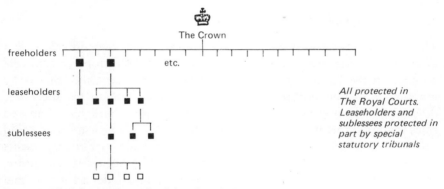

The Crown

freeholders

etc.

leaseholders

sublessees

All protected in The Royal Courts. Leaseholders and sublessees protected in part by special statutory tribunals

Fig. 4.2 The change from feudal to leasehold tenure.

Marlborough to present his sovereign annually with a pennon. Each piece of land is, however, still held in theory from the Crown. It has always been nationalized property. Even a freeholder is a tenant of the Crown.

In Scotland, much more recently than in England, the creation of new feu duties has been banned by the Land Tenure Reform (Scotland) Act 1974, under which anyone subject to existing feu duties is entitled to buy them out and must do so if he sells his land.

The modern type of tenant was developed in the late fifteenth century. He holds land not indefinitely but owns a lease for a set period of time. Such a tenant does technically hold in tenure under the free holder[1] but the statute of

Quia Emptores did not cover such an arrangement. Thus a tenancy under a lease may be subdivided amongst subtenants who take different pieces of the land, or the same parts in succession, provided each succeeding tenant leaves a period after his lease will expire when his head tenant can resume control. The head tenant does not lose his tenure by creating a subtenancy.

4.2.2   Legal estates and arrangements for sharing control over land

Much of the complexity and also flexibility of English land law resulted from a second major concept, that of the *Estate* in land. Because the King owned all the actual land, medieval lawyers developed the idea that those with tenure owned abstract legal estates which could be divided and shared in various ways. By this means, the present and future use of a piece of land was treated as a single existing legal entity, the *fee simple*. This was a bundle of rights to use and dispose of the land which could be split up and shared out between numerous different people in various ways. Section 1 of the Law of Property Act 1925 provides that the only legal estates in land which can exist now are 'an estate in fee simple absolute in possession' or 'a term of years absolute'.

(a) *The fee simple absolute in possession*

The doctrine of estates made it possible to provide for one individual by a grant to him for the length of his life. Alternatively, property could be retained in the family by *entailing* it upon a particular child, that is by granting it to him *in tail* so that it passed from him to his successive descendants. To prevent land being tied up indefinitely, Parliament imposed rules against perpetuity which restricted the period for which an entail could run. More recently, modern Finance Acts have made such arrangements prone to high taxation. The Law of Property Act 1925 ensured that in future, life and entailed interests would always be equitable, under a trust, so that there would always be a current holder of the freehold with a fee simple estate in any piece of land, free to dispose of the land itself, although he might be bound to share the proceeds with others.

The fee simple is an estate which lasts for ever. Under the Law of Property Act 1925 a legal fee simple must also be *absolute*. Previously a legal estate could be formulated so that it would end if some future event, which was possible, but not certain, took place. If the limitation was included in the definition of the fee, such an estate was a *determinable fee*: for example a grant of open country to a local authority 'so long as it remains free from building of any kind'. However, if the limitation was added as a separate clause, the estate was a *conditional fee*, for example a grant of the same land to a local authority 'on condition that no building of any kind shall take place thereon'. A conditional fee is now treated as a legal fee simple absolute.[2] A determinable fee can only be made under a trust. However, in the examples above, if the local authority did build on the land, the effect could be that it would have to return it to the original owner or to anyone who had succeeded to his rights.

The fee simple absolute will survive as a legal entity even if its present owner can not be traced, or dies without any relative who is entitled to take his estate under statutory rules of intestacy. The Crown is entitled to the proceeds of the estate in such a case. The property is treated as being held in trust and could be sold so that the Crown receives the proceeds and the purchaser the fee simple in the land itself. A legal fee simple absolute must be *in possession*. Thus a future estate can only be equitable. For example, a grant 'to X for life, remainder to Y in fee simple' could only be equitable. The grantor would continue to own the legal estate although he would hold the proceeds in trust for X, or, after X died, for Y and Y's successors. Although the fee simple must be in possession, the owner of the fee simple may not have physical control of the land. Possession includes the receipt or right to receive rent or profits from the land,[3] and the person actually in control may be a tenant under a lease. The idea that a freeholder has legal possession, even if he has relinquished control of the land to a tenant, reflects the ancient concept of *seisin*. Under feudal law, the person seised of freehold land had effective control of the land and could use the machinery of the law to evict even a tenant whom he had allowed to use it. Over the centuries, such tenants have been given considerable security by Parliament, but the legal freeholder with seisin and technical possession is still treated as having an interest in the land itself, whereas those with equitable estates are treated as simply having an interest in the value of the land.

The status of freeholder, with a fee simple absolute in possession has several major implications for land use. First, the freeholder may dispose of the land to others at his discretion. The householder is not only secure in his home whilst he lives there but can pass it on to his wife or child. In Britain, the state has not seised a monopoly of dispensing the privilege of a home to live in. The landowner who wishes to beautify and preserve a village and farmland can transfer them to someone he regards as a trustworthy custodian for the future, independent of state control. Second, the freeholder is still able to use the land in its existing form largely as he sees fit. It will be in his interest to keep it in what he regards as as good a condition as possible, although owners may differ over what is a desirable condition. For some, it may mean that the land is run as productively as possible, for others that its amenities are maintained as well as possible. As we have seen in the preceding chapter, public law allows the compulsory acquisition of land which is needed for new purposes, and existing landowners are restricted in their use of land so as to preserve the public interest in both its economic use and its amenity.

However, the underlying principle of private land law remains, that it is in the public interest to harness the motivation and originality of individuals by allowing them to pass on land to their families and to use it creatively in the meantime. As we shall see in the final two sections of this chapter, and in Chapter 7, this principle requires that private land law restricts the use of neighbouring pieces of land so that where there is a conflict between their respective uses a balance is struck between them.

(b) The lease, or term of years absolute

The second form of legal estate possible under s. 1 of the Law of Property Act 1925, is a *term of years absolute*, that is a leasehold estate. By means of this, a legal fee simple may still have a period cut out of it during which someone else has control of the land. Leases are now themselves interests in land. Originally they were simply contractual rights, under which a tenant could recover damages if he was dispossessed but could not recover possession. They are still known by the hybrid name of *chattels real*, chattels being a synonym for personal property based on the word cattle, a major source of wealth in earlier times. Personal rights to use land which do not enjoy the security of a tenancy are *licences*.[4] The expression, *term of years absolute*, is confusing. The tenant or tenants will have exclusive possession of the land during the lease. However, legislation discussed later in this section has ensured that often such tenancies provide more security for resident tenants than do longer than be for any uncertain period,[5] such as until the landlord builds a proposed factory on adjacent ground. However, the term may be very long, such as 2000 years, or very short, such as a month. Usually a long lease will involve an outright payment by the tenant to the landlord, perhaps with additional service charges. It is common for flats to be let in this way, for periods such as ninety-nine years, with the landlord retaining responsibility for painting and cleaning common areas, and for structural maintenance, to be paid for from the service charges. When such leases begin they may cost almost as much as a freehold but by the time they have nearly expired they will have lost most of their value. Leases may also be *periodic*, for short but renewable periods, such as a week or a month. Each period of a week or a month constitutes a renewed lease. However, legislation discussed later in this section has ensured that often such tenancies provide more security for resident tenants than do longer fixed-term leases. Unlike legal fees simple, future leases may be created provided they will take effect within twenty-one years.[6]

4.2.3   Concurrent and consecutive interests in land; and equitable estates

Equity evolved important devices to protect rights in land which were not recognized by the Common Law Courts. In particular, it developed the *Trust* which enabled a person to have the benefit of proceeds from the use of land or to enjoy its use without actually having legal control over it. The trustee with the legal estate might not be entitled to any of the beneficial interest or he might share it with others. The major land law statutes of 1925, the Law of Property Act and the Settled Land Act, used the machinery devised by Equity to provide a uniform system for the straightforward legal control of land, in general allowing for its unhindered sale, and at the same time providing scope for complex arrangements for distributing its economic benefits.

(a) Concurrent interests (Fig. 4.3)

The common law recognized four forms of simultaneous ownership of land by two or more individuals of which the most important were joint tenancies and tenancies in common.[7] *Joint tenancies* required four characteristics known as the *four unities*. Each tenant was equally in possession of the entire land. Each had an identical interest, for example, a lease for the same number of years. The interests had all to be based on the same title, for example a single conveyance or will, and they must normally have come into effect at the

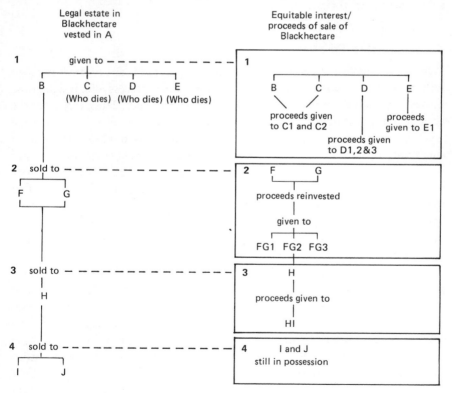

Fig. 4.3 Concurrent interests in land.

same time. When any one tenant died, his interest accrued to the survivors, so that the last survivor was left with the entire estate. By contrast, *tenants in common* shared possession of the land but could have different interests in it which had been created in different ways and at different times. The share of each tenant in common remained intact so that he could sell it or leave it on his death to several individuals. By this means, land held under a tenancy in common could be under the control of an ever increasing number of people and it could be very difficult to get all of them together so as to manage it effectively or sell it. Joint tenants could preserve their shares in the property by severing their interests in various ways and become tenants in common.

The Law of Property Act 1925 created a two-tier system, under which the legal estate in any land can be held by more than one individual only under an unseverable legal joint tenancy. However, the benefit can be shared under an equitable tenancy in common, with the joint tenants acting as trustees. The beneficial interest can be subdivided any number of times. The joint tenants must not number more than four,[8] and they hold, under a statutory trust for sale provided for in the Law of Property Act 1925, on behalf of the beneficiaries. The beneficiaries' rights are provided with some protection against a sale contrary to their wishes or interests.

(b) Consecutive interests

Where a succession of people are given interests in land, one or more persons will be currently *in possession* of each interest. An interest which will come into effect at some time in the future is called a *remainder*. Thus, if X gives the beneficial interest in his farm to his wife for her life, he may at the same time give the remainder to his sons after her death. It is possible to create a succession of remainders, for example, to each of a number of children and finally to the National Trust. If the grantor does not give away the entire interest, so that at some future date he will get back what is left, this is called the *reversion*. If X gives the beneficial interest in his farm to his wife for life and makes no further provision, he will get back the reversion on her death. He may, in the meantime, grant the reversion to someone else or leave it to someone else if he dies before his wife.

Under the legislation of 1925, the *trust for sale* is the normal device for sharing the future benefit of land as well as the present benefit. A major alternative is where a current owner of an estate creates leases out of it. These, as we have seen, may be legal. A landlord or head tenant's right to resume control of land after termination of a lease is a reversion. Leases may be created so that they will give possession to a tenant at some future time within the next twenty-one years. There may be a succession of them taking effect one after the other, as where X grants to Y a lease of his farm for five years terminating on a given date, and a future lease for fifty years to Z, beginning just after the termination of the lease to Y. Alternatively, leases may be subdivided, provided this is not precluded in the deed creating the head lease. Thus, X may grant a lease for five years to Y and of this Y may grant a sublease to Z for four years. Where a lease is created at law, the tenant may be in possession, and the landlord who is receiving the rent will also be in possession, of the fee simple estate.

Future interests, in particular, beneficial interests under a trust for sale of land, fall into a number of categories. A future interest is said to be *vested* if it belongs to an identifiable person and is only prevented from coming into effect immediately because of some intervening interest. Thus, if a landowner grants a park 'to X for life, then to Y for life, remainder to Z', the interests of Y and Z are already vested. However, if there is some further element of uncertainty in a future interest it is said to be *contingent*. Thus, the landowner in our example might grant his park 'to X for life, then to the eldest son of X living at his death'; or he might grant it to 'X for life, then to Y if Y passes his final examinations as a landscape architect'. A future interest may also be vested subject to divesting, as where a grant is made 'to X for life, then to Y, provided Y remains in practice as a surveyor'.

(c) Strict settlements and trusts for sale

The key to the sharing of control of land concurrently or between a succession of people is the concept of the *trust*. This was developed by the Chancery Court to deal with the inflexibility of the ancient common law. Under a trust, the legal control of land, its management and the power to dispose of it, is vested in trustees, for the benefit of beneficiaries. When the law of property was reconstituted in 1925 under the supervision of Lord Chancellor Birkenhead, two forms of trust were used, the strict settlement and the trust for sale.

The *strict settlement* was inspired by the old system of entailing a legal estate in land on successive generations of a family. It is provided for in the Settled Land Act 1925, and involves control of the land at all times by a *statutory owner*. This is usually a current *life tenant*, of full age. Apart from any life tenant there will be at least two and not more than four trustees of the settlement. These are empowered to act as statutory owners if none other is available, for example, if the current life tenant is not yet of age. Also, if the property is sold by the statutory owner the trustees of the settlement take charge of the proceeds until they are laid out on other property. Under s. 18 of the Settled Land Act, no sale of property under a properly constituted strict settlement is valid unless the statutory formalities are properly observed.[9] However, provided the formalities are observed the purchaser need know nothing of any beneficial interests. A strict settlement is set out in two documents. The *vesting deed* confers the legal estate upon the statutory owner, and this is used to convey the estate to the purchaser. The provisions of the settlement are set out in a separate *trust instrument* which the purchaser has no right to see. The rights of the beneficiaries are said to be *overreached* by the transfer. They cease to apply to the original property but are transferred onto the proceeds of sale.[10]

Strict settlements are automatically created in certain special circumstances, as where land is granted to a minor. Generally, s. 1 of the Settled Land Act provides that one arises where land is held on trust for a series of people in succession, or where it is entailed. A strict settlement also arises if land is granted so that it will be divested, or is contingent on a particular event. Thus, a grant of an estate 'to X in fee simple, but if he demolishes any building, thereon to Y', or 'to X if he becomes a member of the Royal Town Planning Institute', could both create strict settlements.

Possible trustees of a strict settlement are specified in s. 30 of the Settled Land Act. They may be appointed under the settlement. In the absence of anyone properly appointed, they may be personal representatives of a deceased settlor. As a last resort, they may be appointed by the court under s. 34. When the person entitled to the final interest under a settlement is able to take the land, if the land is vested in trustees they hold it under a *bare trust*, and the person entitled can require them to transfer it to him absolutely.

Trusts of land which are not strict settlements will be *trusts for sale* under the Law of Property Act 1925, ss. 22–36. Today these are the normal arrangement for sharing estates in land. They do not involve the complexity of a new vesting deed each time one beneficiary succeeds another. They are generally simpler than strict settlements and result in a lower incidence of tax when interests are passed on from one person to another. The trust for sale may be used instead of the strict settlement to provide for a series of owners of land. It is also the method used for the common purpose of sharing concurrent interests, as in the case of a husband and wife with a matrimonial home or of several children inheriting a farm. Shared beneficial interests may be of different sizes, for example one brother might have half the interest in a shop and another two brothers a quarter each. Under a trust for sale, it is the trustees who have the power to dispose of the land. These may or may not themselves be beneficiaries. A common example is the standard trust for sale for a matrimonial home. Husband and wife will be joint owners of the legal estate in their house and trustees for sale on behalf of themselves as beneficiaries.

If anyone wishes to create a succession of interests by means of a trust for sale he must do so expressly, but statute ensures that any attempt to create concurrent interests in land is likely to have the effect of creating an implied trust for sale. Thus, where a house is given to several children or bought by a husband and wife, it will be held by the joint owners on trust for sale.

At first sight, strict settlements are devices for preventing land being sold outside the settlement, but they have been modified by statute so that the land can be disposed of. Trusts for sale, at first sight, seem to be arrangements which require trustees to sell property and distribute the proceeds. In fact, however, they normally contain powers in the trustees to postpone sale, and often have a condition that the sale must not take place unless the trustees have obtained the consent of certain people. A person with a present life interest may be able to live in a home or run a shop subject to a trust for sale and not have it sold by the trustees without his consent. Consent may also be required of the person who will obtain the interest in the house or shop after the present occupant dies. In *Re Inns*,[11] Mr Inns, a prosperous businessman, left his large home, Springfield, in Stevenage, on trust for sale for his widow for life and then to the local council, if they wanted it for a hospital. In the meantime, any sale under the trust was conditional upon the consent of the hospital. When the widow sought additional maintenance because she could not afford to live in the house, Wynn Parry J. treated the condition of consent as valid although it effectively prevented the house being sold. The Courts have a residual power to order a sale under s. 30 of the Law of Property Act 1925 which should prevent the need for consents in cases where these would cause extreme inconvenience by preventing the sale of land. Under a trust for sale, as with a strict settlement, there may be up to four trustees. For a valid sale of land subject to a trust for sale, the Law of Property Act 1925, s. 27 requires at least two trustees, although one is sufficient in the case of a trust corporation or a sole personal representative.[12] If a sale requires consents, under s. 26, it is sufficient if two of them are obtained.

Despite the freedom which the law has provided for the sale of legal estates in land by trustees for sale, the land itself may remain subject to equitable interests. These include lesser interests, such as equitable easements, and some rights of occupants. Chapter 5, Section 5.1, explains how such rights generally need to be protected by registration.

(d) Rules against future restrictions on the use of property

The history of private land law may be seen as the history of those with vested interests in land struggling to impose their control beyond the grave, against judges who saw this as a 'fight against God, by affecting a stability which human providence can never attain to'.[13] The judges also seem to have been conscious from early times of the danger of great dynastic families acquiring excessive power by building up inalienable blocks of property, particularly if the families were to become decadent and fail to use their property efficiently for the wider social good. Thus, in 1285, the English barons obtained a statute known as *De Donis Conditionalibus* which provided that an estate created *in tail* could not be alienated outside the family, but passed from one generation to another indefinitely. However, 200 years later, by the end of the Wars of the Roses, the judges had approved the devices known as *the common recovery* and *the fine* which Shakespeare mentions in his satire on lawyers in *Hamlet* quoted at the beginning of the next chapter. These devices were fictitious sales which were uncontested by those who had current entailed interests and which had the effect of barring or destroying the entail.

Landowners then tried to tie up their estates for the future by specifying a series of individuals through whom the land should pass, such as 'to X [an eldest son] for life, remainder to his eldest surviving son for life . . . and so on for successive surviving eldest sons'. By the Tudor period, in the sixteenth century, the judges were already declaring such arrangements void, or converting them into estates in tail which could be barred. The most significant weapon used by the courts was the *rule against perpetuities*. This was gradually developed from the seventeenth century. Its basic effect was that any contingent future interest in property which might vest after the perpetuity period was void from its outset. The perpetuity period was the length of a human life in being plus twenty-one years. This period was chosen because before 1969 a minor came of age at 21. A life in being included a child in the womb. Thus a grant was just within the rule if it was made 'to X for life and then to the youngest child of X surviving to the age of 21'. The Perpetuities and Accumulation Act 1964 has modified the rule against perpetuities for all instruments coming into effect after 15 July 1964. Now, interests are only void if they are bound to vest outside the perpetuity period. Also, it is now possible to make a valid interest by providing that it will come into effect within a set time of eighty years. This allows for a grant 'to X [an eldest son] for life, then to X's eldest son surviving at his death, remainder to X's eldest surviving grandson or great grandson living 80 years from the date of the grant'. Conveyancers usually take the precaution of always expressly providing that the estate shall in any event vest within the perpetuity period. The present rule against perpetuities ensures that even beneficial interests in land can only be tied up for a limited period in the future. On the other hand, it may remain uncertain for many years where the property will eventually go and this can be an unfortunate disincentive against improvement by those currently in occupation of land.[14]

The details of the rule against remoteness, for example the exact meaning of *a life in being*, are amongst the most complicated and difficult parts of English land law. Broadly, however, the rule ensures that both land itself, and the beneficial interest in it, may only be tied up for the future for a limited period. A separate rule, known as *the rule against accumulations*, further restricts the time during which a trust may provide for income to be kept from distribution to beneficiaries whilst it is being saved up. This rule was introduced by Parliament in 1800 to forestall an arrangement by Peter Thelluson, who had provided in his will that part of his estate was to be held on trust and the income accumulated on such terms that vast sums were likely to be built up in compound interest and not be paid out for two generations.[15] The rule against accumulations is now contained in the Law of Property Act 1925, ss. 164–166 and the Perpetuities and Accumulation Act 1964, ss. 13–14.

A landowner may wish to tie up the future use of his land by transferring it to a corporation, which unlike an individual, may exist indefinitely. However, a corporation may decide to dispose of property unless it is restricted by the terms of a trust. The Victorian courts enforced a further rule against inalienability, the *rule against perpetual trusts*, which made a trust void if it purported to prevent any trustees from ever disposing of the trust property. Thus a gift of land to a farm company upon trust to maintain it as an open space for the recreation of the donor's family, or of money to trustees to maintain a family tomb[16] will be invalid. An important exception to the rule against perpetual trusts is that of gifts made to charities. Thus, land may be transferred to a charitable trust for its indefinite use for charitable purposes, such as providing educational or recreational facilities.[17] The exception may also apply to the rule against perpetuities. The donor may provide that, if the charity fails to carry out his intentions, the property will be transferred to another charity. In *Re Tyler*,[18] the Court of Appeal upheld a condition in a gift by Sir James Tyler to the London Missionary Society that if the society failed to keep his tomb in Highgate Cemetery, the property should pass to the Blue Coat School, Newgate Street London. Today the tomb is still exceptionally well maintained by the London Missionary Society (Fig. 4.4). If

Fig. 4.4 The tomb of Sir James Tyler in Highgate Cemetery during regular maintenance, by kind permission of the London Missionary Society.

a substantial sum is provided and the charity can use the surplus over and above what is needed for the donor's wishes, the first charity is likely to carry out those wishes indefinitely. As in *Re Tyler*, the charity may even be given property on condition that it carries out certain non-charitable purposes of the donor. However, care must be taken in granting such a gift that only that which is itself charitable is made an actual requirement of the trust. In *Re Dalziel*,[19] a legacy to St Bartholemew's hospital failed because a first charge on the legacy itself was to be the upkeep of another mausoleum in Highgate Cemetery.

The rules against future restrictions on the use of property are now mainly of importance in freeing beneficial interests. As we have already seen, land itself is largely freely disposable under the system of trusts for sale. However, a charitable trust may be framed in such a manner that the purposes of the trust can only be carried out if the charity keeps a particular piece of land, such as an area of open country or a grave, which the donor wishes to preserve for the future. Statute also intervenes, notably enabling land to be given to the National Trust on terms which only allow it to be alienated by Parliament.[20]

NOTES: SECTION 4.2

1. Megarry, R.E. (1975) *The Law of Real Property*, 4th edn, Stevens and Sons, London p. 46.
2. Law of Property Act 1925, s. 7 (1) as amended by the Law of Property (Amendment) Act 1926.
3. Law of Property Act 1925, s. 205 (1)(xix).
4. *Post* p. 186f.
5. *Lace* v. *Chantler* [1944] K.B. 368, C.A.
6. Law of Property Act 1925, s. 149 (3).
7. The two less important forms of co-ownership were *tenancy by entireties*, a special form of joint tenancy between husband and wife under which the husband had complete control of the property, and *coparceny*, a special form of tenancy in common between coheirs on intestacy, such as daughters who shared their father's estate in the absence of a son. Tenancies by entireties were abolished in 1926. Coparceny is virtually extinct and can now only exist in equitable interests.
8. The Trustees Act 1925, s. 34 (2) limits the number of trustees generally, to four, and the Law of Property Act 1925, s. 34 (2) provides that if a grant is made to more than four, the first four named act as the joint tenants.
9. Thus in *Weston* v. *Henshaw* [1950] Ch. 510, Dankwerts J. held that a sale was invalid to an honest purchaser who was ignorant of the trust for sale, by a tenant for life who had old deeds which showed him as the present undisputed owner. However, in *Re Morgan's Lease* [1972] Ch. 1 Ungoed-Thomas J. expressed the view that a valid sale may take place to an honest purchaser who is unaware of the settlement, because under the Settled Land Act 1925, s. 110 (1), in such a transaction, proper compliance with the requirements of the Act is to be implied.
10. Where a settlement is made in a will without a separate vesting deed, s. 6 of the Settled Land Act provides for the execution of one by the settlor's personal

representatives. If a settlement is made by the settlor, in his life time, in a document under which he retains an initial life interest, s. 9 provides for the execution of the necessary deed. In the interval before the settlement is properly completed, s. 13 provides that usually a disposition of the property can operate only as a contract by the person purporting to transfer the property, although if it is to an honest purchaser who is unaware of the settlement, he does obtain a good title.

11. *Re Inns* [1947] Ch. 576.
12. A trust for sale may be implied by statute in circumstances where the purchaser has no means of knowing about it. Thus a single legal owner may hold under a statutory trust for sale, e.g. *Caunce* v. *Caunce* [1969] 1 W.L.R. 286. In such a case the single trustee may be able to transfer the estate free from beneficial interests although beneficiaries may be protected by equity if they are in possession, see *post* p. 243f.
13. *Duke of Norfolk's Case* (1681) 3 Chan. Cas. 1, *per* Lord Nottingham L.C., at p. 3.
14. See Gray K.J. and Symes, P.D. (1981) *Real Property and Real People*, Butterworth, London, pp. 186–7.
15. Thelluson's arrangement was upheld by the courts in *Thelluson* v. *Woodford* (1799) 4 Ves. Jur. 227.
16. *Rickard* v. *Robson* (1862) 31 Beav. 244.
17. In *Christ's Hospital* v. *Grainger* (1849) 1 Mac. & G. 460. Lord Cottenham L.C. approved the transfer of property from Reading to London Corporation under a trust originally set up in 1624, because Reading Corporation failed, centuries later, to carry out its responsibilities.
18. *Re Tyler* [1891] 3 Ch. 252.
19. *Re Dalziel* [1943] 1 Ch. 277.
20. National Trust Act 1907, s. 21 and National Trust Act 1939, s. 8.

4.3 Special forms of control: mortgages, leases, licences and charities

As we have seen, a recurring tendency of the law is to treat land as an essentially commercial asset, although in practice economic management frequently involves maintaining its amenity value. However, certain arrangements for the control of land under private law may be more suitable than others for stewarding the amenity value of the landscape.

4.3.1 Mortgages

Mortgages are important legal arrangements which enable land to be pledged in return for money needed by the mortgagor. They treat land as a commercial security. However, it is in the interest of the mortgagee who lends the money to ensure that the property is kept in good condition so that its value is protected. In practice also, mortgages are most frequently used, especially by home buyers, as the means of financing the purchase of the very property which serves as security. A commercial mortgage will involve the mortgagor paying interest on his loan. This may be at regular intervals throughout the mortgage term, or may be added to the capital sum and repaid at the end. Often, the capital is itself paid off in instalments, together with interest on the outstanding sum borrowed. Once the debt is repaid the mortgagor will be entitled to redeem his rights to the property intact, but if he fails to make agreed payments the mortgagee's remedy is to sell the property.[1] In the case of an equitable mortgage this may require an order of the court.[2]

The most common method of mortgaging a legal estate in land is by a *legal mortgage* created by a deed charging the land with the money borrowed. In the case of registered land a deed charging the land should be entered in the register.[3] The land registry will retain the certificate of title.[4] An alternative form of legal mortgage involves the mortgagor granting a lease or sublease of the land to the mortgagee. The mortgagor will in practice normally remain in occupation, but if the mortgage loan or interest is not repaid at the agreed time the mortgagee has the remedy of being able to take over the property under the lease. He is then able to exercise his powers of sale more effectively. In the case of freehold land, a standard term for the lease is 3000 years. If the mortgagor requires more money he may grant a second, slightly longer, lease. If the land is unregistered, the first mortgagee will normally retain the deeds. A later mortgage taken out with someone else will lack this security. Indeed Building Societies are forbidden to grant second or subsequent mortgages unless they made the original loan or loans.[5]

A mortgagor whose own interest is equitable, may create an *equitable mortgage* by assigning his interest in writing to a mortgagee. If the mortgagor's own interest would be overreached[6] on a sale of land and he would have been unable to prevent this sale, neither can the mortgagee. The security here is in the proceeds of sale. An equitable mortgage may also be created where a legal mortgage is intended but not completed with appropriate formality, or where the land certificate or title deeds are simply deposited with the mortgagee as security for the loan. This method is often used to obtain a short-term bank loan. In practice the terms of such a loan are often set out in a *memorandum of deposit under seal,* and if the land is unregistered and the deeds are not deposited, such a memorandum may be registered with the Land Charges Registry as an equitable mortgage in its own right. In the case of registered land, equitable mortgages generally are protected by a notice or caution on the register.

4.3.2 Leases

For the general public who are concerned about the quality of the environment, and for the specialist in land use, seeking to design or protect a scheme of building or landscaping, the manner in which the law divides control over land is vital. For most individuals, what is usually more important is a secure home to live in and a secure place of work. Parallel with developments in the law which have restricted, in the public interest, the use to which landowners may put their own property, has been the introduction of statutory controls to safeguard the security of occupants from eviction or oppressive rents.

However, these provisions have reduced the economic attractiveness of letting property at rent. This has often led to land being managed by employees of the owner rather than by tenants, or to agricultural and residential estates being broken up and sold off. This trend may have distributed control of land more widely in society, but it has left the protection from misuse increasingly with public authorities, or with those who may be entitled to the subsidiary rights in the land of others which we shall look at in the next section.

(a) Security of tenants

A legal lease must be for a specified time, although this may range from a very long term, such as 999 years, to a period shorter than 1 year. Land may be subject to one, or a succession of subtenants provided the time specified in each lease is shorter than the time for which the person granting it is entitled to the land. An essential feature of any lease is that it gives the tenant exclusive possession of the relevant property. Thus, an arrangement granting separately to each of a couple of unmarried people living together the use of a bedsitting room, reserving the right in each case for the landlord to share occupation with them, could not be a lease but only a licence.[7] It would not be covered by the Rent Act which is designed to protect residential tenants.

A long lease will itself provide substantial security. Early in such a lease the lessee may be able to assign the remaining term for almost as much money as if it were a freehold. At the other extreme are *tenancies at will* and *tenancies at sufferance*, which either party may terminate whenever they choose. A *tenancy at will* resembles a licence, and may be created expressly, or may be inferred, for example where a person goes into possession of property during negotiations for a sale or lease, or remains in possession at the conclusion of a lease with the consent of the landlord. If he remains, without the consent of the landlord, he is a *tenant at sufferance* and resembles a trespasser. However, under the Landlord and Tenant Act 1730, he may be required to pay double the rentable value of the land during the time that he remains in possession. *Periodic tenancies* are the most common form of letting. They are created for a set term, often of a year, or a month, but automatically continue into a new term, unless notice is given to terminate. Periodic tenancies are generally implied where a person is allowed to occupy land for the payment of rent and no term is fixed. In particular a tenant at will, or at sufferance, will generally be treated as a periodic tenant where he has paid rent.[8] A periodic tenancy on a yearly basis is a *tenancy from year to year*; unless otherwise agreed, six months notice must be given to terminate it. Often such a letting will be from one of the traditional *quarter days*, Lady Day on 25 March, Midsummer Day on 24 June, Michaelmas on 29 September or Christmas Day on 25 December. Notice must be given for two quarter days ahead, and this may sometimes be slightly less than half a year.[9] Agricultural tenancies are almost invariably from year to year, and, in their case, statute requires a full year's notice which may not be varied by agreement.[10]

At Common Law, a tenant is protected by covenants which are generally implied in any lease. Thus a covenant of *quiet enjoyment* is implied that the landlord will not interfere or authorize anyone else to interfere directly with the tenants' use of his land. For example, the landlord must not cause subsidence to the land by carrying out excavations underneath it to remove minerals which he has retained for himself[11] or harrass a tenant by damaging his premises.[12] Similarly a covenant is implied that the landlord will not *derogate from his grant* by hindering the tenant's use of the premises for the purpose for which he has leased them. Here, a tenant may be better protected than a purchaser who claims an implied easement.[13] For example, the tenant will be entitled to go onto adjacent land belonging to the lessor if this is necessary to carry out repair works which are his responsibility.[14] Again, if the tenant needs a free flow of air for a business which involves storing timber, the landlord may be prevented by the courts from putting up neighbouring buildings which prevent the air circulating freely.[15]

In many respects the security of tenants has been greatly expanded by statute. Thus, *agricultural tenants* will generally be entitled to twelve-months notice and even after vacating the land may remove *emblements*, that is annual crops which they have themselves planted. As we saw in Chapter 2, Section 2.3 statute allows tenants to remove agricultural fixtures. More fundamentally, an agricultural tenant may only be compelled to leave in limited circumstances. Under the Agricultural Holdings (Notices to Quit) Act 1977, s. 2, if the landlord serves a notice to quit the tenant may challenge it within one month by a counter notice. Then, unless he requires the land for non-agricultural purposes and already has any necessary planning consent, the landlord can only require the tenant to leave in limited circumstances, notably where the Agricultural Land Tribunal has ruled that it is satisfied that the tenant has not practiced good husbandry. The tenant may also be compelled to leave if he has failed, after due notice, to pay his rent, or is otherwise guilty of an irremediable breach of the tenancy materially affecting the landlord's interests, or has become bankrupt. The Minister of Agriculture may certify that the land requires reorganizing in the interests of agricultural efficiency and the Agricultural Land Tribunal has power under s. 3, in various circumstances to consent to a notice to quit in the interests of good agriculture. Where a tenant dies, under Part II of the Agriculture (Miscellaneous Provisions) Act 1976, certain close relatives who apply within three months may obtain an order from the Tribunal granting them the right to a substitute tenancy.

Statutory protection for tenants of business premises is provided under the Landlord and Tenant Act 1954, Part II, as amended by the Law of Property

Act 1969. Such a tenant is entitled to renewal of his tenancy when it expires unless the landlord can show one of a number of grounds,[16] including misbehaviour by the tenant, in particular failure to repair the premises or to pay rent. The landlord is also entitled to recover the premises if he provides suitable alternative accommodation, or, in three other cases, where he is prepared to pay compensation. These are, first where the tenancy is a sublease of part of a property and would prevent an economic letting of the whole when the head lease ends; second, where the landlord requires possession to redevelop the site; and thirdly, provided he did not acquire the premises within the five years before the current lease expired, where he intends to occupy the premises for his own business or residential purposes.

The most important and far reaching code for security of tenants is now contained in the Rent Act 1977 and covers *protected residential tenancies*. Protected tenancies do not include those with very low or very high rents, holiday lettings, lettings where the landlord is resident or provides board or personal services or where the landlord is one of a number of public institutions such as educational colleges or housing associations. Local authorities are similarly excluded but their tenants are given security of tenure under the Housing Act 1980. Protected tenants under the Rent Act are entitled to have their rents assessed by an independent rent officer, from whom an appeal lies to a Rent Assessment Committee. If the lease of a protected tenant expires he is entitled to remain in occupation under a statutory tenancy unless he misbehaves, particularly by failing to pay his rent or by breaking some other term of the tenancy; by causing a legal nuisance or by using the premises for immoral purposes. The landlord may also be able to recover possession in certain circumstances if he requires the premises for his own purposes or those of his immediate family, or if alternative accommodation is available to the tenant.

In the case of long tenancies of houses, a different approach to security has been adopted by Parliament, in the Leasehold Reform Act 1967. Generally, where there is a lease for more than twenty-one years, this grants residential occupiers rights to acquire, at an advantageous price, a new fifty-year lease or the freehold. The Housing Act 1980 has now given rights to council tenants of houses to buy the freehold, and to those in flats to buy a long lease.

(b) The control of tenants

Whether he sees leases as a means of making money out of his land, or as a system for conserving for posterity and his own satisfaction an integrated and well managed estate, a landlord will wish to control the use of the land by the tenant. The law protects land from being stripped by a temporary occupant by implying upon tenants an obligation not to cause *waste*. Generally any tenant will be restrained from *equitable waste*, that is, acts of wanton destruction. This is illustrated in *Weld-Blundell* v. *Wolseley*.[17] The Lulworth castle estate was settled in 1869. In 1902, R.J. Weld, the tenant for life, was of unsound mind. Those responsible for his affairs marked 540 mature trees on the estate for felling. The castle was occupied by Weld-Blundell who was likely to succeed to the estate in due course. He sought to prevent the felling and called an expert witness who testified that the trees had obviously been planted over the years as part of a continuous scheme to ornament and shelter the natural amphitheatre containing the castle and the lake by which it stood. The case was referred to Swinten Eady J. who ruled that for the felling to amount to equitable waste the timber must have been planted with the intention that it should be ornamental, it was not enough that it should incidentally serve that purpose. However, the evidence was sufficient to establish such an intention. Many tenants are liable, or *impeachable* for *voluntary waste* which falls short of wanton destruction, for example for structural alterations to a building[18] or cutting down commercial timber, where the land is not a timber estate which depends for its management on regular cutting.[19] However, *meliorating waste* which positively improves the property is permissible, for example where greenhouses have been erected on agricultural land[20] or derelict barracks have been converted into stores and dwelling houses.[21] The courts have to regard improvement in terms of increasing the financial value of the land and not to consider any question of the land being of greater amenity value in its original form. A tenant from year to year is normally under a positive duty to look after the premises leased in a *tenant-like manner*. This seems to include such basic precautions as keeping drains unblocked and keeping electrical wires in a safe condition.[22] It may extend to keeping a building weather-tight.[23] A tenant for a fixed number of years may be under a more substantial obligation to avoid permissive waste.[24]

Apart from implied terms to protect leased land from waste, it is normal for a landlord to include express conditions providing further protection, for example either requiring the tenant to carry out repairs or, as is normal on a short tenancy, retaining the right to do so himself. The landlord may in any event retain a right to inspect the premises to ensure that they are being properly maintained. A tenant is also frequently required to insure the premises against fire and not to assign or underlet the premises or any part of them without the consent of the landlord.

4.3.3   Licences

A person who is authorized to be on land without having any legal interest in it is a licensee. As we shall see in Chapter 7, Section 7.1, anyone else who is in legal occupation of the land owes a duty to safeguard such visitors from harm. However, a licensee may himself occupy and have control of land, for example if he is a contractor in charge of construction work there. A licensee may also occupy premises for his own benefit. A person who wishes to obtain a financial return on land without losing control over it under the Rent Acts or other legislation designed to protect tenants, may grant a licence to use the land in return for a money payment. A licence to occupy land which is less likely to be confused with a lease may be granted as an act of generosity, for example where a retired employee is allowed to live in accommodation rent free,[25] or to protect land whilst it is temporarily not needed, for example where a farmer is allowed to graze animals on wasteland on which the owner hopes in due course to build.

A bare licence may be withdrawn whenever the person entitled to the land chooses. However, in many cases, the courts will protect licensees from expulsion. In particular, a licence coupled with a grant or interest is irrevocable. Thus if a person has an enforceable right to take profits, for example, to cut timber and saw it up on the site[26] or to pump water from someone else's land, this will involve a licence to go on to the land for those purposes and this licence can not be withdrawn. The licence is enforceable against anyone to whom the land to which it is subject is transferred, provided that, where the right to which it is coupled is an equitable one, this is protected by appropriate registration. If a licence is granted under a contract, in equity it can only be withdrawn by the grantor in accordance with the terms of the contract. Thus where Great Yarmouth Borough Council contracted to allow the National Front to use the Wellington pier pavilion for its two-day annual conference and then, after its membership had changed at a local government election, withdrew the licence, the courts granted an order for specific performance to compel the council to honour their agreement.[27]

However, a contractual licence can not generally be enforced against any third party to whom the land affected is transferred. For example, King, the owner of a site at the Royal Canal Bank in Dublin contracted to allow a bill-posting firm to use the side walls of a new cinema on the site for four years. He transferred a lease of the site to a trustee for the cinema who then refused to honour the agreement. The House of Lords held that the original owner was personally liable in contract because the licence could not be enforced against the new owner.[28] On the other hand, a licence to use land may bind someone who purchases the land expressly subject to the licence. King would probably have avoided liability himself, and enabled the bill-posting company to sue the cinema trustee direct, if he had made the lease of the cinema expressly subject to the advertising licence.

A licensee may also be protected under the doctrine of *estoppel*, where he is caused to act to his detriment by relying on the licence. In *Crabb* v. *Arun District Council*,[29] Crabb owned land at the village of Pagham near Bognor Regis. On part of this he had offices and a showroom and a caravan factory. A new road was being built beside the site, for development on neighbouring land, and Arun District Council agreed to allow access onto the road from Crabb's land. However, he then decided to develop an empty part of the land which would need a second access further down the new road. As a result of negotiation the council erected a fence with two gates and Crabb sold off the part of his site which was already developed. He then fell out with the council and it blocked up the access to the part of Crabb's land which he had retained. This was rendered sterile for over five years. The Court of Appeal held that Crabb was entitled to have the access reopened and protected by a permanent easement. In extreme cases the courts may even order the freehold of a piece of land to be transferred to a licensee who has been misled into relying upon the licence.[30]

4.3.4   Charities

As we saw in the last section, someone who puts land in England or Wales into charitable trusts may ensure that it is used indefinitely for particular purposes in the future, despite the general tendency of the law to enable current legal owners to freely dispose of land.[31] The English law of charities has further advantages for protecting future land use. An ordinary trust will be void *for uncertainty of objects* unless individuals who are to benefit can clearly be identified at the time that the trust has to be carried out. These may be a large group, such as the employees of a company, as in *Denley's Trust Deed*[32] where a trust of land in Cheltenham for recreation and as a sports ground was held to be valid. However, a charitable trust may be for much wider purposes, such as providing a country park for the recreational benefit of the public generally. Because there are no individuals who are specified as the beneficiaries of a charity, the Attorney General has the power to compel the trustees to carry out their charitable responsibilities.

A trust could be void in its original form, for example because trustees were named who did not exist, or because the property put in trust was insufficient for the purposes. A gift of £1000 to buy a building to use for certain purposes would probably be impossible to fulfil today if the £1000 was the only money available. A trust may also become invalid at a later date, for example a trust to maintain a particular house in grounds which are later taken over by the state as an army tank range. If such trusts are charitable, the Chancery Division of the High Court has powers which may enable it to prevent their lapsing, by modifying their terms. Under what is known as the *cy-prés* doctrine, it may substitute some similar alternative objects. A small gift to buy premises for a museum might be diverted to support an existing museum of a similar type, or the proceeds from the sale of a nature reserve which is compulsorily purchased might be used to set up another reserve in the neighbourhood. The principles of this doctrine are now contained in the

Charities Act 1960, s. 13. The Chancery Division has power to provide schemes of administration for charities, and the *cy-près* principle can be used to modernize charitable trusts which are obsolete but still legally valid. Charities must normally be registered with the Charity Commission which operates under the Charities Act 1960, and the commissioners may take the initiative in supervising and in modifying charitable trusts.

The most valuable aspect of charities is the tax relief which they enjoy. The various forms of taxation affecting land are outlined in Chapter 3, Section 3.2. Charities are given exemptions from certain of the newer taxes which are aimed at redistributing private wealth and which tend towards the breaking up of large private land holdings, notably capital gains tax, capital transfer tax and development land tax. Charities are also relieved from paying rates to local authorities on their land and buildings. This is now provided for by the General Rate Act 1967, s. 40, which grants 50% relief on all rates and allows local authorities at their discretion to waive the remaining 50%. This discretion allows local authorities to support charities whose activities supplement their own local facilities, as in the case of a charity providing playing fields or a nature centre much frequented by local schools. Charities do not have to pay income tax themselves and also can recover the basic income tax paid by donors on regular gifts under a convenant for four or more years. Thus if I covenant to pay the National Trust £70 a year for four years, after tax, and I pay income tax at 30p in the pound, the National Trust will be able to recover an extra £30 each year from the Inland Revenue. If the donor pays income tax at a higher rate, the charity can only recover the basic rate, but under the Income and Corporation Taxes Act 1970, s. 457 (1A), the tax payer's taxable income is currently treated as excluding up to £5000 which he covenants to charities. Thus his liability to pay higher rates is reduced the more he covenants to charities up to £5000. One form of taxation where charities do not have special privileges is value added tax, which is payable on goods and services. This has meant that charities with large and expensive buildings to maintain, notably churches, have had to face greatly increased bills without being able to obtain any repayment from the state.

The present definition of 'charity' is still based on the early seventeenth-century Charitable Uses Act 1601. This has been interpreted in a mass of cases of which one of the most significant is the late Victorian authority of *Commissioners of Income Tax* v. *Pemsel*[33] It is clear that charity covers relief of poverty and the advancement of education and religion. There is a residual category of purposes of general benefit to the community. This has been held, for example, to include the improvement of agriculture.[34] The Recreational Charities Act 1958 has extended the scope for charities designed to provide recreational facilities. A charity must be for the general public benefit and generally must confine itself to charitable purposes. Thus it must avoid political activity unless this is clearly subsidiary to its main aims. For example, a charity concerned with agricultural education could legitimately advise the government on proposed legislation concerned with agricultural education.[35] On the other hand a charity may further its basic charitable purposes by commercial activities, such as by renting its buildings to other organizations, or running a profit-making shop in its premises, or by charging for the services which it provides.[36]

A charity is not itself a form of legal person. It may be operated by a body of trustees established for the purpose of running it. Alternatively, a body corporate, such as a local authority or a public company, may be made trustee for a particular charity, or a charitable corporation may be set up to act as trustee. A company limited by guarantee is particularly suited to the running of a charity.[37]

NOTES: SECTION 4.3

1. Law of Property Act 1925, s. 10.
2. Ibid. s. 91 (2).
3. Land Registration Act 1925, s. 27.
4. Ibid. s. 65.
5. Building Societies Act 1962, s. 32.
6. *Ante* p. 176.
7. *Somma* v. *Hazelhurst* [1978] 1 W.L.R. 1014, C.A.
8. *Adler* v. *Blackman* [1953] 1 Q.B. 146, C.A.
9. *Sidebotham* v. *Holland* [1895] 1 Q.B. 378.
10. Agricultural Holdings (Notices to Quit) Act 1977, s. 1 (1).
11. *Markham* v. *Paget* [1908] 1 Ch. 697.
12. *Lavender* v. *Betts* [1942] 2 All E.R. 72.
13. *Post* p. 199 and p. 253f.
14. *Ward* v. *Kirkland* [1967] Ch. 194, compare *post*, p. 338.
15. *Aldin* v. *Latimer Clark Muirhead and Co.* [1894] 2 Ch. 437, compare *post* p. 196.
16. Landlord and Tenant Act, 1954, s. 30(1).
17. *Weld-Blundell* v. *Wolseley* [1903] 2 Ch. 664.
18. *Marsden* v. *Edward Heyes Ltd* [1927] 2 K.B. 1, C.A.
19. *Honywood* v. *Honywood* (1874) L.R. 18 Eq. 306, and see *ante* p. 22, note.
20. *Meux* v. *Cobley* [1892] 2 Ch. 253.
21. *Doherty* v. *Allman* [1877] 3 App. Cas. 709, H.L.
22. *Warren* v. *Keen* [1954] 1 Q.B. 15, C.A.
23. *Wedd* v. *Porter* [1916] 2 K.B. 91, C.A.
24. *Yellowly* v. *Gower* (1855) 11 Exch. 274.
25. *Murray, Bull & Co. Ltd* v. *Murray* [1953] 1 Q.B. 211.
26. *James Jones and Sons Ltd* v. *Earl of Tankerville* [1909] 2 Ch. 440. For the meaning of profits see *post* p. 205.
27. *Verrall* v. *Great Yarmouth Borough Council* [1981] Q.B. 202, C.A.
28. *King* v. *David Allen and Sons Billposting Ltd* [1916] 2 A.C. 54, H.L., and see Lord Upjohn and Lord Wilberforce in *National Provincial Bank* v. *Ainsworth* [1965] A.C. 1175, H.L.
29. *Crabb* v. *Arun District Council* [1976] Ch. 179, C.A.
30. *Pascoe* v. *Turner* [1979] 1 W.L.R. 431, C.A.

31. *Ante* p. 179f.
32. Denley's Trust Deed [1969] 1 Ch. 373.
33. *Commissioners of Income Tax* v. *Pemsel* [1891] A.C. 531, H.L.
34. *I.R.C.* v. *Yorkshire Agricultural Society* [1928] 1 K.B. 611, C.A.
35. Ibid. per Atkin, L.J. *obiter dicta*, at p. 632.
36. *The Abbey, Malvern Wells Ltd* v. *Minister of Local Government and Planning* [1951] Ch. 728.
37. *Ante* p. 161f.

4.4   Subsidiary rights over land: natural rights, easements and profits

No piece of land can be used in isolation. It must be possible to get onto it and off it. It will need access to water, and the normal services of modern living, such as electricity, gas and the telephone. Access and similar rights for the benefit of one piece of land may involve restrictions on the use of neighbouring land. Land benefiting from a right over other land is known as the *dominant tenement*. The land subject to the right is the *servient tenement* (Fig. 4.5).

4.4.1   Natural rights

The common law recognized two rights which protected all land in its natural state against damage from misuse of neighbouring land. First, there is a right not to have the land let down by withdrawing the support of neighbouring land. Anyone carrying out excavations for gravel or other materials, recontouring his land, or putting in building foundations, may be liable, if he causes land across his boundary to subside. If the neighbouring land is only liable to collapse because of the weight of buildings on it there is no right preventing excavations which harm the buildings, unless an easement of support has been created for them.

Second, where water runs across land, or along its boundary, in a defined stream, the common law recognized a natural right which prevented others from interfering with the supply, by pollution or by extracting excessive quantities of water. Where water did not run in a defined channel, each landowner could extract as much as he wished, even if this dried up or muddied the supply to neighbouring land. Rights of extraction and the duty not to interfere with rights of running water to other land have both been modified by statute, but the natural right to running water is still important where statute does not apply.

The remedy for interference with a natural right or an easement is an action in private nuisance. As we shall see in Chapter 7, Section 7.2, the law of nuisance protects land from neighbouring activities, which produce excessive noise, smell or other irritations. Although land in its natural state will be entitled to such protection, the level of what is reasonable will depend on the

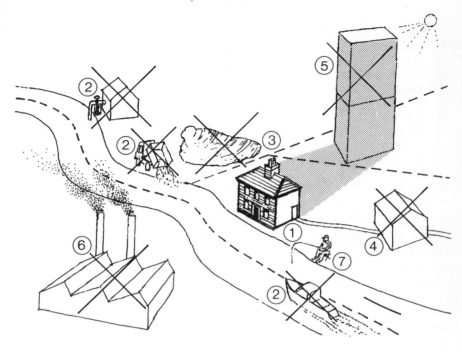

The use of land may be protected by subsidiary rights over neighbouring land or restricted by the subsidiary rights of others.

1. Dominant land and buildings on river
2. Natural rights to water and fishing rights protected
3. Natural rights and easement of support protected
4. Easement of right of way protected
5. Easement of light protected
6. Protection of view by restrictive covenant against building.
7. Profits of fishing restricting use of the land

Fig. 4.5 Examples of subsidiary rights over land.

present user of the area as a whole. Thus, in a built-up area, noisy excavations may have to be confined to the normal working day, whereas this might not be necessary in a remote part of the country. On the other hand, a new permanent activity, such as speedboat racing on a lake, might be unreasonably noisy for a country area whereas it might be acceptable in an urban park.

4.4.2   Easements

An easement is a right to use someone else's land in some limited way without actually taking part of the land or its produce. It may be a positive right, for example a right of access, or it may be essentially a restriction on other property, such as a right to light which prevents building on neighbouring land. Easements are particularly significant because, as we shall see in Chapter 5, Section 5.5 not only may they be expressly created by landowners, but they may be acquired by long use.

(a) Dominant and servient land

An easement must be for the benefit of a dominant tenement. In *Rangeley* v. *Midland Railway Co.*,[1] the railway company diverted a public footpath which lay across the route of their new line, so that it ran through Rangeley's woods instead of across his meadow. It was held that the company had power to do this, but only by buying a strip of the meadow outright under its compulsory purchase powers. The footpath did not benefit the railway line and therefore the company had no dominant tenement to which to attach an easement of access. A dominant tenement does not need to be a tangible piece of land, a *corporeal hereditament*. It may be another right, or *incorporeal hereditament*, such as a profit. Thus someone with fishing rights over a river will need a right of access across the land through which the river runs.[2] A dominant tenement does not need to be adjacent to the servient tenement, but it must be sufficiently close to obtain some real benefit from it. If the owner of an estate in Northumberland were to grant a right of way to the owner of another estate in Kent this could not be an easement but only a personal contract.[3] However, in *Todrick* v. *Western National Omnibus Company*[4] the bus company built a garage on land next to Dr Todrick's house at St Ives in Cornwall. The doctor claimed that the company were not entitled to use an access road across his land because this was not adjacent to the garage but led to it via another piece of land to the north of the garage site. The Court of Appeal held that an easement may exist for the benefit of one piece of land over other land which is not physically contiguous. Nevertheless, the bus company were at fault because they had built a large concrete ramp and were making a heavier use of the access than they were entitled to.

It is sufficient if the benefit from an easement is for some specialized use of the dominant land, for example the right to hang over neighbouring land a sign board advertising a shop. This would not be of any use if the dominant premises became a private house. Thus in *Moody* v. *Steggles*[5] an easement was recognized for hanging a sign from a neighbouring house for the Grosvenor Arms in Newmarket High Street. However, there must be a real benefit for the dominant land. In *Hill* v. *Tupper*,[6] Tupper who had an inn on the Basingstoke canal at Aldershot, put pleasure boats on the canal. Hill had an exclusive licence from the canal company to run boats there but the Court of Exchequer held that this was not an easement, only a personal contract with the company. Thus Hill could not sue Tupper directly. Apart from his licence to run boats, Hill had the lease of land, including a wharf beside the canal, but it could not be said that the right to run boats was a benefit to this land. Rather it was the land which enabled the licence to be carried out. The requirement that an easement must accommodate some dominant tenement has been criticized as outdated under modern circumstances.[7] For example, a business which provided a helicopter service in a city centre or which operated a long-distance lorry service would have to buy or lease sites for a helicopter pad or for regular overnight lorry stops, or depend on personal contracts, although its purposes might be better met by an easement.

(b) Separation of control

The servient and dominant tenements of an easement must be owned and occupied by different people. If an easement is granted to a tenant over his landlord's land it expires when the lease runs out.[8] Similarly, if a landowner buys a neighbouring piece of land over which he has an easement, that easement is extinguished. Thus if the land is later divided again, the old easement will not automatically revive.

(c) A suitable object for a grant

Easements may be created by long use, but most are created under deed. For example, a landlord may let a shop with a right for staff to use a golf course attached to his neighbouring office block, or a developer may buy a right of way over neighbouring land to houses which he is building and then sell the right along with the houses. Even an easement which is created by long use must be capable of forming the subject matter of a grant. Thus it must be possible to state it sufficiently clearly to put in a deed. In *Bass* v. *Gregory*,[9] Bass was owner of the Jolly Anglers' public house in Nottingham. Like many old buildings in that city this had a cellar excavated from solid rock. It was ventilated by a shaft into a well which emerged in Gregory's yard. Bass was held to have an easement for this very specific flow of air. By contrast, in *Harris* v. *De Pinna*[10] the Court of Appeal held that Harris, a timber merchant, could not claim any right to the free flow of air through staging in which he stored timber so as to prevent De Pinna building two large warehouses next door. The general flow of air was too vague to be recognized as an easement.

For an easement to be contained in a valid grant, there would have to be both a capable grantor and grantee. In *Mulliner* v. *Midland Railway Company*,[11] Northampton railway station had been built on arches because of the contours of the site (Fig. 4.6). Land on either side of the line, which had been acquired for the railway, but was now superfluous, was sold off, including a right of communication between the arches. A later purchaser of this land was unable to prevent the arches being filled in with a bonded warehouse, because the railway company which originally purported to

View of station taken from station throat showing relationship of train shed to arches; the latter used as stores

Fig. 4.6 Northampton Railway Station. *Mulliner* v. *Midland Railway Company* (1879) 11 Ch. D. 238.

grant the right of way only had statutory powers to dispose of the actual superfluous land. If an easement is to be created over an extended period, by long user, there must be a capable grantor and grantee throughout that time. In *National Guaranteed Manure Co. Ltd* v. *Donald*,[12] a canal between Carlisle and the Solway Firth was turned into a railway. Water which had previously been extracted from the river Eden for the canal was used to power a bone-grinding mill. This water interfered with Donald's mill so he opened a sluice to let it out. The Court held that the canal company had had no power to acquire any right to extract water except for canal purposes. Therefore, it had not acquired such a right to operate the bone mill by long use. Although its successor, the railway company, had purported to grant this right to the plaintiffs, no such right existed.

Sometimes, something which had been thought incapable of being an easement will, after all, be recognized by the courts. A classic example of an easement is a private right of way, but it was thought for half a century that there could not be a more general right to use someone else's land to walk and take exercise on.[13] Then, just such a right was recognized in 1956 in *Re Ellenborough Park*.[14] An estate had been built in Weston-Super-Mare in 1855, with an open park on the sea front. (Fig. 4.7). Rights were granted, to the new householders fronting onto this park and to some in a nearby street, to use the park as a communal garden. The park was requisitioned by the War Office during the Second World War and the question arose after the war as to whether the householders of the properties who claimed rights over the park were entitled to share in the compensation. The Court of Appeal held that they were as their rights did constitute valid easements.

Fig. 4.7 Ellenborough Park, Weston-Super-Mare, supplied by Aerofilms Ltd.

(d) Avoidance of undue burden

A common reason why the courts may not recognize an alleged easement, is that it would impose an excessive burden upon the servient tenement. Uncertainty would result in an undue burden. So would any expenditure by the owner of the servient tenement. Thus, where there is a right of way or a right to extract water, or a right to use shared chimney flues in the common wall of two adjacent houses, the person entitled to the right is permitted to carry out necessary repairs, but the person over whose land the right is exercised is generally not bound to do any work provided he does not interfere with the right.[15] There is, however, one case where the owner of a servient tenement may be under a duty to keep someone else's right in good condition, that is the *quasi easement* to have boundary fences kept in good repair. In *Lawrence* v. *Jenkins*,[16] some of Lawrence's cows escaped through a hole in a fence and died from eating yew leaves in Jenkin's wood. It was held that Jenkins was liable to keep the fence in good repair because he and his predecessors had acted on this basis for over forty years. The hole was caused by Jenkin's tenant negligently felling a tree across the fence and Jenkins was liable even though he had no reason to know of the damage.

Not only must any expense of maintaining an easement usually be paid by the owner of the dominant land, the easement must not impose so heavy a burden that the owner of the servient land is unable to use it himself. In *Copeland* v. *Greenhalf*[17] Mrs Copeland owned a strip of land at Winchcomb in Gloucestershire next to an orchard called Barebones Orchard. Greenhalf and his predecessors in a wheelwright's business used the land for over 50 years to store vehicles which were being repaired. Upjohn J. held that they must clear the site.

This claim . . . really amounts to a claim to a joint user of the land by the defendant. Practically, the defendant is claiming the whole beneficial use of the strip of land on the South-east side of the track there; he can leave as many or as few lorries there as he likes for as long as he likes; he may enter on it by himself. In my judgment that is not a claim which can be established as an easement. It is virtually a claim to possession of the servient tenement, if necessary to the exclusion of the owner; or at any rate, to a joint user.

4.4.3   Non-derogation from grant

The creation of easements by grant is considered in Chapter 5, Section 5.4, and their creation by prescription, that is long use, in Chapter 5, Section 5.5. It may also be possible to restrict the future use of land in circumstances where the courts would not recognize an easement, either by means of restrictive covenants which are considered later in this chapter, or under the doctrine of non-derogation from grant. This applies where land is transferred for a particular purpose by a grantor who keeps neighbouring land. He and his successors may not derogate from the grant by using the retained land in such a way as to prevent the land which has been granted being used for its intended purpose by the original grantor or his successors.[18] Thus, although no easement has been recognized to a free flow of air, in *Aldin* v. *Latimer Clark, Muirhead & Co.*[19] where Aldin rented premises at Richmond in Surrey to use for a timber business, a firm which became the landlord and built an electricity works next to the timber yard was liable to pay damages for interfering with air flow to Aldin's drying timber. Similarly, in *Grosvenor Hotel Co.* v. *Hamilton,*[20] Hamilton leased a house from the hotel next door. He refused to pay his rent because of vibration from the water pump for a well in the hotel. This made his home so unsafe that eventually he had to move out. The Court of Appeal held that even though the house was so rickety that it might not have been possible for an independent occupier to sue the hotel in nuisance, Hamilton was entitled to damages of considerably more than the rent he owed because the vibrations derogated from his lease.

   Even the doctrine against derogation from grant stops short at implying a grant of a right to privacy. In *Browne* v. *Flower*[21] Mrs Lightbody, the tenant of a twelve-room upstairs flat at Fulthorpe Mansions in Paddington, obtained the consent of her landlords to subdivide the flat and instal a new external open-work iron staircase from the garden. Parker J. refused the tenants of the ground-floor flat an order for the staircase to be removed. It would only have amounted to a derogation from grant if it had rendered the plaintiff's premises 'unfit or materially less fit to be used for the purposes for which they were demised, that is for the purposes of a residential flat'. It was not enough if the plaintiff's comfort was interfered with by loss of privacy or by the need to put up curtains which cut down light.

4.4.4   Classes of easement

The question begging principle that a valid easement must be a suitable object for a grant has given the courts wide scope to decide as a matter of policy that certain rights cannot exist as easements whilst others can. As negative easements are essentially restrictions on the use of servient land, such as rights of support or light which prevent excavation or building, they are vitally important in architectural and landscape work. However, new types of negative easement are unlikely to be recognized, and development control has reduced the need for negative easements generally. Where additional restrictions are appropriate, they may be provided for by restrictive covenants. On the other hand positive easements allows more effective use of dominant land by permitting occupiers to go on to neighbouring land for various purposes, and new forms of positive easement are quite frequently recognized.

(a)   Restrictions which will not be recognized as easements

As we have seen, no easement is recognized for a general free flow of air. Anyone building a windmill,[22] or a chimney,[23] must remember that at some future date the air currents which he needs could be interfered with. An easement may be acquired to project a sign board over neighbouring land but not to project tree branches or roots. The neighbouring land owner may cut these back and does not even have to give notice first provided he does not come on to the tree owner's land. Lord Herschell L.C. justified this in *Lemmon* v. *Webb*,[24] on the grounds that, as a tree is constantly growing, the extent of such a right would never be clear. The courts have also refused to recognize any easement to a view. In *Phipps* v. *Pears*[25] Lord Denning M.R. explained that such a right 'would unduly restrict your neighbour in his enjoyment of his own land. It would hamper legitimate development.' In that case an old house in Warwick, No. 14 Market Street, was demolished, leaving exposed, No. 16, which had been built right up against it in the 1920s. The Court of Appeal ruled that the owner of No. 16 had no cause of action in respect of damage from rain getting in and causing cracking when it froze. 'There is no such easement known to the law as an easement to be protected from the weather.'

(b)   Rights to support

Land is protected by a natural right to support. If a neighbour causes a building or other structure to subside he will be liable for the harm, provided the land would have collapsed even without the extra weight of the building.[26] Otherwise, as Lord Penzance said in *Dalton* v. *Angus*,[27] unless the building is protected by an easement, 'the owner of the adjacent soil may with

Fig. 4.8 St Gabriels Church, Ely Street, Hulme, Manchester, by kind permission of Manchester Local History Library.

perfect legality dig that soil away, and allow his neighbour's house, if supported by it, to fall in ruins to the ground'. If an easement is created, that case shows that the owner of a building may be entitled to protection from both his neighbour's land, and his neighbour's buildings. The neighbour may then be prevented from demolishing his own house unless he provides proper shoring or other protection.

Even an easement of support only entitles a landowner to protection for his property from the removal of earth or another building which supports it. A neighbour is free to alter the water table, for example by exercising his right to pump out water in the course of excavations. *Popplewell* v. *Hodgkinson*[28] is a case reminiscent of the New Testament parable of the two houses, one built on rock and the other on sand. A church was built in Ely Street, Hulme in Manchester, on solid foundations (Fig. 4.8). As a result of the necessary drainage of the spongy site, two poorly constructed cottages next door collapsed. The builder of the church was held not to be liable. However, where subsidence is caused by the extraction of mixed water and solid material,[29] or where solid material, such as salt deposits, is removed by dissolving it artificially in water and pumping it out, there may be liability.[30]

(c) Rights to water

At common law, a landowner was free to extract as much percolating water from under his own land as he liked, whatever the consequences to his neighbour. In *Mayor of Bradford* v. *Pickles*[31] Bradford was supplied with water from land known as Trooper Farm. Mr Pickles apparently wished to force the corporation to buy his neighbouring land, and so pumped out water there to such an extent that the supply to Trooper Farm was substantially affected. The House of Lords ruled that he was entirely within his rights.

A landowner also had a natural right to take water running through or past his land in a river or other defined channel. He could take as much as was necessary for *ordinary* purposes, that is domestic and traditional agricultural use, even if he dried up the supply for others down stream. He was also entitled to take water for extraordinary purposes, such as modern spray irrigation, or cooling industrial machinery, but only if he returned it in substantially the same quantity and quality. Such extraordinary use had to be reasonable depending on the size of the river.[32] Further rights to extract larger quantities of water or to take out water for land which was not adjacent to the stream could be acquired as an easement. Landowners downstream were entitled to bring an action against anyone upstream who extracted more than they were entitled to even if they had not suffered any injury.[33]

Now, as we have seen, in Chapter 3, Section 3.4, the Water Resources Act 1963 forbids most abstraction or impounding of water save under licence from a water authority. The relationship of the statutory and common-law rules on the abstraction of water was highlighted in *Cargill* v. *Gotts*.[34] Mr Cargill occupied Grove Farm at Gimmingham near Mundesley in Norfolk. Originally in a water cart, and eventually in a 900 gallon tanker or *bowser*, he had taken water for the farm from a mill-pond some 500 yards from his boundary since 1927. In 1977, the pond was acquired by Mr Gotts; he promptly prevented any more water being taken. In the Chancery Division of the High Court, Mr Cargill obtained a declaration that he was entitled to abstract water under an easement, £50 damages for the interference, and an injunction to stop interference in the future. The Court of Appeal agreed that there was an easement which had been established before the Water Resources Act 1963 but they discharged the injunction, on the basis that Mr Cargill was not entitled to use his easement until he obtained a licence. Although each load of water was under 1000 gallons, regular use constituted a *series of operations*. The water was used for crop spraying, and on other land than that where it was drawn. Nevertheless, the court allowed Mr Cargill a modified declaration and the majority allowed him damages of £50 on the basis that only the water authority was entitled to take action against an illegal abstraction.

(d) Rights of way

Rights of way are vital forms of easement. They may allow electricity, gas or water to be brought onto the dominant land. Such services are usually provided by statutory undertakers, acting under express statutory powers, but if no statutory power is available, an easement is necessary. In *Simmons* v. *Midford*[35] the owner of a house at New Malden had a drain which ran under neighbouring land. She successfully obtained an injunction to stop another householder linking her house to this drain. The owners of the land where the drain was laid had no right to authorize anyone else to connect into it. However, a right of way normally consists of access to one piece of land across other land. It may provide the only means of reaching the public highway. It may be for limited purposes, for example, removing timber when this is felled,[36] or it may be confined to limited types of traffic, such as pedestrians.[37] The use of a right of way may expand, for example to allow for more customers and delivery vehicles to a growing business,[38] or for an increase in the number of caravans using a caravan site.[39] However, the right may not be used for a completely new purpose. Thus if a field is turned into a camping site, access for agricultural purposes cannot be used to bring in caravans and cars.[40] In *Bracewell* v. *Appleby*,[41] Mr Appleby built himself a new home in a cul-de-sac called Hill Road, Heath End, Surrey, partly on the garden of his previous house, and partly on new land which he had bought for the purpose. Two neighbours sued for an injunction to stop Appleby living in the new house as they considered that it interfered with the amenity of the cul-de-sac. Graham J. held that Appleby's right of access to his original house did not entitle him to get to the new house. However, the judge granted the neighbours damages rather than an injunction since they had delayed in bringing their proceedings until the building was nearly complete.

A right of way will usually lie over a particular route. Users may only make a detour to avoid an obstruction over land belonging to a person who was responsible for the obstruction. In *Stacey* v. *Sherin*,[42] the Great Western Railway Company upgraded one of its lines and made an agreement with Stacey providing him with a new way across the line. Under the agreement, a level-crossing was closed. The King's Bench Divisional Court held that Sherin, who had also been entitled to use the crossing, was not liable in trespass when he used the new route across Stacey's land. Again, a right of way may be over a clearly defined route or it may simply be a right between two points. As Mellish L.J. said in a case concerned with a right across Wimbledon Common:[43] 'If the owner of the servient tenement does not point out the line of way, then the grantee must take the nearest way he can.' The owner of the servient tenement may set out a reasonably specific route, and then the user, 'is not entitled to go out of the way merely because the way is rough and, there are ruts in it and so forth'. The owner of the right of way is responsible for maintaining it in a usable state.

Even if a right of way is along a defined route, the owner of the servient land will be free to build on it provided this does not unreasonably interfere with it. In *Clifford* v. *Hoare*,[44] Colonel Clifford, a gentleman usher of the black rod in the House of Commons, bought building land off Kensington Road in London. Lady Ashburton was sold another site with authority to build a portico with columns whose bases encroached slightly onto Colonel Clifford's access. The Court of Common Pleas held that there had been no breach of the right of way. By contrast, a public right of way will be over a defined route and the owner of the servient land must not encroach upon it. However, a private right of way may follow the same route as a public one, so that for example if the public route is closed the private right may survive.[45]

(e) Access and use of neighbouring land

Often an easement entitles the occupier of one piece of land to go onto other land for some purposes other than that of getting to another place. It is here that new forms of easement are most frequently recognized by the courts. Thus it was established in *Re. Ellenborough Park*,[46] that it is possible to have an easement attached to one piece of land, entitling the occupier to use other land nearby for walking or general recreational purposes. In *Miller* v. *Emcer Products*,[47] the Court of Appeal recognized as an easement the right of a ground-floor tenant to use lavatories on the upper floor of the leased building. Easements may be created to enable a landowner to go onto neighbouring land to repair his building which he cannot reach from his own property,[48] or to safeguard his own land by constructing anti-flood works.[49] Where a right exists which can only be used with access to other land, the necessary right of access will be implied. This will include a right of access to repair the surface of a right of way or a neighbour's building which provides an easement of support.[50] It may allow the person entitled to use drainage pipes on someone else's land to repair these, or even to enlarge or resite them if this is necessary.[51] In *Central Electricity Generating Board* v. *Jennaway*,[52] the Board acquired a statutory easement to run power lines between Castle Donnington in Leicestershire and the borders of Northamptonshire and Buckinghamshire. Lloyd Jacob J. held that this implied the further right to erect three steel pylons on Jennaway's land, under 'the well established doctrine that in the grant of an easement or like right the law will imply the additional grant of what is necessary for the enjoyment of the same'.

(f) Rights to light

Rights to light are an important form of negative easement. In its natural state, land is assumed to be sufficiently well lit from overhead, but an easement may be acquired to protect light to a building from neighbouring land. The right must be acquired in respect of particular windows or some other aperture such as a skylight.[53] Side light to open land such as a garden can only be protected by a covenant.[54] Normally, a landowner cannot prevent the erection of buildings which overlook his property or spoil his view. However, he may prevent the erection of a building close to his boundary which will require light from his land, by opposing this building acquiring *ancient lights*, that is an easement of light by long use. In *Mayor of Paddington* v. *Attorney General*,[55] Paddington Corporation, which managed the church yard of St Mary's church Paddington, passed a resolution to put up screens so as to prevent the builder of a block of flats facing the yard from acquiring ancient lights. The builder failed to obtain an injunction to stop the screen being put up, even though the corporation had no power to put up buildings on the church yard. Today a landowner who wishes to prevent a neighbour acquiring a right to light by long use would have difficulty in obtaining planning permission for such a screen. However, he may protect his land by registering an objection under the Rights of Light Act 1959. This serves as an imaginary screen lasting for up to one year so as to prevent a right to light being established.

Once a building has an established easement for a particular source of light, if the building is altered or replaced by another, the right will survive. Also, if the light to which the building is entitled is reduced, compensation may be obtained for loss of light to other windows which are affected as well. In *Re London Tilbury and Southend Railway Co. and Trustees of Gower's Walk Schools*,[56] in 1884 the school put up new buildings in Lambeth; some of its windows corresponded with windows in the buildings which had been there before, others did not. When, in 1886, the railway company built a warehouse opposite, it had to pay compensation for interference with both types of windows.

The House of Lords stated in *Colls* v. *Home and Colonial Stores*,[57] that the amount of light which may be acquired by uninterrupted use 'is what is required for the ordinary purposes of inhabitants or any business of the tenement according to the ordinary notions of mankind'[58] There, the House concluded that there was no breach of a right to light for an office in Shoreditch when two of five ground-floor windows were obstructed by a new building. In *Ough* v. *King*,[59] the Court of Appeal upheld a county court award of damages for interference of light to one house in Gravesend by additions to the house next door. The court held that in deciding the levels of light required under a particular easement, 'the general nature of the locality could be taken into account, such as whether it is residential or industrial'. The Court of Appeal also agreed with the trial judge that acceptable standards of light could change, and had improved, possibly because of the development of artificial lighting. 'I do not think that ordinary people would accept now [in 1967] for a living room and office on the outskirts of a town like Gravesend, the daylight standard which was accepted 12 years ago for an office in the City of London.' The court rejected a technical test propounded by the defendant's surveyor, who had written a book on the subject jointly with a barrister, that a room could not acquire a right to more light than would illuminate half of it to the level of one lumen at table height.

In *Allen* v. *Greenwood*,[60] Mr and Mrs Allen successfully obtained an injunction to make their neighbour remove a caravan and a close-boarded fence which blocked light to their garden greenhouse in Rochdale and made it of little use for growing anything other than ferns. The Court of Appeal held that, for a greenhouse, an easement of light could include a right to the warmth from direct sunlight needed to grow plants. It also held that a specially high degree of light could be acquired even by long use, provided the owner of the servient land knew of the special need throughout the necessary period. Whether an easement could be acquired for direct sunlight for an indoor swimming pool or for solar panels was left open. It is also unclear whether an easement can be acquired for other special needs such as the proper display of stained glass windows in a church.[61]

In assessing the light needed for a particular building, account is taken of other available sources of light. Thus, where a masonic hall in Sheffield received light from two sides, on one of which Sheffield Corporation wished to build an art gallery and library, Maugham J. ruled that the size of the new building must be so restricted that if an equivalent building were put up on the other side, the two together would still leave adequate light for the masonic hall.[62]

(g) *Easements and the law of trespass and nuisance*

The acquisition of an easement may justify what would otherwise be a trespass to land. Thus an easement may be acquired to walk across a neighbour's land, or to construct a building against his wall. Indeed an easement may be acquired to grow espaliers or climbing plants such as virginia creeper over a neighbour's wall, even though no such easement can be acquired to grow a tree beyond a boundary.[63]

As we shall see in Chapter 7, Section 7.2, the law of nuisance restricts activities which indirectly harm neighbouring land. A right to carry them out may, however, be established as an easement. Thus a right may be established to direct flood water onto neighbouring land,[64] for factory chimneys to pollute the atmosphere,[65] or for an industrial process to pollute a river. However, if such a right is established a nuisance can still be proved, if the quality or quantity of pollution is shown to have significantly increased. Thus in *Baxendale* v. *McMurray*,[66] where a paper-making mill on the river Chess changed from using rags to esparto grass in its processes, The Court of Appeal in Chancery held that Baxendale, the owner of a large house down stream, could obtain an injunction if he showed that there was a greater amount of pollution under the new system.

4.4.5   Rights of common and other profits

A profit, or by its old title a *profit à prendre*, is a right to go onto the soil of another, to take either produce from the soil, or part of the soil itself. The manner in which such rights may significantly restrict the management and development of land is illustrated by the case of *Peech* v. *Best*.[67] In 1921, Best leased to Peech for fourteen years, the exclusive shooting and sporting rights over the 700 acres of Hazeley Farm at Twyford near Winchester. At the time, part of this farm was occupied as an army camp, but shortly afterwards this use ceased. In 1929, Best sold 12 acres on what had been the camp site to de Mestre, a horse trainer, for the erection of stables and related buildings. The courts held that Best had unlawfully interfered with Peech's rights, even though he could still shoot on the remainder of the farm. They did not, however, prevent the stables from being erected, but awarded Best £400 damages, which was one-sixth of the sale price to de Mestre.

(a)   The nature of rights of common and of profits generally

Profits first emerged as *rights of common*, where the inhabitants of a neighbourhood customarily took a particular benefit from certain land. Such customs originated when ancient settlers took over land from the wild and shared it for pasture or other purposes. Following the Norman Conquest of 1066, the manorial system was developed throughout the country, and, especially in lowland areas, land came to be legally vested in the lords of the manors. In the medieval rural economy, villagers relied heavily on rights of pasturing sheep, cattle and draught beasts on part of the land which had come to be vested in their lord. This part of the manorial land was termed the village waste. Other rights suitable for a rural economy were also developed, such as *turbary*, the right to cut peat or turf for fuel, and *estovers*, the right to take wood for domestic purposes, such as fuel, or repairs to buildings or fencing. Another important group of such rights were sporting rights, such as *piscary* for fishing and *auceptary* for fowling. As the manorial system disintegrated, land subject to rights of common generally passed out of the hands of lords of the manor. However, today where more than one person is entitled to take a particular benefit from land, there is still a right of common, even if only one other person shares it with the owner of the soil. Today many pieces of land known as commons are used for public recreation. Such a name will have originated in the shared rights of a restricted group of people rather than of the public at large. However, as we have seen in Chapter 3, Section 3.5, statute has granted certain public rights of access over such land, at any rate in urban areas.

It is often believed that commons are easily recognizable by being open and unfenced. The common law did hold that fences could not be erected on commons. However, surrounding land was often fenced to keep animals on a common. More recently, the destruction of many hedges in arable areas on land not subject to rights of common has also made it hard to distinguish common land. Today, therefore, it may not be easy to judge the legal status of land by whether or not it is hedged or fenced. However, it remains true that rights of common have meant that many areas have been left open and provide a distinctive landscape.[68] Apart from old rights of common, profits came to be recognized as rights which could be claimed by one or more individuals over the land of another, even to the exclusion of the owner himself. These are *sole* or *several* profits.

(b) Registration of rights of common

The Commons Registration Act 1965 required all common land to be entered in a new register together with rights of common over such land and the names of persons entitled to them.[69] For these purposes, sole profits must also be registered as if they were rights in common. However, rights for a term of years or from year to year are not included.[70] The registers are kept by county councils and are available for public inspection. Provisional application for registration of old common land had to be submitted by 2 January 1970.[71] The Act set up Commons Commissioners to adjudicate on disputes. Unchallenged applications have now been confirmed in the register, although the backlog of disputed applications will continue to provide interesting points of ancient law on commons for a long time to come as they are processed by the Commissioners.

Common land may be registered where it is 'waste land of a manor not subject to rights of common'. There may be value in such bare commons for safeguarding public rights of access where these exist. Also, local authorities have power to manage derelict wastes under ss. 8 and 9 of the Act. Where the lord of a manor has not disposed of the soil of the manorial waste but has no other land in the vicinity, it may well be impossible to trace him. Where land is finally registered as common land but no one has been registered as owner of the soil, the Commons Commissioners have jurisdiction to find out who is the owner. Until they have succeeded, a local authority may protect the land from unlawful interference in place of the owner. Where land is registered as a common, even if the public have no right of access, and though the local authority does not take charge of it, the legal restrictions on building on commons will ensure that it remains an open space.

Unless it transpires that the land was part of a highway, final registration is conclusive evidence that it was common land at the date of registration.[72] However, future changes will be possible. Amendments of the register are to be made where rights of common are transferred or otherwise altered, and, more fundamentally, the register may be amended to delete land which ceases to be common land or to add land which becomes common land.[73] Methods for creating and extinguishing such rights are outlined in Chapter 5, Sections 5.4 and 5.5.

The High Court may order amendment of a register of commons where fraud prevented an objection being made or if for some other reason there has been an erroneous entry.[74]

(c) Profits appurtenant or in gross

There is a distinction between profits which benefit the land of the person claiming them and so are *appurtenant* to that land, and profits which are the personal right of the claimant. These are profits *in gross*. A profit in gross where the owner of the soil is excluded from taking the same material, may be *without stint*, that is unlimited save to the extent that it conflicts with other rights of the owner of the soil. Fishing rights, in particular, are often held in gross and may be of considerable financial importance.[75] A land owner selling land by a river may well retain the fishing rights. However, the law has been concerned to protect land from being overburdened by profits which would impair its use by the owner of the soil. Thus, if a profit is held by virtue of title in another piece of land it appears that only where it is specifically quantified may it be detached from that other land and disposed of as a commercial asset in gross. Rights of pasture came to be let or *agisted* by the persons entitled to them,[76] and such rights must now be registered in relation to a specific number of beasts.[77] Whether they are detached or remain attached for the benefit of land, rights of pasture may be subdivided,[78] at least unless they are split amongst so many people that it becomes impracticable to exercise them. Thus if land with rights of pasture still attached were subdivided into tiny freehold plots for sale as souvenirs so that each piece of land would only be entitled to graze a fraction of a cow, this would seem likely to extinguish the right altogether, though even then a number of owners of such fractional rights might combine so as to use them.[79]

Unlike pasture, certain profits are necessarily defined in terms of the land they are to benefit. Turbary is essentially a right of common for providing fuel for the homes of the commoners. It will only be recognized for the benefit of a specific number of hearths. However, if a house entitled to fuel from neighbouring land is demolished and replaced by another building, fuel may be taken for the same number of hearths in the new building.[80] A summer house or studio replacing an old cottage could be fuelled in this way from neighbouring land. A right to turf, or indeed to soil, may exist for the benefit of a garden but it would only be recognized if the exact needs of the garden were clear;[81] for example, if the right were to repair an identifiable lawn with turf, but not if it were claimed to make new banks whenever the owner felt like redesigning his garden. Profits which are attached for the benefit of land and ascertained in terms of the needs of that land can not be turned into commercial enterprises in their own right. Thus it was held in *Bailey* v. *Stephens*[82] that there could be no right appurtenant to the land of the defendant to take two trees from the plaintiff's wood, apparently to sell, rather than for any use connected with the defendant's own land. Similarly in *Clayton* v. *Corby*[83] no right was recognized to take unlimited quantities of clay to feed a brick kiln on the taker's land. Today a commercial agreement to take wood or materials would normally be made for a term of years rather than as a permanent grant of such rights in gross. A permanent grant would have to be registered under the Commons Registration Act 1965.

NOTES: SECTION 4.4

1. *Rangeley* v. *Midland Railway Company* (1868) 3 Ch. App. 306.
2. *Hanbury* v. *Jenkins* (1901) 2 Ch. 401.
3. *Bailey* v. *Stephens* (1862) 12 C.B., N.S. 91, *per* Byles J. at p. 115 *obiter dicta.*
4. *Todrick* v. *Western National Omnibus Company* [1934] Ch. 561.
5. *Moody* v. *Steggles* (1879) L.R. 12 Ch. D. 261.
6. *Hill* v. *Tupper* (1863) 2 Hurl. & Colt. 121.
7. Sturley M.F. (1980) Easements in gross, 96 L.Q.R., 557.
8. *Borman* v. *Griffith* [1930] 1 Ch. 493.
9. *Bass* v. *Gregory* (1890) 25 Q.B.D. 481.
10. *Harris* v. *De Pinna* (1886) 33 Ch.D. 238, C.A.
11. *Mulliner* v. *Midland Railway Company* (1897) 11 Ch.D. 611.
12. *National Guaranteed Manure Co. Ltd* v. *Donald* (1859) 4 Hurls. and Norm. 8.
13. This principle was assumed as a result of *obiter dicta* by Farewell J. in *International Tea Stores Co.* v. *Hobbs* [1903] 2 Ch. 165, and in *A.G.* v. *Antrobus* [1905] 2 Ch. 188. However, a right to walk merely for recreation had in fact been recognized in the older case of *Duncan* v. *Louch* (1845) 6 Q.B. 904.
14. *Re Ellenborough Park* [1956] Ch. 131, C.A.
15. *Jones* v. *Pritchard* [1908] 1 Ch. 630.
16. *Lawrence* v. *Jenkins* (1873) 8 L.R.Q.B. 274. More recently such a quasi easement was recognized by the Court of Appeal in respect of a boundary with common land at Binswood Common in Hampshire, in *Egerton* v. *Harding*, Q.B. 62. [1975] Curiously it is possible that an obligation to repair fences cannot be attached to land by an express covenant even though it can be created by prescription; contrast Wilmer L.J. and Diplock L.J. in *Jones* v. *Price* [1965] 2 Q.B. 618.
17. *Copeland* v. *Greenhalf* [1952] Ch. 488. An easement to store things on someone else's property on a smaller scale does seem to be possible, however. In *Wright* v. *Macadam* [1949] 2 K.B. 744, C.A., the Court of Appeal recognized the right of a tenant to use a coal shed on land retained by the landlord. This is supported by the Privy Council decision of *Attorney General of Southern Nigeria* v. *John Holt & Co. (Liverpool) Ltd* [1915] A.C. 599.
18. *Harmer* v. *Jumbil (Nigeria) Tin Areas Ltd* [1921] 1 Ch. 200.
19. *Aldin* v. *Latimer Clark, Muirhead & Co.* [1894] 2 Ch. 437, compare *Harris* v. *De Pinna, supra* note 10.

20. *Grosvenor Hotel* v. *Hamilton* [1894] 2 Q.B. 836, C.A.
21. *Browne* v. *Flower* [1911] 1 Ch. 219.
22. *Webb* v. *Bird* (1862) 13 C.B. N.S. 841.
23. *Bryant* v. *Lefever* (1879) 4 C.P.D. 172.
24. *Lemmon* v. *Webb* [1895] A.C. 1, *per* Lord Herschell L.C. at p. 6.
25. *Phipps* v. *Pears* [1965] 1 Q.B. 76, C.A., *per* Lord Denning at p. 83.
26. *Ray* v. *Fairway Motor (Barnstaple) Ltd* (1969) 20 P. & C.R. 261.
27. *Dalton* v. *Angus* (1881) 6 L.R. App. Cas. 740, *per* Lord Penzance at p. 804.
28. *Popplewell* v. *Hodgkinson* (1869) 4 L.R. Exch. 248, and see *Langbrook Properties Ltd* v. *Surrey County Council* [1970] 1 W.L.R. 161, *post* p. 348.
29. *Jordeson* v. *Sutton Southcoats and Drypool Gas Co.* [1899] 2 Ch. 217.
30. *Lotus Ltd* v. *British Soda Ltd* [1972] 1 Ch. 123.
31. *Mayor of Bradford* v. *Pickles* [1895] A.C. 587. H.L.
32. *Swindon Waterworks Co.* v. *Wiltshire and Berkshire Canal Navigation Co.* (1875) 7 L.R. H.L. 697, *per*, Lord Cairns L.C. at p. 704.
33. *Rugby Joint Water Board* v. *Walters* [1966] 1 Ch. 397.
34. *Cargill* v. *Gotts* [1981] 1 W.L.R. 441, C.A., *ante* p. 96.
35. *Simmons* v. *Midford* [1969] 2 Ch. 415.
36. *Hollins* v. *Verney* (1834) 13 Q.B.D. 304.
37. *Cousens* v. *Rose* (1871) 12 L.R. Eq. 366.
38. *Woodhouse & Co. Ltd* v. *Kirkland (Derby) Ltd* [1970] 1 W.L.R. 1185.
39. *British Railways Board* v. *Glass* [1964] 1 W.L.R. 538.
40. *R.C.P. Holdings Ltd* v. *Rogers* [1953] 1 All E.R. 1029.
41. *Bracewell* v. *Appleby* [1975] 1 Ch. 408.
42. *Stacey* v. *Sherin* (1913) 29 T. L. R. 555.
43. *Wimbledon and Putney Commons Conservators* v. *Dixon* [1875] 1 Ch. 362, *per* Mellish L.J. at p. 370.
44. *Clifford* v. *Hoare* (1874) 9 L.R. C.P. 362.
45. *Walsh* v. *Oates* (1953) 1 Q.B. 578, C.A.
46. *Re Ellenborough Park* [1956] Ch. 131. see *ante*, p. 195.
47. *Miller* v. *Emcer Products* [1956] Ch. 304.
48. *Philpot* v. *Bath* (1905) 21 T.L.R. 634.
49. *Ward* v. *Kirkland* [1967] Ch. 194.
50. *Bond* v. *Nottingham Corpn* [1940] Ch. 429, *per* Sir Wilfred Greene M.R., at p. 439.
51. *Finlinson* v. *Porter* (1875) 10 L.R. Q.B. 188, see too *Simmons* v. *Midford, supra* note 35, *per* Buckley J. *obiter dicta* at p. 422.
52. *Central Electricity Generating Board* v. *Jennaway* [1959] 1 W.L.R. 937.
53. *Easton* v. *Isted* [1903] 1 Ch. 405.
54. *Potts* v. *Smith* (1867) 6 Eq. 311, *post* p. 210f.
55. *Mayor of Paddington* v. *Attorney General* [1906] A.C. 1, H.L.
56. *Re London Tilbury and Southend Railway Co. and Trustees of Gower's Walk Schools* (1889) 24 Q.B.D. 326, C.A.
57. *Colls* v. *Home and Colonial Stores* [1904] A.C. 179, H.L.
58. *Ibid. per* Lord Davey at p. 204.
59. *Ough* v. *King* [1967] 1 W.L.R. 1547, C.A.
60. *Allen* v. *Greenwood* [1980] 1 W.L.R. 119, C.A.
61. *Newham* v. *Lawson* (1971) 22 P. & C.R. 852.
62. *Sheffield Masonic Hall Co. Ltd* v. *Sheffield Corpn* [1932] 2 Ch. 17.
63. *Simpson* v. *Weber* (1925) 133 L.T.R. 46. cf. *Lemmon* v. *Webb* [1895] A.C. 1, *ante* p. 198 and *supra* note 24.

64. *Simpson* v. *Mayor of Godmanchester* [1897] A.C. 696.
65. *Crump* v. *Lambert* (1867) 3 L.R. Eq. 409.
66. *Baxendale* v. *McMurray* (1867) 2 Ch. App. 790.
67. *Peech* v. *Best* [1931] 1 K.B. 1, C.A.
68. On the influence of commons on the English landscape see Hoskins, W.G. (1955) *The Making of the English Landscape*, Hodder and Stoughton, London, and Stamp L.D. and Hoskins, W.G. (1963) *The Common Lands of England and Wales*, Collins, London.
69. Commons Registration Act 1965, ss. 2 and 3.
70. Ibid. s. 22 (1).
71. S.I. 1966, Nos. 1470 and 1471; S.I. 1968, No. 658.
72. Commons Registration Act 1965, s. 10.
73. Ibid. s. 13, and Commons Registration (New Land) Regulations, 1969, S.I. 1969, No. 1843.
74. Commons Registration Act 1965, s. 14.
75. *Staffordshire and Worcestershire Canal Navigation* v. *Bradley* [1912] 1 Ch. 91.
76. *Bunn* v. *Channen* (1813) 5 Taun. 244.
77. Commons Registration Act 1965, s. 15.
78. *White* v. *Taylor* (No. 2) 1969 1 Ch. 160.
79. *Nichols* v. *Chapman* (1860) 5 Hurl. & Nor. 643.
80. *Attorney General* v. *Reynolds* [1911] 2 K.B. 888.
81. *Lady Wilson* v. *Willes* (1806) 7 East 121.
82. *Bailey* v. *Stephens* (1862) 12 C.B., N.S. 91.
83. *Clayton* v. *Corby* (1843) 5 Q.B. 415.

4.5   Covenants and land use

In 1981, the occupants of five houses in Heddon Banks, a road in the Northumberland village of Heddon-on-the-Wall objected when they learnt that Mr Gilbert, round the corner in Centurion Way, was intending to build three new houses. Mr Gilbert had bought his land in 1954 subject to a restrictive covenant: 'Not to erect on the piece of land hereby conveyed any building whatsoever other than one private dwelling house with proper offices and outbuildings (including at the purchaser's option a private garage). . . .' Below Mr Gilbert's plot was open land in a green belt,[1] and two seats had been placed on Centurion Way for the public to admire the view (Fig. 4.9). Mr Gilbert obtained planning permission for his three proposed houses and applied to the Lands Tribunal for permission to override the restrictive covenant under powers which we shall look at in Chapter 5, Section 5.4. However, his neighbours in Heddon Banks were entitled to the benefit of the covenant and they successfully resisted Mr Gilbert's application in the Lands Tribunal and then in the Court of Appeal.[2] The dispute turned on whether the restrictive covenant gave any practical benefit of substantial value to the objectors.[3] The Court of Appeal held that it did, and that even although the objectors lived round the corner from the site, the covenant 'could be said to touch and concern [their] land'. Its loss could destroy the

Fig. 4.9 The view from Centurion Way, Heddon-on-the-Wall, Northumberland, January 1984.

character of the whole estate by increasing the density of housing and obstructing the view. As Waller L.J. commented: 'the objectors on this estate have the advantage of the view over the Tyne Valley for many miles, a wholly rural view in what is an industrial neighbourhood. A view is not something that can be valued in money terms: indeed it may be, and perhaps I would say in this case is, priceless.'

Covenants are contained in contracts. As we shall see in Chapter 6, Section 6.5, under English Law they are normally personal and can not be enforced against someone who was not a party to the original contract.[4] However, the courts developed principles whereby covenants could be attached to pieces of land, and their benefit and burden passed on to those who later acquired the dominant and servient land respectively.

4.5.1   Transferring the benefits of covenants

(a) At law

At law, it has long been relatively easy to create a covenant which will benefit a particular piece of land, even when that land changes hands. If a property company builds a housing estate, it may agree with those who buy the houses on the estate that it will continue to maintain open spaces and planting. If the houses are resold, successive householders may be able to compel the company to carry out this agreement. For the benefit of a covenant to attach to land, it must be written so as to *touch and concern* that land. Thus in *Dyson* v. *Forster*,[5] Forster successfully sued for compensation for damage caused by mining to the surface of land which he had acquired in County Durham. He was able to enforce a covenant made by the Ecclesiastical Commissioners, from whom he had bought his land, with the person who had acquired and was still exploiting the mining rights. Lord Macnaughten in the House of Lords, said that the test was: 'Does this covenant affect the nature quality or value of the land, or is it a covenant simply collateral?' The covenant here was 'beneficial to the surface owner and no one else'.

A purely personal contract will not touch and concern land. For example if a seed manufacturer agreed to provide free seeds each year to a horticultural expert so that he could try them out over an extended period, this would hardly be a contract which touched and concerned the expert's garden, and so could not be enforced by someone to whom he sold the garden. However, it is often difficult to be certain when a covenant is personal and when it does touch and concern a particular piece of land. A covenant to provide seeds could be attached to a piece of land, at law, if the purpose behind the arrangement was that the seeds should be grown each year in the same ground. Identifying such covenants is the more difficult because it is not necessary for them to state expressly that they are for the benefit of a particular piece of land. It is sufficient if this can be shown by extrinsic evidence. Also, although the covenant must benefit a piece of land, it is only enforceable at law against the original convenantor personally, and he need have no interest in land in the vicinity. Such covenants may be most useful where the covenantee is a corporation, particularly a public one. Thus in *Smith and Snipes Hall Farm Ltd* v. *River Douglas Catchment Board*,[6] farmers with land in Lancashire which was subject to flooding, agreed with a drainage board to contribute to flood protection works. When these failed to contain later floods because they had been carried out defectively, the Court of Appeal held that Mr Smith, who had acquired some of the land intended to be protected, was entitled to receive compensation under the covenant, even though the agreement had not actually identified the land.

A legally enforceable covenant, therefore, may be made, to carry out specific works, such as new flood banks, or to provide a regular service such as supplying water to a house.[7] However, in some circumstances, the benefit of a covenant can not pass at law. For example the covenant may be for the benefit of an equitable interest only. A landscape gardener with a life interest in a piece of land where he carried on his business might make a covenant for his neighbour to provide water and electricity for the business. Even if this was clearly intended to benefit the land used by the landscape gardener, it would only be an equitable interest. If the landscape gardener sold his interest, the benefit of the covenant would not pass, at law, to the purchaser.

Also, at law, a benefit will only pass if the original estate is kept intact. If a farmer sells a building site to a developer and agrees not to build on the remainder of his farm, at law, the householders who buy individual plots from the developer can not enforce the covenant against the farmer.

(b) In equity

Where the law failed to transfer the benefit of a covenant with the land it was intended to benefit, then equity often stepped in. Now, as we shall see under the next heading, statute may provide a much more extensive solution, but in any case where the statutory provisions do not apply, the equitable rules may still be important. It is clear that where equity makes the burden of a restrictive covenant pass on the transfer of servient land,[8] for example a covenant not to build on an open space, it will also be prepared to treat the benefit as passing on the transfer of the dominant land. It is possible that, even where the burden is positive, as in the example of the landscape gardener in the previous paragraph, equity may enable the benefit, although not the burden, to change hands. Thus, if a landscape gardener, with the benefit of rights to water and power from adjacent land, for use on land over which he had a life interest, sold that life interest, in equity his successor would be able to claim the water and power from the original owner of the adjacent land. Again, if a person entitled to the benefit of a positive covenant splits up his land, in equity the individuals who acquire each plot may be able to enforce the covenant, against the original covenantor.[9]

For the benefit of a covenant to pass in equity, just as at law, the covenant must *touch and concern* the land which is to benefit. In addition the benefit must either be annexed initially to the land, or the original covenantee must assign it clearly at the same time as passing on his own interest in the dominant land. However, courts have progressively taken the view that provided a covenant clearly does *touch and concern* a piece of land, it is implicitly attached for its benefit.[10]

(c) Under the Law of Property Act 1925, s. 78

The Law of Property Act 1925, s. 78 reads:

A covenant relating to any land shall be deemed to be made with the covenantee and his successors in title and the persons deriving title under him or them, and shall have the effect as if such successors and other persons were expressed. For the purposes of this subsection in connection with covenants restrictive of the user of land *successors in title* shall be deemed to include the owners and occupiers for the time being of the land of the covenantee intended to be benefitted.

Thus, in *Smith and Snipes Hall Farm Ltd* v. *River Douglas Catchment Board*,[11] where breach of a covenant to provide flood protection works resulted in a farm being flooded, both Mr Smith, as owner, and Snipe Hall Farm Ltd, which was the tenant of the flooded farm, were entitled to recover damages from the Board which had broken the covenant.

In *Federated Homes Ltd* v. *Mill Lodge Properties Ltd*,[12] in 1980, the Court of Appeal held that, where a restrictive covenant was written so that it was for the benefit of a given piece of land, s. 78 had the effect of annexing the covenant to that land. Federated Homes and Mill Lodge both bought sections of land at Newport Pagnall in Buckinghamshire with outline planning permission for dwelling houses. Mill Lodge bought its section from the development company which obtained the planning permission, subject to a covenant that it should not build more than 300 dwellings 'so as not to reduce the number of units which the vendor might eventually erect on the retained land under the existing planning consent'. 'The retained land' was treated by the court as meaning 'any adjoining or adjacent land retained by the vendor', an expression used elsewhere in the conveyance. Federated Homes obtained their part of the site after it had passed through the hands of two intermediary developers, but the Court of Appeal held that s. 78 had the effect of passing on to them the benefit of the covenant against Mill Lodge's land and that they were entitled to prevent Mill Lodge from building an extra thirty-two houses for which that company had obtained new planning permission. This interpretation of s. 78 has been strongly criticized.[13] It had previously been thought that all the section was intended to do was to save time in conveyancing. Once a covenant was clearly annexed to the benefit of land, the section ensured that it would automatically pass with the land each time it was transferred. The *Federated Homes* case means that the section has the effect of annexing the benefit of a covenant in the first place. Indeed it may have that effect even if the parties make clear that they only want the present owner of the land to benefit. In the same case, the Court of Appeal also approved the view that once a covenant is attached for the benefit of one area of land it continues to benefit the individual parts of the estate if the estate is later subdivided.

4.5.2 Transferring the burdens of covenants

The burden of a covenant has always been harder to attach to land than the benefit. However, at law there are means of ensuring that even a positive burden is passed on to successive owners of servient land. In the case of restrictive covenants equity now enables the burden to be attached quite easily.

(a) Restrictive covenants

Unless it states otherwise, a restrictive covenant will bind the original covenantor, even after he has ceased to control the relevant land.[14] Thus, if the owner of a factory covenants that no building shall take place on a garden in the factory grounds, and building is carried out by a later purchaser, the original owner can be sued for damages, unless he expressly provided in the covenant that he would not be responsible for successors in title. However, equity also allows the covenant to be directly enforced against the purchaser, and may stop him building, by means of an injunction.[15]

The modern equitable restrictive covenant was established in 1848, in *Tulk v. Moxhay*.[16] In 1808 Tulk had sold the open space in Leicester Square (Fig. 4.10) 'with the equestrian statue then standing in the centre thereof, and the iron railing and stone work round the same' to one Elms. This land was eventually acquired by Moxhay, who proposed building on it. Tulk still owned houses on the square and claimed that Moxhay was bound by a covenant which he had imposed when he sold the open space, that Elms and his successors should 'keep and maintain the said piece of ground and square garden, and the iron railing round the same in its then form, and in sufficient and proper repair as a square garden and pleasure ground, in an open state, uncovered with any buildings, in neat and ornamental order'. Lord Cottenham L.C. approved an injunction to prevent building, because it was inequitable to allow a person to use land in a manner inconsistent with a contract which he knew had been made by the previous owner of the land.

The covenant which was enforced in Tulk's case looks like a positive one but it was enforced because it included what was essentially an agreement not to build on open land. An essentially positive covenant will not attach to land

Fig. 4.10 Leicester Square, London, January 1984.

even in equity. Thus if a piece of land is sold to a developer, on condition that buildings of a certain quality and type are to be erected and maintained there, those who subsequently acquire that land can not be compelled to build or maintain such buildings.[17] Where a covenant includes both positive and negative elements the negative parts may still be enforced after the positive parts have been severed, provided they are still meaningful. In *Shepherd Homes Ltd* v. *Sandham* (No. 2)[18] a covenant on an open-plan housing estate required householders both to maintain their gardens and to refrain from erecting fences. Although maintenance could not be enforced, Meggary J. held that the obligation not to fence could be. However, if a covenant is essentially negative, as in Tulk's case itself, it does not matter if it is framed in a positive form. Thus in *Powell* v. *Hemsley*,[19] Powell, who owned Lenton Hall near Nottingham, claimed that there had been a breach of a covenant, on part of the estate which had previously been sold off, that no building was to be carried out unless plans were first approved by the owners of the Hall. Eve J. held that this was a valid covenant. Where a restrictive covenant has been broken, the courts will readily make a positive order in the form of a mandatory injunction, for example requiring the demolition of buildings erected in breach of covenant.[20]

Restrictive covenants have been treated by the courts as an extended form of negative easement. Normally, like an easement,[21] a restrictive covenant must benefit some dominant land. In *London County Council* v *Allen*,[22] to get building approval to lay out two new streets, Allen entered into a deed against putting up any building on part of the relevant land, so as to leave space for future extensions of the streets. The county council later tried to make the then owners of the relevant land, including Allen's wife, pull down houses they had put up in breach of the covenant. The Court of Appeal held that the covenant was not enforceable against anyone other than the original covenantor, because the local authority had no land in the vicinity which the covenant was designed to benefit. Today, under statute, local authorities, and also the National Trust, are empowered to enforce such covenants in the general public interest and not just where they control nearby land.[23] However, ordinary sellers of land and others who take out restrictive covenants to control development can still enforce these if they retain land nearby which benefits from the protection of the covenants. Courts may also treat a covenant as invalid if it is drafted for the benefit of an excessively wide area. Thus, in *Re Ballard's Conveyance*,[24] when part of an estate at Chiswick in Hertfordshire was sold off, the sale included a covenant against building on the remainder of the estate, which consisted of some 1700 acres. Clarkson J. held that by far the larger part of this acreage, 'could not possibly be affected by any breach of the stipulations', and therefore the whole covenant was invalid. However, a court may uphold a wide covenant on the basis that the original covenantee reasonably took the view that it was of value to the estate as a whole. In *Wrotham Park* v. *Parkside Homes*,[25] Brightman J. treated as valid a covenant against building on a plot of land in Hertfordshire, where the estate which was to be protected was some 4000 acres scattered in three main areas in the county.

(b) Positive covenants

The special equitable rules which enable the burden of restrictive covenants to run with land do not apply to positive covenants, such as an agreement to maintain planting in a park or to maintain a monument for the benefit of surrounding houses. Nevertheless, as we have seen in Chapter 3, Section 3.2, if a local authority is a party to such an agreement made under special statutory powers, it may be enforceable against subsequent owners of the servient land.[26] There are also certain arrangements whereby private parties may effectively use positive covenants to protect land. The traditional means of doing so is by a chain of related contracts. If a developer builds a housing estate and agrees to keep up a park for the benefit of each plot on the estate, the individual householders and their successors may be able to recover compensation from the developer if the maintenance is not carried out, even if he no longer has any interest in the land.[27] To ensure that he is not out of pocket when he sells the land, the developer may obtain a new covenant from the purchaser. The purchaser may do the same when he re-sells the land. Such arrangements have limitations. The original covenantor may die or cease to exist. Even if he is still available to be sued, the only remedy which the courts will grant under any of the contracts is damages. If one link in the chain is missing, as when a later purchaser can not be found, or is dead, there will be no means of bringing pressure on the present owner of the servient land to carry out the covenant. Chain covenants may be made more effective if each current owner of the servient land who sells it brings in the current owner of the dominant land as a party to the renewed covenant with the purchaser.[28]

Another arrangement for maintaining positive covenants is to ensure that the occupiers entitled to their benefit themselves control the servient land. For example, they may each be allocated shares in a property company holding that land. Again, it may be possible to make use of the Law of Property Act 1925, s. 153. This provides for enlargement of leases for more than 300 years with over 200 years to run, provided no more than a nominal rent is paid for the lease. The tenant may simply make a deed giving himself the fee simple. However, the section stipulates that he is still bound by any covenants which would have applied under the lease. These may include positive obligations. Thus a developer wishing to dispose of land which he had retained on an estate may sell a long lease on the land. The purchaser enlarges this but his successors will then be subject to any positive covenants included in the long lease. A further device which may be used to protect positive covenants is for the original owner of the servient land to make the estate which he grants, conditional upon the observance of the covenant and to reserve a right of re-entry if it is not observed.[29] Thus, positive covenants may also be enforced where the owner of the servient land is taking some reciprocal benefit. In *Halsall* v. *Brizell*,[30] an estate in Liverpool, called Cressington Park, had been built in 1851 behind a sea wall. Covenants were made with the purchasers of each plot to contribute to the maintenance of communal services, including roads and a promenade on the sea wall. In 1950, the proprietors who managed the estate, and held the roads and sea wall as trustees, imposed an extra contribution on one of the plots because it had been let to a number of tenants. Upjohn J. held that the covenant did not allow for this higher contribution. However, he regarded the basic require- ment of paying to provide for services as enforceable against householders who had succeeded to the servient plots. They were taking advantage of services provided under the deed containing the covenant and, it would appear, by accepting these, had implicitly agreed to contribute towards their cost.

NOTES: SECTION 4.5

1. *Ante* p. 132.
2. *Gilbert* v. *Spoor* [1982] 2 All E.R. 576, C.A.
3. Law of Property Act 1925. s. 84 (1A) *post* p. 259.
4. *Post* p. 318.
5. *Dyson* v. *Forster* [1909] A.C. 98, H.L.
6. *Smith and Snipes Hall Farm Ltd* v. *River Douglas Catchment Board* [1949] 2 K.B. 500, C.A.
7. *Shayler* v. *Woolf* [1946] Ch. 320, C.A.
8. *Post* p. 214f.
9. In the case of negative covenants, see *Rogers* v. *Hosegood* [1900] 2 Ch 389, C.A.
10. The exact circumstances where the benefit of a covenant may be annexed to land or assigned with it in equity are matters of some uncertainty. See detailed discussions in Megarry, R.E. and Wade, H.W.E. (1975), *The Law of Real Property*, 4th edn, Stevens and Sons, London, p. 762 f; and Gray K.J. and Symes P.D., (1981), *Real Property and Real People*, Butterworth, London, p. 621 f.
11. *Supra* note 6.
12. *Federated Homes Ltd* v. *Mill Lodge Properties Ltd* [1980] 1 W.L.R. 594, C.A.
13. Newson G.H. (1981) *Universal Annexation*, 97 L.Q.R. 32.
14. Law of Property Act 1925, s. 79.
15. *Post* p. 382f.
16. *Tulk* v. *Moxhay* (1848) 2 Ph. 774.
17. *Haywood* v. *Brunswick Building Society* (1881) 8 Q.B.D. 403.
18. *Shepherd Homes Ltd* v. *Sandham* (No. 2.) [1971] 1 W.L.R. 1062.
19. *Powell* v. *Hemsley* [1909] 1 Ch. 680.
20. *Jackson* v. *Normanby Brick Co.* [1899] 1 Ch. 438. C.A.
21. *Ante* p. 193.
22. *London County Council* v. *Allen* [1914] 3 K.B. 642, C.A.

23. *Ante* p. 99f.
24. *Re Ballard's Conveyance* [1937] 1 Ch. 473.
25. *Wrotham Park* v. *Parkside Homes* [1974] 1 W.L.R. 798.
26. *Ante* p. 99f.
27. Provided the covenant did not exclude liability after the covenantee disposed of the property; Law of Property Act 1925, s. 79.
28. See further on the doctrine of Privity of Contract, *post* p. 318.
29. See *Shiloh Spinners Ltd* v. *Harding* [1973] A.C. 691, H.L.
30. *Halsall* v. *Brizell* [1957] Ch 169.

Chapter 5

MEANS OF ACQUIRING AND EXTINGUISHING CONTROL OF LAND

A Serjeant at the law who paid his calls,
Wary and wise, for clients at St. Paul's
There also was, of noted excellence.
Discreet he was, a man of reverence,
Or so he seemed, his sayings were so wise.
He often had been justice of Assize
By letters patent, and in full commission.
His fame and learning and his high position
Had won him many a robe and many a fee.
There was no such Conveyancer as he
All was fee-simple to his strong digestion,
Not one Conveyance could be called in question.
   Geoffrey Chaucer: The Prologue to *The Canterbury Tales*,
      (translated into modern English by Nevill Coghill)

Why may not that be the skull of a lawyer? Where be his
quiddits now, his quillets, his cases, his tenures, and his tricks
. . . Hum! This fellow might be in's time a great buyer of land,
with his statutes, his recognizances, his fines, his double
vouchers, his recoveries: is this the fine of his fines, and the
recovery of his recoveries, to have his fine pate full of fine dirt?
. . . The very conveyance of his lands will hardly lie in this box;
and must the inheritor himself have no more, ha?
    William Shakespeare, *Hamlet*, Act V, Scene I

Probably the work of lawyers which has always been most apparent to the
ordinary member of the public is the transfer of land. When the greatest
English writers refer to lawyers they often represent them as conveyancers of
land, and today private conveyancing is the monopoly of the legal profession.

Under the Solicitors Act 1974, s. 22 it is an offence for a legally unqualified person to draw or prepare an instrument relating to real or personal estate unless he shows that it was not done in expectation of any gain or reward. This monopoly is one of the means whereby the state provides control over the transfer of land today. However, the most extreme aspect of state intervention is in its own powers of compulsory acquisition.

5.1   The acquisition of control of land by public authorities

Of the methods of public control of land discussed in Chapter 3, the most sweeping is outright compulsory purchase. If a public authority has powers of compulsory purchase it usually has alternative powers to buy the land by a voluntary agreement with the existing owner, using the methods of land transfer outlined in Section 5.3. Whether it acquires a site voluntarily or compulsorily, a public authority will generally have special powers to extinguish subsidiary rights over that land and to acquire any new rights which it may need over other land so as to use effectively the land which it has acquired. The private landowner may have little hope of resisting the compulsory acquisition of his land, but he can delay the acquisition and ensure that it is done openly so that political pressures may be brought on the acquiring authority to change its mind. Special procedural safeguards are given to landowners who may themselves be seen as acting on behalf of the public, such as local authorities, statutory undertakers and the National Trust. The manner in which public bodies are prevented from acting outside their statutory powers and are compelled to follow fair procedural requirements is discussed in Chapter 8.

Today, land is still regarded as essentially private property, but existing owners may be seen on the one hand as custodians or stewards for the public benefit, or on the other as persons who hold it as essentially a private economic benefit. On the first view, the representatives of the public should be free to take over control where they decide that this is in the public interest. Because of the second view they may only do so if they pay compensation to the deprived owner for his economic loss.

5.1.1.   Methods of compulsory purchase

(a) Statutes authorizing compulsory purchase

From early days, Parliament could appropriate land by means of a specific Act. Occasionally such acts are still used today. Thus the Roosevelt Memorial Act 1946, provided for the erection of a memorial statue to President Franklin Roosevelt of the United States of America in Grosvenor Square, London, and expressly extinguished the exclusive rights of adjacent property

Fig. 5.1 Grosvenor Square, London, showing the Roosevelt Statue, January 1984.

owners over the square (Fig. 5.1). More often, express powers for extinguishing private rights or for acquiring public rights over land are provided in local Acts of Parliament authorizing the construction of major engineering works such as the Milford Haven oil refinery set up under the Gulf Oil Refinery Act 1965.[1]

By the middle of the nineteenth century, the need for public land had become so frequent that standardized procedures were introduced. Acts were passed providing general powers for the acquisition of land for certain purposes. The Acquisition of Land (Authorization Procedure) Act 1946 provided a single standard procedure which could be incorporated into other statutes giving powers of compulsory purchase for particular purposes. The standard procedure is now provided by the Acquisition of Land Act 1981. Normally, therefore, the authority for a particular compulsory purchase order today, will depend partly on the procedures set out in the Act of 1981 and partly on special statutory powers to make the order, given in another Act. Important examples of such special powers are found in the Town and Country Planning Act 1971, s. 112, whereby local authorities may take over land for development and other planning purposes, and s. 113 whereby the Secretary of State for the Environment may take land for the public service. Some statutes still provide their own procedures rather than relying upon the 1981 Act. Important examples are local authority powers to take land for slum clearance under the Housing Act 1957, Part III, Ministry of Agriculture powers to take land for afforestation or other forestry purposes under the

Forestry Act 1967, s. 40, and powers for the construction of new towns under the New Towns Act 1981.

(b) Compulsory purchase orders

Whether the statutory authority is contained in one special Act, or incorporates the standard procedure under the Acquisition of Land Act 1981, a compulsory purchase order is made, initially, by the acquiring authority. Then it is usually necessary for it to be confirmed by a higher authority. Thus a local planning authority order to take land for development, under the Town and Country Planning Act 1971, s. 112, must be confirmed by the Secretary of State for the Department of the Environment. However, when it is a Minister who makes an order, he will normally be able to confirm it himself after giving it publicity and taking account of objections. Under Part III of the 1981 Act, a confirming authority will normally be required to hold a public inquiry to consider any objections unless none are raised, or unless any objections which are made are really no more than claims for suitable compensation. Also, an inquiry may not be necessary where the issue has already been decided, notably where it has already been written into a development plan.[2]

Special protection is provided where certain types of land are taken under compulsory powers. Thus orders may have to be laid before Parliament, and may be annulled by Parliament, where they are intended to take local authority or National Trust land or the sites of ancient monuments. However, once an order has been made, it will probably be too late to protect land by transferring it to a body which enjoys special protection. In 1949 Islington Borough Council made a compulsory purchase order on 123 acres, for a cemetery. That summer, Middlesex County Council made a compulsory purchase order on a large area called Trent Park, including the 123 acres. An inquiry was due to be held on the orders made by both councils, but, in November, the county council acquired the entire area by agreement with the owners. The inquiry was held solely with regard to the proposed cemetery. The county council demanded that the special Parliamentary procedure be followed, but the Minister refused this and confirmed the cemetery order. This decision was upheld by the Court of Appeal. The owners of land affected by a compulsory purchase order have a limited period in which to object to, or to challenge, an order in the High Court. If Middlesex County Council had acquired the estate after the cemetery order had been made, but before these rights of appeal had expired, the land might have been protected by the special procedure.[3] As it was they were certainly too late when they bought the proposed cemetery land.

A compulsory purchase order may be challenged in the High Court if it has not been made in accordance with the necessary procedures. More fundamentally, it may be challenged if it is *ultra vires*, that is outwith the powers granted by the statute under which it is made. Thus, although many powers of compulsory purchase, notably those under the Town and Country Planning Act 1971, ss. 112 and 113, are very wide, some are much narrower. For example, the Coast Protection Act 1949 authorizes coast protection authorities to acquire land for coast protection works by compulsion, where it appears to such an authority that the work cannot be carried out otherwise. In 1962 Bognor Regis Urban District Council made such an order, which was confirmed by the Minister of Housing and Local Government, to acquire land at Felpham. However, landowners with adjoining houses whose property was involved, complained successfully to the courts that the authorities had exceeded their statutory powers. Part of the land was being taken to erect a promenade, rather than for coast protection, and in any event, it did not appear that compulsion was necessary, as adequate provision for the works could probably have been made with the consent of the landowners.[4]

(c) Notice to treat

The usual procedure for actually appropriating land under a compulsory purchase order is contained in the Compulsory Purchase Act 1965, although occasionally the old Land Clauses Consolidation Act 1845 still applies. Under the 1965 Act, s. 5, a notice to treat must give particulars of the land to which it relates, demand particulars of the recipient's estate and interest in the land and of the claim made by him in respect of the land, and state that the acquiring authority are willing to treat for the purchase of the land and as to compensation. Under s. 4, a notice to treat will be ineffective unless it is served within three years of the date on which the compulsory purchase order becomes operative. Like the initial compulsory purchase order, a notice to treat may be challenged if it is served for purposes different from those originally authorized. Here, even an order made under wide powers may specify a particular scheme and the notice to treat will be invalid unless it is for essentially the same scheme. Indeed, if the acquiring authority indicates that it now proposes to take the land for a different purpose, it may be treated as abandoning the compulsory purchase order. Even after a notice to treat has been served, if it becomes clear that the acquiring authority intends to use it for an improper purpose, it may be prevented from doing so. In 1937, Dudley Corporation made a compulsory purchase order to acquire an island site in Dudley, for road widening and the construction of a market hall. A notice to treat was served and compensation agreed but the scheme was called to a halt by the onset of the Second World War. After the War, the council sought to revive its powers under the order but the owners of the land successfully obtained, from the Chancery Division of the High Court, a declaration that the powers had been abandoned. The council had not fully decided exactly what to do with the land but was going to use part of it as a car park and had certainly dropped its original scheme.[5]

Some latitude is given in allowing land to be used for different purposes from those specified in a notice to treat. Thus, Wednesfield Urban District Council acquired land for a housing estate under a number of compulsory purchase orders, and served a notice to treat in respect of one plot on Capital Investments Ltd., on the basis that that plot would be used for building houses. The council then changed its mind and decided to build a school on the site. Wilberforce J. refused Capital Investments a declaration that the notice to treat was void despite their argument that the council was now using it for *ultra vires* purposes. In the judge's view the relevant land was being acquired as part of a balanced housing estate, somewhere on which a school would clearly be required.[6]

A notice to treat has similarities with a private contract for the sale of land, but under the Land Compensation Act 1961, s. 31, when any person served with a notice to treat submits details of the compensation which he claims, the acquiring authority may withdraw within six weeks. If no such claim is submitted, unless it has actively taken possession of the land, the acquiring authority may withdraw up to six weeks after compensation has been assessed by the land tribunal.

(d) Conveyance or vesting

For land to be effectively transferred to an acquiring authority, there must usually be a conveyance. Under s. 23 of the 1965 Act, the cost of this will be borne by the acquiring authority. If anyone refuses to transfer his title voluntarily, under s. 9, the acquiring authority pays compensation into court and may then execute a deed poll transferring the necessary title to itself. In such a case it is likely that the compensation will have been assessed by the Lands Tribunal. There is a simplified procedure under the Compulsory Purchase (Vesting Declarations) Act 1981, whereby once a compulsory purchase order has been made, the acquiring authority may execute a declaration vesting the land directly in itself. There are safeguards to ensure that no declaration is made until there has been opportunity for objections. This will in practice allow at least two months. Then the declaration cannot come into effect sooner than twenty-eight days from when it is made.

(e) Entry

Once a compulsory purchase has been made, under s. 11 of the 1965 Act, after giving between three and fourteen days notice to the owners or other occupiers, an acquiring authority may enter the affected land, 'for the purpose of surveying and taking land . . . of probing or boring to ascertain the nature of the soil and of setting out the line of the works'. Once the notice to treat has been served, after giving fourteen days notice to any owner, lessee and occupier, the acquiring authority may enter and take possession of the land. Under s. 14 (4), the acquiring authority may also enter on the land, once compensation has been agreed and paid, or earlier, with the consent of the owner and occupier. Once consent has been given it cannot be withdrawn.[7] Where there is a general vesting declaration, under the Compulsory Purchase (Vesting Declarations) Act 1981, s. 8, the acquiring authority may take over the land as soon as the declaration becomes effective.

5.1.2 Subsidiary rights

(a) Overriding subsidiary rights

Power to acquire land will normally enable the acquiring authority to override subsidiary rights which restrict its use of the land. Thus, where land is acquired compulsorily under the Town and Country Planning Act 1971, Part VI, s. 118 provides that, 'all private rights of way and rights of laying down, erecting, continuing or maintaining any apparatus on, under or over the land shall be extinguished, and any such apparatus shall vest in the acquiring authority'. Section 127 goes further where works are carried out under planning permission on land acquired by a local planning authority for planning purposes, even if it has been transferred to some other developer. Section 127 authorizes the overriding of any easements and of any other rights or advantages affecting the land, including rights of support and any other natural rights for the benefit of neighbouring land. This power applies even when the development land has been acquired by agreement and not by compulsory power. Neither s. 118 nor s. 127 provide for the overriding of the rights of statutory undertakers or of public rights of way, but these may be dealt with separately, if necessary by the Secretary of State, under ss. 230 and 214 respectively.

Although compulsory purchase of land often has the effect of overriding existing rights over that land, these will not necessarily be extinguished. During the Second World War, the Air Ministry requisitioned part of a farm on the Crichel Estate in Dorset. Shortly afterwards the trustees of the estate conveyed the entire farm to its tenant, subject to a covenant against using any of it for non-agricultural purposes. In 1954 the Air Ministry compulsorily purchased most of the requisitioned land, but the conveyance was made subject to the restrictive covenant, 'so far as it was valid subsisting and capable of being enforced'. Since 1947, the land had actually been used by Flight Refuelling Ltd, a private commercial firm doing Air Ministry work. Mrs Marten, who had become the absolute owner of the Crichel Estate, obtained a declaration backed up with an injunction, from Wilberforce J., that Flight Refuelling should not use the land subject to the covenant otherwise than for works connected with the Royal Air Force.[8]

It may be possible to insert new restrictions on the use of land where it is transferred to a public authority. Thus in *Earl of Leicester* v. *Wells-next-the-Sea Urban District Council*,[9] in 1948, the fourth Earl sold some 19 acres of the Holkham Estate to the council, subject to a covenant that the land should not be used for any purpose other than that of small holdings and allotments. In 1963 the demand for allotments had declined. The council obtained a necessary consent from the Ministry of Agriculture to use the land for housing and obtained planning permission to do so. However the fifth Earl, who had now inherited the Holkham Estate, obtained an injunction from Plowman J., which prevented the housing development going ahead. The covenant was valid because it did not restrict the council in using the land for the particular purpose for which it had been acquired.

(b) Creating subsidiary rights

Just as public authorities may need to overcome restrictions on land which they have acquired for their purposes, they may need to create new rights for the benefit of that land over property remaining in private hands. Whether or not they can do so will depend on the rights which they are authorized to acquire. The Local Government (Miscellaneous Provisions) Act 1976, s. 13 provides that, where a local authority is authorized to make a compulsory purchase order over any land, this includes a power to create any new rights not previously in existence. Before this provision was introduced, Camden London Borough Council had run into difficulties when it sought to ease its housing shortage by compulsory purchase, under the Housing Act 1957, Part V, of a group of maisonettes constructed on top of the Earnshaw Wing of the Centre Point office block complex in St Giles Circus in London (Fig. 5.2). In *Sovmots Investments Ltd* v. *Secretary of State for the Environment*,[10] the House of Lords ruled that the purchase was invalid because it depended upon various new rights which would have to be created over the remainder of the block, such as rights of support, rights of way for emergency exits, window cleaning and maintenance, the use of a lift for removing rubbish, and passage for the essential services of water, sewage, electricity and gas. The definition of *land* which could be acquired under the Housing Act did not include such subsidiary rights where they had not previously existed. By comparison, in certain cases, statutes have envisaged the creation of subsidiary rights rather than the outright purchase of land. Thus the Mineral Workings Act 1951, s. 26 specifically provides that where a local authority, or the Minister of Agriculture, acquire worked ironstone land so as to restore it, they may create access by compulsorily acquiring easements for rights of way.

Fig. 5.2 Centre Point office block, St Giles Circus, London, January 1984.

5.1.3 Compulsory purchase in reverse

(a) Severance

In certain circumstances a public authority may be obliged to relieve a landowner of land which has become a burden to him. Thus, under the Compulsory Purchase Act 1965, s. 8, where there is compulsory purchase of part of a house, building or manufactory, and the remainder will suffer material detriment, or where there is compulsory purchase of a part of a park or garden belonging to a house, the amenity or convenience of which will be seriously affected, the person being required to sell may serve a *counter notice* requiring the whole property to be taken. Provided the authority has not taken possession of the land it may withdraw its notice to treat,[11] but must otherwise take the whole unless it can satisfy the Lands Tribunal that the detriment claimed will not occur. In 1964 the London Borough of Hillingdon made a compulsory purchase order on the centre of Uxbridge with a view to comprehensive redevelopment. The order was confirmed, and in 1967 a notice to treat was served on part of the garden and driveway of Old Bank House in the High Street, which was described as 'the cradle of Barclay's Bank'. The house itself was already let to the council on a three-year lease and the owners served a counter notice requiring the council to buy their entire remaining interest in the property. The Lands Tribunal ruled that the Old Bank House was a house, even though it was not now used for residential purposes, and that the house included the garden and driveway so that the notice to treat did apply to part of a house, the remainder of which would suffer material detriment. The counter notice was therefore valid.[12]

Where open land is cut in two, under the 1965 Act the acquiring authority may be required to take small isolated pieces. The Land Compensation Act 1973, s. 53 enables those being deprived of agricultural land to serve a counter notice obliging the acquiring authority to take other farmland which it will no longer be possible to farm as a result of the compulsory purchase.

(b) Adverse planning decisions

Under the Town and Country Planning Act 1971, Part IX, those affected by various sorts of planning decisions may also require a planning authority to take land from them. Under s. 180 an owner of land may serve a purchase notice on a local planning authority requiring it to take land which has become incapable of reasonably beneficial use in its existing state where appropriate planning consent for alternative use cannot be obtained. If the authority serves a notice stating that it or another local authority, or a statutory undertaker, is prepared to take the land, they are automatically authorized to purchase it. Otherwise the authority should refer the case to the

Secretary of State who may confirm the purchase notice or give appropriate planning permission to enable the land to be used. Under s. 184, landowners are not able to use this provision to dispose of land which has a restricted use only because of planning conditions imposed on it at the time when permission was given to redevelop a site of which it formed part. Thus if a developer is required to landscape an open strip of land between new housing and a public road, the Secretary of State may decline to relieve him of that open strip, even though permission to build on it has been refused.[13] Similar provisions for purchase notices are available; under s. 188, where planning consent has been revoked or modified; under s. 189, after a discontinuance order; and under s. 190, on refusal to grant satisfactory listed building consent. By virtue of s. 191, purchase notices are also available where tree preservation orders or restrictions on advertisements render land unuseable.

For land to be incapable of reasonably beneficial use, it is not sufficient that it could be used more effectively or profitably than in its present form. In 1958 a Mr Bunn sought planning permission to develop 2½ acres of land on the coast at Selsey in Sussex for permanent residential use. The land had temporary permission for fourteen bungalows and seventeen caravans but was threatened by coastal erosion. Mr Bunn wanted to carry out protection work using the profits from his proposed development. When he was refused planning consent he served a purchase notice on Chichester Rural District Council. The Minister of Housing and Local Government confirmed this on the basis that 'the land in its existing state and with its existing permissions is substantially less useful to [Mr Bunn] than it would be with permission for the permanent redevelopment for residential purposes'. The Divisional Court quashed the notice. As Lord Parker C.J. observed: 'I suppose that in every case where land is worth developing and permission to develop is refused, the existing use of the land will be of less beneficial use, it will be less useful to the owner, than if it were developed. The test is whether it has become incapable of reasonably beneficial use in its existing state.'

(c) Planning blight

Where land is affected by planning blight, so that it cannot be sold except at a substantially reduced price, the Town and Country Planning Act 1971, s. 193 enables a person whose rights are affected to serve a blight notice requiring purchase of the land by the authority responsible for the blight. If the authority serves a counter notice declining to purchase, the landowner may refer the dispute to the Lands Tribunal. Section 192 sets out the circumstances where a blight notice may be served, in particular where land is earmarked in a development or highway plan, to be acquired for the purposes of central government or of statutory undertakers or the National Coal Board, or as part of an action area or housing general improvement area, or is likely to be affected by road building. This section also provides for purchase notices where land is subject to a compulsory purchase order but no notice to treat has yet been served. The Land Compensation Act 1973 extended eligible land so that a notice may be served in various cases where blight is more remote, for example, under s. 68, if it is earmarked in a proposed development plan, or, under s. 70, where it is covered by a compulsory purchase order which has not yet been confirmed.

5.1.4   Compensation for compulsory purchase

Where land or any right over land is acquired by a public body, the dispossessed landowner will be entitled to compensation. The higher the compensation the less reluctant he may be to hand over his land, but the less likely the public body will be to take it. Thus, public development is more likely to take place on land where compensation is low or where the land can be acquired by agreement at a modest price, avoiding the expense of compulsory purchase procedures. Even so, if a public body chooses to embark on an expensive scheme, the tax payers or rate payers who have to provide the money have little hope of stopping it. In *J. Murphy and Sons* v. *Secretary of State*,[14] Camden Borough Council made a compulsory purchase order under the Housing Act 1957 to buy industrial land along Highgate Road in London and applied for outline planning permission to develop it for residential purposes. The Secretary of State for the Environment approved both the purchase and the planning consent. J. Murphy and Sons had a 10-acre depot for vehicles and equipment next to the site and wished to expand onto it. They applied to the High Court to quash the decisions on the grounds that the Secretary of State had failed to consider the high cost of developing the site which would involve expensive precautions to contain noise. Ackner J. refused to interfere with the decisions on the ground that the Secretary of State had rightly taken the view that cost was not a relevant consideration. In fact however the scheme was eventually carried out without problems of undue cost in any event.

If compensation is not agreed it will be determined by the Lands Tribunal. The relationship of this with the court structure is discussed in Chapter 1, Section 1.2. The basic rules for assessing compensation are set out in the Land Compensation Act 1961, s. 5. The two approaches to assessment are value on the open market and alternatively the reasonable cost of equivalent reinstatement.

(a)   Value on the open market

Value on the open market is the normal basis for assessing compensation for compulsory purchase. Land valuation is an art practised by professional estate agents and land valuers. It consists largely in drawing comparisons with properties which have recently been sold, or in working out capital values based on the rent which could be charged for the property being assessed. In assessing market value a key factor is the development potential of the land. Section 14 of the 1961 Act makes clear that value is to be given for any existing planning permission. Also, under s. 15, it is to be assumed that planning permission would have been given for the type of development for which the land is being acquired. However, this has to be read in the light of s. 6, which provides that no account shall be taken of any increase or diminution in value which is attributable to the carrying out, or the prospect of, development, which would not have been likely to have taken place if it had not been for the compulsory purchase. The effect of this is that the land is assumed to have planning permission for the type of development for which it is being compulsorily acquired, but the fact that the acquiring authority actually intends to carry out the development is ignored. A private developer on the open market might be unlikely to want to take up the opportunity and so the extra value may be small. The principle in s. 6 had been established long before the 1961 act, and is particularly associated with the case of *Pointe Gourde Quarrying and Transport Co. Ltd* v. *Sub-Intendant of Crown Lands*.[16] There, land in Trinidad, including a limestone quarry, was compulsorily acquired to enable the United States to establish a naval base. An extra $15 000 was allowed because the quarry was particularly suitable for the needs of constructing the base. The Privy Council agreed with the full court of Trinidad and Tobago that this sum must be cut out because, irrespective of the wording of the relevant legislation, 'it is well settled that compensation for the compulsory acquisition of land cannot include an increase in value which is entirely due to the scheme underlying the acquisition.'

A further assumption is made, under s. 16, that planning permission would have been granted for any development for which the land is designated in the current development plans. If it is within an area designated for alternative uses, say industrial or office development, the dispossessed owner is entitled to the higher value. However, the assumption is only made if permission might reasonably have been expected on the relevant site. In *Provincial Properties (London) Ltd* v. *Caterham and Warlingham Urban District Council*,[17] there was a dispute over the level of compensation to be paid in respect of a two-third-acre site on top of a ridge in the grounds of a vanished house called Bleak House at Whyteleafe in Surrey (Fig. 5.3) The Court of Appeal agreed with the Lands Tribunal that even though the site was in an area scheduled for residential development, no permission was to be assumed, because the site was far too obtrusive. Indeed no less than six applications to build there had already been turned down. On the other hand, even where there is no indication in a development plan that a site could be used for a

Proposed development

Fig. 5.3 View of compensation site. *Provincial Properties (London) Ltd* v. *Caterham and Warlingham U.D.C.* [1972] 1 Q.B. 453.

particular purpose, s. 14 (3) ensures that higher compensation may still be awarded on the grounds that planning permission might have been granted. Under s. 17 there is a special procedure whereby a local planning authority may be asked for a *certificate of appropriate alternative development*, stating what planning consent would have been given had the compulsory purchase not taken place. Either party may appeal to the Secretary of State for the Department of the Environment against the form of such a certificate. Even if an assumption is made that permission would be given for a particular type of development, this will not add to the value of compensation if the development clearly would never have been carried out. In *Bromilow* v. *Greater Manchester Council*,[18] the Lands Tribunal made no allowance for a certificate of appropriate alternative development which stated that an office block would have been permitted on a site at Westhoughton in Lancashire, because there would have been no demand for such an office block on the site. It was in an industrial area close to a large engineering works and an ugly, smelly, bone factory.

Where a person is required to move, in addition to compensation for the value of the land taken, s. 5, Rule 6, of the 1961 Act recognizes that a disturbance payment may be made to cover necessary expenses.

(b) Reasonable cost of equivalent reinstatement

Instead of market value, s. 5, Rule 5, of the Land Compensation Act 1961, allows the Lands Tribunal, in its discretion, to award the reasonable cost of equivalent reinstatement, where a site is devoted, at the time of the notice to treat, 'to a purpose of such a nature that there is no general demand or market for land of that purpose'. This provision protects those, like the trustees of churches, who would not normally be able to sell their premises for their existing use but would find it very costly to set up elsewhere. The courts have interpreted the rule to mean that this basis of assessment may be used even if the land is not actively in use at the time of the notice to treat, provided the intention is to keep it for its special purpose. Thus it has been possible for trustees of churches which are in a derelict state to be relieved of their old premises and to set up elsewhere where a church is needed.[19] However, the Lands Tribunal must be satisfied that at the date of the notice to treat there is a genuine intention to set up elsewhere, and even then may refuse to give more than the market value, if it regards the increased compensation as disproportionate to the public value of the present use.[20]

5.1.5   Compensation for public works

Where a person is deprived of part of his land, rather than requiring the authority concerned to take the remainder as well, under the Compulsory Purchase Act 1965, s. 7, he may seek compensation for its reduced value as a result of it being severed or injuriously affected. Section 10 of the same Act has been treated as providing a more general right to compensation, even for persons who have not actually been deprived of land, but who have suffered *injurious affection*, as a result of public works causing harm which would have been actionable at common law had they not been carried out under statutory power. The Land Compensation Act 1973, Part 1, provides for compensation for depreciation in the value of land after works have been carried out, where harm has been caused through operating the new activities for which they were constructed. Again, this provision only applies if no action could have been brought were the works not being used under statutory authority. Today, therefore, if a building is deprived of access by the construction of a new road, its owner may obtain compensation for the harm caused by the construction of the road, and he may obtain further compensation for nuisance resulting from the noise and fumes generated on the road.

NOTES: SECTION 5.1

1. See *ante* p. 19 and the case of *Allen* v. *Gulf Refinery Ltd* [1980] Q.B. 156.
2. Town and Country Planning Act 1971, s. 132.
3. *Middlesex County Council* v. *Minister of Housing and Local Government* [1953] 1 Q.B. 12.
4. *Webb etc.* v. *Minister of Housing and Local Government* [1965] 1 W.L.R. 755, C.A. See further Chapter 8, Sections 8.2 and 8.3.
5. *Grice* v. *Dudley Corporation* [1958] Ch. 329.
6. *Capital Investments Ltd* v. *Wednesfield Urban District Council* [1965] Ch. 774.
7. *Doe d. Hudson* v. *Leeds and Bradford Railway* (1851) 16 Q.B. 796.
8. *Marten* v. *Flight Refuelling Ltd* [1962] Ch. 115.
9. *Earl of Leicester* v. *Wells-next-the-sea Urban District Council* [1973] Ch. 110.

10. *Sovmots Investments Ltd* v. *Secretary of State for the Environment* [1979] A.C. 144, H.L.
11. *King* v. *The Wycombe Railway Co.* (1860) 29 L.J.R. Ch. 462.
12. *Ravenseft Properties Ltd* v. *London Borough of Hillingdon* (1968) 20 P. & C.R. 483, L.T.
13. Before this provision was introduced the Secretary of State would have been obliged to confirm a purchase notice on such amenity land. See *Adams and Wade, Ltd* v. *Minister of Housing and Local Government* (1965) 10 P. & C.R. 60.
14. *J. Murphy and Sons* v. *Secretary of State* [1973] 1 W.L.R. 560 and see *ante* p. 119f.
15. However, cost of proposed development may sometimes be a reason for refusing planning permission. See *ante* p. 119f.
16. *Pointe Gourde Quarrying and Transport Co. Ltd* v. *Sub-Intendent of Crown Lands* [1947] A.C. 565. On appeal from the Supreme Court of Trinidad and Tobago.
17. *Provincial Properties (London) Ltd* v. *Caterham and Warlingham Urban District Council* [1972] 1 Q.B. 453.
18. *Bromilow* v. *Greater Manchester Council* (1975) 31 P. & C.R. 398, C.A.
19. *Trustees of Zoar Independent Church* v. *Rochester Corporation* [1975] Q.B. 246.
20. *Festiniog Railway Co.* v. *Central Electricity Generating Board* (1962) 13 P. & C.R. 248, C.A. See *ante* p. 23f.

5.2   Systems of registration

In many situations, a person may need to find what rights others have over a piece of land. In particular, if he is buying some land he will need to know whether the seller is entitled to transfer it and also whether there are any rights which will restrict or assist his use of it. Thus there might be a right of way enjoyed by a neighbouring land owner which would prevent his building in the middle of the property, or the seller's separated wife may still be using the land as her matrimonial home. Conversely, there may be a restrictive covenant over adjacent land which will ensure that the property will continue to enjoy a fine view in the future.

The state may protect those who are likely to be affected by the rights of others by requiring those rights to be registered. An effective register will make clear to an inquirer what rights there are over any particular piece of land. Ideally it should be possible to identify a piece of land on an index map and to find a list of all the rights over it. If land is registered in such a manner it may be transferred simply by altering the name of the owner in the register and by passing to the new owner a certificate of title to the land rather like a company shares certificate.

5.2.1   Forms of registration

Registration can take various forms. Land surveys have been conducted by the state from early times for purposes of taxation. In 1085, following the

Norman Conquest, William I ordered the famous Domesday Book which was completed the following year and identified by name and size each plot of land in most of the old administrative divisions of England known as Hundreds. The Domesday Book gave the names of the proprietors of each plot, but it contained no maps. In the eighteenth century the army Board of Ordnance began to produce what have developed into comprehensive Ordnance Survey maps of the entire country. By contrast on the continent of Europe, state surveys, known as *cadastres*, have long been used to mark out entire countries in map form showing how property is divided between different individuals. Cadastres were originally intended as a basis for taxation but may now provide a general index for identifying rights in land. A comparable system of registration, specifically for the benefit of landowners and the public, known as the *Torrens system*, was named after Sir Robert Torrens, who in 1857 became first Prime Minister of South Australia. After setting up the system, he resigned to administer it as Registrar General. The Torrens system was adopted, with various modifications, in other British territories, such as Canada, and also in some French and Belgian dependencies. With less success it was also tried in parts of the United States. In Australia, land was acquired by individuals through a grant from the Crown. The Torrens system required all new grants to be registered. The Register was available for public inspection. In Australia it was already required that when grants of land were made, boundaries had to be accurately surveyed. With registered land, accurate boundaries were marked in the Register, and this came to be regarded as a hallmark of the Torrens system. In some countries where the system was adopted, such as New Zealand, previously granted land was also included, although there titles were not necessarily provided with such clearly defined boundaries.

In Scotland a different system had been operated since 1617. This consisted of registration of deeds creating or transferring interests in land rather than of the title to particular parcels of land.[1] For the Scottish equivalent of a deed, known as a Writ, to be effective it had to be entered in the *Register of Sasines*. In 1871 this Register was supplemented by a system of search sheets, so that each piece of land was recorded on a separate sheet. If a piece of land was subdivided, a new sheet was opened for each part. The register was provided with indexes of place names and of the names of those with interests in land. A major disadvantage of the Register of Sasines was that anyone acquiring an interest in land had to check the register for a ten-year limitation period,[2] for the details of any title having priority over that of the vendor. Also the search sheets did not necessarily provide a clear location or description of the land.

A system of *Registration of Title* has now been introduced in Scotland by the Land Registration (Scotland) Act 1979 to supercede registration of Sasines. In England, registration of title was introduced on a voluntary basis in 1862. In 1925 provision was made for it to be compulsorily applied in stages throughout England and Wales. For land where the title was not registered, separate provision had already been made for the registration of a number of subsidiary interests in land in *land charges registers*.

5.2.2   Registration of title

(a) The extent of registration

Title to land is registered under the Land Registration Act 1925 and its accompanying rules, S.R. & O. 1925, No 1093 and later amendments. In 1980, 74% of the population of England and Wales was covered by compulsory registration of title to the land where they lived.[3] By 31 March 1982, there were 7 727 357 registered titles.[4] The Land Registry Headquarters is based in London at Lincoln's Inn Fields. Registers are kept at thirteen centres (Fig. 5.4). Registration is being made compulsory in areas by a succession of

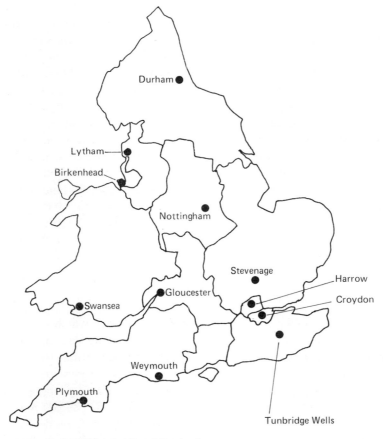

Fig. 5.4 Location of District Land Registries.

Orders in Council. The main conurbations have already been included but much of the more extensive rural areas have not. In compulsory areas registration is only required for the conveyance on sale of a fee simple or for the creation or transfer of a lease which will run for at least twenty-one years unless the freehold has not yet been registered in which case the lease must have at least forty years to run. Land which is inherited by successive generations of a family may never come to be registered. Outside the compulsory areas, freehold titles of council houses must be registered where these are bought by tenants under the provisions of the Housing Act 1980. Also, the owner of any legal estate may voluntarily apply for a title to be registered, provided the Chief Land Registrar has indicated that he is prepared to register property in the class to which it belongs.

(b) The terms of registration in the Land Registry

Each entry in the Land Register is in three parts. The *property register* identifies and describes each piece of land for which title is registered. It includes details of interests such as easements and restrictive covenants over or for the benefit of the land. The *proprietorship register* gives the names of proprietors with details of their land and title. A title may be registered as *absolute* subject to other interests recorded in the register. On the other hand if there is some question as to its validity it may be registered as a *qualified title* or, when it is based on adverse possession,[5] as a *possessory title*. In either case, it will be unprotected against other possible prior interests which can not be discounted or ascertained for certain. A qualified or possessory title may later be converted to an absolute title. If a tenant is able to establish fully both his own leasehold title and any superior titles, his leasehold title may be registered as *absolute*, but as a tenant has no right to see his landlord's title in the register, he may well not be able to establish its validity. Nevertheless his own title may be registered as a *good leasehold title*. The third part of the register is the *charges register* which gives details of incumbrances over registered land and details of dealings with these.

(c) Use of the Land Register

The Land Register is used by means of an index map which is open to the public and shows each separate registered plot of land with its own parcel number. Parcel numbers are allocated in order of registration. There is also an index of proprietors which shows the names both of those with titles and of those with charges. However, a veil of secrecy is drawn over these names. Normally, under the Land Registration Act 1925, s. 112, no-one may look at entries on the register without the permission of the title holder, although, under s. 110, an intending purchaser must be given permission. By contrast someone like a prospective lessee has no such right. He might find that land he had leased was bound, for example by restrictive covenants he had not expected.

The main value of registration of title is that it makes conveyancing much easier. Traditional conveyancing requires a detailed check on title for at least the previous fifteen years. A legal estate owner of registered land is given a certificate of title known as a *land certificate*, corresponding to the entry for his land in the property register. If he transfers his estate in the land he passes the land certificate to the purchaser. Under s. 123 of the 1925 Act, unless the property register is then changed to show the new name, the conveyance is ineffective. After two months it is normally treated as void. However, once the register is changed, the purchaser has a good title even against anyone who actually had a better title than the vendor.

(d) Protection provided by the Land Register

Minor interests, which are shown on the register, such as restrictive covenants and contracts for the sale of a legal estate in land, known as estate contracts, are similarly protected and bind a purchaser. A person claiming such an interest who can produce the land certificate may have it recorded on the charges register as a *notice*. If he cannot produce the land certificate, because he is unable to obtain the co-operation of the person with the legal title to the land, he may enter a *caution* on the register. This entitles him to notice of any prospective conflicting entry and an opportunity to challenge it. If necessary, an order called an *inhibition* may be obtained from the court or from the registrar to prevent dealings with a piece of registered land. A similar order, called a *restriction*, may be made on the application of the registered proprietor of the land or with his support.

Under s. 82 of the 1925 Act, the registrar or the court have jurisdiction to rectify entries in the register, for example if these were made as a result of fraud, or to exclude a piece of land to which a squatter has obtained a good title.[6] If anyone suffers loss as a result of errors in the register or in an official search made in it, under s. 83, he may be able to obtain an indemnity from the registry through the court. Here again, rights in land are treated as primarily financial interests. They are sacrificed to the certainty of a clear ruling on title. The register also fails to provide protection against a class known as *overriding interests*. These are provided for in s. 70, and are generally the types of right which, in the case of non-registered land, are not registrable as incumbrances in the land charges registries. They include rights being acquired under the Prescription Act 1832,[7] such as profits and legal easements, and rights of persons in actual occupation of the land. Generally tenants will be protected on this basis even if their leases are not entered on the register. Since leases for not more then twenty-one years are unregistrable, provided these are legal rather then equitable, they are generally treated as overriding interests. Certain examples of overriding interests may be registered as minor interests in which case they are treated as such.[8] For example if a right of way were acquired by long use over a piece of land, it would bind a purchaser of that land even if it were not registered. If it were registered it would normally bind him, but if an official search made on his behalf by the Land Registry failed to reveal it, he would not be bound and the person entitled to the right of way would have to rely on compensation against the registry.

5.2.3   Registration of land charges

Before the major reform of land law in the first quarter of the twentieth century, central registers were already kept of certain incumbrances of land such as actions claiming a right in land and also writs and orders enforcing judgements of any court affecting land. A new Register of Land Charges covering many common interests over land was set up in 1922 and is now provided for in the Land Charges Act 1972.

(a)   Contents of the Land Charges Register

Today a total of five registers are kept by the Land Charges department of the Land Registry at Plymouth under the Land Charges Act 1972. The public, or more often their solicitors, may make searches in the registers. Usually this is done by asking the registry to carry out an official search for incumbrances against named title holders. Of the five registers, that known as the Register of Land Charges is divided into classes A to F. Classes C and D are the most important and sub-divided. Class C contains interests made both before and after the end of 1925. Those in Class D have all been created since 1925. Particularly important charges are those under C (i), puisne mortgages, that is legal mortgages which are unprotected by the deposit of documents; C (iii), general equitable charges not registered under any other head, for example equitable mortgages of any legal estate; C (iv), estate contracts, that is enforceable agreements to convey or create a legal estate in land by those entitled to do so; D (i), Inland Revenue charges for payment of capital transfer tax; D (ii) restrictive covenants, other than those in leases; D (iii), equitable easements and other rights or privileges such as profits.

(b)   The significance of registration of land charges

The practical importance of the five land charges registers is that under the Law of Property Act 1925, s. 198, if an interest is registrable in one of them, once it is registered this is generally treated as actual notice to anyone who later purchases, that is obtains any interest in, the affected land. Such a person is therefore bound by an interest which has been registered. If such an interest is not registered, a later purchaser may not be bound by it even if he actually is aware of it. However, it may be difficult to find whether or not a piece of land is subject to any incumbrances even if there are some which have been registered. Registration is made under the name of the person who, at the time, owns the legal estate in the land affected by the charge, and there is no index or map relating to pieces of land affected. As we shall see in Section 5.5, a person transferring land only has to establish a good title for some fifteen years. Therefore interests may be registered against the names of people who are not on the available title deeds because they had the estate at an earlier period. Furthermore registration may be effective even if the name against which it is entered is given in an unexpected form, provided it 'may be fairly described as a version' of the relevant full names. Thus in *Oak Co-operative Building Society* v. *Blackburn*,[9] a building society seeking to foreclose on a mortgage for a house was held to be bound by an estate contract made by the mortgagor to sell the house to a purchaser who was occupying it. It did not matter that the estate contract was registered against the mortgagor in the name of 'Frank David Blackburn', whereas his true name was 'Francis David Blackburn'.

A remedy has been provided in many cases for purchasers who suffer loss because an incumbrance in the name of an earlier estate owner could not be discovered. Provided the purchaser had no actual knowledge of the incumbrance, he may be able to obtain compensation from the Chief Land Registrar.[10] There are also powers vested in the courts under the Land Charges Act 1972, s. 1 (6) to vacate, that is remove, from the register, entries which are defective. The court may even intervene when this statutory power does not apply. In *Heywood* v. *B.D.C. Builders*,[11] B.D.C. Builders negotiated with Heywood to buy land for development near Exeter. When the negotiations fell through, B.D.C. Builders claimed that there had actually been an agreement to sell the house, and registered an estate contract. Heywood successfully applied to have this vacated, B.D.C. Builders then appealed and registered their dispute in the separate Register of Pending Actions. Heywood applied for this to be vacated too and the Court of Appeal did as he asked on the basis that there was in fact no claim which could properly have been registered. The court's statutory power would only have applied if the builders themselves had brought a claim for possession of the land. However, this did not matter, the builders were in effect abusing the register by using it simply to prevent Heywood selling the land to someone else.

(c) The effect of non-registration of land charges

If a registrable incumbrance is not registered, there is consolation for the person entitled to it, that it may still be enforced as a personal contract against whoever originally made it. In *Hollington Bros. Ltd* v. *Rhodes*,[12] Rhodes was one of the head tenants of an office block who negotiated to sublet their premises to Hollington Bros. and allowed them to take possession. The head lease was transferred to another company which only allowed Hollingtons to stay provided they paid considerably more money. Hollingtons had not registered any agreement for the sublease and therefore they sued Rhodes. Harman J. held that in fact no agreement had been reached to sublet, but if it had been, Hollingtons could have recovered their extra expenditure in full from Rhodes.

In the *Hollington Bros.* case, the new head lessees had actually been notified in the documents transferring the head lease that Hollingtons had a subtenancy. The significance of non-registration was that despite such notice purchasers in their position are not bound by any contract to create a subtenancy, unless it has been registered under class C (iv) of the Register of Land Charges. The Land Charges Act 1972 provides that any unregistered interests which fall into this heading or under any of the headings in Class D are unenforceable against any purchaser for money or moneys worth of a legal estate in the land affected. By contrast, unregistered interests which should have been registered in the Register of Pending Actions are unenforceable against any purchaser for value of an interest in the same land but only if he does not have express notice. Value is rather wider than money or moneys worth and includes the acquisition of land as part of a marriage settlement in consideration of a future marriage. Other interests which should have been but are not registered are generally unenforceable against any purchaser for value of any later interest even if he has had express notice.

5.2.4   Local land charges

In addition to the incumbrances which are registered at Plymouth, the Local Land Charges Act 1975, provides for charges or restrictions on land together with positive obligations, enforceable by ministers of the Crown, government departments, or local authorities, to be recorded in local land charges registers which are maintained with indexes by district councils, London borough councils and the Common Council of the City of London. Although certain matters, such as covenants in leases, or for the benefit of specific public land, do not have to be included, many important burdens on land will be found in these registers. These include planning conditions attached to planning consents granted since August 1977, and covenants for the general public benefit under the Town and Country Planning Act 1971, s. 52 and the Local Government (Miscellaneous Provisions) Act 1982, s. 33.[13]

The Local Land Charges Act 1975 provides that charges to which it relates will still be valid even if they are not registered, previously they would have been invalid unless they were registered. Now, however, under s. 10 any purchaser for valuable consideration of an interest in land or the proceeds of sale of land who is misled can obtain compensation from the registering authority if he suffers loss because a local land charge has been omitted from the register or an official search carried out for him has failed to reveal it.

Local land charges are registered by reference to each relevant piece of land and are available for searches by the public. Local authorities also keep certain other records which may not directly relate to the land of interested persons but which may reveal matters likely to affect it. These include development plans,[14] registers of planning applications and decisions in the vicinity[15] and definitive maps showing public footpaths and bridleways.[16]

5.2.5   The effect of unregistered interests

Certain types of interest in land are essentially irrelevant for a purchaser. Thus the purpose of both strict settlements[17] and trusts for sale[18] is to treat those with beneficial interests in land as entitled only to its financial value. In any dealing with such land their interests are *overreached*, that is persons acquiring a new interest are unaffected by them. However, on registered land, such interests should be entered as minor interests to ensure that purchase money is paid to at least two trustees for the protection of beneficial owners.[19] There are other interests which may significantly restrict the use of the land by a purchaser and which are not registrable. Thus on unregistered land, neither restrictive covenants made before 1925 nor legal easements, are to be found in the Land Charges Register. In the case of registered land they should be shown in the register, but if by oversight they are omitted, such overriding interests are still effective. A legal interest, in land whose title is registered, is binding on a purchaser of that land, even though the legal interest itself is not registrable, and could not have been discovered without some considerable difficulty. Thus if a person acquires a legal right of way by long use over a piece of land, whether its title is registered or unregistered, and the land is sold to a builder, the builder may be bound by the right of way even though he has no idea of its existence. The most he can hope for is to recover compensation from the vendor who sold him the land without telling him about the right of way.

To some extent the protection provided for purchasers of registered land actually seems to be weaker than that for purchasers of unregistered land. In *Williams and Glyn's Bank* v. *Boland*,[20] the House of Lords dealt with two cases of wives whose husbands had mortgaged to the bank the matrimonial home, which was registered land, and had defaulted on the mortgage instalments. The House of Lords held that as the wives were in actual occupation, each of them had overriding interests under the Land Registration Act 1925, s. 70. These could have been registered as minor interests, but although they had not been, they took priority over the bank mortgage. A person who acquires land subject to such equitable rights of others in actual possession may have little indication of their presence unless he employs a private investigator. By contrast an equitable interest in unregistered land, such as a pre-1925 restrictive covenant, which is not registrable under the Land Charges Act 1972, is enforceable but under the Law of Property Act 1925, s. 199, not against any *bona fide* purchaser for value of a legal estate in the land who did not have notice of it. The value may be any acceptable legal consideration. It could be money, whether or not amounting to the market value, or other land or a prospective marriage. The concept of consideration is further discussed in Chapter 6, Section 6.5. In such a case a purchaser is bound by an interest if he heard of it before he had paid the purchase price, but he is entitled to renounce the contract.[21] Notice may be actual or imputed through the knowledge of the parties' agent, normally a solicitor, acquired in dealing with the same transaction. Notice may also be constructive in that the incumbrance would have come to the knowledge of the purchaser or his agent if they had made such enquiries and inspections of the land as ought reasonably to have been made.

NOTES: SECTION 5.2

1. In England, registers of deeds were operated from the early eighteenth century in Middlesex and Yorkshire but have now been closed.
2. Prescription and Limitation (Scotland) Act 1977, s. 1.
3. Report to the Lord Chancellor of Her Majesty's Land Registry 1979–1980, p. 3.
4. Ibid. 1981–1982, p. 4.
5. *Post* p. 261f.
6. *Chowood Ltd* v. *Lyall* [1930] 2 Ch. 156.
7. *Post* p. 265f.
8. *Williams and Glyn's Bank Ltd* v. *Boland* [1981] A.C. 487, H.L.,*per* Lord Wilberforce at p. 507.
9. *Oak Cooperative Building Society* v. *Blackburn* [1968] 1 Ch. 730. The building society solicitor compounded his client's difficulties by asking for a search in the name of, 'Francis Davis Blackburn'. Had the search been in the correct name the client would not have been bound.
10. Law of Property Act 1969, s. 25.
11. *Heywood* v. *B.D.C. Builders* [1964] 1 W.L.R. 971 CA.
12. *Hollington Bros. Ltd* v. *Rhodes* [1951] 2 T.L.R. 691.
13. *Ante* p. 99f.
14. *Ante* p. 57f.
15. Town and Country Planning Act 1971, s. 34, *ante* p. 153.
16. Wildlife and Countryside Act 1981, s. 57, *ante* p. 153.
17. *Ante* p. 175.
18. *Ante* p. 176.
19. Such interests may be protected even without registration. See *Peffer* v. *Rigg* [1977] 1 W.L.R. 285.
20. *Williams and Glyn's Bank Ltd* v. *Boland supra* note 8. In the case of unregistered land, a right to occupation of a matrimonial home is registrable under the

Martimonial Homes Act 1967, s. 2, in the Land Charges Register as a Class F land charge. In the case of registered land such a right is registerable as a minor interest.

21. *Tourville* v. *Naish* [1734] 3 Peere Wms. 307.

5.3   Methods of transferring land

The system of registration of title has greatly simplified the transfer of land. As we have seen in Chapter 4, Section 4.2, strictly what is transferred will be an estate or interest in land. Whether land is registered or unregistered, the negotiations before it is actually conveyed remain much more complicated than in most other contractual dealings (Fig. 5.5).

REGISTERED LAND	UNREGISTERED LAND
Conveyance of the land lodging certificate and Transfer of Land Certificate	Conveyance of the land by deed prepared by vendor's solicitor
Change of proprietor's name in the Land Registry	Search in Land Charges Register by purchaser
Requisitions (questions put by purchaser as to the validity of the vendor's title)	Requisitions (questions put by purchaser as to validity of vendor's title)
Transfer of title prepared by vendor. Purchaser authorized to carry out search in Land Registry	Abstract of Title prepared by vendor and submitted to purchaser
Exchange of contracts	Exchange of contracts
Enquiries to vendor by purchaser	Enquiries to vendor by purchaser
Draft contract Copy sent to purchaser	Draft Contract Copy sent to purchaser
Structural survey by purchaser's surveyor (valuation by valuer for building society or other mortgagee) Inspection of site. Searches in local land charges register and requests for information from local authorities etc.	Structural survey by purchaser's surveyor (valuation by valuer for building society or other mortgagee) Inspection of site. Searches in local land charges register and requests for information from local authorities etc.
Preliminary negotiations between prospective vendor and purchaser, usually through vendor's estate agent	Preliminary negotiations between prospective vendor and purchaser, usually through vendor's estate agent

Fig. 5.5 The normal stages in sale of registered and unregistered land.

5.3.1   Contracts for sale

(a) The need for writing

'[A]ny contract for the sale or disposition of land or any interest in land', is unenforceable in the courts, 'unless the agreement upon which such action is brought, or some memorandum thereof, is in writing, and signed by the party to be charged', or by some other person who has been lawfully authorized. This rule is now found in the Law of Property Act 1925, s. 40. It makes contracts concerned with real property inherently more formal than most other sorts of contract. A contract for the transfer of a legal estate in land is an *estate contract* and should be protected by appropriate registration depending upon whether the title to the land is registered or unregistered. The contract itself need not be in writing, although in practice it generally is. However, the writing relied on must contain all the terms agreed. Otherwise the contract will be void. Thus the writing must state the identity of the vendor and the purchaser, the property to be transferred, and the price. If these are all that is agreed there is an *open contract*, in which case additional terms will be implied by the law, for example that the vendor must prove his good title to what he claims to convey and must carry out the conveyance within a reasonable time. Normally the parties will agree expressly on detailed terms. In *Beckett* v. *Nurse*,[1] Mrs Beckett sought specific performance of a contract with Nurse to transfer to her late husband a field at Thorpe Audlin in the West Riding of Yorkshire. She relied on a receipt for £17 which had been given to her husband. It was signed by Nurse and also bore the name of her husband together with a sketch plan of the field and stated that it was a deposit 'for a field situated near the Fox Inn. Sold for £50'. Nurse claimed that the agreement was on the basis that Mr Beckett would build a bungalow on the field and would look after Nurse's adjoining land. The Court of Appeal held that if this was so the memorandum was insufficient and sent the case back to the County Court for further investigation.

An agreement concerned with a transfer of land may be contained in several documents but only if these refer to one another. In *Timmins* v. *Moreland Street Property Co. Ltd*,[2] Timmins, a vendor, sought to enforce the sale of a property in Shoreditch for £39 000. He relied on a cheque for a deposit of £3 900. However the cheque gave no indication of the purpose for which it had been paid. Therefore it could not be read together with Timmins' own receipt which provided the additional details. The courts have been liberal over the requirement that a contract dealing with land will only be enforced against a person who has signed it. For example it may be sufficient if headed notepaper is used with the name of the party against whom it is sought to enforce the contract.[3] The reason for requiring a signed memorandum for any contract concerned with land is so as to avoid the risk of fraud.

However, the precaution itself gives scope for unscrupulous behaviour by a party who refuses to go ahead with an agreement which he has led others to rely on. A notable example is *gazumping*, where a vendor withdraws from an original agreement so as to sell to a new purchaser who makes a higher offer. As Sachs J. has commented, a gentlemen's agreement to sell 'is only too often a transaction in which each side hopes the other will act as a gentleman and neither intends so to act if it is against his material interests'.[4] Nevertheless, a contract without an adequate memorandum is not void. Anyone wishing to escape liability on this ground must specifically plead the point before the courts.[5] Otherwise a court will enforce a contract even though there is no written evidence of its existence. Also, equity, in any case, enables a court to enforce an oral contract concerned with land of which there has been *part performance*. Here the greater risk is seen to be that of a person fraudulently trying to evade his obligations.

(b) Part performance

Part performance may occur where a purchaser has taken possession of premises, provided he did so with the consent of the other party.[6] It may consist in certain circumstances of a payment of money,[7] or of making alterations to property. Thus in *Broughton* v. *Snook*,[8] Mr Broughton gave up the flourishing Museum Hotel in Sheffield for semi-retirement in the Bridge Inn at Calver in Derbyshire. Mr Snook, the elderly owner of the Bridge had orally agreed that Broughton should buy it when an existing tenancy finished. The tenant wanted to transfer to another public house early and Broughton then moved in with Snook's approval, decorated the premises and altered a doorway and a fireplace. Snook became incapacitated and died shortly afterwards. His executors tried to resell the Bridge but Farewell J. ordered that they should carry out the agreement with Broughton.

5.3.2 Negotiations leading to contract

(a) Preliminaries

In practice, someone buying land in England will not bind himself by a written contract until a number of investigations have been made, usually by his solicitors. These preliminary negotiations will be carried out, *subject to contract*, making clear that no binding agreement has yet been reached. If a purchaser pays a deposit and the agreement is not concluded his deposit will generally be recoverable.[9] In the course of negotiations the purchaser will make a search in the local land charges register. It is preferable here as with all searches for the registry to be asked to carry out an official search so that it will be liable for any negligent errors.[10] In addition requests will be put to the appropriate local authority, normally the district council, for details which are not included in the register, notably of planning matters such as compulsory purchase orders, and applications for planning permission which have been made in respect of neighbouring property. Details will also be sought on such matters as whether the roads past the property to be conveyed have been adopted and whether any new road-building scheme is planned in the vicinity.

Normally a purchaser will commission a structural survey. As we shall see in Chapter 7, Section 7.1, the vendor is generally not responsible for any defects in the state of the premises. His main duty is to ensure that the title which he offers to transfer is good. The purchaser's solicitor should also carefully inspect the site, to check such matters as the location of boundaries, possible rights of way over the land, rights to light which it may need or to which it may be subject, and the presence of any occupant such as a deserted wife who may have rights to remain in occupation.[11]

(b) Draft contract

Whilst the purchaser is carrying out his investigations, the vendor's solicitor will draft the contract. He will retain one copy for the vendor to sign and send a second copy to the purchaser's solicitor for the purchaser to sign. The contract is normally in a standard form, such as the Law Society's Conditions of Sale, which sets out details of the land, the legal rights to be transferred and rights to which the land is subject. Appropriate additions will be made, for example a specific date for completion, provision for a deposit and the terms of any new burdens to be imposed, such as easements and restrictive covenants. If there are a number of prospective purchasers, the vendor may initiate a *contract race*, by sending copies of the agreement to each purchaser. The one who first exchanges contracts wins the sale. Where there is a contract race, the vendor may not be entitled to withdraw, as he may want to if yet another purchaser appears and is ready to pay a large sum immediately.[12]

On receiving the draft contract, the purchaser's solicitor will put to the vendor's solicitor a number of further enquiries. Normally these will be mainly in a standard form covering such matters as the location of boundaries, fixtures which are to be left on the land and any other items which are not fixtures but which are to be included in the sale. The vendor is not required to provide evidence of title at this stage but if the land is unregistered generally does send the details, in an abstract of title, which he will in any event be required to provide after the contract has been finalized.

(c) Exchange of contracts

The transfer contract becomes binding when the two copies are formally exchanged. Once this would have been at a meeting of the parties' solicitors, but is now usually done in the course of a telephone conversation,[13] followed by a postal exchange of the two copies. When contracts are exchanged, the purchaser will normally be required to pay a 10% deposit which is retained by the vendor's solicitor until the conveyance is complete. Where land is auctioned, the vendor's solicitor will have deposited the draft contract with the auctioneer for prospective purchasers to look at. It will be signed by the successful bidder at the end of the auction. From the date when contracts are exchanged, the purchaser is normally entitled to the property at the agreed price whether its value increases or decreases. If for example it is burned down he will be responsible for its insurance.[14] He will also be responsible for any damage caused by the property to neighbouring land.[15] If a party refuses to go ahead with the conveyance the courts may compel him to do so by the remedy of specific performance.

5.3.3   Conveyance

Following the exchange of contracts the vendor is responsible for proving his good title to the land and for *completing* the contract by executing the conveyance. This must be done by a deed,[16] or the purchaser's interest will remain merely equitable. If the land were then transferred by the vendor to someone else, the original purchaser would merely be entitled to damages, including any increase in the value of the property. It is at the conveyancing stage that the system of registered land has greatly simplified many transactions. Once land is registered it may be conveyed by transferring the land certificate and by changing the name of the proprietor of the land entered in the register. The vendor authorizes the purchaser to check the title in the land registry, which he does in practice by asking for an official search. The vendor's solicitor prepares a transfer of title which authorizes the change in the register. If the title is not registered as absolute, the vendor will be served with *requisitions* requiring him to provide additional evidence of its validity. He will also be required to furnish full details of incumbrances referred to in the register such as restrictive covenants. In the case of unregistered land, the vendor provides an *abstract of title*, setting out the history of the land with a précis of all relevant documents of title for at least fifteen years back to the root of title. In practice most vendors' solicitors now tend to bundle up photocopies of all the relevant documents and send them to their purchaser's solicitor to sort out. The purchaser's solicitor will in any event search the relevant registers and may raise requisitions from the vendor so as to clear away any doubt on the title. An actual conveyance of unregistered land must be carried out in a deed signed and sealed by the vendor and delivered to the purchaser. At the time of the conveyance, other necessary steps will be concluded, notably payment of the outstanding price, paying off of previous mortgages, and the creation of new mortgages. Appropriate stamp duty must be paid under the Stamp Act 1891 on conveyances of property worth more than £30 000. The conveyance must be stamped by the Inland Revenue Commissioners within thirty days.

5.3.4 Leasehold conveyancing

A new lease may be created or an existing lease assigned, by means very similar to the conveyance of freehold land. However, a major difference is that under the Law of Property Act 1925,[17] leases for no more than three years and at the best rent reasonably available may be created orally. As the majority of leases are from year to year or on a shorter periodic basis, such as monthly or even weekly, this concession greatly simplifies the leasing of land. However, there may be other requirements of formality. Thus under the Landlord and Tenant Act 1962,[18] where premises are let on a weekly tenancy, the landlord must provide the tenant with a rent book containing details including the name and address of the landlord, the rent and the terms.

5.3.4 Non-commercial transfers

Land may be transferred voluntarily as a gift, in which case a conveyance is necessary, although the normal preliminaries to a sale will not be carried out. Where a person dies leaving real property this passes to his personal representatives, that is executors under the Will or in the absence of executors, administrators. In the case of intestacy there will be administrators. Where the personal representatives transfer a legal estate in land direct to a beneficiary they are required by the Administration of Estates Act 1925, s. 36 (4) to sign a written *assent*. On a subsequent sale these events are recorded in the abstract of title. When the deceased leaves registered land the register must be amended to show the name of the beneficiary or trustees to whom the land is left.

NOTES: SECTION 5.3

1. *Beckett* v. *Nurse* [1948] 1 K.B. 535, C.A.
2. *Timmins* v. *Moreland Street Property Co. Ltd* [1958] 1 Ch. 110.
3. *Tourret* v. *Cripps* (1879) 48 L.J. Ch. 567.
4. *Goding* v. *Frazer* [1966] 3 All E.R. 234, *per* Sachs J. at p. 239. Quoted in *Barnsley's Conveyancing Law and Practice*, 2nd edn (1982) Butterworths, London, p. 241.
5. Rules of the Supreme Court, Order 18, Rule 8.
6. *Delaney* v. *T.P. Smith Ltd* [1946] K.B. 393.
7. *Steadman* v. *Steadman* [1976] A.C. 536, H.L.
8. *Broughton* v. *Snook* [1938] 1 All E.R. 411.
9. *Chillingworth* v. *Esche* [1924] 1 Ch. 97.
10. *Coats Patons (Retail) Ltd* v. *Birmingham Corporation* (1971) 69 L.G.R. 356, and see *ante* p. 243.

11. *Williams and Glyn's Bank Ltd* v. *Boland* [1981] A.C. 487, H.L., *ante* p. 243.
12. *Daulia Ltd* v. *Four Millbank Nominees Ltd* [1978] Ch. 231 C.A.
13. *Domb* v. *Isoz* [1980] Ch. 548, C.A.
14. *Paine* v. *Meller* (1801) 6 Ves. Jun. 349.
15. *Robertson* v. *Skelton* (1849) 12 Beav. 260.
16. Law of Property Act 1925, s. 52 (2).
17. Ibid. s. 54 (2).
18. Landlord and Tenant Act 1962 s. 1.

5.4   The creation and extinction of subsidiary rights

Subsidiary rights over land, notably easements, profits and restrictive covenants, may be created by statute, or, as is usually the case, by agreement. There may be such an agreement specifically for the purpose, or, as we shall see in the next section, a voluntary grant may be assumed by prescription after long use. Often, however, subsidiary rights over land are created as part of a well-documented larger arrangement, for example where the owner of a large piece of ground sells off part to a builder, retaining rights of light and rights of way over it and creating restrictive covenants to prevent any buildings which might spoil the enjoyment of his own neighbouring house. An agreement to create a subsidiary interest should be expressed in writing to comply with the Law of Property Act 1925, s. 40. An actual grant of a legal easement or profit must be by deed to comply with s. 52. However, rights may be created in equity with less formality.

5.4.1   Grants of easements

An easement may be created expressly or by implication as part of a larger transaction. As a general principle in interpreting a grant, any doubt is decided in favour of the grantee since he was in the weaker position in deciding the form which the right should take. In 1863 the South Metropolitan Cemetery Company bought some 30 acres of meadow land at Norwood on the outskirts of London for a cemetery. A subsidiary access to the site existed off a private road through two gates in a hedge. To replace the hedge the company built a wall with two newly positioned gates. Eden, who had bought the land on the other side of the private road, dug a hole to prevent access to one of the new gates. When sued for obstruction he claimed that the company had only been granted a right of way to the original gates.[1] However, the court held that the grant should be construed as a general one to use every part of the road and was not limited to access to the original gates.

(a)   Equitable easements and profits

If parties agree in writing to create an easement for some payment of value, equity will normally treat this as actually being done and a valid deed made.[2]

If there is a merely oral agreement this may be enforced in equity under the doctrine of *part performance* in favour of a party who has acted on it. Thus in 1885 McManus and Cooke who owned adjacent houses in Gutter Lane in London agreed orally to replace a party wall in an area between the properties so as to allow improved skylights for each. McManus built the wall and erected his skylight but Cooke built a higher skylight which interfered with McManus's light. Kay J. upheld McManus's claim that, because he had acted on the agreement, it gave him an enforceable right to light with which Cooke had interfered. Similarly in *Mason* v. *Clarke*,[4] a Shepton Mallet transport company let a farm on the borders of Northamptonshire and Leicestershire to Clarke but reserved the rights to game. Subsequently they granted to Mason, a garage proprietor and rabbit catcher, a right to catch rabbits. Clarke was worried by the growing rabbit population, and, apparently fearful that Mason would cultivate it, became violent. When he was sued for interfering with Mason's rabbit-catching, Clarke relied on the fact that Mason had only been given the rabbitting rights orally. However, the House of Lords held that, as the rabbit catcher had been on the land and set snares, he had acquired an enforceable right in equity.

(b) Grantors and grantees

Because a grant is normally construed in favour of the grantee against the grantor, it is normally important to be able to tell which is which. However, where pieces of land are sold by the same owner to different purchasers at the same time, in respect of rights over the other land, each purchaser is in the position of a grantee. In 1919 four cottages in Bonnett Lane at Wareham in Dorset were sold individually, but at the same auction. At the back of the cottages with a wooden and corrugated iron fence. The other cottagers pulled access and for emptying cesspools from the cottage yards. Hansford who bought the end cottage, number 1, blocked this access to the other three cottages with a wooden and corrugated iron fence. The other cottagers pulled the fence down. When Hansford sued them in trespass, Russell J. held that easements had been granted for the other three cottages at the time of the sale.[5]

Where land has been divided for a long time, it may be difficult to show whether one piece was separated before another and if so which was disposed of first. However, this may cause less problems than might be expected, because a reserved right, like a grant, is construed in favour of the person who claims its benefits. Thus a right will be construed in favour of dominant land over land to which it was once attached whether it is claimed that the right was originally reserved when the servient land was disposed or, or was granted by someone who retained the servient land. The reason for this exception to the normal rule is that, before 1926, when a landowner wished to reserve a right over land of which he was disposing, it was necessary for the purchaser to make a separate grant back to the original owner of the right which he required. The Law of Property Act 1925, s. 65 (1), has abolished the need for a separate conveyance. However, reservation is still treated as if it were a re-grant. The Court of Appeal confirmed this in *St Edmundsbury* v. *Clark* (No. 2).[6] The Anchorage at Iken, 4 miles inland from Aldeburgh in Suffolk, was the old rectory of the parish church of St Botolph. In 1945 the rectory and glebe were sold to Mr Clark and a right of way was retained through the grounds to the church. In 1971 Mr Clark and the church authorities fell out. Mr Clark claimed that the church was only entitled to access on foot. He put up gates with concrete posts where the access led off the highway onto his land and bolted the gate, which he had himself once donated, into the churchyard itself. The Court of Appeal construed the original reservation of a right of way as clearly applying only to foot traffic but they disagreed with Megarry J. who had ruled that a reservation should, as a general principle, be construed against the initial grantor. The Court of Appeal reaffirmed that had it been necessary the term would have been construed against Mr Clark.

(c) Implied easements and profits

Where land is divided up, if an easement has not been expressly created, one may be implicitly reserved in favour of the part retained, or, more frequently, implied in favour of the part disposed of. Thus a right of way of necessity may be implicitly reserved or implicitly included in a grant where land would otherwise be inaccessible for the purpose for which it was used at the time of the grant. In *Pinnington* v. *Galland*,[7] land at Sutton-upon-Trent was sold in three lots on the same day in 1839 but there was no indication that the conveyances were made at exactly the same time or that they were made in any particular order (Fig. 5.6). Of the three lots, that known as Rye Holme Closes was reached from the highway across one of the other properties. In 1845, Galland, who had now acquired this other property disputed the access. The court held that if the Rye Holme Closes were the later property sold a right of way had nevertheless been retained in their favour. If they had been sold first a right had been implicitly granted to them. However, a right of necessity will not be upheld if the relevant access was not essential at the time the land was divided but only became so later, for example if there was an alternative road along the sea shore or a hill top which was later washed away or collapsed. Similarly a right of necessity cannot be used for new purposes such as access to new houses or factories.[8] Also the Court of Appeal has held that a right of necessity may be expressly excluded by the words of a grant.[9]

An easement may be implied, even as a reserved right, where this is necessary to carry out the common intentions of the original parties. Thus a

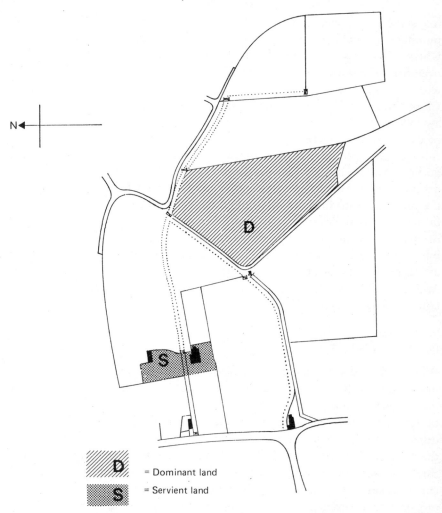

N◄

D = Dominant land
S = Servient land

Fig. 5.6 Implied easements in the case of *Pinnington* v. *Galland* [1853] 9 Ex. 1.

landowner will be deemed to reserve a right of support to his existing buildings where he sells off neighbouring land.[10] In *Cory* v. *Davies*,[11] a plot of land in Cardiff was let in 1857 on a ninety-nine-year building lease to three builders who between them constructed a terrace of seven houses set back with an access drive on to the main Newport road. In 1920 Davies bought the easternmost house and locked the east drive gates. The lessees of the other houses in the terrace successfully obtained an injunction from Lawrence J. requiring the gate to be re-opened. Although no rights of way had been reserved in the leases, it was the clear intention of the parties that all the properties should use the drive. Work had been begun on laying it out even before the leases were executed.

The courts show greater readiness to recognize implied grants of easements in accordance with the clear intentions of the two parties. In 1961 Mr Wai Man Wong bought the remaining years of a twenty-one-year lease, which had begun in 1957, of a restaurant in Exeter which he converted into a Chinese restaurant called the *Chop Sticks*. Beaumont Property Trust Ltd, the landlords, refused to allow the construction of a new ventilation system attached to the back of the building even though this was necessary to comply with public health regulations and with terms of the lease, in particular that the lessees should control and eliminate smells and odours. When Mr Wong claimed from the courts the right to erect the system they held that although the need for an external venting duct was not apparent when the lease was made, to comply with the intentions of the parties it had in fact been necessary from the beginning.[12]

The Law of Property Act 1925, s. 62, is designed to shorten conveyances by providing that unless otherwise stated a conveyance, whether the grant of a freehold or a lease, will automatically include all existing 'liberties, privileges, easements, rights and advantages whatsoever' currently enjoyed by the land conveyed. Not only does this confirm the transfer of existing easements and profits, it can also upgrade lesser rights, such as licences, where these are capable of being created as easements or profits. Thus, where a tenant has a licence to a short cut across his landlord's adjacent land, if the tenant buys the reversion of the lease,[13] or the lease is renewed,[14] the right of way will automatically become an easement. In such circumstances landlords and vendors must be careful to exclude any such rights by which they do not want to be bound permanently. A rather different principle is known as the rule in *Wheeldon* v. *Burrows*.[15] There the Court of Appeal held that, on the sale of a piece of land in Derby, no right to light had been implicitly reserved for the benefit of workshops retained by the vendor. However, Thesiger L.J. said *obiter dicta* that, on a grant of part of a tenement, the grantee is entitled to 'all the continuous and apparent' rights which are capable of being made as easements and which were in regular use by the grantor at the time of the grant. The judge also spoke of the right being necessary to the reasonable enjoyment of the property granted. He clearly envisaged that it might be possible to use the land without it but he did not make clear whether this more restricted form of necessity was an alternative to or an addition to the requirement that the right should be continuous and apparent. To be continuous and apparent there must be some clear permanent sign of the existence of the right such as windows receiving light,[16] or a defined access. Thus in *Brown* v. *Alabaster*,[17] three houses had been constructed under building leases on Park Road, Mosely, Worcestershire with a back access lane on land at the end of gardens belonging to two of the houses. Brown the owner of the lease to the outer house, Normanhurst, sought to stop Alabaster who owned the leases to the other two houses using this lane. Although it had not been expressly provided in the original leases of Alabaster's houses, Cottisbrook and Westbourne, Kay J. held that a right to use the access was implied because it had been continuous and apparent.

5.4.2 The voluntary and involuntary extinction of rights

Subsidiary rights can be extinguished or varied if those entitled to their benefit expressly so agree with those subject to them. Thus it is normally possible to buy up rights, for example a right of way or a right to light, which would otherwise hamper development. Where there is an agreement to release an easement or profit but no deed has been executed, in equity, the courts will uphold the agreement if, in reliance upon it, the person whose land is subject to the right acts to his detriment, for example by putting up a building.[18] Even in the absence of agreement, a subsidiary right may be abandoned provided there is a clear indication from the circumstances that this must have been intended. However, mere non-use is not enough. In about 1824 the occupier of number 14 Bath Street, in Bath, bricked up a back doorway to Cross Back Lane, later known as White Hart Lane, which led to Stall Street. The door had been there since the house was built in 1793. In 1864, after it had been closed for longer than it had originally been used the door was reopened by Cook, who was now the owner. Three years after that, he successfully obtained an injunction to stop Bath Corporation building across the access into Stall Street.[19] Assuming that Cook's access was a private right of way, on the facts, the previous blocking up was only a non-user and not an abandonment. By contrast, in *Ankerson* v. *Connelly*,[20] the owner of a house with ancient lights pulled it down and built a much larger structure which depended entirely on light from the servient land. The court held that the original right to light had been abandoned. Such of the original window space as was retained could have been blocked before the rebuilding without substantially affecting the lighting of the old dominant building.

A profit may not be regarded as abandoned even where it has been unexercised for many years, and even where it is for the benefit of land which has been put to a different use, provided that that land could easily be restored to a condition in which it required the profit. Thus in *Carr* v. *Lambert*,[21] rights of pasture were held not to have been abandoned even though for fifty years the land entitled to them had ceased to be a cattle toft and had been used as an orchard with a house and stable. However, it was said by the court that the rights probably would have been extinguished had a town of considerable extent or a reservoir been put on the land. In *Lascelles* v. *Lord Onslow*,[22] Lush J. seemed to envisage that rather less drastic changes in land use might diminish demand on a common and lead to a reduction of rights over it. He listed changes in the mode of managing farms, in the description of cattle kept, and the kind of food given, and in the produce raised; also the appropriation of the land to other uses such as its conversion into nurseries, hop gardens, market gardens or building ground.

It appears that restrictive covenants may be abandoned if they are not enforced,[23] and subsidiary rights generally may become unenforceable if those entitled to them fail to begin using them over a considerable period.[24] A subsidiary right will in any event be extinguished where the fee simples of both the servient land and the dominant land become vested in the same person. Thus in *Lord Dynevor* v. *Tennant*,[25] Lord Dynevor, and other co-owners of the Neath Abbey Estate in Ireland, granted, in 1820, a 1000-year lease of a strip of land for a canal, reserving rights of access across it. In 1838 the estate was divided up. The reversion of the strip of land with the canal on it was later conveyed to the canal owner. Lord Dynevor, as tenant for life of the land on either side, claimed the right of access across the canal, but it was held by the House of Lords that this right had been created with regard to the reversion of the canal land and not of the adjoining land. As the fee simple and the leasehold estates in the canal land had merged, the rights had ceased to exist.

Uncertainty as to whether a right has ceased to exist may arise where the land subject to it can no longer support it. If land subject to profits has long been built over or covered by the sea or by shingle the rights will doubtless have been lost.[26] However, temporary use inconsistent with a profit may not extinguish it. Thus if gravel or clay are removed and the land is then returfed, rights of pasture may continue.[27]

5.4.3   Statutory relief from subsidiary rights

Those whose land is subject to subsidiary rights may occasionally be able to invoke public powers to overcome them. If land is ripe for development, an owner might arrange for it to be acquired for this purpose by a local authority under the Town and Country Planning Act 1971, s. 119. The land could then be transferred back to him so that he could carry out development. Under s. 127 he would then be authorized to override subsidiary rights over the land. In the case of rights of common, and more recently of restrictive covenants, Parliament has given private citizens powers to have inconvenient rights of others terminated.

(a)   Statutory relief and rights of common

At common law it was possible for the lord of a manor to *approve* manorial waste subject to rights of pasture, that is to fence off parts for his own use, provided he could establish that he was leaving enough to satisfy the commoner's rights. Today this right is subject to the consent of the Secretary of State for the Environment. Fencing off of part of common land or building on it are only permitted with his approval.[28] More drastically, under the Commons Act 1876, applications may be made to the Secretary of State to enclose common land and to extinguish all rights of common, if it is shown that this would be for the benefit of the neighbourhood as well as in the private interest of the applicant. However, the procedure is a cumbersome one. It involves a public local inquiry and if the Secretary of State supports the application, the order by which he implements it must be laid before Parliament.

(b) The Lands Tribunal's powers over restrictive covenants

The Law of Property Act 1925, s. 84 (1) gives those whose freehold land is subject to restrictive covenants a relatively simple procedure for dealing with them by applying to the Lands Tribunal for their discharge or modification. If appropriate, suitable compensation must be paid and new conditions may be imposed. The powers also apply to covenants in leases for more than forty years of which at least twenty-five years has expired, and it appears that they apply to covenants made for the benefit of the covenantor personally.[29] Jurisdiction is discretionary but is only available if the Lands Tribunal is satisfied that the applicant has made out grounds specified in the section.

Under paragraph (b) of these provisions, the Lands Tribunal may endorse an agreement to waive a restrictive covenant or rule that it has been implicitly abandoned. Under paragraph (a) it may act where 'by reason of changes in the character of the property or the neighbourhood or other circumstances of the case which the Lands Tribunal may deem material, the restriction ought to be deemed obsolete'. Here, if planning policy has led to a change in the character of a neighbourhood, say from that of large private houses to flats or offices, covenants against such uses may have become obsolete. However, a person benefiting from a covenant may still be entitled to protection even if the neighbourhood has changed. In *Truman Hanbury and Buxton Co. Ltd Application*,[30] a large estate on London Road at Leigh-on-Sea was built in 1848, with covenants against non-residential use, and specifically forbidding any of the premises to be used for the trade of a hotel keeper, inn keeper, or victualler of wine, spirits or beer. By the 1950s London Road contained many shops and an application was made to discharge the restrictions against hotels and related uses on two plots. The Court of Appeal upheld the Lands Tribunal's refusal to discharge the covenant. Romer L.J. held that: 'if serious injury would result to the opponents and others if the covenant was discharged . . . I cannot see how on any view the covenant can be described as obsolete because the object of the covenant is still capable of fulfilment and the covenant still affords a real protection to those who are entitled to it.'

Because obsolescence has been interpreted in terms of covenants ceasing to benefit the dominant property, generally, obsolete covenants may also be discharged under paragraph (c). This allows for discharge, or more commonly modification, where this 'will not injure the person entitled to the benefit of the restriction'. Here a covenant may be modified even though those entitled to its benefit fear some indirect harm as a result. In 1940 the owner of an estate on the Helford River near the village of Helford in Cornwall granted a restrictive covenant against non-agricultural building over her land in favour of the National Trust. Over the following years the Trust allowed some building on the estate, but in the 1960s opposed the erection of a new house planned by Gee who had acquired a site with an existing house on the estate. The proposed house was described by the planning inspector who recommended planning approval as a building which would be comparatively unobtrusive, on a site, 'which offers great scope and challenge for an interesting architectural scheme'. Although the Lands Tribunal refused to modify the covenant, the Court of Appeal did so.[31] The National Trust had not opposed the scheme for aesthetic reasons but on the unsubstantiated grounds that the house set a precedent for further breaches of National Trust covenants and would discourage people from making further covenants with the Trust or from contributing to its work, notably to Enterprise Neptune, by which it was seeking to protect as much as possible of the British Coastline.

The most far-reaching grounds for the Lands Tribunal to act in discharging or modifying covenants are in paragraph (aa) and ss. 1 A, B and C which were inserted into s. 84 of the 1925 Act by the Law of Property Act 1969. These grounds apply where the continued existence of a covenant in its present form would impede some reasonable user of the land for public or private purposes. The Lands Tribunal is required to 'take into account the development plan and any declared or ascertainable pattern for the grant or refusal of planning permission in the relevant area as well as the period at which and the context in which the restrictions were created or imposed and any other material circumstances'. The Tribunal must be satisfied that any persons who will be deprived of benefit from the covenant can be adequately compensated by a money payment and as to one of two further alternative requirements. The first alternative is that the covenant 'does not secure to persons entitled to the benefit of it any practical benefits of substantial value or advantage to them'. This extends the jurisdiction under paragraphs (a) and (c). However, a benefit may be of substantial value or advantage if it is of importance to those protected by it whatever its financial value. Thus the Lands Tribunal refused to discharge a covenant imposed on a cottage and adjacent land in a quiet rural backwater of the Isle of Wight near Ryde, which forbade non-residential and non-agricultural uses so as to protect the adjacent home of the original vendor. The cottage had been turned into a riding school so that a field was churned up, the vicinity was defouled with manure and children using the riding school made it noisy. The Lands Tribunal appears to have discounted evidence that similar interference with the covenantee's enjoyment could have been caused by permissible agricultural uses.[32]

The second alternative under paragraph (aa) is that, in impeding the proposed reasonable use, the continued existence of a covenant in its present form is contrary to the public interest. Even here, although account must be taken of planning patterns in the neighbourhood, these are not conclusive. Before the First World War a site was acquired by a brewery company which was later taken over by Bass Ltd. A covenant was imposed to prevent non-residential building so as to provide a 'cordon sanitaire of residential buildings masking any new industrial development'. In 1972 Bass Ltd applied for the covenant to be overridden so as to enable it to construct an improved trunker park for its vehicles. Although the site was zoned for industrial use and planning permission had been granted, the Lands Tribunal refused to override the covenant. The Chairman, J. D. Daniel Q.C. commented that: 'the proposition that this operation is in the public interest is strange indeed unless the public interest is to be equated to the economic benefits of this particular part of the beer trade.'[33] On the other hand in *S.J.C. Construction Co. Ltd Application*,[34] Sir Douglas Frank Q.C., the President of the Lands Tribunal, modified a covenant against flats on the site of a large demolished house in Cheam to allow for these to be built even although they would interfere with the view from old people's accommodation which was to be built on adjacent local authority land. The local authority had itself given planning permission for the flats. These were needed and there was a scarcity of suitable land on which to provide them. Also, £47 000 worth of work had already been done as a result of apparent acquiescence by the local authority and this should not be wasted.

NOTES: SECTION 5.4

1. *South Metropolitan Cemetery Co.* v. *Eden* (1855) 16 C.B. 42.
2. *May* v. *Belleville* [1905] 2 Ch. 605.
3. *McManus* v. *Cooke* (1887) 35 Ch.D. 681.
4. *Mason* v. *Clarke* [1955] A.C. 778, H.L.
5. *Hansford* v. *Jago* [1921] 1 Ch. 332.
6. *St Edmundsbury* v. *Clark* [1975] 1 W.L.R. 468, C.A.
7. *Pinnington* v. *Galland* (1853) 9 Ex. 1.
8. *London Corporation* v. *Riggs* (1880) 13 Ch.D. 799.
9. *Nickerson* v. *Barraclough* [1981] Ch. 426.
10. *Shubrook* v. *Tufnell* (1882) 46 T.L.R. 886.
11. *Cory* v. *Davies* [1923] 2 Ch. 95.
12. *Wong* v. *Beaumont Trust* [1965] 1 Q.B. 173.
13. *International Tea Stores Co.* v. *Hobbs* [1903] 2 Ch. 165.
14. *Goldberg* v. *Edwards* [1950] 1 Ch. 247.
15. *Wheeldon* v. *Burrows* (1878) 12 Ch.D. 31, C.A.
16. *Phillips* v. *Low* [1892] 1 Ch. 47.
17. *Brown* v. *Alabaster* (1887) 37 Ch.D. 490.

18. *Waterlow* v. *Bacon* (1866) 2 L.R. Eq. 514.
19. *Cook* v. *Bath Corporation* (1868) 6 L.R. Eq. 177.
20. *Ankerson* v. *Connelly* [1907] 1 Ch. 678, C.A.
21. *Carr* v. *Lambert* (1866) 1 L.R. Exch. 168.
22. *Lascelles* v. *Lord Onslow* (1877) 2 Q.B.D. 433.
23. See discussion in *Lloyds Bank Ltd* v. *Jones* [1955] 2 Q.B. 298, *per* Singleton L.J. at p. 320–2.
24. *Swan* v. *Sinclair* [1925] A.C. 227.
25. *Lord Dynevor* v. *Tennant* (1888) 13 App. Cas. 279.
26. *Scrutton* v. *Stone* (1893) 9 T.L.R. 478.
27. *Robertson* v. *Hartopp* (1889) 43 Ch.D. 484.
28. Law of Commons (Amendment) Act 1893.
29. *Shepherd Homes Ltd* v. *Sandham* (No. 2) [1971] 1 W.L.R. 1062, *per* Megarry J. at p. 1070 f.
30. *Truman Hanbury and Buxton Co. Ltd Application* [1956] 1 Q.B. 261, C.A.
31. *Gee* v. *National Trust* [1966] 1 W.L.R. 170, C.A.
32. *Re Bailey's Application* (1981) 42 P. & C.R. 108.
33. *Re Bass Ltd's Application* (1973) 26 P. & C.R. 157, at p. 161.
34. *S.J.C. Construction Co. Ltd Application* (1975) 29 P. & C.R. 322, C.A.

5.5 How time affects the control of land

There is an underlying principle of law that peoples' rights and obligations should be clear and in particular should not be left in any state of uncertainty because of ancient disputes. For this reason it has been provided in a number of ways that when circumstances have existed for a long time they will be protected at the expense of earlier rights.

5.5.1 Good title and the limitation act

Where freehold land is sold, the vendor is generally required to show a good title, either by producing the land certificate[1] if the land is registered, or, if it is not, by a *root of title* at least fifteen years old proving a sale or other disposition of the entire legal and equitable interest and clearly identifying the land concerned. In the case of unregistered land, all documents must be produced showing dealings in the land from the date of the root of title. The relevant time has been steadily reduced over the last century and is now stipulated in the Law of Property Act 1969, s. 23. Where a lease is transferred the transferror will normally only be required to prove his title to the lease itself and not the title under which the lease was granted originally.[2] If a title is subject to subsidiary interests the purchaser will normally be protected because these will be registered in some form. Purely equitable interest affecting proceeds of sale of land will not normally concern him.[3]

(a) The effect of possession

Although a person disposing of land will normally be required to prove his title for fifteen years or more, where he has been in possession for a shorter time he may, nevertheless, dispose of his right to possession, and those who have been in possession of land for any period may bring an action in the courts relying on the fact of possession to recover the land from anyone who dispossesses them of it and who does not have a prior title. Thus, if one squatter is evicted by another he may enlist the help of the court to recover possession. Where a person has been in possession of land for a sufficient time that will prevent even a person with an earlier title recovering the land. Currently the Limitation Act 1980 s. 15, provides a limitation period of twelve years in the case of land. Where land is unregistered the act simply extinguishes rights of action to recover possession. Where land is registered, after the expiration of the limitation period the owner of the registered title holds the land on trust for the new possessor until the register has been amended.[4] However, although an old title may be extinguished and a new possessory title protected by the Limitation Act, subsidiary rights such as easements are not affected.

(b) When time runs

The limitation period begins to run against a person from the time when he is dispossessed, or, if he is not in possession, from the date when he becomes entitled to possession. Thus, if a house is built so as to intrude onto neighbouring land which has been let under a twenty-year lease, time begins to run against the tenant immediately. It does not begin to run against the owner until the lease expires. The owner then has twelve years in which to sue. In *Spectrum Investments Co.* v. *Holmes*,[5] it was held that if a squatter on registered land has a possessory title entered on the register, the landlord may not evict him until the original lease would have expired. However, where the land is unregistered, if the original tenant relinquishes the lease to the landlord at an earlier date, the landlord is immediately entitled to repossession. A tenant who stays in possession after the expiration of the lease as a tenant at sufferance,[6] may eventually obtain a squatter's title himself.[7] However, a tenant who takes possession of adjacent land belonging to the landlord and not included in the lease will only acquire a possessory title to this for the remainder of the lease,[8] and on the same terms. We have seen in Chapter 4, Section 4.2, that future interests under trusts for sale and strict settlements are treated as essentially interests in the value of land rather than in the land itself.[9] However, for the purposes of the Limitation Act 1980, by s. 38 (1), such interests are themselves treated as land. By itself, this provision would mean that if a life tenant were dispossessed, time would begin to run immediately against both the life tenant and those entitled to the property after him in equity. However, s. 18, provides that the legal estate survives with the tenant for life so that, although he loses his own right to recover possession, only when he dies does time begin to run against his successor. Section 15 (2b) stipulates that an action must then be brought within twelve years of the original dispossession of the life tenant or within six years of his death if that is longer.

Normally, under s. 15 (6) and Sched. 1, Part I, even if a person in possession of land ceases to exercise any form of control over it, time only begins to run against him when someone else actively enters into adverse possession. However, where adverse possession has begun whilst land is vacant following the death of the estate owner, or in other circumstances where there has been a grant of the land to some other person who has not yet taken possession, the adverse possession is backdated to the death or grant. If one trespasser who has excluded the owner from land then abandons it, and after an interval a separate person begins adverse possession, then time only begins running in favour of the second trespasser from when he enters the land and not from the earlier trespass.[10] On the other hand if an initial trespasser passes on his possession directly to someone else or even if he is in turn dispossessed directly by another trespasser, time continues to run against the original owner. In *Asher* v. *Whitlock*,[11] in 1842 and again in 1852, one Williamson enclosed successive pieces of waste land in the Bedfordshire village of Keysoe and built a cottage, which, on his death in 1860, he left to his wife Lucy till her death or remarriage, and then to his daughter Mary Ann. Lucy remarried in 1861 a man called Whitlock. They lived in the cottage with Mary Ann who died in 1863. By 1865 Lucy had also died. Mrs Asher, who was heir to Mary Ann, then successfully brought an action to recover the land. Cockburn C.J. ruled that Thomas Williamson's possession of the land was sufficient to get him a good title against anyone other than the original owner. His right to possession had passed to Mrs Asher. Whitlock had not remained in possession long enough on his own account for Mrs Asher's action to be out of time. Probably the lord of the manor who originally owned the waste would have been too late to sue anyone, although if the property had been left abandoned and he had taken it over again no-one could have challenged him and he would have been able to pass on his original title without any difficulty.[12]

(c) Dispossession

For a person to be dispossessed by another for the purposes of adverse possession, he must be excluded clearly from the land. It is not enough that the new occupant shares it with him.[13] However, if the owner uses the land in some capacity where he does not rely upon his title he may not be regarded as retaining possession. In *Bligh* v. *Martin*,[14] Mr Martin bought an estate called

Roffy House at Horsham in 1945. Not until 1965 did he look closely enough at his conveyance to notice that what he had bought included a certain plot of 3.817 acres. The original owner had also included this plot in a later sale of an adjacent farm called Greenfields. The plot was farmed with Greenfields for nearly five years until this was sold to Mr Bligh who then employed Martin through estate agents to plough and harvest the disputed plot as a contractor. Each winter Martin let his cattle on to the land and in 1960 took a grazing tenancy or licence to use it entirely for grazing. When he discovered his own paper title he fenced off the land but he was too late. Bligh successfully sued him in trespass.

Someone with an original title may retain possession by minimal acts of control. 'In the case of vacant and unenclosed land which is not being cultivated there is little that can be done on the land to indicate possession',[15] and adverse possession does not occur where the original owner has given up direct control but has left a new occupier in possession with his express or implied permission as a licensee. In *Wallis's Cayton Bay Holiday Camp Ltd v. Shell Mex*,[16] $1\frac{1}{3}$ acres of land near the sea at Cayton Bay between Scarborough and Filey in Yorkshire had been sold by a farmer for a garage on a proposed new road. Some years later, in 1961, Wallis's bought the remainder of the farm to extend its camp. The line of the road which had been acquired by the local authority and the garage site were clearly excluded in the conveyance to Wallis's but there were no boundaries on the ground separating these three pieces of land. Wallis's used the road and the garage sites, first for farm purposes, cutting the grass and cropping wheat, then as a playground and football field for the camp, still cutting the grass and also collecting litter, and painting the outer fence white like the outer fence of the camp. They obtained an express licence to use the land for the road but merely treated the garage site as their own. The road was then abandoned and Shell Mex who were now owners of the garage site offered to sell it to Wallis's. They, however, ignored the offer, hoping to obtain a squatters' title to the land which was now worth £8000. In 1973 Shell Mex, in the words of Lord Denning M.R., 'smelt a rat', and fenced off the land. Wallis's then sued for interference with a possessory title which they claimed after twelve years occupation. The county court and a majority of the Court of Appeal rejected this claim. As Lord Denning stated:

when the true owner of land intends to use it for a particular purpose in the future but in the meanwhile has no immediate use for it, and so leaves it unoccupied, he does not lose his title to it if it is used for some temporary purpose, like stacking materials; or for some seasonal purpose like growing vegetables. Not even if this temporary or seasonal purpose continues year after year for 12 years or more.

As Ormrod L.J. commented, if Wallis's had built chalets on the land, that probably would have amounted to adverse possession. What they actually had done was trivial if regarded as an interference with the proposed use of the disputed site for a future garage. On the other hand the same acts of trespass might have been highly significant if carried out in the garden of a house.

The amount of control which is required of a squatter to extinguish a previous title and to obtain a possessory one is much greater than that required of the original owner in retaining possession. The squatter must also have a clear intention to take possession throughout the limitation period. Thus it may well not be enough if he merely makes use of the land to take produce such as hay, timber or pigeons. Such behaviour is likely at the most to be regarded as the exercise of a right to take profits.[17]

5.5.2   Prescription

There are distinct time rules which allow for the prescription by long use of easements and profits for the benefit of neighbouring land. Here the legal theory is that, if someone has exercised a use for long enough, it must be presumed that he or his predecessors were once granted a right to do so. These rules make it particularly important that those concerned with advising on changes in land use should check whether the change will interfere with any right which has been acquired by long use. For example new building or landscape work may prove to be impracticable because it would block an established right of way. In such a case an architect or landscape architect advising on the scheme could well be negligent if he failed at an early stage to check for evidence of such rights being exercised over the land and to make sure that the position had been checked by his client's solicitor.

This is a difficult part of the law. Today prescription is normally claimed under the Prescription Act 1832 which has been described as 'one of the worst-drafted acts on the statute book'.[18] The Act provides that generally, under s. 2, an easement may be obtained by twenty years use and, under s. 1, a profit by thirty years use. Easements of light are subject to special rules.

(a)   Prescription is related to fee simple estates

Normally prescription can only be over one fee simple estate for the benefit of another. Thus it is not possible for a profit in gross[19] to be acquired by prescription.[20] However, a tenant may acquire an easement or profit over neighbouring land for the benefit of his landlord. Also, provided prescription starts at a time when the servient land is in the hands of a fee simple owner it can continue although the land is later let. In *Pugh* v. *Savage*,[21] Pugh had owned Church Villa Farm at Loppington near Wem in Shropshire since 1950. Savage became tenant of the neighbouring Factory Farm in 1966 and was told that he was entitled to take farm vehicles from one of the fields over a footpath on Pugh's farm. In 1968 Pugh blocked this route. When Savage made a detour on Pugh's land, Pugh sued him for trespass. The Court of Appeal held that Savage was entitled to the right of way. It had been exercised by previous occupants of the dominant fields. It did not matter that both they and Savage were tenants, as a tenant may acquire a prescriptive right of way for his landlord by using it whilst he is a tenant. Also it did not matter that during part of the relevant period there had been a tenancy of the servient land. By contrast, s. 7 of the Act provides that any period during which the owner of servient land is a tenant for life or is an infant or mentally disabled is to be deducted from the time of adverse possession. However, time starts to run again when the disability ends and does not have to be restarted from the beginning.

(b) User as of right

For prescription to be effective, the right claimed must be exercised as a right. This involves use according to the Latin tag, *nec clam, nec vi, nec precario*, that is it must not be, 'clandestine, contentious or by sufferance'.[22] Thus no right will be acquired by a secret use. In *Union Lighterage Co.* v. *London Graving Dock*,[23] the owner of a dock at Blackwall secured it by underground rods fixed to piles some 15 feet 6 inches away. The intervening land was subsequently sold without notice of the rods and a later owner removed them. A majority in the Court of Appeal held that no easement had been acquired to keep the rods in position since they had been hidden apart from two nuts showing on the outside of the piles to which they were fixed. Romer L.J. said that the right claimed must be 'of such a character than an ordinary owner of the servient land diligent in the protection of his interests, would have, or must be taken to have, a reasonable opportunity of becoming aware of that enjoyment'.[24]

Secondly the use must not be contentious. In particular it must not be challenged in legal proceedings during the prescription period.[25] Finally, a use will not be exercised as of right if it is carried out under permission. In *Gardner* v. *Hodgson's Kingston Brewery Co. Ltd*,[26] the owner of stable used an access through the yard of an adjacent inn. Although this use had been carried on for some sixty years it was held not to be an easement since an annual sum of 15 shillings had been paid in respect of it. Thus, if a landowner grants a neighbour some licence such as a temporary access it is wise to safeguard its becoming an established right by exacting some nominal annual sum of money.

(c) Continuous uninterrupted use

The exercise of a right claimed under the Prescription Act 1832, must have been asserted continuously for the necessary period and, s. 4 requires this to have been continued up to immediately before the cause of action in which the right is tested. What is continuous is a question of fact and will vary with the circumstances. Thus to exercise a right of way, a claimant does not need to be using it ceaselessly. However in *Hollins* v. *Verney*,[27] Verney claimed a right of way across Hollins' land for carting timber from his wood. When Hollins sued in trespass, the Court of Appeal refused to recognize the right claimed because evidence only showed the use to have been exercised on the occasion leading to the action and on two previous occasions at intervals of twelve years. Under s. 4, to prevent a right being acquired, an interruption of the continuous period must be submitted to, or acquiesced in, for one year by the claimant after he has received notice of it. An interruption requires some overt act such as fencing off the land where the right is claimed. Resistance preventing the interruption taking effect does not need to be so drastic. In *Davies* v. *Du Paver*,[28] Davies and Jones claimed the right after sixty years use to sheep walks on 12½ acres of land at Festiniog in Wales called Hafod Ysbyyty. Du Paver had bought the land in 1949 and fenced it off. The plaintiffs objected fiercely at the time and even although they then did nothing for thirteen months, when an action was brought a majority of the Court of Appeal agreed with the County Court judge that it was right not to regard them as acquiescing in the interruption. However, the Court of Appeal held that no right to the sheep walks had been acquired in the first place because the owner of the servient land had not been shown to know or have means of knowledge of the use, or power to object to it. If objection is taken to a use which has been carried on for so long that there is less than one year of the statutory period left to run, it is too late for it to be interrupted under the terms of the Act. Nevertheless during that year the owner of the land affected may still be able to bring an action in trespass to expel the person exercising the use and so put an end to it.[29]

(d) Easements of light

Under the Prescription Act 1832, easements of light are provided for in s. 3, separately from other rights. A person with windows receiving light from land which is tenanted can acquire a right against both the tenant and the landlord.[30] A tenant can acquire a right to light for the remainder of his lease against land let to another tenant by the same landlord.[31] Generally, the Act does not require that the enjoyment of light should be as of right. Also, such an easement may be acquired after only twenty years in circumstances where other rights could be acquired only after forty years or not even then. However, adverse possession of a right to light will not occur if the light is enjoyed only under an express written agreement,[32] or, under s. 4, if it is interrupted for at least one year without submission or acquiescence by the person claiming the right. An interruption would normally involve erecting unsightly and expensive barriers to block off the light. Thus the Rights of Light Act 1959 allows for the creation of an imaginary obstruction for one year by registration with the district council. A landowner who wishes to keep open the option of building next to land on which someone else has erected buildings may therefore need to register an objection every nineteen years. If he does not register until the twentieth year it may be too late. Interruption must be for a full year. Unlike a use such as a right of way, adverse possession of a right to light cannot be stopped by an action in trespass, since the enjoyment of light does not involve going on to the servient land. In the twentieth year, s. 3 (4) of the 1959 Act allows the owner of the dominant land to sue to protect a right to light as soon as an objection is registered. On the other hand if he fails to sue he is treated as acquiescing in the interruption and at the end of a year will have lost his claim since, as with other claims under the Prescription Act 1832, he must show an uninterrupted twenty years immediately before an action in which the right is tested.

(e) Other means of prescription

Before the Prescription Act 1832, easements or profits would be recognized at *common law* if they had been exercised throughout living memory, but only if there was no evidence showing that this use did not go right back to 1189.[33] It was therefore virtually impossible at common law to claim rights to light or to support of buildings, few of which date back to the twelfth century. To protect long-established uses which must have been more recent than 1189 the courts evolved what has been called 'a revolting fiction',[34] and 'the final consummation of judicial legislation,[35] in the form of the doctrine of *lost modern grant*. Where a use had been exercised for twenty years it was assumed that this was under a proper grant even if evidence was given by those who would have known that no such grant had been made. However, the assumption was not made if the grant would have been impossible, for example because it would have contravened a statute. Today, certain sorts of easement, such as a right to pollute water, have become increasingly difficult to create because of modern legislation.[36] Both at common law and under the doctrine of lost modern grant, an easement or profit can only be claimed if it has been exercised for the benefit of, and against, fee simple estates as of right and continuously.

Today common law, or the doctrine of lost modern grant may still be used occasionally to establish a right to an easement or profit in circumstances where the Prescription Act 1832 does not apply, notably where profits have been taken for over twenty years but not for a full thirty years.[37] The Prescription Act, 1832 itself provides more liberal provisions under s. 2, where an easement is claimed after forty years use, or under s. 1 where a profit is claimed after sixty years. Thus in such cases the use will become a right even if it has been exercised under permission where that permission was merely given orally when the use began and has not been reaffirmed since, for example by regular payments. Also no account is taken of any part of the forty- or sixty-year periods during which the servient owner was subject to legal disability.[38]

NOTES: SECTION 5.5

1. *Ante* p. 239.
2. *Ante* p. 238.
3. *Ante* p. 243.
4. Land Registration Act 1925, s. 75 (1).
5. *Spectrum Investments Co.* v. *Holmes* [1981] 1 W.L.R. 221.
6. *Ante* p. 183.
7. *Re Jolly* (1900) 2 Ch. 616, C.A.
8. *Smirk* v. *Lyndale Developments Ltd* [1975] Ch. 317.
9. *Ante* p. 175.
10. Limitation Act 1980, s. 15 (6), Sched. 1, Para. 8 (2).
11. *Asher* v. *Whitlock* (1865) 1 L.R. Q.B. 1.
12. In *Willis* v. *Earl Howe* [1893] 2 Ch. 545, Kay L.J. said, *obiter dicta*, at p. 553, 'a continuous adverse possession for the statutory period, though by a succession of persons not claiming under one another, does, in my opinion, bar the true owner'.
13. *Treloar* v. *Nute* [1976] 1 W.L.R. 1295, *per* Sir John Pennycuick at p. 1300.
14. *Bligh* v. *Martin* [1968] 1 W.L.R. 804.
15. *Wuta-Ofei* v. *Danquah* [1961] 1 W.L.R. 1238, at p. 1243, P.C., on appeal from the West African Court of Appeal.
16. *Wallis's Cayton Bay Holiday Camp Ltd* v. *Shell Mex* [1975] 1 Q.B. 94, C.A.
17. *Powell* v. *McFarlane* (1977) 38 P. & C.R. 452.
18. Law Reform Committee (1966) 14th Report, Cmnd. 3100 para. 40.
19. *Ante* p. 207.
20. *Shuttleworth* v. *Le Fleming* (1865) 19 C.B., N.S. 687.
21. *Pugh* v. *Savage* [1970] 2 Q.B. 373, C.A.
22. *Eaton* v. *The Swansea Waterworks Co.* (1851) 17 Q.B. 267, *per* Erle J. at p. 275.
23. *Union Lighterage Co.* v. *London Graving Dock* [1902] 2 Ch. 557, C.A.
24. *Ibid* at p. 571.
25. *Eaton* v. *The Swansea Waterworks Co. ante*, note. 22.
26. *Gardner* v. *Hodgson's Kingston Brewery Co. Ltd* [1903] A.C. 229, H.L.
27. *Hollins* v. *Verney* (1884) 13 Q.B.D. 304, C.A.
28. *Davies* v. *Du Paver* [1953] 1 Q.B. 184, C.A.
29. *Reilley* v. *Orange* [1955] 2 Q.B. 112, C.A.
30. *Simper* v. *Foley* (1862) 2 Johns. & Hem. 555.
31. *Morgan* v. *Fear* [1907] A.C. 425, H.L.
32. *Colls* v. *Home and Colonial Stores* [1904] A.C. 179, H.L. *per* Lord Lindley at p. 205, and see *ante* p. 203.
33. *Hulbert* v. *Dale* [1909] 2 Ch. 570, *per* Joyce J. at p. 577. (affirmed in the Court of Appeal without reference to the point).
34. *Angus & Co.* v. *Dalton* (1871) 3 Q.B.D. 85, *per* Lush J. at p. 94, quoted in Megarry R.E. and Wade H.W.R. (1975), *The Law of Real Property*, 4th edn, Stevens and Sons, London p. 848.

35. *Bryant* v. *Foot* (1867) 2 L.R. Q.B. 161, *per* Cockburn C.J. at p. 181.
36. *Hulley* v. *Silver Springs Bleaching and Dyeing Co. Ltd* [1922] 2 Ch. 268.
37. *Tehidy Minerals Ltd* v. *Norman* [1971] 2 Q.B. 528, C.A.
38. However, under s. 8, periods during which the servient land is held under a life tenancy are deducted even from a forty- or sixty-year period of prescription.

Chapter 6

LAND USE AND LEGAL RESPONSIBILITY FOR HARM

[I]n English law there must be, and is, some general conception of relations giving rise to a duty of care, of which the particular cases found in the books are but instances ... [A]cts or omissions which any moral code would censure cannot in a practical world be treated so as to give a right to every person injured by them to demand relief. In this way rules of law arise which limit the range of complainants and the extent of their remedy. The rule that you are to love your neighbour becomes in law, you must not injure your neighbour; and the lawyer's question, Who is my neighbour? receives a restricted reply. You must take reasonable care to avoid acts or omissions which you can reasonably foresee would be likely to injure your neighbour. Who, then, in law is my neighbour? The answer seems to be — persons who are so closely and directly affected by my act that I ought reasonably to have them in contemplation as being so affected when I am directing my mind to the acts or omissions which are called in question.

Lord Atkin in *Donoghue* v. *Stevenson* [1932]
A.C. 562, at p. 580

Whoever may have the power over a piece of land, they or others may suffer harm or cause harm in the course of the many uses to which the land may be put. The law enforces the responsibility for such harm in three main ways, by criminal law, tort and under contract.

Criminal law provides rules which normally restrict everyone in their manner of behaviour. In the public interest it punishes those who fail to comply with its standards. The law of tort also lays down general standards, but as a basis for individuals to protect their rights by bringing court proceedings for an appropriate remedy rather than for the purpose of punishing the interferer. By contrast, the law of contract provides a framework whereby individuals may restrict their general responsibility to each other, or, more often, may take on special responsibilities, for example to provide services or materials. It is important to bear in mind that these three areas of the law all depend for their effectiveness on the manner in which they may be enforced: Chapter 8, Section 8.1 outlines the remedies available from the courts.

6.1   Land use and the criminal law

The criminal law provides direct protection for the landscape by punishing those who harm the property of others, notably by arson or other forms of criminal damage. Those who misbehave in the course of work on land may commit other offences. A trespasser who attacks a landowner trying to evict him will be guilty of assault. The landowner will himself be guilty of assault if he uses excessive force in the eviction. A surveyor or other professional person who acts dishonestly in the course of his work may be guilty of various forms of fraud. The criminal law also provides the teeth for various forms of public control over land use and may be used against landowners themselves. Thus, those who carry out unlawful development may be ordered by an enforcement notice to restore the land to its previous condition. If they fail to do so they will be guilty of a criminal offence. Breaches of certain special planning controls, for example cutting down a tree which is protected by a tree preservation order or demolishing a listed building, are themselves criminal offences.

In the autumn of 1971, Barnet London Borough Council were widening Oakleigh Road North at Whetstone. The Eastern Electricity Board instructed private contractors, Madden Duggan Co Ltd to relay underground cables beneath the road. Despite warnings by the council to take care of trees next to the road, which were subject to preservation orders, the contractors severely damaged the root systems of six trees (Figs 6.1 and 6.2). Four, on the highway itself, were felled by the council, and the two others, which were on private property, were lopped. The council prosecuted the Electricity Board and their contractor for the offence of 'wilful destruction' of the six trees.[1] The Magistrates' Court ruled that there was no evidence that the defendants had wilfully destroyed the trees. The Divisional Court allowed the councils' appeal and sent the case back to the magistrates, with the ruling that to destroy a tree it did not need to be, 'obliterated'. It was enough if it was 'rendered useless . . . when as a result of that which is done to it, it ceases to have any use as amenity, as something worth preserving. For example, if a person intentionally inflicts on a tree so radical an injury that in all the circumstances any reasonably competent forester would in consequence decide that it ought to be felled . . .'

Fig. 6.1 The site of *Barnet L.B.C.* v. *E.E.B.* [1973] 1 W.L.R. 430, by kind permission of the London Borough of Barnett.

The Barnet case presents the somewhat curious prospect of one public body being prosecuted in the courts by another. Where the law is used to punish an offence rather than to compensate an injured party it might seem more appropriate for the individual directly responsible to be prosecuted. Nevertheless, as we shall see, this case also illustrates the form of a typical environmental offence.

When it is available, the criminal law may be a more powerful deterrent than the civil law against abuses of the landscape, because of the heavier sanctions available, including imprisonment. In practice, however, it is harder to obtain a conviction for a criminal offence than a civil judgment against the wrongdoer, because of the tougher rules of evidence and procedure. Statutory offences against the environment may be easier to prove because they are usually *strict*, that is they may not require the offender to have intended or been aware of the consequences of his actions. However, the sanctions actually imposed by the courts for these offences tend to be modest fines. Also there is little stigma attached to such offences in the public eye, so that developers and others who are tempted to commit them may decide to ignore the risk of prosecution. Although private citizens such as members of a conservation group could in many cases prosecute someone who has abused

Fig. 6.2 Severed tree roots in the case of *Barnet L.B.C.* v. *E.E.B* [1973] 1 W.L.R. 430, by kind permission of the London Borough of Barnet.

the landscape, because of the expense, prosecutions are usually left to the police or other public bodies such as local authorities. These tend to give a low priority to this use of their resources.

6.1.1   General principles of criminal law

The criminal law consists of a wide range of offences, most of which are defined by statute. The most common offences are triable by magistrates' courts, although more serious examples may be committed to the Crown Court for trial. Wherever anyone is charged with an offence the prosecution must prove appropriate, 'conduct of the accused and his state of mind at the time of that conduct'.[2] In the Barnet case of the trees at Whetstone what was in issue was the meaning of 'destroy', part of the necessary conduct. If the trees had been a hedge of saplings, the issue might have been over whether these amounted to trees, another aspect of conduct. However, a case of this sort is more likely to be contested on the grounds that there was no appropriate state of mind or that the defendant was in some way justified by a legal defence in what he did.

(a) State of mind

The clearest form of a guilty state of mind is where an offender intends what he does. A person may intend an event without actually desiring it, provided he foresees that it will probably happen as a result of what he does.[3] Thus, if an offence requires the accused to have acted *wilfully*, as in the Barnet tree case, it would seem to be sufficient if he was aware that his act would cause a risk of the relevant sort of harm, or if he did not care whether or not there was a risk and shut his eyes to the possibility.[4] A similar standard is applied where an offence requires the accused to have acted *maliciously*,[5] However, many modern statutory offences provide for *strict liability*, where a person may be guilty even although he had no means of realizing that he was committing an offence. In particular, strict liability often applies where a person is treated as vicariously responsible for an offence committed by someone else.[6] On the other hand, there are circumstances where a person charged with a crime can escape liability by proving a generally recognized defence, and some of these are available on charges of strict liability.

Rather than making an accused strictly liable, the law may vary the normal rules of evidence. Thus, by the law of evidence, the prosecution is under a general burden to prove its case, 'beyond reasonable doubt', on each necessary element.[7] Where an accused person raises a special defence, it is then normally necessary for the prosecution to prove that this does not apply. Sometimes, particularly in modern statutory offences, the accused must prove his defence, but even then, only on the balance of probabilities,[8] that is he must prove that what he claims is more likely than not. This is the standard used in civil cases.

Many offences may be committed *intentionally* or *recklessly*. Under the Criminal Damage Act 1971, s. 1 (1): 'A person who without lawful excuse destroys or damages any property belonging to another intending to destroy or damage any such property or being reckless as to whether any such property would be destroyed or damaged shall be guilty of an offence.' Where it is expressly provided that an offence may be committed recklessly, it is sufficient if the offender's act creates an obvious risk, that is if objectively a reasonable person in his position would recognize it. It does not matter whether the accused has himself recognized the risk and carried on regardless or has simply not given any thought to the possibility.[9]

Although recklessness involves an objective standard of responsibility, an offence may only rarely be committed by a negligent act. *Negligence* does not require the risk to be obvious but merely reasonably foreseeable. It is the normal basis for liability in tort and is discussed in Section 6.2. The idea of negligence is used in criminal law where it is provided that a person accused of an otherwise strict offence may raise a defence that he took all reasonable or reasonably practical precautions. Thus under the Control of Pollution Act

1974, s. 3, it is an offence to dispose of most sorts of solid waste except in compliance with a licence. However, a number of defences are available. For example, if someone with a licence failed to comply with its conditions, he is not liable if he shows 'that he took all such steps as were reasonably open to him to ensure that the conditions were complied with'.

Offences aimed at protecting the environment are often strict. The prosecution is spared what may be a very difficult task of proving any particular mental state. Because conviction is far more likely, it makes those who might be responsible for strict offences take greater care to ensure that they do not occur. Although there is a presumption against an offence being strict,[10] pollution offences and other offences under environmental legislation do not seem to be regarded as morally very reprehensible. They are punished relatively slightly, and there is a corresponding readiness by the courts to treat them as strict. If those who are not morally at fault happen to be convicted it is believed that this will not impose a lasting slur on their reputations.

Often the word *knowingly* is used in modern statutory offences to show that mental responsibility is required. If no such term is used the courts may hold that an offence is strict. Thus the Rivers (Prevention of Pollution) Act 1951, s. 2 (1), makes a person guilty of an offence, 'if he causes or knowingly permits to enter a stream any poisonous, noxious or polluting matter'. In *Alphacell Ltd* v. *Woodward*,[11] Alphacell ran a paper manufacturing works called Mount Zion by the river Irwell in Lancashire. Polluted water from their works was pumped into the river when the water circulating system became clogged with brambles and other vegetation. Alphacell were charged with causing the overflow and the House of Lords held that they were rightly convicted, even though it was not clear that they had any reason to know that the overflow was likely. With this offence knowledge was only required for the passive responsibility of permitting an overflow. Nevertheless, for a charge of actively causing pollution the prosecution must prove that this was caused by the accused. Thus, by contrast with the Alphacell case, in *Impress (Worcester) Ltd* v. *Rees*,[12] Impress were held by the Queen's Bench Divisional Court not to be liable for causing the escape of oil from a fuel storage tank into the river Severn because the valve releasing the oil had been opened by some unknown person. Again, in *Price* v. *Cromack*,[13] the Divisional Court held that Price was not liable for *causing* pollution where effluent escaped by natural causes from two lagoons built on his land. The lagoons had been constructed with his consent but by a separate company. Had he been charged with *knowingly permitting* the escape it appears that he might have been successfully convicted.

(b) Participants in crime

In addition to the *principals in the first degree*, that is those who directly commit a criminal act, those who *aid, abet, counsel or procure* the offence will also be liable.[14] Thus someone who acts as lookout during a theft or who sends a thief to steal someone else's property for him will be as guilty of theft as the thief himself. Under the Criminal Law Act 1977, s. 1, if two or more people agree that a course of conduct shall be pursued which would amount to or involve an offence, they are guilty of *conspiracy*, even though the course of conduct is not actually carried through and even if there are facts which actually render the commission of the offence impossible. Thus, if a group of vandals agree to steal or destroy a statue in a public park, they will be guilty of conspiracy even if they find when they arrive at the park that the statue has been shipped to America. Similarly, under the Criminal Attempts Act 1981, an individual may be guilty of an *attempt* to commit an indictable offence or certain summary offences if he does 'an act which is more than merely preparatory' to its commission,[15] 'even though the facts are such that the commission of the offence is impossible'[16] He will be liable if he intends to do something which would be an offence if the facts were as he believed them to be, even though they are actually different. Thus a person who sets out to burn down his neighbour's wood may be guilty of attempted criminal damage if he starts a fire on his own land which, because the wind changes, does not spread across the boundary as he expected. Similarly, he will be guilty if he burns a wood, which he believes to be his neighbour's, but which turns out, because of an error over the boundary, to be part of his own property.

There is no general rule that an employer is responsible for his servant's crimes, although as explained in Section 6.6, he is vicariously responsible for his servant's torts. However, at common law an employer is criminally liable for any acts of public nuisance committed by his servant and numerous modern statutory offences which impose strict liability have been treated as making employers vicariously liable for the offences of their employees.[17] Thus in *G. Gabriel Ltd* v. *Enfield London Borough Council*,[18] Gabriel's conviction of wilfully obstructing a highway was upheld by the Queen's Bench Divisional Court. They had supplied an empty skip to a customer who had told their driver to put it in the road. The contract with the customer provided that where the skip was to be deposited was at the sole discretion of the customer and for the purpose of the deposit the driver was to be treated as the customer's agent. The court took the view that this merely had the effect that the customer was probably guilty of an offence as well. The employer was liable because he had chosen 'to delegate the conduct of his business to a servant who [did] an act in the course of conducting the business which [was] absolutely prohibited'.[19] If a person has a statutory duty he may be vicariously liable if he delegates it to someone who is not even a servant and who commits an offence of strict liability.[20]

If trespassers carry out an act on someone else's land which it is an offence to cause or permit, the landowner will not be liable for permitting this if he has taken reasonable steps to keep them off. Thus in *Bromsgrove District Council* v. *Carthy*[21] a landowner was held by the Divisional Court to have been rightly acquitted of permitting gypsies to use, as an unlicenced caravan site, a piece of land which he owned a considerable distance from where he lived. He had been refused planning consent to build a house on this land and it was looked after by a local agent who had asked the gypsies to leave but had not gone to the lengths of physically evicting them or bringing court proceedings.

A corporation can be criminally liable even for an offence requiring mental awareness, but only through an act or default of its officers or employees. Provided it can be shown that these had control of the company or corporation or had ultimate responsibility within it for what they did, they can make the corporation liable for any offence which they commit and for which the corporation can effectively be penalized by a fine.[22] However, as the officer or employee who was directly responsible will usually be personally liable, the value of prosecuting a corporation is questionable save as a means of providing compensation for injured parties who wish to be spared the expense of bringing court proceedings.[23] This is particularly so when the prosecution is brought by one public body against another as in the case of *Barnet London Borough Council* v. *Eastern Electricity Board*.[24]

(c) Justified crimes: general defences

Certain persons, notably children under 10 and those who are mentally incapacitated, cannot be criminally liable although they may be subject to other forms of compulsory public control. Others may avoid liability by raising one or more defences. Generally even a strict offence cannot be *committed involuntarily*.[25] Thus a person who is pushed against a valve so as to open it and release poisonous waste into a river will not be guilty of causing pollution. It is probably also a defence to any offence short of murder that the accused was compelled to do the act charged, by *duress* consisting of threats of death or serious injury to himself or someone else, at least if these were imminent and any reasonable person would have been swayed by them.[26] Otherwise there seems to be no general defence in English law that the act charged was necessary even to protect life,[27] although this will often be provided for in particular offences. For example if a man burnt his neighbour's wood to protect his property or his neighbour's house from a larger fire this would normally be a lawful excuse to an offence of criminal damage.[28]

It is often said that ignorance of the law is no defence, and people have been convicted of offences of which they could not possibly have been aware.[29] However the Statutory Instruments Act 1946, s. 3 provides that it is a defence to a charge under a statutory instrument[30] that the instrument has not been published. It is no defence that the accused had obtained legal advice that his act would not constitute a crime,[31] even if the advice was obtained from a public official.[32] Even in cases where an offence consists in breaking a special order rather than breaking a general rule, such a defence has been held not to apply. Thus in *Maidstone Borough Council* v. *Mortimer*,[33] a professional tree feller was held by the Divisional Court to be guilty of contravening a tree preservation order on an oak tree although he had been expressly told by the owner of the tree, a Mrs Twydell, that she had received permission from the local authority to fell it. Nevertheless, where an accused person is mistaken as to the effect of a provision of the civil as opposed to the criminal law, provided the offence is one requiring mental awareness he may well escape liability, for example where he destroys someone else's property, such as fixtures in a house which he rents, honestly believing these to be his own property.[34] Similarly he may escape liability if he makes a mistake as to the location of a boundary.[35]

6.1.2   Offences affecting the landscape

The criminal law has always been used to protect property, but in the interests of those with private property rights rather than of the general public. The essence of crimes against property tends to be the level of dishonesty involved rather than the loss to the community of the property affected. There is now also a range of modern statutory offences which are specifically designed to protect the environment. These may often be committed by persons who actually own the property concerned. Although proceedings are relatively rare for such offences and the punishment is often low they provide an essential last resort to back up public control of the environment.

(a) Offences against private property

The main offences against private property are now provided for in the Theft Act 1968, and the Criminal Damage Act 1971. The Theft Act 1968, s. 1 (1) provides that a person is guilty of *theft* 'if he dishonestly appropriates property belonging to another with the intention of permanently depriving the other of it'. The Criminal Damage Act 1971, s. 1 (1) provides that, 'a person who without lawful excuse *destroys or damages any property* belonging to another intending to destroy or damage any such property or being reckless as to whether any such property would be destroyed or damaged shall be guilty of an offence'. In each case there are special provisions as to offences involving real property. Under the Theft Act 1968, s. 4, if a person removes a fixture from land he cannot be guilty of stealing it if he was in possession of the land unless he was a tenant or held the land on trust for someone else. Except when he steals for commercial purposes, a person cannot be charged with theft or criminal damage of wild mushrooms, which include any fungus, or for picking the flowers fruit or foliage from any wild plant including any shrub or tree,[36] although it could be an offence to steal or destroy such a plant by uprooting it entire. Similarly either offence could be committed by cutting branches off a tree in the wild.

Generally a person may commit an offence against property in which he has a part share, such as partnership property.[37] However in such a case, the prosecution may have more difficulty in showing that there was the dishonesty required under the Theft Act 1968, s. 2 or that there was no lawful excuse as provided for in the Criminal Damage Act 1971, s. 5. In particular, someone is not dishonest if he believes that he has a legal right to take the property which he appropriates, or that the person entitled to the property would consent to his taking it or that the person to whom the property belongs cannot be discovered by taking reasonable steps. There is a lawful excuse for someone damaging property who believes that he had or would have been given permission by someone entitled to give it,[38] or for someone honestly believing that the destruction or damage was needed as a reasonable means for the immediate protection of other property. The general defences already discussed would also be available, for example if property was destroyed under duress. Curiously, however, it appears possible that damaging property to save life, for example demolishing a wall to rescue a trapped child could amount to criminal damage if the property owner objected. In such a case if a prosecution were brought, a court would doubtless only impose an absolute discharge.

The Theft Act provides for a number of offences in addition to theft which may serve to protect the condition of land. Thus, under s. 9, *burglary* includes entering a building or part of a building as a trespasser with intent to steal or commit unlawful damage, and having entered a building or part of a building stealing or attempting to steal. Section 11 provides a special offence of unauthorized removing of articles on display or kept for display to the public from any building or its associated grounds which are open to the public. This protects articles where a thief is entitled to visit the building and so could not be a trespasser. It was designed in particular to cover cases where works of art may be taken and held for ransom with no intention to permanently deprive the owner, as required for theft. Concern had arisen particularly following the removal of Goya's portrait of the Duke of Wellington from the National Gallery. This was recovered four years later.[39]

The Criminal Damage Act 1971, also provides for a number of special offences. Thus under s. 1 (3), criminal damage by fire is treated as arson and is punishable with life imprisonment rather than the ten years maximum for straightforward criminal damage. There is a widely held superstition that it is a crime to trespass on private land. This is fostered by numerous notices warning that trespassers will be prosecuted. However, with a few exceptions trespass is not a crime. The main exceptions are found in the Criminal Law Act 1977. Section 6 makes it an offence for anyone, unless he is, or is acting on behalf of, a displaced residential occupier, to use or threaten violence against anyone else or against property, for the purpose of securing entry to premises where he knows that there is someone present on the premises who opposes his entry. Under s. 7 it is an offence for anyone who has entered residential premises as a trespasser to refuse to leave at the request of the displaced occupier or of someone with similar rights. More specialized examples of criminal trespass are provided where property is particularly vulnerable or dangerous. Thus it is a summary offence under the Towns Gardens Protection Act 1863, s. 5 to trespass in a town garden. It is an offence under the Railway Regulations Act 1840, s. 16 to trespass on a railway. Those who are allowed onto land for recreation and similar purposes may commit an offence if they break any bye-laws. Thus the National Trust has power to make bye-laws under the National Trust Act 1971, s. 24 to prohibit numerous abuses of their land, such as lighting fires or posting advertisements.[40] These bye-laws are made and enforced in the same manner as local authority bye-laws under the Local Government Act 1972, ss. 235–238.

(b) Offences for the protection of the environment

The system of development control and the other public law controls discussed in Chapter 3, Sections 3.3 and 3.4 use the criminal law to provide sanctions, usually relying on offences of strict liability. Thus although unlawful development is not itself a criminal offence, under the Town and Country Planning Act 1971, s. 89 it is an offence to fail to comply with an enforcement notice ordering the restoration of land after unlawful development. A breach of special restrictions under the same Act may also constitute an offence, as under s. 102 where there is a breach of a tree preservation order or under s. 55 where there is damage to a listed building. Under the Ancient Monuments and Archaeological Areas Act 1979, s. 28, it is an offence even for an owner to destroy or damage a protected monument. Under the Wildlife and Countryside Act 1981, s. 28 it may be an offence to carry out operations which have been forbidden by the Nature Conservancy Council as likely to damage flora or fauna or geological or physiographical features which led to a site being designated as an area of special scientific interest.

Other environmental offences apply generally. Thus it is an offence punishable under the Water Resources Act 1963, s. 49 to unlawfully abstract or impound water. Breaches of various controls of pollution under the Control of Pollution Act 1974 also constitute a criminal offence. Occasionally the criminal law is used to protect the environment by forbidding behaviour without providing a scheme for it to be licensed. Under the Litter Act 1983 it is an offence for anyone in public places to leave litter in the open unless this is authorized by the general law or by the occupier or similar person with authority over the land where the litter is left.

NOTES: SECTION 6.1

1. *Barnet London Borough Council* v. *Eastern Electricity Board* [1973] 1 W.L.R. 430, D.C. The offence was under the Town and Country Planning Act 1962, s. 62, now replaced by the Town and Country Planning Act 1971, s. 102.
2. *R.* v. *Miller* [1983] 1 All E.R. 978, *per* Lord Diplock at p. 980.
3. *Hyam* v. *D.P.P.* [1975] A.C. 55, H.L.
4. *R.* v. *Sheppard* [1981] A.C. 394, H.L.
5. *R.* v. *Cunningham* [1957] 2 Q.B. 396, C.A. In *R.* v. *Mowatt* [1968] 1 Q.B. 421, C.A., it was held by the Court of Appeal that on a charge of maliciously wounding a person, it was sufficient if the accused person foresaw some harm of the relevant type even if he was not proved to have appreciated how serious that might be.
6. In civil law see *post* p. 310f.
7. *Woolmington* v. *D.P.P.* [1935] A.C. 462, H.L.
8. *R.* v. *Carr-Briant* [1943] K.B. 607, Court of Criminal Appeal, at p. 87.
9. *R.* v. *Caldwell* [1982] A.C. 341, H.L., and *R.* v. *Lawrence* [1982] A.C. 510, H.L.
10. *Sweet* v. *Parsley* [1970] A.C. 132, H.L.
11. *Alphacell Ltd* v. *Woodward* [1972] A.C. 824, H.L.
12. *Impress Worcester Ltd* v. *Rees* [1971] 2 All E.R. 357, D.C.
13. *Price* v. *Cromack* [1975] 1 W.L.R. 988, D.C.
14. Accessories and Abettors Act 1861, s. 8. amended by Criminal Law Act 1977. For summary proceedings see Magistrates' Courts Act 1980, s. 44.
15. Criminal Attempts Act 1981, s. 1 (1).
16. Ibid. s. 1 (2).
17. A statute may create vicarious liability where the person who actually committed the crime must have had mental responsibilities. *Mullins* v. *Collins* [1874] 9 L.R. Q.B. 292.
18. *G. Gabriel Ltd* v. *Enfield London Borough Council* [1971] 69 L.G.R. 382, D.C. the offence was contrary to the Highways Act 1959, s. 121 (1), now replaced by the Highways Act 1980, s. 137. In the 1980 act, ss. 139, and 140 now make special provisions for controlling builders' skips on the highway.
19. Following *Barker* v. *Levinson* [1951] 1 K.B. 342, D.C., *per* Lord Goddard C.J. at p. 349.
20. *Linnett* v. *Metropolitan Police Commissioner* [1946] K.B. 290, C.A.
21. *Bromsgrove District Council* v. *Carthy* [1975] 30 P. & C.R. 34.
22. *Tesco Supermarkets Ltd* v. *Nattrass* [1972] A.C. 153, H.L. There the company was not liable under the Trades Description Act 1968, for an offence by one of its branch managers since his role was a subordinate one.
23. For powers of compensation vested in criminal courts see *post* p. 380.
24. *Ante* p. 272.
25. Smith J.C., and Hogan B. (1978), *Criminal Law*, 4th edn, Butterworth, London, p. 38.
26. For a major discussion on the offence of duress see *D.P.P. for Northern Ireland* v. *Lynch* [1975] A.C. 653, H.L.
27. *Buckoke* v. *Greater London Council* [1971] Ch. 655, C.A.
28. Criminal Damage Act 1971, s. 5 (2). For the position in tort see *post* p. 301 and *post* p. 338.
29. In *R.* v. *Bailey* [1800] R. and R. the relevant offence had been created whilst the accused was at sea and in no position to hear of it.
30. *Ante* p. 39.
31. *Shaw* v. *D.P.P.* [1962] A.C. 220, H.L.

32. *Cambridgeshire and Isle of Ely County Council* v. *Rust* [1972] 1 Q.B. 426.
33. *Maidstone Borough Council* v. *Mortimer* [1980] 3 All E.R. 552, D.C.
34. *R.* v. *David Smith* [1974] Q.B. 354, C.A.
35. In *Roberts* v. *Inverness Local Authority* [1889] 27 S.L.R. 198, a farmer was charged with moving a cow from one district to another contrary to regulations, designed to prevent spread of infection. He was found not guilty as he had been told by a local authority official that the districts had been amalgamated.
36. Theft Act 1968, s. 4 (3) and Criminal Damage Act 1971, s. 10.
37. *R.* v. *Bonner* [1970] 1 W.L.R. 838, C.A.
38. Even if consent was in the hope of fraudulently recovering insurance payments, *R.* v. *Denton* [1981] 1 W.L.R. 1446, C.A.
39. Smith, J.C. (1979) *The Law of Theft*, 4th edn, Butterworth, London, p. 137.
40. *Ante* p. 40.

6.2 Land use, negligence and statutory and strict liability in tort

The foundation for legal liability for harm in modern English law is the Scottish case of *Donoghue* v. *Stevenson*,[1] heard in the House of Lords in 1932, where Lord Atkin made the famous statement at the beginning of this chapter. The tort of negligence is based on the principle that each person owes a duty to all those whom his behaviour may affect, to take the care not to harm them which a reasonable person would be expected to take. In *Donoghue* v. *Stevenson*, a preliminary point was raised in the Scottish civil courts, as to whether an action could lie against a manufacturer where an ultimate consumer had been injured by the manufacturer's product. Mrs Donoghue had been treated to a bottle of ginger beer which was bought for her by a friend at a café in Paisley. After drinking some of the ginger beer she alleged that she discovered a decomposed snail in the bottle, as a result of which she suffered shock and also gastroenteritis because of what she had already drunk. The House of Lords ruled that in both Scottish and English law a manufacturer, in such circumstances, did owe a duty of care to the ultimate consumer. However, they went further and laid down that this was part of a wider duty which each person owes to take care for the safety of anyone else whom he ought reasonably to foresee as likely to be affected by his acts or ommissions.

Anyone who fails to act like a reasonable person will be at fault even though he personally, perhaps through limited intelligence, was honestly unaware that he might cause harm. However, although the duty not to be negligent is therefore very wide-ranging, the courts have contained it within limits. Various ways in which they have restricted liability both for negligence and for other torts relevant to land use are the subject of the next two sections. However, the judges have also restricted liability for negligence by holding that in certain situations the general duty to take care does not apply, and that in others it will only be broken in restricted circumstances.

Even after the House of Lords laid down the general principles of responsibility enshrined in *Donoghue* v. *Stevenson*, there was a tendency to consider claims for negligence in terms of specific categories, and to see whether each new situation fitted into or could properly be added to existing categories. However, in *Junior Books Ltd* v. *Veitchi Co. Ltd*,[2] the House clearly adopted a more flexible approach of applying the basic principles of liability directly to each dispute rather than seeing how it compared with previous examples. Veitchi Co. were specialist flooring contractors who constructed a floor at Junior Books' factory in Grangemouth during 1970. The floor began to break up in 1972. Veitchi had been employed as sub-contractors and had no direct contract with Junior Books. Nevertheless, they were sued directly and on a preliminary point of whether they owed a duty to the client in the absence of contract with them, the House of Lords agreed with the lower courts that such a duty was owed. Lord Roskill in particular said that:

rather than to ask whether the particular situation which has arisen does or does not resemble some earlier and different situation where a duty of care has been held or has not been held to exist, I look for reasons why, it being conceded that the appellants owed a duty of care to others not to construct the flooring so that those others were in peril of suffering loss or damage to their persons or their property, that duty of care should not be equally owed to the respondents.[3]

There were two tests to apply by way of general principle; first whether there was 'sufficient relationship of proximity', and secondly whether there were 'any considerations negativing, reducing or limiting the scope of the duty or the class of person to whom it is owed or the damages to which a breach of duty may give rise'.

6.2.1 Acts and omissions

Lord Atkin stated in *Donoghue* v. *Stevenson* that there is a general duty to take care, both in acts and omissions. However, in practice, no general responsibility has been recognized for omissions, although sometimes, what appears to be an omission may properly be seen as a negligent manner of carrying out a positive act. Thus a builder who leaves cement out of his mortar, or omits steel supports inside foundations is likely to be in breach of duty to those on whom the building later falls. On the other hand an architect who sees a dangerous building and walks past on the other side of the road without warning anyone, or a forester who notices that someone else's tree is rotten and is likely to shed a branch on a passer-by, but fails to tell the tree owner, may be morally at fault but will not be liable legally to anyone, if the building or the branch do fall. However, where there is a positive duty to act, neglect to do so will give rise to liability. An architect would clearly be liable in contract if he failed to survey a client's building when he had contracted to do so, but told the client that it was sound where a proper survey would have shown it to be dangerous. Equally an architect could be under a positive duty to act in circumstances where he had no contract or after his contract had expired. For example if he were consulted on the alteration of a building and advised that it would be safe to build an extra storey, but three weeks later, after his involvement with the project had ceased, and just before building began, he happened to learn of underground workings which would make the extra storey dangerous, a court might then well regard him as owing a positive duty to warn the building owner. Chapter 7 of this book deals with a number of situations where the law recognizes relationships which require positive steps to be taken to protect the safety of other people.

6.2.2 Relationships giving rise to a duty of care

If the law recognizes a duty in principle to take care for the safety of others, this is known as a *notional duty*. However, in some circumstances, as a matter of policy, the law will not recognize a duty to prevent harm even in carrying out a positive act. Thus where a landowner has an absolute right to do something on his land, he has no duty to avoid harming his neighbour in the exercise of that right. For example at common law a landowner had an absolute right to abstract percolating water from his soil even if he knew very well that this would dry up the supply to his neighbour's reservoir. Neither would he be liable if he affected the water table and damaged the foundations of his neighbour's buildings.[4] Similarly there still is generally an absolute right to cut off tree branches or roots projecting from neighbouring land, without even the need to give notice to the tree owner.[5] Even so it may be unwise to assume that a person who practises such behaviour will always escape liability for any harm which results. The change in the water table or the damage to the tree could lead to a building or to the tree collapsing onto someone who was oblivious to the danger, but where this was clearly foreseeable by the person who brought about the collapse. Especially where it was not foreseeable to anyone else, the courts might be prepared to find whoever brought about the collapse liable to anyone injured by it.

In some circumstances, the courts will not recognize a duty because the relationship between the parties involved is regarded as one which, as a matter of policy, should not give rise to a duty. For example before the wide principle of liability for negligence was laid down in 1932, the courts had established that, except under an express agreement, no duty was owed by sellers or landlords of land to protect purchasers of the land or anyone else who might later acquire any interest in it from any structural defect even if they clearly should have known that the premises were unsafe. Although this immunity has been modified by the Defective Premises Act 1972,[6] it may still apply in some cases. For example, under the present law, a seller who has not actually done any repair work on his home, but knows that it is unsafe, perhaps that a ceiling is likely to collapse, will not owe a duty to anyone who is injured by the defect after he has sold the house. However, it may be that this is very much an area of law which the House of Lords might decide to reshape even if Parliament cannot find time to do so.[7]

Generally, as Lord Macmillan said in *Donoghue* v. *Stevenson,*

in the daily contacts of social and business life human beings are thrown into, or place themselves in, an infinite variety of relations with their fellows; . . . the grounds of action may be as various and manifold as human errancy; and the conception of legal responsibility may develop in adaption to altering social conditions and standards. The criterion of judgment must adjust and adapt itself to the changing circumstances of life. The categories of negligence are never closed.[8]

One such new category was recently developed by the House of Lords in the case of *Home Office* v. *Dorset Yacht Co. Ltd.*[9] There seven borstal boys escaped from a party camping on Brownsea Island in Poole Harbour, Dorset, and unmoored a yacht. This collided with another yacht which they then boarded and further damaged. The yacht owners claimed that the three borstal officers who were in charge of the boys were responsible for the harm because they had gone to bed leaving the boys to their own devices. The Home Office raised a preliminary issue that it owed no duty to the yacht owners to prevent their charges from causing damage. With the one exception of Viscount Dilhorne, who was one of five judges in the House of Lords, all the judges who heard the case rejected this argument. The borstal officers did owe a duty to take reasonable care to protect other people's property from their charges, even though these were young men of full age and capacity. Also, there was no public policy under which prison authorities needed immunity from the risk of civil liability if they were to carry out their work effectively.

In the Dorset Yacht Company case the Home Office was acting under a statutory duty to control the borstal boys. This duty included the power to contain and supervise them. As we shall see in Chapter 7, Section 7.5.3, public authorities have considerable discretion as to how they carry out their duties and use the powers committed to them by statute. However, where an authority or its subordinates acts outside its powers by displaying negligence it is now clear that it may be liable to compensate those who are foreseeably injured as a result.

6.2.3 Emotional distress, economic loss and harm caused by bad advice

In some circumstances the courts avoid holding a person liable for negligence by not recognizing a duty to prevent a particular type of harm or to prevent harm arising in a particular manner.

(a) Emotional distress

The courts have always tended to concentrate on tangible harm which can be calculated in financial terms. It has only recently become clear that, even where there is initial liability for some physical harm to person or property, a duty may also be recognized not to cause emotional distress to the person affected. Thus in *Perry* v. *Sydney Phillips & Son*,[10] chartered surveyors, who negligently advised that a house in Taunton was in good condition when it had a leaking roof, smelly septic tank, and bulging interior supporting wall, were liable under their contract, and also independently in negligence, both for the cost of the repairs and also for distress and discomfort suffered by the home owner during the time that he had to live in the house whilst worrying about its condition. Where a person suffers physical injuries, it has long been established that he is entitled to compensation for his pain and suffering as well as for the injury itself. Thus, if a person lost an arm when a tree fell on him, and this prevented him from practising his hobby of water-colour painting, he would be granted damages to reflect this special loss. However, where injury is caused indirectly, by shock, the duty to prevent harm is less likely to be recognized than where the injury is caused directly. If a negligently built wall collapses it certainly may be foreseeable that it is likely to injure or kill a passer-by. It might seem almost equally foreseeable that the family of the passer-by would suffer severe distress as a result. However, although the courts may recognize a duty to those who are indirectly affected, they look closely at their relationship to the person directly injured and the circumstances in which they were affected, for example whether they actually witnessed the accident or heard about it very shortly afterwards.[11] Thus someone who has little or no personal connection with the person who was directly injured is only likely to be able to recover damages for his own shock if he witnessed the accident or its immediate aftermath.[12] Even then the person indirectly affected will only be able to recover damages if he establishes that he has been caused, 'not merely grief, distress or other normal emotion, but a positive psychiatric illness'.[13]

(b) Economic loss

Economic loss is another sort of harm which the courts have been reluctant to recognize any duty to avoid, unless it is associated with direct physical harm. Thus, if a workman on a building site is negligently injured, it has long been recognized that he can recover for loss of his future wages. However, it has been held that there is no duty to prevent construction work causing economic loss in isolation. For example in *Cattle* v. *Stockton Waterworks Co*,[14] the court held that there was no cause of action available to a contractor cutting a tunnel under a road, who was held up and lost profit, as a result of water which had escaped from a water main and made the soil harder to work. If an injured party suffers physical harm as well as economic loss, it has been held that he can only recover for economic loss which is closely related to the physical harm. Thus, where a labourer on a construction site cut a cable, and so shut off power to a neighbouring factory, his employers were treated as liable for damage to machinery in the factory and for products in the course of manufacture which were spoiled, but the factory owner was not able to recover loss of profit for further products which he could not make during the time that his machinery was out of action.[15] On the other hand, if dangerous construction work puts neighbouring property at risk, it has been recognized that the owner of that property may be able to recover damages for its reduced value, even although it has not yet suffered any physical harm. In *Batty* v. *Metropolitan Property Realisation Ltd*,[16] houses were negligently erected on land subject to landslides. The builders, and the developers who had employed them, were held liable to the owners of one of the houses which became unsellable. At the time the case was decided there had been physical damage to the plaintiff's garden but his house was still completely intact.

In the light of *Junior Books Ltd* v. *Veitchi Co. Ltd.*,[17] the distinction in tort between physical harm and economic harm may largely have been broken down.

(c) Harm caused by bad advice

Often economic loss is caused by negligent advice. For example an architect or consultant planner may advise a prospective house purchaser that he does not need planning permission to build an extension to a house he wants to buy. The purchaser may suffer loss if he buys the house, finds he does need permission after all, can not get it, and sells at a loss. In the major case of *Hedley Byrne & Co Ltd* v. *Heller & Partners Ltd*,[18] the House of Lords recognized that in making formal statements there is a duty not to cause pure economic loss. Hedley Byrne and Co were advertising agents who prepared an advertising programme for a firm called Easipower Ltd. This went into liquidation leaving Hedley Byrne to pay the costs of the programme. Hedley Byrne had relied on confidential reports from Heller and Partners Ltd, who were merchant bankers. The House of Lords held that Hellers had made an express disclaimer of responsibility which protected them from liability. Nevertheless the Lords also ruled that the bank, and persons in a similar position, did owe a duty to take care in giving advice. If they broke such a duty, they would be answerable for resulting economic loss. The judges differed over the exact circumstances where a duty would arise in giving advice. Lord Reid suggested that the obvious difference between negligent words and negligent acts is that, 'quite careful people often express definite opinions on social or informal occasions even when they see that others are likely to be influenced by them; and that they often do that without taking care which they would take if asked for their opinion professionally or in a business connection'.[19] A duty of care would arise only if there were some form of special relationship. Lord Reid suggested that a reasonable man knowing that he was being trusted or that his skill and judgment were being relied on must generally be held to have accepted some responsibility for his answer being given truthfully and carefully, that is he must be treated as having accepted a relationship with the enquirer which obliged him to exercise appropriate care. However, there would only have been liability if the enquirer acted reasonably in relying on the advice.

There were some indications that the courts might restrict the duty of care in making statements to those made either on request and by a person whose business would include advising on such matters,[20] or in circumstances where the person giving the advice had some personal financial interest in the matter on which he was advising.[21] However, the Court of Appeal appears to prefer the wider view that a duty arises wherever a person 'who has or professes to have special knowledge or skill makes a representation by virtue thereof to another — be it advice, information of opinion . . .'[22] Thus there is little doubt that a professional planner would be liable for negligence if he inaccurately told someone who came to his office for advice that a particular sort of building work would not need planning permission where this was incorrect and the person to whom the advice was given acted on it by erecting a building which he was later obliged by an enforcement notice to pull down. It is equally clear that the planner would not be liable if he gave the same advice to a casual acquaintance in the course of a general conversation during a sherry party. The position would be less clear if the advice were given to a witness in the course of a discussion during a luncheon adjournment at a planning inquiry concerned with a different property. As we shall see in Chapter 7, Section 7.5.3 liability for careless advice is particularly important where a member of the public has been misinformed by a public official such as a planning officer. For example if such an officer inaccurately and without proper authorization advises a member of the public that he does not require planning consent for some proposed development the planning authority will usually be free to stop that development going ahead or to require the developer to remove any work which he has carried out in reliance on the advice. Nevertheless it may be obliged to pay for the expense which the developer has incurred.

There may be liability for advice given at second hand to a particular person provided whoever gave the advice knew that it would be passed on to that person. In *Yianni* v. *Edwin Evans & Sons*,[23] surveyors were held to be liable to the purchaser of a defective house who had relied on their valuation made for his building society. The survey had valued the house at £15 000, but it later required £18 000 to repair it. There may even be a duty owed to persons who are clearly likely to be affected by bad advice even though they do not themselves rely on it.[24] For example if a person intent on buying a piece of land withdrew from the purchase, preventing a profitable deal, because he was negligently advised by his own architect that the land was unsuitable for building, it is possible that the disappointed vendor might have a cause of action against that architect. In *Ministry of Housing and Local Government v. Sharp*,[25] a firm of builders bought some land with planning permission for building in Hemel Hempstead. Some years earlier planning permission had been refused and the previous owners were paid compensation to which they were statutorily entitled. Now that planning permission had been granted, the compensation would normally have been repayable to the ministry by the current landowner. This obligation was recorded in the local land charges registry. However, a clerk working for the relevant district council negligently gave a certificate to the purchaser that there was no such charge. As a result he could not later be made to pay. The Court of Appeal held that the district council was liable to the ministry for their compensation repayment which had been lost because of the erroneous certificate given to the purchaser. Sharp was the official who signed the defective certificate. He was held not to be personally liable for the search which was done by one of his subordinates. It is possible to regard the negligent issuing of a certificate in this case as an act which directly terminated the ministry's right to the repayment rather than as a mis-statement, but this underlines how it is often unrealistic to distinguish the damaging effects of words from harm caused by acts. Today, under the Local Land Charges Act 1975, the purchaser in Sharp's case would have to repay the compensation but would claim it back from the local authority.[26]

Where advice is given to a wide audience, although it may be foreseeable that many may be affected, it is unlikely that the courts would recognize a duty of care. For example if a book on trees inaccurately stated that tree preservation orders had been abolished and that it was safe for anyone who owned a tree to cut it down it would be reasonably foreseeable that, as a result, people reading the book might cut down trees and then be fined or ordered to replant. Nevertheless the courts would be unlikely to hold the author liable to such an unlimited public. In a dissenting judgment in the case of *Candler v. Crane Christmas*,[27] Denning L.J. stated that: 'a scientist or expert . . . is not liable to his readers for careless mis-statements in his published works. He publishes his work simply for the purpose of giving information, and not with any particular transaction in mind at all.' Denning L.J. gave the example of a marine hydrographer whose inaccurate maps might cause untold harm. Similarly a surveyor would not owe a duty to the general public to ensure that plans he drew were accurate. However, if he drew them up for a seller of land as the basis for the sale he probably would be liable to the subsequent purchaser if he marked the boundary in the wrong place and as a result the purchaser put up new buildings which a neighbour then compelled him to pull down. By contrast a duty not to cause physical harm by careless statements may be owed to all those in a group who could forseeably be affected, rather than just to individuals known to be personally at risk.[28]

6.2.4 Duty in fact and breach of duty

Even where a notional duty exists, that is where liability not to cause harm is recognized in principle, a person will only be liable for damage he causes if he personally owed a duty in fact, and was in breach of it. Thus the law recognizes that a building inspector may owe a duty to subsequent purchasers of a house which he inspects whilst it is being built to ensure that work has been carried out properly. However, such a duty will not arise in a particular case if the inspector properly exercises his discretion not to inspect a building at all.[29]

(a) Duties to individuals

A person who acts dangerously may not be aware that any specific individual is likely to be endangered, but for him to be liable to any such individual it is sufficient if he is aware of risk to people generally or to some particularly vulnerable class including the person whom he injures.[30] Thus a landscape architect who planted yew trees in a children's playground might well be liable if any child was poisoned by eating yew berries, as it should have been foreseeable that some child would do this. On the other hand there would probably be no breach of duty in planting yew trees in places where small children would not normally play unattended, such as in the grounds of old people's sheltered accommodation or in the traditional setting of a churchyard.

(b) Standards of care

What amounts to a breach of duty depends very much on the circumstances of each case. However, a number of considerations are likely to be relevant. Thus, as we shall see in Chapter 7, Section 7.5, a person with special skills or knowledge of danger is expected to show a higher standard of care than the ordinary person. Conversely, someone who follows normal practices accepted by his profession or at his workplace is unlikely to be in breach of duty if, retrospectively, the practice is shown to be unsafe. Generally the more risky a particular act is the more the care that must be taken. However, what is risky depends partly on the likely seriousness of any harm which might occur, as well as on how likely it is that there will be harm of any sort.[31] Thus, if with his clients' approval and to reduce costs a builder uses a cheap and untried new flooring material which soon after cracks slightly, he may not be liable to a person who trips over on the floor and breaks an arm, if the risk that the material would cause such harm might be regarded as slight since the type of injury which could result is relatively slight. However, if untried materials were used for the walls of a concrete block of flats, even if the likelihood of their collapsing was just as slight, since the harm they could cause if they did collapse was likely to be devastating the courts would be much more likely to find that there was liability in the event of such a collapse. The courts are also less likely to find somebody liable where an accident resulted from taking a slight risk, if this was for some purpose of particular public benefit,[32] or if the expense of protective precautions would have been very high.[33] Thus the director of an archaeological rescue dig might escape liability in negligence for pumping out water from the excavations in a hurry so that to his consternation it flooded tents on a nearby campsite, although had he been working on a more leisurely dig he would have gone to the time and expense of making a more thorough study and realized that the flooding was likely.

6.2.5   Strict and statutory duty

Although the law of negligence requires people, in most circumstances to act in a reasonable manner, and if they fail to, makes them responsible for harm which they may cause, in some circumstances either common law or statute impose strict liability. As we shall see in Chapter 7, sometimes the special common law torts of trespass and nuisance, and in particular the rule in *Rylands* v. *Fletcher*,[34] may make someone liable for harm which no reasonable person would have expected. On the other hand, statutes such as the Occupiers' Liability Act 1957 impose a duty in particular circumstances which is essentially the same duty of reasonable care as is normally applied in negligence. However, the main development of strict liability in tort has been by statute. Statutes are often used to ensure that various activities are carried out safely, by laying down detailed duties of care. Often these are further amplified by statutory instruments. Such legislation frequently specifies absolute duties. If these are broken there will be no room for any dispute over whether a reasonable person might have behaved in the manner which caused the breach. Where the breach of duty gives rise to liability in tort to a person who has been injured, the person who is responsible under the statute is in effect required to make sure that the risk is covered by insurance, so that anyone who is injured will be compensated. For his own part he will have the extra incentive to obey the statute that this will keep down his premiums.

(a) Examples of statutory duty

In Chapter 3, we have considered a number of statutes designed to protect the environment from pollution and other abuses. However, some of the best-known statutory duties are laid down in the Health and Safety at Work Act 1974. This provides very general requirements for employers and employees to maintain the safety of people at work. Thus s. 2 stipulates that 'it shall be the duty of every employer to ensure, so far as is reasonably practical, the health, safety and welfare at work of all his employees'. The section sets out examples of where the duty must be exercised, such as with regard to plant, storage and handling of materials, and safe access and egress. Section 7 lays a corresponding duty on employees to take care for their own safety and that of their fellows. The standards, therefore, are the traditional ones of reasonable care. However, the Act specifically provides that no breach of either of these general duties confers any right of action in civil proceedings.[35] Rather, the Act provides a framework under which those responsible for working arrangements must follow general standards set out in codes of practice, overseen by a national Health and Safety Commission and enforced by a national Health and Safety Executive and by local authorities. These act through inspectors,[36] who may serve improvement notices,[37] or prohibition notices,[38] to ensure that standards of safety are complied with and may if necessary bring prosecutions to punish any breach of the Act and related legislation.[39] On the other hand, however, the Act authorizes the making of many detailed regulations which are often strict. It provides that generally where these are broken and any injury results this will give rise to civil proceedings. Many such regulations were made under previous legislation and remain in force. Thus the Construction (Working Places) Regulations, 1966,[40] were made originally under the Factories Act, 1961 and relate to commercially executed building and engineering works. A typical example is regulation 29 (2)(a): 'Every side of any gangway, run or stairs from which a person is likely to fall a distance of more than 6 feet 6 inches shall be provided – (a) with a suitable guard-rail or guard-rails of adequate strength to a height of between 3 feet and 3 feet 9 inches above the gangway, run or stairs; . . .'. Thus if a man falls off a gangway 6 feet 7 inches above the ground, where there is no guard-rail or a rail only 2 feet tall, he can rely on his employers' breach of this duty. It will be irrelevant if the employer argues that the conditions were such that a handrail was not necessary or that an accident was not reasonably foreseeable in the circumstances.

(b) Which statutes give rise to claims in tort?

Generally, statutory duties are public standards of duty laid down as part of the criminal law. A breach of such a duty will be an offence, normally punishable by a fine. At common law, if a public nuisance causes particular harm to some individual, as we shall see in Chapter 7, Section 7.2, that person may bring an action in tort. However, where a statutory duty has been broken, a person injured by the breach will normally only be permitted to bring an action based on it if the statute was designed to protect from the specific sort of harm which the injured person has suffered, a class, of which he is a member, rather than the public as a whole. Some statutes specifically provide for civil proceedings where there is a breach. Thus the Control of Pollution Act 1974 expressly authorizes civil actions for harm resulting from an offence of depositing poisonous, noxious or polluting waste on land. Often, however, statutory duties are treated as entirely public affairs which give no new right to interested private individuals. Thus, as we have seen, if a person abstracts water without obtaining an abstraction licence this failure cannot be relied on in any legal action by a person who claims rights to the same supply.[41]

Even where a breach of statutory duty may give rise to civil proceedings, it cannot be relied on for harm which is different from that against which the statute was directed. Thus where sheep were washed off the deck of a ship on which they were being transported it was held that no action for their loss could be brought in respect of the breach of a statutory duty to provide pens, since the statute in question was intended to contain the spread of contagious diseases.[42]

NOTES: SECTION 6.2

1. *Donoghue* v. *Stevenson* [1932] A.C. 562, H.L.
2. *Junior Books Ltd* v. *Veitchi Co. Ltd* [1983] 1 A.C. 520, H.L.
3. Ibid. at p. 542.
4. See *ante* p. 199 and *post* p. 348.
5. See *post* p. 389.
6. See *post* p. 332.
7. As to the House of Lords powers to change law established by previous precedent see *ante* p. 48 and *British Railways Board* v. *Herrington* [1972] A.C. 877, *post* 329.
8. *Supra* note 1 at p. 619.
9. *Home Office* v. *Dorset Yacht Co. Ltd* [1970] A.C. 1004, H.L.
10. *Perry* v. *Sidney Phillips & Son* [1982] 1 W.L.R. 1297, C.A. The case followed *obiter dicta* in the Court of Appeal in *Hutchinson* v. *Harris* (1978) 10 Build. L. R. 19.
11. *McLoughlin* v. *O'Brian* [1982] 2 All E.R. 298.
12. *Chadwick* v. *British Railways Board* [1967] 1 W.L.R. 912.
13. *McLoughlin* v. *O'Brian, supra*, note 11, *per* Lord Bridge, at p. 311.
14. *Cattle* v. *Stockton Water Works* (1875) L.R. 10 Q.B. 453.
15. *Spartan Steel & Alloys Ltd* v. *Martin & Co (Contractors) Ltd* [1973] Q.B. 27, C.A. However in *H. Parsons (Livestock) Ltd* v. *Uttley Ingham & Co Ltd* [1978] Q.B. 791, C.A., Lord Denning M.R. said that in both contract and tort there is a duty to avoid causing economic loss provided it is a 'serious possibility'. There is a duty to avoid physical harm which is merely foreseeably possible.

16. *Batty* v. *Metropolitan Property Realisation Ltd* [1978] Q.B. 554, C.A.
17. *Supra* note 2.
18. *Hedley Byrne & Co. Ltd* v. *Heller & Partners Ltd* [1964] A.C. 465, H.L. The
    right to exclude liability for careless statements as well as for careless acts has been
    restricted by the Unfair Contract Terms Act 1977, see *post* p. 308.
19. Ibid. at p. 482.
20. *Mutual Life and Citizens Assurance Co Ltd* v. *Evatt* [1971] A.C. 792, P.C., from
    Australia.
21. *W.B. Anderson and Sons Ltd* v. *Rhodes (Liverpool) Ltd* [1967] 2 All E.R. 850.
22. *Esso Petroleum* v. *Mardon* [1976] Q.B. 801.
23. *Yianni* v. *Edwin Evans & Sons* [1982] Q.B. 438.
24. *Ross* v. *Caunters* [1980] Ch. 297.
25. *Ministry of Housing and Local Government* v. *Sharp* [1970] 2 Q.B. 223, C.A.
26. *Ante* p. 243.
27. *Candler* v. *Crane Christmas* [1951] 2 Q.B. 164, C.A. The dissenting judgement
    was later approved by the House of Lords in *Hedley Byrne* v. *Heller, supra* note
    18.
28. *Clay* v. *A.J. Crump and Sons* [1964] 1 Q.B. 533, C.A., *post* p. 306.
29. *Dutton* v. *Bognor Regis Urban District Council* [1972] 1 Q.B. 373, see *post*
    p. 373.
30. *Haley* v. *London Electricity Board* [1965] A.C. 778, H.L.
31. *Paris* v. *Stepney Borough Council* [1950] A.C. 367, H.L.
32. *Daborn* v. *Bath Tramways Motor Co Ltd* [1946] 2 All E.R. 333, C.A.
33. *Latimer* v. *A.E.C. Ltd* [1953] A.C. 643, H.L.
34. *Rylands* v. *Fletcher* (1868) 3 L.R. H.L., see *post* p. 344.
35. Health and Safety at Work Act 1974, s. 47.
36. Ibid. ss. 19 and 20.
37. Ibid. s. 21.
38. Ibid. s. 22.
39. Ibid. s. 39.
40. S.I. 1966, No. 94.
41. *Cargill* v. *Gotts* [1981] 1 W.L.R. 441 C.A., *ante* p. 200.
42. *Gorris* v. *Scott* (1874) 9 L.R. Ex. 125.

6.3   Limits to liability

A person who suffers harm will not necessarily be able to obtain a remedy
from the courts. It may not be possible to show that any other person was
legally responsible. Even if someone else has been negligent or in breach of
some strict duty it does not follow that they will be treated as responsible in
law for the harm. In any case, even if the legal rules are clear it may be
impossible to produce sufficient evidence to establish liability. It is also
important to appreciate, as we shall see in Chapter 8, that where there is legal
responsibility the courts may be more ready to grant certain remedies than
others.

6.3.1   Causation and foresight of harm

In some torts, notably trespass, which we consider in Chapter 7, Section 7.2,
an action may be brought in the courts even though no harm has been caused.

Thus it is a trespass to build a shed so that it touches a neighbour's wall even without doing the wall any harm.[1] Normally, however, no action may be brought in tort unless there has been harm. The harm must actually have been caused by the tort and must be of a type which was not too remote.

(a) Causation in fact

Where a claim depends upon proving harm, courts often ask whether the harm would not have occurred *but for* some act or omission for which the defendant is responsible. Thus in *Dutton* v. *Bognor Regis Urban District Council*,[2] the Court of Appeal upheld a decision that a district council was liable for the negligence of its building inspector in approving the inadequate foundations of a house built on a filled-in rubbish dump. In the words of Stamp L.J., 'the house would on the balance of probability never have been built *but for* the carelessness of the defendant council'. However, this test is not always adequate. For example, if harm results from two or more causes, those responsible for each may be liable even although the harm would still have occurred in the absence of one or another. Thus a person walking along a road might be killed by the simultaneous fall of a rotten branch from a tree and by a skidding car. In other cases, harm may result from a combination of faults. Thus in *Hale* v. *Hampshire and Dorset Motor Services Ltd.*,[3] under its statutory powers Poole Corporation had planted trees beside a road. A bus ran into an overhanging branch and the eye of Hale, a passenger, was so badly injured by broken glass that it had to be removed. The Court of Appeal affirmed the decision that the corporation was two-thirds to blame for allowing the tree to overhang the road in a dangerous manner and the bus company one-third to blame for the negligence of their driver in running the bus into it.

In some cases the courts treat a particular cause as ceasing to have any effect if the chain linking it with later harm is broken by an intervening event or if some other person becomes responsible for the situation. Thus in *Buckner* v. *Ashby and Homer Ltd.*,[4] Mr Buckner was injured in wartime London. He fell as he was using a passage in Shoe Lane, which had been roofed in as a shelter from bombs. He tripped over a raised plate which had been left lying on the ground by the contractors, but, nevertheless, he failed in his claim against them for negligence. The courts held that the contractors' work had been approved by a London County Council supervisor. In the words of Atkinson J., the trial judge:

It may very well be said that the inspection was perfunctory and hurried, but none the less there was an intervening conscious agency which might and should have averted the mischief. I think that the defendants were well entitled to take it for granted that when once their work had been examined and passed by people competent to examine it, their responsibility would cease.

In addition the defendants were entitled to assume that proper lighting would have been provided in the passage.

(b) Acts of third parties and acts of God

There will not be liability for a breach of duty which leads to harm if the chain of causation from the initial fault was broken by a later act of the plaintiff himself,[5] or of some third party,[6] or by an intervening natural event.[7] For example if a contractor were to leave a dangerous hole on a building site it is unlikely that he would be liable for the injuries of a workman on the site who fell into it whilst walking across it on a plank for his own amusement or who was pushed in by a companion. However, the possibility of misbehaviour by others may itself be foreseeable and it may be a breach of duty not to guard against it.[8] For example, if plants with tempting poisonous berries are grown in a public park on an open site it should be foreseeable that children may eat them.[9] If a surveyor leaves his employer's equipment unattended in the open it may be foreseeable that it will be stolen or that children may play with it and injure each other.

Where harm is caused directly by a third party, particularly an unexpected trespasser, this may even be a defence in an action based on strict liability, as in the case of *Box* v. *Jubb*.[10] Box occupied premises at Batley in Yorkshire. When these were flooded by Jubb's nearby reservoir he was not able to recover damages because the overflow resulted from the owner of another reservoir emptying excess water higher up the main drain which fed both, and a blockage further down the drain. Normally it might have been expected that Jubb would have been strictly liable under the rule in *Rylands* v. *Fletcher*.[11] In that case, which we shall consider further in Chapter 7, Section 7.2, there was liability for the escape of water which had been accumulated in a reservoir by the defendant, because water collected in such circumstances was inherently likely to cause mischief if it escaped. Nevertheless, Blackburn J. said that there may be a defence to such a claim of strict liability where the plaintiff himself caused the escape or perhaps if 'the escape was the consequence of *vis major* or the Act of God'. An Act of God appears to be an overriding natural disaster such as an earthquake or an extraordinary flood.[12] It may seem surprising that strict liability should not apply in these cases since the person who collects harmful things is likely to be in the best position to insure against harm which they may cause should they escape for any reason.

(c) The concept of remoteness

Where a particular fault has led to harm, if the courts take the view that it would be unjust to hold the person responsible for the fault liable for the harm, they may decline to do so by means of several devices. Thus, as we have seen in Section 6.2 they may hold that there was no duty in the first place. Another rationalization for not holding a defendant liable is that the harm was too remote from his act. For example, if an architect directed a workman on a building site to remove the support from a wall which later fell down as a result, normally the architect clearly would be liable to any workman on whom the wall fell.[13] However, would he be liable to the workman's mother if she suffered a heart attack when hearing of the accident or would he be liable to a window cleaner at a nearby house who was so startled by the sound of the wall collapsing that he fell off his ladder?

The courts are reluctant to hold even negligent people liable for such far-reaching consequences. In the case of the workman's mother they would probably hold that the architect did not owe her a duty.[14] If they did not hold the architect liable to the window cleaner it could be on the basis that his injury was too remote. It was once said that liability for an injury depended on whether it was a *direct* consequence of a breach of duty.[15] Today, however, in negligence, the formulation is the same as that used for establishing whether there is a duty in the first place; that is whether the harm was a *reasonably foreseeable* consequence of the breach of duty. This rule was laid down by the Privy Council on an appeal from the Supreme Court of New South Wales in what is commonly known as the *Wagon Mound* (No. 1).[16] Although the precedent of this case is not strictly binding on English courts it is now generally accepted as if it were.[17]

On 1 November 1951 there was a great fire in Sydney Harbour which severely damaged the Sheerlegs Wharf which belonged to Morts Dock and Engineering Co. Ltd. The previous day, the SS. *Wagon Mound* had been moored some 600 feet away at the Caltex wharf, discharging gasolene products and taking on bunkering oil. Her crew carelessly allowed a large quantity of oil to spill into the harbour and to spread across the bay. Welding work was being carried out at the Sheerlegs Wharf and molten metal fell onto debris in the oil, starting the fire. The trial judge had found that those responsible for the *Wagon Mound* did not know, and could not reasonably be expected to have known, that the oil was capable of being set alight when spread on water. However, he decided that they were liable for the fire on the basis that it was a direct consequence of their negligence. The Supreme Court of New South Wales upheld this decision but it was reversed by the Privy Council. In its advice, given by Viscount Simonds, the Privy Council said that:

the essential factor in determining liability is whether the damage is of such a kind as the reasonable man should have foreseen . . . Who knows or can be assumed to know all the processes of nature? But if it would be wrong that a man should be held liable for damage, unpredictable by a reasonable man, because it was nevertheless *direct* or *natural*, equally it would be wrong that he should escape liability, however *indirect* the damage, if he foresaw or could reasonably foresee the intervening events which led to its being done.

On this basis the owners of the *Wagon Mound* were not liable for the fire.

In the *Wagon Mound* (No. 1), the Privy Council remarked that the test of foreseeability would not necessarily be appropriate for determining remoteness in cases of strict liability, such as *Rylands* v. *Fletcher*.[18] Nevertheless, in such cases it should be possible to apply the test by asking what sort of harm a reasonable man would have foreseen if he were told what was going to go wrong.[19] Thus a farmer may be strictly liable for the escape of water which he has accumulated in a reservoir, even though he would not have foreseen the escape. However, there may not be liability for harm which a reasonable man would not have expected even if he had known that there was going to be an escape. For example even if he had known that there was going to be an escape, the farmer might not have foreseen the loss of cattle which were not in the path of the water, stampeding over a cliff because they heard the sound of it.

In Chapter 7, Section 7.2 we shall see that where damages are sought in an action based on the tort of private nuisance, which is of particular relevance to the use of land, liability seems virtually equated with that in negligence. In the *Wagon Mound* (No. 2),[20] the Privy Council underlined this. The fire at Sheerlegs Wharf in Sydney Harbour, caused by the oil discharged from the *Wagon Mound*, severely damaged two other ships, the *Corrimal* and the *Audrey D.*, belonging to the Miller Steamship Company. This company's claim in negligence against the owners of the *Wagon Mound* was dismissed by the Australian Courts as a result of the earlier decision of the Privy Council, but their claim in nuisance was upheld on the basis that for this tort damage need only be direct and not necessarily foreseeable. The Privy Council rejected this distinction and held that foreseeability is the correct test in nuisance as well as for negligence. Paradoxically, the Privy Council then advised that the fire was foreseeable after all and the ship owners were entitled to succeed in both nuisance and negligence. The reason for the outcome differing from that of the earlier case seems to have been the manner in which the evidence was presented. Morts Dock and Engineering Company were at pains to show that the fire was a direct consequence of the spillage of oil but that it was not reasonably foreseeable. If it had been foreseeable they would have been at fault in allowing welding to continue and, under the then law in Australia on contributory negligence,[21] would have recovered nothing.

In practice it is often difficult to tell how judges will apply the test of reasonable foresight. In the *Wagon Mound* (No. 1) it was accepted by the courts that some damage to the plaintiffs was foreseeable, in the form of interference with the use of slipways as a result of oil. However, this was entirely different from fire damage. From subsequent cases, it appears that provided some damage is foreseeable, it may not matter if what is actually suffered is of a different form or if the harm occurs in a rather different way from that which was foreseeable.[22] As Lord Denning M.R. has said:

It is not necessary that the precise concatenation of circumstances should be envisaged. If the consequence was one which was within the general range which any reasonable person might foresee (and was not of an entirely different kind which no one would anticipate) then it is within the rule that a person who has been guilty of negligence is liable for the consequences.[23]

Further, once liability has been established for a particular type of harm, it does not matter if this is more extensive than was foreseeable.[24] So, if a tree owner is responsible for a branch falling on the head of a visitor to his land he must pay for the full extent of the harm, even if the visitor has an 'egg shell skull', as a result of which he suffers far worse injuries than could have been expected.

(d) Policy considerations

A difficulty in telling when a court will hold someone liable for a particular harm and how it will rationalize this, seems, at root to be that, applying the law involves the judges making decisions of policy. As Lord Denning M.R. has said in *Lamb* v. *Camden Borough Council;*[25]

The truth is that all these three – duty, remoteness and causation – are all devices by which the courts limit the range of liability for negligence or nuisance. As I said recently ... *it is not every consequence of a wrongful act which is the subject of compensation. The law has to draw a line somewhere.* Sometimes it is done by saying that there is a break in the chain of causation. At other times it is done by saying that the consequence is too remote to be a head of damage. All these devices are useful in their way. But ultimately it is a question of policy for the judges to decide.

Mrs Lamb and her father owned number 6, Villas on the Heath, in the Vale of Health at Hampstead. In October 1973, whilst Mrs Lamb was in New York, Camden Borough Council had a trench dug nearby to replace a sewer. A water main was fractured and water washed away the foundation of the house, causing subsidence. The house was left empty pending repair, and over the next eighteen months there were two invasions by squatters. Mrs Lamb recovered £50 000 damages for the subsidence. However, the Court of Appeal held that she could not recover a further £30 000 for damage caused by the squatters. Oliver and Watkins L.J.J. stressed the absence of foreseeability of such damage, but Lord Denning relied openly on the policy consideration, that in practice it was eminently a householder's job to guard against squatters, or to get rid of them and also to provide insurance against their depredations.

6.3.2 Justified harm

As we shall see in Section 6.4, in various circumstances, harm may be regarded, at least in part, as the responsibility of the person who suffers it.

Indeed, as we have already seen,[26] a plaintiff may be regarded as the essential cause of his own misfortune. However, there are circumstances where a person causes harm to another which is a foreseeable consequence of his own behaviour and cannot be absolved by any acceptance of responsibility on the part of his victim, but where he is nevertheless justified by some other defence.

(a) Mistake

If a person harms another as a result of a reasonable mistake this may mean that his act was not negligent. For example, if a surveyor has drawn up plans of a garden for a householder, and based the location of the boundaries on measurements given him by his client, he could well be acting reasonably, even if the measurements were wrong. If he showed the plans to the owner of a neighbouring garden, who was thus led to believe that the position of his property was several feet further in one direction than it in fact was, the surveyor would probably not be liable in negligence if that neighbour proceeded to put up a garage on the far side of his property which projected across the boundary so that he later had to demolish it. On the other hand, the garage builder himself could not rely on his mistake to avoid liability in trespass. For this it is sufficient for there to be a voluntary intrusion on someone else's land.[27]

(b) Necessity

What would otherwise be a tort may be justified where it is reasonably necessary to protect one's own life or person or that of one's family, or even one's own property. A tort may also be justified where it is shown that it was necessary to protect the public in general or possibly any other person. Thus in *Dewey* v. *White*,[28] a house in High Holborn, London, was in a dangerous condition because of a fire. A group of firemen were held to be justified when they threw over a chimney stack on to Dewey's neighbouring house, because they did so to avoid the immediate danger of it falling on the highway and on to other occupied houses. It may even be justifiable to cause harm to a person so as to protect him or his own property from some worse form of harm.[29]

If harm to an innocent person is to be justified under the defence of necessity, it must be shown that the steps taken to cause harm were proportionate to the risk which they were intended to avoid.[30] Drastic forms of protection against burglars or other trespassers may themselves be illegal. Thus under the Offences Against the Person Act 1861,[31] it is an offence to use, 'any spring-gun, man-trap, or other engine calculated to destroy human life or inflict grievous bodily harm, with the intent that the same or whereby the same may destroy or inflict grievous bodily harm upon a trespasser or other person coming into contact therewith'. Also, now, under the Guard Dogs Act

1975, a guard dog may not be let loose in premises unless there is a handler present to control it. Generally where a person harms another so as to protect himself he may be obliged to recompense that person for the benefit he has himself received at the expense of the other, under special principles known as *quasi-contract*.

(c) Statutory authority

Large-scale public works are often set up under express statutory authority.[32] Such statutes often provide a defence against possible claims in tort, particularly nuisance, at least provided care is taken to avoid harm where this is reasonably possible. In *Allen* v. *Gulf Oil Ltd*[33] an oil refinery was built at Milford Haven in South Wales on 400 acres next to the village of Waterstone consisting 'of a vast complex of jetties on Milford Haven harbour, where the largest oil tankers can deliver crude oil, refining plant, pipes and pumping apparatus, storage tanks, a petrochemical plant, and a private railway with sidings . . .'. Mrs Allen, who lived in Waterstone, claimed that this amounted to a nuisance by smell, noise and vibration. A preliminary point was argued up to the House of Lords as to whether Gulf Oil Ltd had a defence that they were authorized to construct and operate the refinery under the private Gulf Oil Refinery Act 1965. This Act gave authority to compulsorily acquire land together with detailed power to construct certain works. The House of Lords held that it also contained the necessary implication that the refinery could be constructed and operated. In the words of Lord Wilberforce it conferred: 'Immunity against proceedings for any nuisance which can be shown [by Gulf Oil Ltd] to be the inevitable result of erecting a refinery upon the site . . . any refinery – however carefully and with however great a regard for the interest of adjoining occupiers it is sited, constructed and operated.'[34] Lord Wilberforce pointed out that in any event,

the establishment of an oil refinery was bound to involve some alteration of the environment and so of the standard of amenity and comfort which neighbouring occupiers might expect. To the extent that the environment has been changed from that of a peaceful unpolluted countryside to an industrial complex . . . Parliament must be taken to have authorised it.

6.3.3   Time and the ending of liability

In about March 1969, Pirelli General Cable Works Ltd engaged the firm of consultant engineers, Oscar Faber and Partners to advise on the construction of a new services block at their Southampton works. This included a pre-cast concrete chimney with four flues. It was erected by sub-contractors in June and July 1969 but Oscar Faber were responsible for the design. They made use of a new lining material called Lytag which proved defective so that the chimney eventually had to be replaced entirely. It was established that cracks must first have existed at the top of the flues by April 1970 although they were not discovered by Pirelli until November 1977. Pirelli began an action for damages against Oscar Faber on 17 October 1978. As we have seen in Chapter 5, Section 5.5, rights in law may be affected by the passage of time. Under the Limitation Acts it has long been necessary for most actions to be brought within six years from the date when they accrue, that is the date when the person bringing an action would first be able to succeed in his claim. The law is now set out in the Limitation Act 1980. With regard to actions including a claim for damages for personal injuries, the limitation period is three years.[35]

In any sort of claim there is often uncertainty as to when the action does accrue and the period begins to run within which the claim must be brought. Thus, the Pirelli claim against Oscar Faber would have been too late if the action had accrued when the original advice was given, or when the chimney was completed or even when damage could first have been identified. The Judge who initially dealt with the claim, and the Court of Appeal, regarded themselves as bound by earlier case law,[36] to hold that the cause of action only arose when the plaintiffs discovered, or ought with reasonable diligence to have discovered, damage. On this basis Pirelli would have been within the six year limitation period. However, the House of Lords overruled the previous case law,[37] and held that it was bound by yet earlier authority of its own,[38] to conclude that the cause of action accrued when the structure first became defective, even although this was not in fact apparent until later. On this basis the action was out of time, as it should have been brought within six years of when there must in fact have been cracks in the chimney. Lord Fraser,[39] in the House of Lords, also ruled *obiter dicta* that owners of a particular property form a single class, so that if time begins running against an original owner it goes on running against anyone who subsequently acquires the property. 'Otherwise it would mean that if the property happened to be owned by several owners in quick succession, each owning it for less than 6 years, the date when action would be time barred might be postponed indefinitely'.

Although the House of Lords reached their decision in the Pirelli case unanimously, they also unreservedly condemned it as unsatisfactory and hoped that Parliament would change the law. Such a change had already been made with regard to personal injuries claims,[40] by providing that there a cause of action only accrues once the plaintiff has knowledge that he is entitled to it. The meaning of knowledge is elaborated in the Act in considerable detail but includes awareness that a significant injury has been suffered or the presence of circumstances where there ought reasonably to have been such an awareness.[41] Despite the concern of judges for plaintiffs whom they may have deprived of their opportunity to sue for damages, as a result of the Pirelli case consulting engineers and many other professional groups involved in construction work were highly relieved that generally they would be safe from liability within a settled time from finishing any project. However, even since the Pirelli case, possible causes of action remain dormant so long as damage is entirely latent. As Lord Fraser suggested, there could be a defect in a structure which does not amount to damage. For example if a building is erected on defective foundations no cause of action will accrue until these result in the building above cracking, unless at least the foundations are 'so gross that the building is doomed from the start'![42] Again, if a building collapses as a result of some defect, injuring people and their property such as neighbouring houses, those affected will clearly not have suffered harm until that point. Thus their cause of action could commence very many years after the building was completed. However, if a defect in a structure has actually become known to its owner, a court would probably consider that, on its later collapse, the effective cause of any damage to third parties was the owner's failure to take proper precautions rather than the original negligence.

In respect of claims for personal injuries, the Limitation Act 1980 gives the courts considerable discretion to allow an action to proceed even outside the limitation period, where this would be equitable.[43] More generally, where a cause of action accrues to a person under a disability, time does not normally begin running until the plaintiff has ceased to be disabled.[44] Also, where a cause of action is based upon fraud of the defendant, or any fact relevant to the plaintiff's right of action has been deliberately concealed by the defendant, time does not begin to run until the plaintiff discovers or could with reasonable diligence have discovered the mistake.[45]

NOTES: SECTION 6.3

1. *Westripp* v. *Baldock* [1938] 2 All E.R. 779, affirmed [1939] 1 All E.R. 297, CA.
2. *Dutton* v. *Bognor Regis Urban District Council* [1972] 1 Q.B. 373, C.A., at p. 413. See *post* p. 737.
3. *Hale* v. *Hampshire and Dorset Motor Services Ltd* [1947] 2 All E.R. 628, C.A.
4. *Buckner* v. *Ashby and Homer Ltd* [1941] 1 K.B. 321, C.A. See Atkinson J. at p. 335.
5. *McKew* v. *Holland and Hannen and Cubitts (Scotland) Ltd* [1969] 3 All E.R. 1621, H.L. See further *post* p. 306f, where the plaintiff contributes to his harm by his own negligence.
6. *Weld-Blundell* v. *Stephens* [1920] A.C. 956, H.L.
7. *Carslogie Steamship Co. Ltd* v. *Royal Norwegian Government* [1952] A.C. 292, H.L.
8. *Stansbie* v. *Troman* [1948] 2 K.B. 48, and see *Home Office* v. *Dorset Yacht Co.* [1970] A.C. 1004, H.L. *ante* p. 286.
9. *Glasgow Corporation* v. *Taylor* [1922] 1 A.C. 44, H.L.
10. *Box* v. *Jubb* (1879) 4 Ex. Div. 76.
11. *Rylands* v. *Fletcher* [1866] 1 Ex. Cas. 265, *post* p. 344.
12. *Nichols* v. *Marsland* (1876) 2 Ex.D. 1, C.A.
13. *Clay* v. *A.J. Crump & Sons* [1964] 1 Q.B. 533. See *post* p. 306.

14. See the problem of nervous shock mentioned *ante* at p. 287.
15. *Re Polemis* [1921] 3 K.B. 560, C.A.
16. *Overseas Tankship (U.K.) Ltd* v. *Morts Dock and Engineering Co. Ltd* [1961] A.C. 388, P.C.
17. For example, *Doughty* v. *Turner Manufacturing Co. Ltd* [1964] 1 Q.B. 518, C.A.
18. *Ante* note 11.
19. See Rogers W.V.H. (1979), *Winfield and Jolowicz on Tort*, 11th edn, London. Sweet and Maxwell, p. 121.
20. *Overseas Tankship (U.K.) Ltd* v. *Miller Steamship Co. Pty* [1967] 1 A.C. 617, P.C.
21. *Post* p. 306f.
22. *Hughes* v. *Lord Advocate* [1963] A.C. 837, H.L., from Scotland.
23. *Stewart* v. *West African Terminals Ltd* [1964] 2 Lloyd's Rep. 371, C.A. *per* Lord Denning M.R. at p. 375.
24. *Smith* v. *Leech Brain and Co. Ltd* [1962] 2 Q.B. 405.
25. *Lamb* v. *Camden Borough Council* [1981] 1 Q.B. 625 at p. 636.
26. *Ante*, p. 297.
27. *Post*, p. 327f.
28. *Dewey* v. *White* (1827) Moo. & M. 56.
29. See *Cope* v. *Sharp* (No. 2) [1912 1 K.B. 496, C.A., *post* p. 338.
30. *Sarch* v. *Blackburn* (1830) 4 C. & P. 297.
31. Offences Against the Person Act 1861, s. 31.
32. *Ante* p. 19.
33. *Allen* v. *Gulf Oil Ltd* [1981] A.C. 1001, H.L. Lord Kelvin dissenting took the view that the Act did not implicitly provide a defence.
34. Ibid. *per* Lord Wilberforce at p. 1014.
35. Limitation Act 1980 s. 11. The basic period of six years is set out in s. 2.
36. *Sparham-Souter* v. *Town and Country Developments (Essex) Ltd* [1976] 1 Q.B. 858, C.A.
37. *Pirelli General Cable Works Ltd* v. *Oscar Faber and Partners* [1983] 1 All E.R. 65, H.L.
38. *Cartledge* v. *E. Jopling and Sons Ltd* [1963] A.C. 758, H.L.
39. *Supra* note 37 at p. 71.
40. Limitation Act 1980, s. 11.
41. Ibid. s. 14 (3), and see *Dove* v. *Banhams Patent Locks Ltd* [1983] 2 All E.R. 833.
42. *Supra* note 37, at p. 12.
43. Limitation Act 1980, s. 33.
44. Ibid. s. 28.
45. Ibid. s. 32.

6.4 Spreading the burden of harm

Many accidents or other circumstances which give rise to a legal claim may involve a number of individuals. Several people may be injured at the same time, for example where a badly built structure collapses. Again, the same fault may lead to a succession of injuries. For example, the collapsing structure may have to be rebuilt and in the meantime the owner may not be able to use his property. Later, a neighbouring building may be found to have suffered from the collapse and its owner may incur the cost of repairs.

Conversely a number of people may contribute to the same injury and may have to share in compensating those who had been injured.

Garage proprietors in Dudley had a site cleared by demolition contractors prior to redevelopment. The demolition and reconstruction were supervised by an architect named Young. The two contractors and the architect each had independent contracts direct with the client. To protect the site from trespassers during demolition, the client asked the contractors not to take down a wall. They consulted the architect by telephone and without visiting the site he authorized the retention of the wall. The wall was in fact clearly unsafe, as it had been left on a precipice 5 to 7 feet high. Two months later the building contractor had taken over the site, and three workmen were having breakfast in a hut which they had erected under the wall, when it collapsed. Two of the workmen were killed. In *Clay* v. *A.J. Crump & Sons Ltd*,[1] the survivor claimed damages from the courts for his injuries. The building owner who had left everything to his architect and contractors was cleared of liability. The demolition contractor was held to be 38% at fault, the building contractor 20% at fault for letting their men work on a dangerous site and the architect 42%. A further complication may arise if a plaintiff contributes to his own harm. In that case he may have to bear all or part of the burden of what he suffers.

6.4.1   The responsibility of plaintiffs for their own injuries

As we have considered in section 6.1, a person who has suffered some form of harm may effectively have caused his own misfortune in which case he will not be entitled to any damages from someone else who has been in breach of duty to him. For example, if a building contractor put up an insecure gate and it fell on a passer-by who had taken it upon himself to move it, knowing that it was dangerous, the passer-by might well be regarded as entirely responsible for his own injury. Thus in *Norris* v. *W. Moss & Sons Ltd*,[2] a scaffolder working on a building found that some scaffolding already in position was defective and tried to correct it, in what the trial judge called 'a fantastically wrong manner'. The scaffolder was held to be solely responsible for injuries which he suffered although his employers were in breach of statutory regulations because of the initial defects in the scaffolding. In other cases a plaintiff may have contributed to his injury without being entirely responsible, or, although not contributing to it, may have acquiesced in the risk that he might be harmed.

(a)   Contributory negligence

If a plaintiff contributed to his own injury this used to be a complete defence for anyone else whom he sued in respect of it.[3] Now, under the Law Reform

(Contributory Negligence) Act 1945,[4] the plaintiff's damages 'shall be reduced to such extent as the court thinks just and equitable having regard to the claimant's share in the responsibility for the damage'. The Act applies where the plaintiff claims that he has been injured by the fault of someone else consisting of 'negligence, breach of statutory duty or other act or omission which gives rise to liability in tort or would apart from this act give rise to the defence of contributory negligence'[5]. Apart from breach of statutory duty,[6] which is expressly included, contributory negligence may, for example, be a defence to an action in nuisance. In *Trevett* v. *Lee*,[7] Mrs Trevett was delivering milk in the village of Puncknoll in Dorset. The Lees had laid a hosepipe across the road, which she saw, but nevertheless tripped over. The courts held that the Lees were not negligent and that the hosepipe was there for a reasonable purpose of feeding water into their house. However, if they had been at fault they would have had the defence of Mrs Trevett's contributory negligence which would have applied to her claim in nuisance as well as to her claim in negligence.

Even if a contract imposes a duty on someone to exercise some particular care, that person may be able to rely on the contributory negligence of another party whom he injured in breach of the contracted duty.[8] However, a person who intentionally injures another will not be able to rely on a defence of contributory negligence.[9] If a man intentionally runs someone over in his car it will be no defence that his victim was not looking where he was going and could have jumped out of the way.

'A person is guilty of contributory negligence if he ought reasonably to have foreseen that, if he did not act as a reasonable, prudent man, he might be hurt himself; and in his reckonings he must take into account the possibility of others being careless.'[10] The amount by which damages will be reduced under the defence of contributory negligence will depend partly on how careless the plaintiff was and partly on how significant such carelessness was as a cause of his injury. That is, account is taken both of his blameworthiness and of the relative importance of his act in causing the damage irrespective of his blameworthiness.[11]

(b) Acquiescence

A person may consent to behaviour which would otherwise be a tort. If ramblers picnic in the gardens of a country house which is closed to the public, they will normally be trespassers, but obviously they will not be so if they are invited to eat there by the owner of the house. In other cases, without actually inviting harm, a person who has been injured may have debarred himself from claiming compensation because he had accepted the risk of possible negligence.[12] Thus if two workmen agree to demolish a building in an unsafe manner and one of them pushes a wall over on top of the other, the injured man may be debarred from suing their common employer in vicarious liability.[13] However, this defence will only be available if the injured person accepts the risk willingly, in full knowledge of the circumstances, and without any external pressures. Therefore, it is rarely that an employer will be able to escape liability to an injured workman on this basis since an employee is likely to be in a weak position to object to any risk which his employer requires him to take.[14] In other cases, where a person accepts a risk of danger, he may be unable to recover compensation if he is injured. This may be because the person who might otherwise have been responsible has discharged his duty by making the risk clear, or because the injured person is himself an expert called in to deal with the very danger which causes his injury. For example, if an engineer employed to repair a collapsed culvert fell into it, he would be unlikely to have a cause of action against the owner of the culvert for putting him in a dangerous position.

Difficulties over whether a person has genuinely accepted the risk of harm which he later suffers often occur where the person who is alleged to be at fault claims that a warning notice had been put up or that the injured person had agreed to accept the risk of harm, for example by signing a disclaimer notice. Here, the Unfair Contract Terms Act 1977 provides that no notice nor any term of a contract can be used to exclude liability by someone who, in the course of a business, causes death or personal injury as a result of negligence.[15] Negligence for this purpose includes a breach of any obligation to take reasonable care whether under a contract or in tort including a breach of the Occupiers' Liability Act 1957.[16] Business includes work done in pursuance of a profession and the activities of any government department or local or public authority.[17] Also, the Act applies to harm resulting from the occupation of premises for business purposes. Liability for loss or damage other than for personal injuries, for example for harm to goods or buildings, can only be excluded or restricted so far as is reasonable in the circumstances.[18]

Even in the non-business context a person may not always be able to protect himself from liability in negligence to another person who explicitly agrees to accept the risk. Thus the Occupiers Liability Act 1957 specifies that, 'where damage is caused to a visitor by a danger of which he had been warned by the occupier, the warning is not to be treated without more as absolving the occupier from liability, unless in all the circumstances it was enough to enable the visitor to be reasonably safe'.[19] On the other hand that Act also affirms that an occupier is not liable in respect of a risk which was willingly accepted by a visitor,[20] and that 'an occupier may expect that a person, in the exercise of his calling, will appreciate and guard against any special risks ordinarily incident to it, so far as the occupier leaves him free to do so'.[21]

6.4.2   Defendants with shared liability

Two or more individuals may be jointly responsible for an accident caused by the act of one of them. Notably, as we shall see in the next sub-section, an employer may be jointly responsible for harm caused by his employee. Again, as illustrated in *Clay* v. *Crump*,[22] at the beginning of this section, several individuals may contribute to an accident in different ways. Where an individual is jointly responsible for particular harm or is one of several contributing to the harm, he may be liable to compensate an injured plaintiff for his entire injury. Thus if all but one of a number of defendants in a case like *Clay* v. *Crump* have died or lost all their money, the injured plaintiff will not lose part of his compensation.

(a)   Contribution between joint and several tort feasors

Since 1935, those who have contributed to a single harm have been able to spread the burden of their liability by obtaining contributions from each other. This could amount to a complete indemnity of the whole sum, as where an employer had paid damages for an accident which his employee caused by disobeying express instructions.[23] Principles for claiming contributions or indemnities are now provided in the Civil Liability (Contribution) Act 1978. Normally an injured plaintiff will sue all possible defendants in the same action. Otherwise he will probably have to pay the costs of bringing any separate action later.[24] By serving *contribution notices*, those who are sued may claim contributions from other defendants to the same action.[25] If a defendant wishes to blame someone who is not yet a party, he may serve a *third party notice* bringing that person into the action.[26]

   As we have seen in the previous section, there are strict limitation periods, that is time limits, for bringing actions in the courts. An injured person may obtain judgment against a defendant just within such a time limit. If the defendant then seeks contribution from someone else, the Limitation Act 1980 requires that he must make his claim within two years.[27] However if a defendant is entitled to an indemnity under a contract, for example with an insurer or fellow contractor, he will normally have six years in which to sue. Contributions from others may be obtained by a defendant who has agreed to compensate an injured person without going to court.[28]

(b)   Successive wrongs

Where a person suffers two or more quite distinct injuries, the person responsible for the later ones will only have to pay compensation for the additional harm which he causes.[29] Thus if a contractor, working in a school, negligently sets fire to it so that the entire interior will need to be restored, and then a helicopter crashes into the roof, so that it has to be replaced as well, those responsible for the helicopter will only be liable to pay for the restortation of the roof and not for that of the interior. However, the first tort-feasor in such a case may object to paying the full cost of restoration on the grounds that the second accident would have made this necessary in any event. The law now appears to be that if there is some underlying defect which appears after an injury, and which would have occurred in any event, damages awarded against the person who caused the earlier injury will be reduced.[30] Thus if a visitor to a house set it on fire and gutted the interior but the foundations of an offshoot to the house were defective, so that it was bound to collapse at some time in the near future, and it did, two weeks after the fire, the fire raiser would escape paying damages for the rebuilding of the offshoot. On the other hand if a later injury is the result of an independent tort, for example if the offshoot in the last example was later blown up by a terrorist, there is authority that the person who caused the earlier harm may be required to pay compensation on the same basis as if the later harm had not occurred.[31] Otherwise the terrorist in our example could claim that he need only pay damages for the restoration of an already gutted building and the original fire raiser could escape liability on the basis that the harm he caused was swallowed up in the later damage.

(c) Contracts creating or restricting shared liability

A contract may create responsibility to pay compensation for ensuing harm and shift the expense from one person to another. Thus a landscape architect could employ an assistant on the terms that, if the assistant negligently caused any harm to a client, the employer would pay any damages in full and would indemnify the assistant if any claim were brought against him. Again, when a number of specialists are involved on a project, it may be agreed that one or other will accept liability for any damage in the course of the work and will take out appropriate insurance. In *Spalding* v. *Tarmac Civil Engineering Ltd*,[32] Spalding was a local authority engineer who was hit by the boom of a mechanical excavator during site work at Thornaby-on-Tees airfield. The real dispute in the case was between Arthur White (Contractors) Ltd, the owners of the excavator, and Tarmac, the hirers, who were using it on site with a driver provided by the owners. The House of Lords held that although there was fault by both, under the hiring contract the hirers had to bear the entire claim.

6.4.3   Vicarious liability

An important means of ensuring that a person who has suffered harm will be able to obtain compensation is the concept of vicarious liability, whereby an employer is treated as responsible for torts of his employees. The employer is likely to have more resources to meet damages, and is in the best position both to provide insurance cover and to exercise supervision so as to prevent harm occurring in the first place. Vicarious liability is related to strict liability in that it may make an employer liable who has personally been in no way at fault. However, it presupposes some tort by an employee. If no employee is at fault, the employer will generally not be liable either. Thus, if a tree surgeon negligently prunes a tree in such a manner that a branch later falls on a passer-by, he and his employer will be liable to the passer by. However, if there was no reason for anyone to expect that the pruning would cause the branch to fall, and the accident was no-one's fault, neither will be liable.

(a) Relationships giving rise to vicarious liability

Employers are generally only vicariously responsible for acts of their servants, that is employees over whose work they have significant control. However, the degree of control necessary varies depending upon the work involved. Even the employers of a labourer would hardly risk telling him how to use his shovel. The employers of an experienced professional person such as an architect or surveyor, or a clerk of works,[33] may give very little supervision over how he does his work. Ultimately the key question in identifying whether someone is an employer for the purposes of vicarious liability often is whether he has the power to dismiss. Thus where a servant of a regular employer, such as one of its bulldozer drivers, is delegated to work with a bulldozer on a site under a building contractor, the driver is likely to remain the employee of the firm providing the machine. That firm will be vicariously liable if the driver carelessly knocks over somebody or something with the bulldozer. It may be immaterial that, in the contract between the two firms, the driver is described as the servant of the contractors.[34] Various factors which may be relevant in determining whether an employee is a servant or an independent contractor include the extent to which he provides his own tools and arranges for subordinate assistance, and the manner of his payment, notably whether this is in a lump sum or in the form of a regular wage including employers' contributions to compulsory insurance schemes.[35] Overall it has been said that: 'under a contract of *service* a man is employed as *part of the business*, and his work is done as an integral part of the business; whereas under a contract for *services*, his work, although done for the business, is not integrated into it, but is only accessory to it.'[36]

(b) Scope of employment

Even where the person who causes an injury is clearly an employee of someone else, there will only be vicarious liability if he was acting within the scope of the employment when he caused the injury. Thus, if an engineer, working for contractors carrying out a construction scheme at an atomic power station, returned at night to sabotage the site, his employers would not be vicariously liable. However, an act may still be within the scope of employment even though it would clearly never have been tolerated by the employer, as where it was a criminal offence,[37] or even if it had been expressly forbidden[38]. Thus if a landscape contractor, employed to remove spoil tips, expressly instructed one of his workmen to cut down a tree before starting to excavate, and instead the workman began work on a bank without removing the tree so that it fell on someone else, the contractor would be vicariously liable. On the other hand if an employee takes it upon himself to do something which is not part of his job at all, the employer may not be vicariously liable.[39] Thus if a labourer who had been told never, on any account, to use earth-moving equipment, filled in a hole with a mechanical shovel, and whilst so doing knocked over a visitor to the site, his employer would probably not be vicariously liable.

(c) Employers' personal liability

It is important to appreciate that quite apart from vicarious liability, an employer may sometimes be liable personally for harm caused by his employee. Here it makes no difference if the employee is an independent contractor rather than a servant, or if the tort is committed by the employee outside the scope of his employment. For example a landowner could be liable for an accident resulting from his employing the village drunk to cut down some trees next to a highway, since he would be negligent to choose a clearly incompetent contractor.[40]

In some cases a person has a strict duty for which he may not delegate responsibility. Such duties are often imposed by statute, and particularly upon public bodies. Thus in *Hardaker* v. *Idle District Council*,[41] under their statutory powers, the district council employed a contractor to construct a sewer. They were liable when the contractor negligently damaged a gas main and blew up the Hardakers' house. Similarly, at common law, a person may be strictly liable in various circumstances which are particularly prone to danger, for example where he orders works to be carried out on a building adjacent to a highway.[42]

(d) The responsibility of employees to employers

Where an employer is liable to a third person who has been injured by the fault of an employee, he may be able to recover a contribution or a full indemnity from the employee.[43] Generally, employers' insurance companies do not require employees to pay compensation, but if an employee behaves outrageously, or if his employer is not covered by insurance, the employee may be required to pay. Often large organizations, particularly public bodies, do not take out insurance against certain risks because it is cheaper to pay compensation where necessary than to incur large regular premiums. It is generally of great importance for an employee to make certain that under his contract of employment, he is protected by his employer, or by his employer's insurance, from liability for any harm which he may cause in the course of his work, or that he has satisfactory insurance cover on his own account, whether through a union or other professional body, or privately.

6.4.4 Insurance

Although the law of tort may make a particular person liable for harm, it is often possible to guard against such liability by contract. Thus, as we have seen, an employer may agree to cover any liability for damages which one of his employees incurs during the course of the employment. Usually such protection involves a contract of insurance. A person who fears that he may become liable to a third party may take out a *third party policy* of insurance to cover this risk. Often someone who is likely to share liability with someone else may agree to obtain insurance cover for both. To some extent, in deciding whether a duty of care exists in particular circumstances, the courts may take account of the realities of insurance and the convenience of one person rather than another providing insurance against a particular risk.[44]

(a) Situations where insurance is required

It is vital for anyone who is likely to be held legally responsible for some harm connected with land use to be provided with adequate insurance cover. Occasionally a person is required by statute to be insured. The main example of compulsory insurance is the requirement that all car drivers be covered against risks to *third parties* including their passengers.[45] The requirement also applies to those who cause or permit others to use a vehicle. Thus an employer must provide cover for an employee driving a firm vehicle. Under the Employers' Liability (Compulsory Insurance) Act 1969,[46] most employers must be covered against liability for bodily injury or disease sustained by employees and arising out of their employment whilst in Britain. The employer is not generally required by law to insure against any harm which his employees may cause, but he would be wise to do so. Again the occupier of property is not required to insure against risk to his visitors but he would be wise to do so and also to cover himself against any liability for harm to neighbours or to the public from nuisance or any other cause. It is important for anyone with an interest in land to have *first party cover*, that is a policy which will compensate him personally if his property is damaged or destroyed. As we have seen in Chapter 5, Section 5.3, the risk in a piece of land passes to a new owner at the time when a contract of sale is agreed and not at the stage when the land is actually conveyed.[47]

(b) Interests which may be insured

Insurance contracts are subject to much specialized law built up in decided cases. An important feature is the requirement that the person who is insured should have an *insurable interest*. Thus an insurance policy for money to be paid if some property or person is harmed cannot be validly taken out by someone who could in no way be liable for the harm or suffer financial loss himself. For example if a person took out a policy against the possible destruction of a country house belonging to somebody else but which he merely happened to like, this would be regarded as a gamble or wager and would be void under the Gaming Act 1845.[48] Unfortunately it is not clear to what extent a person with a limited interest may insure, for example whether a tenant can insure against the entire value of the house in which he lives, where the main financial loss in the event of destruction would in fact fall on the landlord.[49]

(c) 'Uberrimae fides'

Another important feature of insurance contracts is that a policy is voidable by the insurer if the insured does not show the utmost good faith in that he fails to disclose some material fact such as would influence the judgment of a reasonable or prudent insurer in deciding whether or not to accept the risk or what premium to charge.[50] Thus a person insuring a building should reveal any defect such as weak foundations. It is particularly important to disclose any previous loss of a sort similar to that covered,[51] or any previous refusal of cover by an insurance company.[52] An insurance policy often requires the insurer to reveal any new element of risk which arises after the contract has begun. However, if no such provision is made the insured does not need to warn of new risks.[53] Even if the policy does require disclosure of new risks it will not be voidable if temporary risks are undisclosed unless the clause expressly refers to these as well.[54]

NOTES: SECTION 6.4

1. *Clay* v. *A.J. Crump & Sons Ltd* [1964] 1 Q.B. 533, C.A. However, compare *Clayton* v. *Woodman & Son (Builders) Ltd* [1962] 1 W.L.R. 585, *post* p. 371.
2. *Norris* v. *W. Moss & Sons Ltd* [1954] 1 W.L.R. 346, C.A.
3. See the difference in outcome between the two *Wagon Mound* cases *ante* p. 298f.

4. Law Reform (Contributory Negligence) Act 1945, s. 1 (1).
5. Ibid. s. 4.
6. *Caswell* v. *Powell Duffryn Colliery Co.* [1940] A.C. 152, H.L.
7. *Trevett* v. *Lee* 1 W.L.R. 113 C.A.
8. *Quinn* v. *Burch Bros. (Builders) Ltd* [1966] 2 Q.B. 370, C.A.
9. *Lane* v. *Holloway* [1968] 1 Q.B. 379, C.A.
10. *Jones* v. *Livox Quarries Ltd* [1952] 2 Q.B. 608, C.A., *per* Denning L.J. at p. 615.
11. *Stapley* v. *Gypsum Mines Ltd* [1953] A.C. 663, H.L. *per* Lord Reid at p. 682.
12. *ICI Ltd* v. *Shatwell* [1965] A.C. 656, H.L.
13. See *post* p. 310f.
14. *Bowater* v. *Rowley Regis Corporation* [1944] K.B. 476, C.A.
15. Unfair Contract Terms Act 1977, s. 2 (1).
16. Ibid. s. 1. For liability under the Occupiers' Liability Act 1957, see *post* p. 327.
17. Ibid. s. 14.
18. Ibid. ss. 2 (2) and 11.
19. Occupiers' Liability Act 1957, s. 2 (4)(a).
20. Ibid. s. 2 (5).
21. Ibid. s. 2 (3)(b)
22. *Ante* p. 306, and, *supra* note 1.
23. *Lister* v. *Romford Ice and Cold Storage Co.* [1957] A.C. 555, H.L. see *post* p. 312.
24. Civil Liability (Contribution) Act 1978, s. 4.
25. Rules of the Supreme Court, 1965, Order 16, Rule 8.
26. Ibid. Rule 1.
27. Limitation Act 1980, s. 10.
28. Civil Liability (Contribution) Act 1978, s. 1 (4).
29. *Performance Cars Ltd* v. *Abraham* [1962] 1 Q.B. 33, C.A.
30. *Jobling* v. *Associated Dairies Ltd* [1982] A.C. 794, H.L.
31. *Baker* v. *Willoughby* [1970] A.C. 467, H.L.; questioned in *Jobling* v. *Associated Dairies*, *supra* note 30.
32. *Spalding* v. *Tarmac Civil Engineering Ltd* [1967] 1 W.L.R. 1508, H.L.
33. *Morren* v. *Swinton and Pendlebury District Council* [1965] 1 W.L.R. 576.
34. *Mersey Docks and Harbour Board* v. *Coggins and Griffiths (Liverpool) Ltd* [1947] A.C. 1, H.L.
35. Whether such payments are to be made may itself depend on whether the employee is a servant. See *Morren* v. *Swinton and Pendlebury District Council*, *ante* note 33.
36. *Stevenson, Jordan and Harrison* v. *Macdonald* [1952] 1 T.L.R. 101, C.A., *per* Denning L.J. at p. 111.
37. *Lloyd* v. *Grace, Smith & Co.* [1912] A.C. 716, H.L.
38. *London County Council* v. *Cattermoles (Garages) Ltd* [1953] 1 W.L.R. 997, C.A.
39. *Beard* v. *London General Omnibus Co.* [1900] 2 Q.B. 530.
40. *Staveley Iron and Chemical Co. Ltd* v. *Jones* [1950] A.C. 627, H.L.
41. *Hardaker* v. *Idle District Council* [1896] 1 Q.B. 335.
42. *Tarry* v. *Ashton* (1876) 1 Q.B.D. 314. See further *post* p. 343.
43. *Lister* v. *Romford Ice and Cold Storage Co.*, *ante*, note 23.
44. However, the use of policy considerations with regard to insurance will not justify the courts changing established legal principles; *Launchbury* v. *Morgans* [1973] A.C. 127 H.L.
45. Road Traffic Act 1972, s. 144.
46. Employers Liability (Compulsory Insurance) Act 1969, s. 1 (1).

47. *Ante* p. 249.
48. Gaming Act 1845, s. 18.
49. For a more detailed discussion see Birds, J. (1982) *Modern Insurance Law* Sweet and Maxwell, London. pp. 37 f.
50. *Lambert* v. *Co-operative Insurance Society* [1975] 2 Lloyd's Rep. 485, C.A. There are exceptions; material facts which diminish the risk and which are public knowledge or of which the insurer waives disclosure need not be disclosed.
51. *Arterial Caravans Ltd* v. *Yorkshire Insurance Co.* [1973] 1 Lloyd's Rep. 169.
52. *Locker and Wolfe Ltd* v. *Western Australian Insurance Co.* [1936] 1 K.B. 408.
53. *Pim* v. *Reid* (1843) 6 Man. & G.1.
54. *Shaw* v. *Robberds* (1837) 6 A. & E. 75.

6.5   Responsibility under contract

Although the law lays down general standards of care in all activities which may affect other people, by means of a contract individuals may agree to vary those standards or may create a duty where one might not otherwise exist. A contract is a legally enforceable agreement, and the general law provides a framework which determines when its terms will be recognized as enforceable.

6.5.1   The creation of contracts

It is often assumed by the layman that a contract must be in writing. However, this is not generally true, although as we have seen in Chapter 5, Section 5.3, under the Law of Property Act 1925, s. 40, such requirements do apply to a contract to sell or otherwise dispose of land or any interest in land. Such a contract can only be enforced against a party who has signed or whose agent has signed a written note or memorandum setting out the subject matter of the agreement with the relevant terms, the identity of the parties and the consideration which each is contributing. However even then, under the doctrine of part performance, an informal contract for the transfer of land may be enforceable once the parties have begun to perform it. Nevertheless, it is always desirable for any contract of complexity to be agreed in writing so as to provide solid evidence that it was made and as to what it contains. Also there are a number of requirements for any enforceable contract.

(a) Offer and acceptance

The first requirement of an enforceable contract is that the offer of one party to enter into an agreement must have been accepted by the other. Sometimes, especially where there has been a number of letters exchanged or meetings between the parties, it is difficult to tell which party is the offeror and which the offeree. Nevertheless, until the parties have both agreed to be bound, there can be no contract. Thus if the owner of a tree invites tenders from tree surgeons to prune it, he is not making an offer but merely an *invitation to treat*. The tenders constitute offers. For one of them to become binding the tree owner must normally inform the offeror that his offer has been accepted.[1] In the interval the offeror may withdraw or vary his offer. If the offeree proposes some variation on the original offer this is treated as a counter offer and has the effect of cancelling the original offer.[2]

(b) Consideration

A feature of English contract law which is not found in other systems of law is the requirement that, either the contract must be made formally in a deed under seal, or each party must give some consideration to the other.[3] The consideration does not have to be equal on each side, although it must consist of something which may be regarded as of money value. For example if a landscape architect gratuitously promises to give a landowner some plans for a golf course which he drew up for a previous owner of the site and which were never implemented, the landowner cannot compel him to carry out his promise. On the other hand, there will be consideration if the parties agree that the landowner will pay a stipulated or a reasonable sum of money, hand over a case of wine or make the landscape architect a life member of the proposed golf course. The recompense may even be derisory.[4] Thus if the parties in our example wish to make a binding contract it is enough for them to agree that the landowner will pay £1 even though the plans involved many days' work. However, consideration must involve something which a party is not already obliged to do.[5] Thus, for example, a person who is owed a debt for fees of £1000 will not normally bind himself by accepting £500 in settlement but may still recover the balance.[6] Similarly, if, for example, a farmer agrees to pay £200 to a surveying student who has previously given him a copy of a survey carried out on a vacation exercise, the survey may be regarded as a gift and the farmer will not be bound to pay the £200.[7] However, in such circumstances it is often possible to imply an agreement at the time when work is done or property handed over that a reasonable price will be paid.[8] If a later price is then agreed this will be enforceable. If no price is agreed, the courts will be prepared to fix one on what is known as a *quantum meruit*.

(c) Intent to create legal relations

The parties to an agreement with all the hallmarks of a contract, may nevertheless not intend that it should be legally binding. In such a case, if for example the parties fall out, one will not be able to enforce the agreement in the courts. There is a presumption that agreements made in a professional or business context are intended to create legal relations and that those in a purely family or social context are not. However, each case will depend on its facts.[10] If an architect agrees to design a new house for his brother, even to a detailed specification, but with no mention of payment, it is unlikely that the brother could compel him to do the work. However, if a specific sum is agreed for the work, the intent to create legal relations will be apparent. In some circumstances the parties may intend a unilateral contract, that is one which depends on one of the parties in particular taking the initiative to make it enforceable. Notably, if an estate agent agrees to sell a building, his client can not normally compel him to perform the agreement but if the estate agent finds a buyer willing and able to buy, the client will normally be bound to pay the agent a commission.[11]

6.5.2   Enforcement of contracts

A contract may be defective and unenforceable in a number of circumstances. Thus, as we have seen in Chapter 4, Section 4.1, a party may lack legal capacity, for example because of his youth.

(a) Privity

Another special feature of English law is the rule of privity. Under this, a contract may generally only be enforced by someone who is a party to it.[12] Thus, if a contractor agrees with a demolition subcontractor that the sub-contractor may take away building materials from the client's site after carrying out demolition, and the client who owns the site prevents the subcontractor from taking the materials, the subcontractor has no claim against the client unless he also has a direct contract with him. The sub-contractor must sue the main contractor. This may be unsatisfactory for example if the main contractor has gone into liquidation. As we shall see in Chapter 7, Section 7.5, such problems may be avoided by multiple contracts directly involving the various parties to construction works. A notable exception to the rule of privity which we have seen in Chapter 4, Section 4.5 is that restrictive covenants may be attached to land and therefore benefit and bind later owners who are not parties to the original agreement.

(b) Void and voidable contracts

A contract may be void, that is in law it will be regarded as if it had never existed, or it may be voidable, in which case it may be rescinded by a court. The most obvious example of a void contract is an *illegal agreement* such as a commission for a thief to steal a statue. Any agreement to commit an immoral act,[13] or a tort,[14] is also illegal. Normally money paid under an illegal contract can not be recovered.[15] Other contracts may be void on grounds of *public policy* such as contracts in restraint of trade which are not reasonably necessary to protect the interests of the other party.[16] Thus an agreement by a trainee architect not to practise in the same area as his employers when he finished his training would be void unless it were confined to a sufficiently narrow district and time.

In exceptional circumstances, a contract will be void because of some fundamental *mistake* by the parties. Thus they may have agreed in the shared belief that the subject matter of the contract exists when it does not.[17] For example, a demolition contractor might agree with a local authority to remove an unsightly scrap heap from private land in the belief that the owner had failed to comply with an enforcement notice to do so himself. If, just before the agreement was made, the owner had removed the scrap heap, the contract would be void. However, where parties both mistakenly believe that something exists when it does not, there may be an effective agreement for one to bear the risk if there is a mistake.[18] For example a demolition contractor might agree with a client to clear the site of an old building in return for keeping the materials from it, neither party realizing that the old dressed-stone foundations had been removed years before. In such a case, the contractor might well be treated as accepting the risk that the materials were less than he hoped for, or alternatively the site owner might be treated as giving a warranty that the foundations were there. If parties share some less fundamental mistake about the substance of the contract, it is less likely to be treated as void, although in equity a court may still set it aside.[19] Thus if an architect were employed to design a house on a site which neither he nor his client realized was subject to a restrictive covenant or to some statutory control, the courts would probably rescind the contract if the error was discovered before the architect began to draw up his designs. However, once he had carried out some work, a court would be less likely to allow rescission at least without ensuring that the architect was paid for what he had done.

A contract will also be void if the parties each intend something totally different from each other and objectively the agreement could cover either,[20] or one is aware that the other is mistaken.[21] Thus an agreement by a landscape gardener to plant trees on a named site could be regarded as void where each party had in mind different sites with the same name or where the landscape gardener knew that his client was under the misapprehension that the trees to be planted were of a different species with a similar name. Here, in less extreme cases, the courts may refuse equitable remedies, such as specific performance, to enforce a contract based on a mistake by one of the parties.[22]

A party may be induced to enter into a contract by a *misrepresentation*, for example a landscape architect offering to provide plans for a new golf course might inaccurately state that the site was suitable because of its soil qualities. A misrepresentation may itself become a term of the contract or it may merely induce the other party to enter into the contract. In either case that party will be entitled to rescind the contract,[23] unless this is inequitable, for example because it is impossible to restore the situation to what it was before, as in the case of a contract concerned with a mine which has been worked out.[24] In a case of innocent misrepresentation, provided recision could still have been granted a court may award damages instead, if these appear a more equitable remedy, in particular where the party who made the misrepresentation would suffer disproportionately if the contract were rescinded.[25] If the misrepresentation was fraudulent or negligent both remedies may be awarded. Under the Misrepresentation Act 1967, s. 2 (1) there is a presumption that any misrepresentation was negligent.

A contract may also be rescinded if it was made under *duress* by the threat of some illegal act or as a result of undue influence. Unless provided otherwise this is presumed to exist where a contract is made between persons in fiduciary relationships, that is certain relationships of special trust such as between parent and child,[26] or doctor and patient.[27]

(c) Termination of contracts

A contract will be discharged where it has been performed by the parties, where the parties agree to terminate it, or where one repudiates it and this is accepted by the other.[28] If one party fails to perform his part, under the Limitation Act 1980, s. 5, he normally becomes immune from legal proceedings after six years have elapsed. A contract may also be discharged under the doctrine of *frustration* where it becomes impossible to fulfil as the parties had intended. It is difficult to tell what will amount to a frustrating event with regard to a particular contract. In one example, where a warehouse was being sold on the express understanding that the site would be redeveloped, the agreement was not treated as frustrated where, after contracts had been exchanged, the building was listed by the Department of the Environment so that development was no longer likely to be possible.[29] On the other hand if, for example, an architect agreed to make certain alterations to a building the contract would be frustrated if the building burnt down before the work was carried out. However, in such a case the architect might be able to recover payment for work carried out before the fire.[30]

6.5.3   The relationship of contract and tort

The formalized rules of contract law were largely developed by judges during the nineteenth century, when great emphasis was put on freedom of contract, to a considerable extent enabling parties to exclude or vary liability for causing harm to each other. Today, however, it is recognized that parties to a contract are frequently unequal, and as we have seen in the previous sections of this chapter, statutes, such as the Unfair Contract Terms Act 1977 and the

Occupiers' Liability Act 1957, limit the extent to which a person can agree in advance to deprive himself of a remedy where injured through the fault of someone else.[31] Often a relationship between one party to a contract and another whom he has injured is such that, even in the absence of the contract, there would still have been a duty to take care. In such a case an injured person may have alternative or concurrent claims in contract and tort. It used to be thought that where an injury was caused by a breach of contract resulting in injury confined to financial loss, the injured person could not sue in tort, but now, particularly in the light of the important case of *Junior Books Ltd* v. *Veitchi Co. Ltd*[32] it is clear that he may also be able to.

(a) Limitation of actions

As we have seen,[33] the Limitation Act 1980, requires that an action in tort must usually be brought within six years of liability arising, or within three years when the claim is for injury or death of a person. These periods also apply when an action is brought in respect of a breach of contract.[34] However, an action in contract accrues, and the period for bringing that action begins at the time when the contract is broken, whereas in tort time begins to run only from when damage occurs. For example a landscaping contractor might be employed by the owners of a factory who are extending their premises to create banks on adjacent land under an agreement by the factory to compensate a neighbour for relinquishing the benefit of a restrictive covenant. If the banks were constructed negligently, the neighbour's action in tort could well not accrue until the banks collapsed onto his land. If the factory owner were to bring an action in contract they would be obliged to do so within six years of the construction work. If the bank collapsed onto their land a considerable number of years after it was built they would be too late to sue in contract but might in some circumstances still be able to do so in tort.[35]

Where there is a contract this may restrict the time in which an action may be brought. Thus, subject to any relevant statutory restrictions against evading liability, the owner of land could bind himself not to bring an action in respect of defective work under a landscape contract other than an action in contract started within the time laid down by the Limitation Act 1980.

(b) Remoteness and measure of damages

Another area where liability in contract and tort may differ is that of the damages which may be recovered. There are two stages in assessing damages which tend to be confused. First both in contract and in tort there will only be liability for harm of a type which is not too remote. On the one hand there has never been difficulty in principle in recovering compensation for purely financial loss in contract as there has been in tort.[36] On the other hand the test for what is too remote in tort is generally very liberal[37] whereas it is much stricter in contract. Thus in *Koufos* v. *C. Czarnikow Ltd* known as *The Heron* (No. 2),[38] Lord Reid said that in contract

the crucial question is whether, on the information available to the defendant when the contract was made, he should, or the reasonable man in his position would, have realised that such loss was sufficiently likely to result from the breach of contract to make it proper to hold that the loss flowed naturally from the breach or that loss of that kind should have been within his contemplation.

The modern rule of tort is quite different and imposes a much wider liability. A defendant will be liable for any type of damage which is reasonably foreseeable as is liable to happen even in the most unusual case, unless the risk is so small that a reasonable man would in the whole circumstances feel justified in neglecting it. And there is good reason for the difference. In contract, if one party wishes to protect himself against a risk which to the other party would appear unusual, he can direct the other party's attention to it before the contract is made . . . but in tort there is no opportunity for the injured party to protect himself in that way and the tortfeasor cannot reasonably complain if he has to pay for some very unusual but nevertheless forseeable damage which results from his wrongdoing.[39]

In *The Heron* (No. 2), although they all recognized that the test in contract differed from that in tort, the members of the House of Lords applied somewhat varying tests as to remoteness of damage in contract. Lord Reid said that it was generally sufficient that the event causing any particular type of damage claimed 'would have appeared to the defendant as not unlikely to occur'. By contrast Lord Upjohn, for example, adopted the test that there must be a 'real danger', or a 'serious possibility', of the type of harm claimed for occurring.[40] If a party to a contract is aware at the time when he entered into the contract of special circumstances that make a particular type of harm likely, then he will be liable for such harm if it does result from his breach of contract.[41]

The second aspect of assessing damages is the measurement of the amount to be awarded for any particular harm. The principles for awarding damages are considered further in Chapter 8, Section 8.1.3. The manner in which these may be difficult to separate from the initial question of whether there is liability for any particular form of harm is illustrated by the case of *Cottrill* v. *Steyning & Littlehampton Building Society*.[42] There the building society, as mortgagees of a property known as Highcliffe, at Seaton in Devon, granted Cottrill an option to purchase the property for £5000 subject to his successfully obtaining planning permission to convert the house into flats and to build six houses on the adjacent land. Whilst Cottrill was abroad on holiday, the building society sold the property to a third party for £6250. They contended that, if they were liable for breach of contract, they need only pay the difference of £1250 between the purchase price agreed with Cottrill and that which they had actually obtained. However Elwes J. ruled that assessment should include Cottrill's loss of profit which he had expected to make on the conversion and on the six houses.

In Cottrill's case the judge treated the crucial question as one of measuring the proper market price of the property which Cottrill had lost. However, in assessing this he ruled that the loss of profit which was reasonably foreseeable because the defendants knew of Cottrill's intention at the time of the contract, was a form of loss for which Cottrill was entitled to compensation.

NOTES: SECTION 6.5

1. *Robophone Facilities Ltd* v. *Blank* [1966] 1 W.L.R. 1428, C.A.
2. *Hyde* v. *Wrench* (1840) 3 Beav. 334.
3. *Morley* v. *Boothby* (1825) 3 Bing. 107.
4. *Chappell and Co. Ltd* v. *Nestlé Co. Ltd* [1960] A.C. 87, H.L.
5. *Stilk* v. *Myrick* [1809] 2 Camp. 317.
6. See *Foakes* v. *Beer* (1884) 9 App. Cas. 605, H.L.
7. See *Lampleigh* v. *Brathwait* (1615) Hob. 105.
8. *Pao On* v. *Lau Yiu Long* [1980] A.C. 614, P.C., from Hong Kong.
9. *Powell* v. *Braun* [1954] 1 All E.R. 484, C.A.
10. *Snelling* v. *John G. Snelling Ltd* [1973] Q.B. 87 and *Rose and Frank Company* v. *J.R. Crompton and Bros. Ltd* [1923] 2 K.B., C.A., reversed [1925] A.C. 445, H.L.
11. *Luxor (Eastbourne) Ltd* v. *Cooper* [1941] A.C. 108, H.L.
12. *Dunlop* v. *Selfridge & Co.* [1915] A.C. 847, H.L.
13. *Pearce* v. *Brooks* (1866) L.R. 1 Ex. 213.
14. *Apthorp* v. *Neville and Co.* (1907) 23 T.L.R. 575.
15. *Parkinson* v. *College of Ambulance Ltd* [1925] 2 K.B. 1.
16. *Fitch* v. *Dewes* [1921] 2 A.C. 158, H.L.
17. *Griffith* v. *Brymer* (1903) 19 T.L.R. 434.
18. *McRae* v. *Commonwealth Disposals Commission* (1950) 84 C.L.R. 377, High Court of Australia.
19. *Solle* v. *Butcher* [1950] 1 K.B. 671, C.A.
20. *Raffles* v. *Wichelhaus* (1864) 2 Hurl. & Col. 906.
21. *Hartog* v. *Colin and Shields* [1939] 3 All E.R. 566.
22. *Wood* v. *Scarth* (1855) 2 K. & J. 33. cf. (1858) 1 Fost. & Fin. 293, where damages were later awarded in the common law courts.
23. Misrepresentation Act 1967, s. 1, cf *Redgrave* v. *Hurd* (1881) 20 Ch. D. 1.
24. *Vigers* v. *Pike* (1842) 8 Cl. & F. 562.
25. Misrepresentation Act 1967, s. 2 (2).
26. *Lancashire Loans Ltd* v. *Black* [1934] 1 K.B. 380, C.A.
27. *Re. CMG* [1970] Ch. 574.
28. *Hochster* v. *De La Tour* (1853) 2 E. & B. 678.
29. *Amalgamated Investment and Property Co. Ltd* v. *John Walker and Sons Ltd* [1977] 1 W.L.R. 164, and see *ante*, p. 143.
30. Law Reform (Frustrated Contracts) Act 1943, s. 1.
31. *Ante* p. 308.
32. *Junior Books Ltd* v. *Vietchi Co. Ltd* [1983] 1 A.C. 520. H.L. See *ante* p. 284 and *post* p. 370. See, in particular, the case of *Batty* v. *Metrolpolitan Property Realisations Ltd* [1978] Q.B. 554, C.A.

33. *Ante* p. 303.
34. Limitation Act 1980, s. 5.
35. See here *Pirelli General Cable Works Ltd* v. *Oscar Faber and Partners* [1983] 1 All E.R. 65, H.L., *ante* p. 302f.
36. *Victoria Laundry (Windsor) Ltd* v. *Newman Industries Ltd*, [1949] 2 K.B. 528, C.A. Cf. in tort see *ante* p. 287f.
37. *Ante* p. 297f.
38. See *Koufos* v. *C. Czarnikow Ltd* (*The Heron* (No. 2)) [1969] 1 A.C. 350, H.L.
39. Ibid. at p. 385–6.
40. Ibid. at p. 425.
41. *Hadley* v. *Baxendale* (1854) 9 Exch. 341.
42. *Cottrill* v. *Steyning & Littlehampton Building Society* [1966] 1 W.L.R. 753.

Chapter 7

SPECIAL ASPECTS OF LEGAL RESPONSIBILITY IN LAND USE

The person whose grass or corn is eaten down by the escaping cattle of his neighbour, or whose mine is flooded by the water from his neighbour's reservoir, or whose cellar is invaded by the filth of his neighbour's privy, or whose habitation is made unhealthy by the fumes and noisome vapours of his neighbour's alkali works, is damnified without any fault of his own; and it seems but reasonable and just that the neighbour, who has brought something on his own property which was not naturally there, harmless so long as it is confined to his own property, but which he knows to be mischievous if it gets on his neighbour's, should be obliged to make good the damage which ensues if he does not succeed in confining it to his own property.

Rylands v. *Fletcher* (1866) 1 L.R. Exch. 265, Exchequer Chamber, *per* Blackburn J. at p. 280

it is the law, I believe I may say without question, that at any time within twenty years after [a] house is built the owner of the adjacent soil may with perfect legality dig that soil away, and allow his neighbour's house, if supported by it, to fall in ruins to the ground.

Dalton v. *Angus* (1881) 6 App. Cas. 740, *per* Lord Penzance at p. 804

Judges sometimes reach startlingly different conclusions in what appear to be similar cases. This is hardly surprising in view of the difficulties involved in balancing consistently the conflicting interests of different parties. Thus, we have seen in Chapter 4, Section 4.4, that the natural rights of land for protection against adjacent property are limited, although greater rights, for example to support of buildings, may be obtained by long use. However, restrictions on activity which may cause something or some substance to escape and interfere with neighbouring land are more stringent. So also are the duties imposed on occupants of land to prevent accidents on the land itself.

7.1 Harm on land: occupiers and others

One way in which the law greatly restricts the use of land is by laying down requirements that it should be kept safe. This is an area where statute law has spelled out much of the responsibility of occupiers, landlords and builders, but the common law has been left to fill gaps in this responsibility and to regulate the duties of others who may create hazards (Fig. 7.1).

7.1.1 The occupier and his duty

Many mishaps may result from land or buildings which are in an unsafe state. A badly-built wall may fall down; an insecurely constructed bank may collapse; or an unwitting visitor may trip on an uneven path. The common law duty of care which was stated in *Donoghue* v. *Stevenson*[1] in 1932 might have been expected to make those in charge of any piece of land and those who leave it unsafe, after working on it, liable to anyone who was foreseeably

1. The occupier/builder/landlord
2. Visitors
3. Trespassers
4. Purchasers and their successors
5. Tenants

Fig. 7.1 Harm on land.

likely to suffer harm from its defective condition. However, case law had developed complicated rules which meant that an occupier of land owed a stricter duty to those whom he positively invited onto his land for some reason of benefit to himself, such as employees or delivery men, than to those whom he merely allowed to be there. The Occupiers' Liability Act, 1957, abolished this distinction between invitees and licensees. It provides that all occupiers of land now owe a duty similar to that owed generally at common law to any visitor who is entitled to be there.[2] The Act imposes responsibility for the safety of land on occupiers rather than on those with any particular estate or title in the land.[3] An occupier is a person with practical control of the land and control may be shared between two or more persons.[4] Thus, where a site is being developed by a number of contractors, the owner and the contractors may share control. If the owner invites a friend or business associate to come and look at the new layout, the owner and the contractors may all owe a duty under the Act to take care for the safety of the visitor.

(a) Occupiers and visitors

The common duty of care under the Occupiers' Liability Act is now owed to all visitors whether they would have been regarded as invitees or licencees at common law. However, if a visitor enters the land under an express contract, this may alter the duty owed to him.[5] For example, a workman on a landscape site might be expressly required under his contract to provide his own safety helmet. If the workman failed to wear a helmet and was hit by a falling stone he might be unable to claim that his employers were at fault, whereas a visiting friend of the owner who was injured because he was not provided with a helmet might be able to recover damages. Where a visitor comes onto land under a contract which does not specifically affect the form of duty owed to him by any occupier there will be a term of the contract implied, under the Act,[6] that the occupier owes to him the same common duty of care as to any other visitor. In any event the injured person may bring an action as a visitor and ignore the fact that he may also have a claim in contract. Thus in *Sole* v. *W.J. Hallt*,[7] a workman tacking up plaster boards in a partly-built house stepped back to look at his work and fell down the open stair well. Swanwick J. held that there was a breach of contract by the employers who were in occupation of the estate but Sole could not rely on this because his own carelessness was the cause of the accident. However, he was entitled to recover in tort for two-thirds of the damages attributable to his accident.

Visitors include people who have been expressly allowed onto land, but also those with implied permission. A salesman who visits a home offering to sell double glazing or grass seed will normally be owed a duty by the occupier unless he had been warned by a notice that tradesmen were forbidden. Nevertheless, it may be uncertain whether someone using a well-known short cut is a visitor. He may not be if the owner has clearly warned trespassers to keep out by a notice or a fence, but if the occupier does nothing to warn them off those who use his land are more likely to be treated as legitimate visitors. However, in *Lowery* v. *Walker*[8] a man was bitten and stamped on by a horse whilst walking along a track, which the public had used for thirty or more years, across a farm to a railway station. The House of Lords held that the farmer who occupied the land was liable even though he had objected to the police about the short cut and had warned people off. By contrast, in *Edwards* v. *Railway Executive*,[9] the House of Lords held that the Railway Executive was not liable to a boy of nine who lost his arm after being run over by a train when he got onto a railway line from an adjacent playground belonging to Woolwich Corporation. Lord Goddard commented that,

repeated trespass of itself confers no licence. The owner of a park in the neighbour-hood of a town knows probably only too well that it will be raided by young and old to gather flowers, nuts or mushrooms whenever they get an opportunity. But because he does not cover his park wall with *chevaux de friese* or post a number of keepers to chase away intruders how is it to be said that he has licensed what he can not prevent?[10]

Since an occupier does now owe some duty to trespassers[11] the courts are less likely to imply a licence to come onto premises unless there has been clear acquiescence by the occupier, for example, on a building site where roads have been laid out and are already being used by the public, although not yet dedicated to them.[12]

The common duty of care owed by occupiers to visitors under the Occupiers' Liability Act 1957 is set out in s. 2 (2), as 'a duty to take such care as is reasonable to see that the visitor will be reasonably safe in using the premises for the purpose for which he is invited or permitted by the occupier to be there'. The duty imposes liability for omissions to repair unsafe premises. Not only will an occupier be responsible if he dangerously performs some activity such as by running over a visitor with a piece of machinery or by constructing an unsafe bank which later collapses on a visitor. He will also be responsible for harm caused by his failure to properly maintain the premises. Thus he may be liable if a foot bridge collapses because it has naturally decayed or if a tree which vandals have killed later falls onto a visitor. The Act makes clear that the duty owed to different visitors will vary. Thus, it provides that 'an occupier must be prepared for children to be less careful than adults'.[13] Therefore, an occupier may be liable to a visiting child who is injured whilst climbing a wall with loose stones,[14] or a tree which grows close to an overhead electric cable.[15] Again where a child of seven died from eating berries of a specimen shrub *Atropa belladona* in the Botanic Gardens at Glasgow, the House of Lords held the Corporation liable for her death.[16] The duty owed to children will be greater in places such as public parks where they may be expected to play without strict supervision from adults.[17]

The Occupiers' Liability Act[18] concedes that the occupier 'may expect that a person in the exercise of his calling, will appreciate and guard against any special risks ordinarily incident to it, so far as the occupier leaves him free to do so'. If a landowner asks a contractor to make a wall or bank safe he will hardly owe the contractor the same duty as he would owe to a friend on whom the wall or bank fell during a walk on the land. Generally an occupier may be able to cover himself against liability to visitors simply by warning them of a danger on his land, but the Act provides that such a warning is not enough, 'unless in all the circumstances it was enough to enable the visitor to be reasonably safe'.[19] Thus a notice which warned that there was a trench across a footpath used at night would be no defence if the notice was not visible in the dark.

(b) The duty of occupiers to trespassers and others

Outside the Occupiers' Liability Act 1957, an occupier may owe a duty to people who are not visitors. *British Railways Board* v. *Herrington*[20] established that a duty is owed even to trespassers. There a 6-year-old boy, playing on National Trust Land at Mitcham in Surrey called Bunce's Meadow, strayed onto an electric railway line through a defective fence belonging to the Railways Board. He was badly burned. The House of Lords held that there had been a duty owed to him. The exact nature of the duty which may be owed to a trespasser is not clear. Lord Morris described it as one of, 'acting with common humanity'.[21] Lord Reid stated that it was subjective and must vary according to the 'knowledge, ability and resources' of the relevant occupier: 'The occupier might often reasonably think, weighing the seriousness of the danger and the degree of likelihood of trespassers coming against the burden he would have to incur in preventing their entry or making his premises safe, or curtailing his activities on his land, that he could not fairly be expected to do anything.' Where the presence of children is forseeable, the duty to act with common humanity is higher than with adults. In practice if an occupier owes a duty to trespassers this will usually involve him taking steps to warn them away from any hazard on the land or to keep them out. If children are likely to come onto the land a mere warning notice is unlikely to be enough. Generally if the occupier 'could at small trouble and expense take some effective action, . . . most people would think it inhumane and culpable not to do that'. However, 'an impecunious occupier with little assistance at hand would often be excused from doing something which a large organisation with an ample staff would be expected to do'.[22] in the later Privy Council case from Australia of *Southern Portland Cement Ltd.* v. *Cooper*,[23] a boy of 13 was compensated for injuries suffered when playing on sand which had been stacked to such a height around the poles carrying an electric cable that he could reach the cable. Lord Reid indicated that where the occupier created the hazard himself he had a higher duty than when he simply failed to remedy one which arose otherwise. Even where he caused the danger, the occupier could be given some leeway to avoid his being hampered in the conduct of his affairs by any obligation to take elaborate precautions.

Some persons who are not trespassers on land are not visitors either. Thus, someone using a public or a private right of way is not a visitor of the occupier of the land over which the right of way lies.[24] The Occupiers' Liability Act expressly provides that it creates no duty to members of the public who come on private land where an access agreement has been made under the National Parks and Access to the Countryside Act 1949.[25] In *Greenhalgh* v. *British Railways Board*,[26] Mrs Greenhalgh, a housewife, fell over in a pothole whilst taking a short cut on a public footpath across an old railway bridge near Little Hutton in Lancashire. The Court of Appeal held that the Railways Board owed her no duty to keep the bridge in good repair. Similarly in *Holden* v. *White*,[27] no duty was owed by a householder who owned a footpath which gave access to neighbouring houses, to a milkman who put his foot through a defective manhole. In such cases, however, it may be assumed that an occupier owes a similar duty of common humanity as he owes to trespassers. He will also owe a duty, which is the same as to legitimate visitors, to avoid activity causing harm,[28] for example by running down with his tractor a member of the public enjoying the view from an access across one of his fields.

Legitimate visitors may become trespassers if they go beyond the purpose for which they were allowed onto the land. As Scrutton L.J. once commented: 'When you invite a person into your house to use the staircase, you do not invite him to slide down the bannisters.'[29] A contractor employed to dig out some ditches on a farm would become a trespasser if he took the opportunity to shoot some pheasants in the farmer's adjacent wood. However, provided a person comes onto land as a legitimate visitor, he only becomes a trespasser when he knowingly goes beyond what he is entitled to do.[30] Once he does this he may be treated as a trespasser from the time when he came onto the land in the first place.[31] Thus, if a visitor to a country house vandalized a statue, he might find that he could not recover damages from the occupier if his car had collapsed in the meantime into an unsafe drain under the car park.

7.1.2 Responsibility of landlords

In certain circumstances a landlord may share occupation of premises with a tenant. For example he may retain control of communal hallways and stairs.[32] Even where a landlord has no current control of property he may be responsible for harm caused by its defective condition. First, where he has created the defect himself, he is liable on a footing similar to a vendor.

However, if he is responsible for repairing the premises, or even if he has a right to do so, under the Defective Premises Act 1972, s. 4, he may also be liable for defects which he did not himself cause. There the landlord will only be responsible if he knew of the defect, whether or not from the tenant, or if he ought in all the circumstances to have known of it. The duty is to take reasonable care in all the circumstances to see that all persons who might reasonably be expected to be affected by the defects are reasonably safe from personal injury or from damage caused by them to their property. The duty also applies to premises occupied under rights in any contract or statute which do not amount to a tenancy. A landlord is often responsible for maintaining at least the exterior of premises, especially under periodic tenancies[33] and may be required to maintain them by statute, notably in the case of agricultural tenancies[34] and of residential tenancies for less than seven years.[35] Often a landlord retains the right to carry out repairs even if he has no duty to the tenant to do so. Here, under the Defective Premises Act, 1972, he is again liable provided he knows or ought to know of the defect, but only from the time when he is in a position or can put himself in a position to exercise his right of entry. Under the tenancy agreement he may only be entitled to enter the premises after giving notice to the tenants. If a tenant is responsible under his lease for repairs which the landlord is entitled to carry out on his default, although the landlord will be liable to third parties, he will not be liable for any harm to the tenant himself.

7.1.3   The duties of contractors and others not in occupation

Where an occupier has done work on his premises which has left them in a dangerous state he will be liable as occupier for any harm which results, and, as we have seen, a contractor may temporarily displace the landowner as the person in occupation and responsible for the safety of the premises.[37] However, before the modern duty of care was established in 1932, the courts had developed an immunity for vendors of land from liability for any harm which later arose on the land.

(a) The duty of builder vendors in tort

Under the principle of *caveat emplor*, unless it was agreed to the contrary, a purchaser of land was responsible for making sure that what he bought was safe.[38] The vendor was not responsible even for defective work he had carried out himself, and the sale precluded any question of his later liability to third parties. It remains true that a vendor of land is not responsible for any defects even though he knew about them, provided he did not himself bring them about for example by doing defective repairs himself. However, vendors of land which they themselves have made dangerous are now treated on essentially the same footing as contractors who had no interest in the land. These were regarded as under a duty to anyone who might subsequently be harmed by their negligent workmanship. Thus in *Sharpe* v. *E.T. Sweeting and Son Ltd.*,[39] Sweeting built some council houses for Middlesbrough Corporation. A year later, as Mrs Sharpe, who had been living there ever since as wife of the tenant, went out of the house to take the evening air, the concrete canopy over the front door collapsed on top of her. Neild J. held Sweeting liable for her injuries. In *Dutton* v. *Bognor Regis Urban District Council*,[40] the Court of Appeal rejected the distinction that owner-builders were not responsible for the state of houses which they sold. Subsequently, 'do-it-yourself' builders have similarly been treated as responsible for defective workmanship after the premises have been sold.[41]

Concurrent with the hearing in *Dutton's Case*, Parliament was passing the Defective Premises Act 1972, which provides[42] that, where there is a duty of care in respect of 'construction, repair, maintenance or demolition or any other work . . . done on or in relation to premises', this is not abated by any subsequent disposal of the premises. Thus any architect, engineer or landscape architect who creates a dangerously defective scheme is now likely to be liable in negligence to anyone who is subsequently injured as a result. However, one caveat which Lord Denning M.R. indicated in *Dutton's Case*[43] was that where the defect was one which could be discovered on inspection the chain of liability would be broken by such inspection or even an opportunity for one. Thus there could be liability to a later occupant for dangerously inadequate foundations which were not apparent above ground, but not for an earth work at an angle of repose which was clearly too steep for safety.

(b) Warranted standards in building work

In *Hancock* v. *B.W. Brazier (Anerly) Ltd*,[44] Brazier built an estate of 40 homes, one of which was bought by Hancock. At the time of the conveyance, the house was partly constructed. The foundations included hard core which contained lumps of sodium sulphate. This soaked up water and expanded. It also caused a chemical reaction with concrete which disintegrated as a result. The courts upheld Hancock's claim for damages. As Lord Denning M.R. held in the Court of Appeal, on a contract for the actual building of a house by a vendor, unless they were expressly excluded there were implied warranties 'that the builder will do his work in a good and workmanlike manner; that he will supply good and proper materials; and that it will be reasonably fit for human habitation'. Although the builders had not been negligent and had bought the defective hard core in good faith, they were strictly liable in contract to the purchasers. Again, statute has extended the common law. Here the Defective Premises Act 1972, s. 1, provides that, 'a person taking on work for or in connection with the provision of a dwelling (whether the dwelling is provided by the erection or by the conversion or enlargement of a building) owes a duty' to the initial person ordering the work and also to anyone acquiring a later interest in it whether legal or equitable. The duty is very similar to that recognized in *Hancock's Case*. In each case the duty is a strict one and damages may be recovered from a builder or other responsible person who has been in no way negligent. However, the duty under the Act only applies to work for the provision of dwellings, whereas the common law contractual duty will be applied in all sorts of construction work on land. However, the statutory duty is owed by all those involved in providing dwellings, such as developers and not just builders. On the other hand, although it is not restricted by the doctrine of privity of contract[45] to those who initially contract for the building work to be carried out, the Act does not create a duty to persons who have no interest in the land. These must rely on the duty owed in tort for negligent construction. As a result of s. 3 of the Act, this duty is now unaffected by any subsequent sale.[46]

In 1937 the National House-Builders' Registration Council was established to provide for good standards in the building industry. It established contractual standards for its members, and the Building Societies Association supported this by recommending that building societies should only grant mortgages guaranteed by these standards. Now, the Defective Premises Act 1972, s. 2 allows builders of dwellings to substitute to the duties under s. 1 alternative duties to purchasers and to those who have a later interest in a dwelling, under a building scheme approved by the Secretary of State for the Department of the Environment. Under this provision many builders are now bound, not by s. 1, but by the National House-Builders' Council Scheme. This has certain advantages for homeowners. For example it gives the initial purchaser a right to make spot checks during the building period. Protection lasts for ten years rather than the normal six years under the Limitation Act 1980,[47] and is guaranteed by the Council if the builder responsible goes bankrupt. On the other hand liability under the statutory scheme is in certain ways more extensive. For example it allows direct action against sub-contractors who would not be covered by the voluntary scheme. Also the statutory scheme allows those to whom a duty is owed to recover damages for personal injuries. The voluntary scheme does not cover these, although it does not prevent anyone bringing an action to recover damages for them in negligence, if that can be established.

(c) Negligence by non-occupiers

A person who creates a dangerous situation on someone else's land owes a duty of care to third parties who might foreseeably be injured as a result, whether legitimate visitors or trespassers. In *A.C. Billings and Sons Ltd* v.

Riden[48] Mrs Riden, a lady of 71, visited friends who were caretakers at a house in Cheltenham, used as government offices, where the front steps were being restored. Because of the building works she left by an awkward route and fell into the area of the neighbouring house. The contractors were held liable to her for failing to provide safe access. In *Buckland* v. *Guildford Gas Light and Coke Co.*[49] a girl of 13 climbed an oak tree on a farm where she often went to watch cows being milked. She was electrocuted by 91 000-volt electric wires supplying the farm. The electricity suppliers were held liable whether or not the girl was a traspasser on the tree. However in *British Railways Board* v. *Herrington*, Lord Wilberforce and Lord Pearson implied that now that an occupier owes a duty to trespassers[50] non-occupiers will owe the same duty whereas Lord Diplock indicated that the duty may be different.

As we shall see in the final section of this chapter, the contractors and other specialists concerned with work on a particular construction site may be numerous. Public officials, such as local authority planning officers and building inspectors may be involved and will owe a duty not to be negligent to later occupiers and their visitors or even to trespassers. On the other hand, those who may be responsible for a harmful state of affairs on a piece of land include trespassers. Indeed they may be particularly prone to negligence although they are likely to be difficult to catch and even then may well have no money to pay damages for any harm they have caused. One other group which may be responsible for injuries on land consists of suppliers of materials. Under the Sale of Goods Act 1979 these have a statutory responsibility to purchasers for the quality of their goods. Where goods are supplied as part of a contract for work and materials, similar warranties as to fitness are now provided by the Supply of Goods and Services Act 1982.

NOTES: SECTION 7.1

1. *Donoghue* v. *Stevenson* [1932] A.C. 562 H.L. *ante* p. 283.
2. Occupiers' Liability Act 1957, s. 2 (2).
3. The Act in fact imposes responsibility not only on occupiers of land but also on occupiers of structures, including moveable structures such as excavating machinery; see s. 1 (3)(a) and *Bunker* v. *Charles Brand and Son Ltd* [1969] 2 Q.B. 480.
4. *Wheat* v. *E. Lacon & Co. Ltd* [1966]A.C. 552, H.L., and *AMF International Ltd* v. *Magnet Bowling Ltd* [1968] 1 W.L.R. 1028. see *ante*, p. 309.
5. The Unfair Contract Terms Act 1977, has restricted the use of contracts for reducing occupiers' liability. See *ante* p. 308.
6. Occupiers' Liability Act 1957, s. 5 (1).
7. *Sole* v. *W. J. Hallt* [1973] Q.B. 574, and see *ante*, p. 327.
8. *Lowery* v. *Walker* [1911] A.C. 10, H.L.
9. *Edwards* v. *Railway Executive* [1952] A.C. 737, H.L.
10. Ibid. at p. 746.
11. *Post* p. 329.

12. In *Coleshill* v. *Manchester Corpn.* [1928] 1 K.B. 776, C.A., a member of the public using an incomplete road was treated as a licensee, although under the law before 1957 the occupiers of the road had not broken their duty to him.
13. Occupiers' Liability Act 1957, s. 2 (3)(a).
14. *Boyd* v. *Glasgow Iron and Steel Co. Ltd* 1923 S.C. 758.
15. *Buckland* v. *Guildford Gas Light and Coke Co.* [1948] 1 K.B. 410.
16. *Glasgow Corpn.* v. *Taylor* [1922] 1 A.C. 44. H. L., from Scotland.
17. *Phipps* v. *Rochester Corpn.* [1955] 1 Q.B. 450, *per* Devlin J. at p. 472.
18. Occupiers' Liability Act 1957, s. 2 (3)(b), and see *ante* p. 308.
19. Ibid. s. 2 (4).
20. *British Railways Board* v. *Herrington* [1972] A.C. 877, H.L.
21. Ibid. p. 909.
22. Ibid. p. 899.
23. *Southern Portland Cement Ltd* v. *Cooper* [1974] A.C. 623, P.C.
24. Occupiers' Liability Act 1957, s. 1 (4).
25. National Parks and Access to the Countryside Act 1949, s. 60. See *ante* p. 151.
26. *Greenhalgh* v. *British Railways Board* [1969] 2 Q.B. 286, C.A.
27. *Holden* v. *White* [1982] Q.B. 679, C.A.
28. *Thomas* v. *British Railways Board* [1976] 1 Q.B. 912, C.A., *per* Scarman L.J. at p. 297.
29. *The Calgarth* [1927] P. 93, at p. 110.
30. *Stone* v. *Taffe* [1974] 1 W.L.R. 1575, C.A.
31. This principle dates back to the *Six Carpenters Case* (1610) 8 C.R. 146a. It has been applied recently in *Cinnamond* v. *British Airports Authority* [1980] 1 W.L.R. 582, C.A.
32. *Wheat* v. *Lacon and Co. Ltd, ante* note 4.
33. *Ante* p. 183.
34. Agricultural Holdings Act 1948, s. 6 and The Agriculture (Maintenance, Repair and Insurance of Fixed Equipment) Regulations, 1973, S.I. 1973, No. 1473, and see *ante* p. 184.
35. Housing Act 1961, s. 32, and see *ante* p. 185.
36. Defective Premises Act 1972, s. 4.
37. *Ante* p. 327.
38. For example, *Otto* v. *Bolton and Norris* [1936] 2 K.B. 46, and see *ante* p. 248.
39. *Sharp* v. *E.T. Sweeting and Son Ltd* [1963] 1 W.L.R. 665.
40. *Dutton* v. *Bognor Regis Urban District Council* [1972] 1 Q.B. 373, C.A., approved by the House of Lords in *Anns* v. *Merton London Borough Council* [1978] A.C. 728 and *Batty* v. *Metropolitan Property Realisations Ltd* [1978] Q.B. 554, C.A.
41. *Hone* v. *Benson* (1978) 248 E.G. 1013.
42. Defective Premises Act 1972, s. 3 (1).
43. *Supra* note 40 at p. 396.
44. *Hancock* v. *B.W. Brazier (Anerley) Ltd* [1966] 2 All E.R. 901, C.A.
45. *Ante* p. 318.
46. *Supra* note 42.
47. See *ante* p. 302f.
48. *A.C. Billings and Sons Ltd* v. *Riden* [1958] A.C. 240, H.L.
49. *Ante* note 15.
50. *British Railways Board* v. *Herrington, supra* note 20.

7.2 Torts controlling harm across boundaries: trespass, nuisance, and the rule in Rylands v. Fletcher

Although landowners and those who work for them must avoid the risk of unpleasant accident on any land for which they are responsible, the law of tort probably has a greater effect on the way land is used because of the manner in which it deals with harm caused to other land. Many activities may cause damage beyond the boundaries of the land where they are carried out. A cliff or a bank may slip, or a building collapse onto its neighbour; water may flood, or fire spread from one piece of land on to another; trees may fall on passers-by; their roots may damage adjacent buildings. Anyone responsible for such events may be liable under the principles of negligence which we have already considered in Chapter 6, Section 6.2, but normally a range of older torts are still used to protect land. With some variations, the principles for limiting and spreading liability which we have considered in Chapter 6 are relevant to these torts (Fig. 7.2).

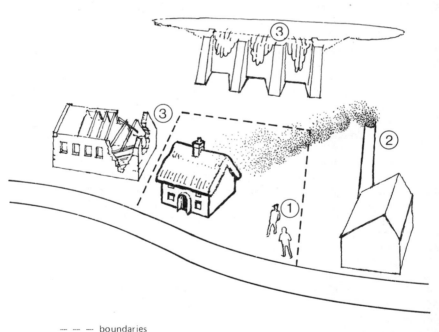

--- --- --- boundaries

1. Trespass
2. Nuisance
3. Strict liability

Fig. 7.2 Harm across boundaries.

7.2.1   Trespass

Long before there was an all embracing concept of negligence, the law protected landowners by giving them rights of action in trespass. The tort of trespass still provides an important restraint on land use. Like the word *tort*, itself, *trespass* originally meant, simply, a legal wrong. It could take several forms, trespass to the person, to goods or to land. Today, actions in trespass to land are available to protect land from interference by outsiders, particularly where this is intentional, for example by squatters in an empty house, by those who trample a farmer's crops, or by those who come to spy on the private homes of the rich and famous. By comparison, as we have seen in Chapter 2, Section 2.2, an action in trespass may be used amicably to establish the line of a disputed boundary. It is also the means of stopping substantial intrusions, such as the erection of a sign board so that it projects into a neighbour's air space,[1] or of a building actually constructed on his land. Since a profit is a right to remove something tangible from land, interference with it is also treated as a trespass.[2]

(a)   The protection provided by actions in trespass

A trespass to land is an unjustifiable, direct, interference with another person's possession of land. It is a tort, but it is generally not a crime, despite frequently encountered notices warning that, 'trespassers will be prosecuted'.[3] However, actions in trespass were originally intended to prevent breaches of the peace, where people dispossessed from land might take the law into their own hands. As a result such actions may still be brought even where no actual harm has been caused. If a trespass does cause harm, greater damages will be awarded. Also, as a trespass is a continuing wrong, a series of actions may be brought if it is not stopped. In the old case of *Holmes* v. *Wilson*,[4] Holmes accepted a payment to compensate her for a trespass by building buttresses on her land, for a road. Later she successfully sued for damages, because the buttresses had not been removed.

If several people are in possession of one piece of land at the same time for different purposes, each may be able to sue in trespass. If a trespass affects land permanently, an action may be brought by someone, such as a landlord, who does not have immediate control, but is entitled to the reversion in the land.[5] Thus a landlord may sue a trespasser who cuts down large trees which his tenant would not have been entitled to remove.[6] Even a trespasser may himself be trespassed against.[7] For example if a man unlawfully builds a garage on his neighbour's land, he may sue a stranger who parks his car in it without anyone's permission.

(b) Trespass and other torts

To be a trespass, interference with possession must be direct. If it is indirect, it may be a legal nuisance, but then it will only be actionable if it causes harm. The line between direct and indirect interference is difficult to draw. It can be a trespass to grow a creeper up a neighbour's wall,[8] whereas allowing branches of a tree to grow over a boundary, or roots to grow beneath, can only be a nuisance.[9] Throwing rubbish or earth onto someone else's land or against his wall would be a trespass,[10] but discharging oil so that it was carried onto the land by water would seem not to be.[11]

An intrusion onto someone else's land is not a trespass if it is involuntary, as where a person falls or is pushed on to it.[12] However, it is a trespass to interfere intentionally with someone else's land, as a result of a mistake, however reasonable,[13] and whether of fact or law. Thus it is a trespass to use a neighbour's land for access without his permission, even in the genuine belief that it is one's own land, or on the mistaken view of the law that there is a legal right to use adjacent land if this is necessary to carry out essential maintenance to one's own buildings. There is at present no such right to go onto neighbouring land, without permission, to carry out essential maintenance on one's own property. However, the Law Commission has suggested that authority to do so should be obtainable from a court.[14] A negligent intrusion on to neighbouring land would probably be regarded by the courts as negligence rather than trespass.[15] Thus if building materials were stacked carelessly so that they collapsed across a boundary, the injured neighbour should probably sue in negligence.

(c) The limits to liability in trespass

An intrusion on to someone else's land will not be a trespass if it is authorized by the person in possession or by some general legal authority. Thus, a person who is entitled to a right of way, obviously, cannot be sued in trespass for using it. Again, there may be a right to go on to land of another in cases of extreme necessity, to preserve life or property, or to prevent damage from a nuisance on the neighbouring land. In *Cope* v. *Sharpe* (No. 2),[16] Sharpe was a gamekeeper whose master had shooting rights on Cope's land. To protect nesting birds from an existing fire, he created a flame belt by starting a smaller fire himself. The original fire was extinguished before it could have harmed the birds, but the Court of Appeal held that Sharpe was not liable in trespass, as 'his acts were reasonably necessary in the sense of acts which a reasonable man would properly do to meet danger'. However, a legitimate right of entry becomes a trespass if it is exceeded. Thus users of a public highway become trespassers against adjacent landowners who own the sub-soil if they use the way for purposes other than passing or repassing along it. In the late nineteenth century, one Harrison had a grudge against the Duke of Rutland. On a public path across the Duke's grouse moors, he violently waved a pocket handkerchief, and fiercely opened and shut his umbrella, so as to scare grouse away from the butts where the Duke was shooting. The Duke sent his minions to eject Harrison from the moor and Harrison sued the Duke for assault and false imprisonment. The Court of Appeal had no hesitation in holding that Harrison was a trespasser and had been properly evicted from the moor.[17]

7.2.2 Private nuisance

If an unjustifiable interference with land in someone else's possession is indirect, it will be a private nuisance. The law concerned with this tort has been developed by the courts to extend the protection afforded by the action in trespass, to cover a multitude of situations, resulting in physical harm across boundaries, or in interference with the reasonable enjoyment of neighbouring land. Nuisance can be found in major industrial processes, on the one hand, and on the other, in small scale anti-social acts. It may consist of unpleasant smells, excessive noise, or vibrations, dirt or offensive vapour. A typical example of a nuisance dispute was *Halsey* v. *Esso Petroleum Co. Ltd*[18] Mr Halsey lived in a terraced house in Fulham. He successfully sued the proprietors of an oil depot on the edge of a neighbouring industrial area. Its boilers made his doors and windows vibrate during the night and his sleep was punctuated by the arrival and departure of heavy tankers. The atmosphere was polluted with the smell of oil and acid smuts damaged washing in the garden.

Large-scale demolition, building and other construction work is also particularly likely to generate nuisance,[19] but very different activities may be controlled on the same principles, such as carrying on the business of prostitution,[20] or operating sex shops.[21] A separate sort of private nuisance consists in substantial interference with easements or profits. Easements, in particular, depend for protection on the law of nuisance, because interference with an easement, unlike a profit, cannot amount to trespass.[22] However, in a case of interference with an easement, there will be no liability for damages, if the defendant could not have been expected to know that the easement existed, for example where he has damaged cables or sewers under his land, of whose presence he had no reason to be aware.[23]

(a) Nuisance and reasonableness

Where there is an interference with the amenity of neighbouring land, whether it amounts to a nuisance depends on what is a reasonable balance between the rights of the parties. Thus, in *Pettey* v. *Parsons*,[24] the Court of Appeal showed what could amount to a substantial interference with a private right of way. Mrs Pettey bought a shop in Bournemouth, from Parsons, to use as a dairy. The premises included a footpath between the dairy and other shops retained by Parsons. To make it secure from marauders, Mrs Pettey put a fence down the far side of this path and a gate across its entrance. Mr Parsons pulled these down. The Court of Appeal held that Mrs Pettey was entitled to erect the fence and gate, but, to prevent substantial interference with Parson's right of way, the fence had to contain a gate for him, and the gate across the entrance to the footpath had to be kept open during business hours and unlocked at other times. The manner in which the courts draw the line between what are reasonable uses of land and what amount to nuisances, are considered in more detail in Section 7.3.

(b) Nuisance and harm

Actions in nuisance are important because they are less concerned with compensating those injured by some harm, than with protecting their land from harmful states of affairs. Nevertheless by contrast with trespass, no action may be brought for a nuisance, unless it has caused harm. However, as harm may be an intangible interference with surrounding amenities, or obstruction of a right such as access, the practical distinction is not great. Furthermore, where harm cannot be proved, a court may presume it. Thus if it is shown that someone has constructed a drainage system, or erected a building with cornices which will deflect water on to neighbouring property, this may be treated as a nuisance even before any rain has fallen.[25] Indeed it is often said that a nuisance must be a continuing state of affairs. Thus if someone drove a single golf ball out of his garden and hit a passer-by there would not be a nuisance, although there might be liability in negligence, whereas running a golf course or a cricket club in circumstances where harm was likely to occur probably would amount to a nuisance.[26] If a dangerous state of affairs exists, even before any damage has occurred, a *quia timet* injunction could be obtained to forestall the risk of injury.[27] A nuisance action is often most valuable in obtaining an injunction to prevent the continuance of a harmful state of affairs. The action itself will have ensured that both parties are fully aware of the cause of complaint, although they may disagree over whether it is harmful or unreasonable. However, where private nuisance actions are used to obtain compensation for harm which has already occurred, they have become closely identified with claims in negligence. A plaintiff must show that such harm as he suffered was of a type reasonably forseeable by the defendant, which is tantamount to showing that the defendant has been negligent.[28]

7.2.3 Public nuisance

(a) The nature of public nuisance

A public nuisance is a crime,[29] rather than a civil wrong, and it consists in interference with public rights, as where a highway is blocked,[30] or where some harmful or offensive activity is carried on, which affects the public at large, and not merely one of a small number of adjacent property owners. Thus P.Y.A. Quarries Ltd carried on a quarrying business at Penyralltwen near Pontardawe, in what was then Glamorgan. The quarrying significantly expanded, and local people petitioned the Pontardawe Rural District Council, objecting to flying stones and dirt. Eventually proceedings were taken on their behalf by the Attorney General, who obtained an injunction, restricting the quarrying.[31] In the Court of Appeal, Romer L.J. said that a public nuisance involved affecting a representative cross-section of 'a sufficient number of persons to constitute a class of the public'.[32] Denning L.J. said that it must be, 'so widespread in its range or so indiscriminate in its effect that it would not be reasonable to expect one person to take proceedings on his own responsibility to put a stop to it, but that it should be taken on the responsibility of the community at large'.[33]

(b) Private claims in public nuisance

Public nuisance often overlaps with private nuisance. The individual householders affected by P.Y.A. Quarries could have sued in private nuisance. However, an exclusively public nuisance may only be stopped by an injunction sought by the Attorney General, or, by a local authority.[34] Nevertheless, any individual who suffers some particular damage, over and above that inflicted on the public at large, may bring an action based on a public nuisance, irrespective of whether he has any property rights which would have entitled him to sue in private nuisance. In such cases, public nuisance appears very similar to the tort of negligence, since there will only be liability to the injured member of the public for harm of a sort which was reasonably foreseeable. However, there may be the important practical difference, that once the injured party has proved that the defendant caused him harm through a public nuisance, he may not have to prove that his harm was a reasonably forseeable consequence. Instead the defendant may only escape liability if he proves that it was not reasonably foreseeable.[35]

7.2.4 Statutory Duties

Many activities which are a risk to neighbouring property have been regulated by statute,[36] including many which would amount to public nuisances at common law, such as pollution in various forms, and noise. Certain activities are treated as statutory nuisances, even if their effect would not have been sufficiently wide spread to amount to a public nuisance. The Public Health Act 1936, s. 92 treats as a *statutory nuisance*, 'any premises in such a state as to be prejudicial to health or a nuisance'. In *National Coal Board* v. *Thorne*,[37] the Board was convicted of failing to abate a nuisance order under this provision, at a house they owned at Banwen in South Wales. The alleged nuisance consisted of defective windows, guttering and skirting boards. The Divisional Court quashed the conviction, because it had been made on the basis that the house was simply in a defective state amounting to a nuisance. The Divisional Court held that this must mean either a public or private nuisance, and, as Watkin J. explained, these 'cannot arise if what has taken place affects only the person or persons occupying the premises where the nuisance is said to take place'. On the other hand, it appears that there would still have been a statutory nuisance if it had been proved that there was, 'some injury or an anticipated injury to the health of persons residing either in the premises or in any premises adjoining them'. An individual harmed in such circumstances might be able to bring an action for breach of statutory duty.[38]

(a) Fire

Statutes are sometimes used expressly to regulate compensation for harm across boundaries. The Fires Prevention (Metropolis) Act 1774, which in fact applies throughout England and Wales, provides that, 'no action, suit or process whatever, shall be had, maintained or prosecuted against any person in whose home, chamber, stable, barn or other building or on whose estate any fire shall accidentally begin'. Where this does not apply, for example if fire starts from a vehicle on the highway, the person starting it and the person on whose property it occurs, are strictly liable at common law.[39] Also, the courts have held that no fire is *accidental* if it is begun intentionally or negligently by anyone.[40] On the other hand, an occupier may have a good defence, if he can show that the fire was created by a total stranger, although even then, the fire will be regarded as a nuisance for which the occupier becomes responsible once he knows or ought reasonably to know that it has started. Similarly an occupier will become responsible for a fire which was caused accidently, for example by lightening, once he ought to have become aware of it.[41]

(b) Danger from public undertakings

Often public bodies statutorily responsible for dangerous activities are strictly liable for any harm which these cause. Thus the statutory undertakers who supply water are strictly liable, under the Water Act 1981, s. 6, for the escape of water from any of their communication pipes or drains. Only the United Kingdom Atomic Energy Authority is entitled to carry out operations involving nuclear plant, and under the Nuclear Installations Act 1965 it is strictly liable to compensate anyone injured by radiation, or through any other peculiar property of nuclear matter. Again the Civil Aviation Act 1949 allows civil aircraft to fly over private property irrespective of the rights of landowners,[42] but by s. 40 (2), it also provides strict liability 'where material damage or loss is caused to any person or property on land or water by, or by a person in, or by an article or person falling from, an aircraft while in flight, taking off or landing'.

(c) Animals

In the countryside, a major statutory intervention in liability for harm across boundaries was the Animals Act 1971. This makes persons in possession of livestock which stray onto anyone else's land strictly liable for any harm suffered by that land, or by property on it, although not for personal injuries.[43] There are defences, for example where the other landowner has a duty to fence his land,[44] but in contrast to other cases of strict liability,[45] no defence is provided where animals cause harm after being let out by a trespasser, or even as a result of a natural disaster, such as an earthquake. If animals stray onto the highway,[46] or if they are being driven on the highway and stray onto neighbouring land,[47] liability is not strict, but depends on the normal principles of negligence.

7.2.5   Strict liability and the rule in Rylands v. Fletcher

(a) Liability for dangerous structures

In certain situations, the law of private nuisance has been developed to make landowners strictly responsible for harm caused across a boundary by their premises. In *Wringe* v. *Cohen*,[48] the Court of Appeal imposed a strict duty on those responsible for premises next to a highway, to keep them in good repair and to prevent them falling, whether onto the highway or onto neighbouring premises. Wringe recovered damages for the collapse, onto his lock-up shop in Sheffield, of Cohen's gable end. Thus the person responsible for a defective building will be liable for harm which it causes, although he did not know of the danger and was not negligent in his ignorance. However, the Court of Appeal held that if danger is caused by a third party or by a latent defect, such as crumbling foundations, the duty is not strict but is the same as for a normal nuisance. The person responsible for the premises only becomes liable if he knows, or ought reasonably to know of the defects.[49]

(b) The rule in Rylands v. Fletcher

The case of *Rylands* v. *Fletcher*,[50] is the key authority for a second and major area of strict liability. John Rylands and Jehu Horrocks owned a mill at Ainsworth on the road between Bury and Bolton in Lancashire. They had a reservoir built for them nearby, on land belonging to Lord Wilton. Water from the reservoir burst through into Thomas Fletcher's Red House Colliery workings. The contractors who had built the reservoir appear to have been negligent. They had failed to take proper account of five old pit shafts encountered during the construction work. However, it was the mill owners who had accumulated the water who were sued, and they were held to be liable. The justification for the rule laid down in the case was given by Blackburn J., in the old court of Exchequer Chamber, in the words at the beginning of this chapter. He stated the rule thus:

> We think that the true rule of law is, that the person who for his own purposes brings on his lands and collects and keeps there anything likely to do mischief if it escapes, must keep it in at his peril, and, if he does not do so is prima facie answerable for all the damage which is the natural consequence of its escape.[51]

The rule does not apply to injuries on the land where the accumulation takes place. In *Read* v. *J. Lyons & Co Ltd*,[52] it was not applied to an explosion in a munitions factory which caused injuries in the factory itself. Furthermore, not all Blackburn J.'s examples would necessarily give rise to liability today. If a modern water closet flooded, its owner would probably only be liable if he knew or ought to know that it was defective,[53] and such commonplace domestic features as electric wiring would not be covered.[54] The essential requirement is that the substance or thing stored should be potentially *mischievous* if it should escape. However, it is difficult to tell in advance what a court would regard as potentially mischievous. The thing or substance which escapes must also be a *non-natural* use of the relevant land. In *Rylands* v. *Fletcher* in the House of Lords, Lord Cairns, the Lord Chancellor, laid down, that a non-natural user was one which would not have taken place 'in the ordinary course of the enjoyment' of the relevant land.[55] It seems that it must therefore be something out of keeping with the normal uses of the neighbourhood, but again the exact meaning of this term is unclear.

Since it may be impossible to tell in advance what a court would regard as both inherently dangerous and a non-natural use of land, the rule in *Rylands* v. *Fletcher* may seem unfair to land users. It has been said in the House of Lords that even explosives do not necessarily involve an inherently dangerous use.[56] However, for certain types of land use, it is wise to take out insurance on the basis that there may be strict liability. Apart from the accumulation of large quantities of water, the rule has been applied to sewage,[57] and to gas.[58] It can apply to the growth of plants, such as a yew tree projecting over a boundary and poisoning cattle,[59] and to accumulations of solid material, such as mining spoil.[60] It also includes things which do not themselves escape, but which generate harm across boundaries, such as electricity,[61] or explosives used for blasting which shower stones.[62] Strict liability has also been applied where pile-driving equipment caused vibrations which damaged a neighbouring house,[63] and where creosoted wooden blocks gave off creosote fumes which damaged neighbouring trees and shrubs.[64]

The possibility of strict liability applies to building and to many construction and landscaping activities such as tree planting, accumulation of water and the dumping of large quantities of soil and similar materials. Ironically, however, as we have seen in Chapter 6, Section 6.3, liability is not strict in those very cases where there is in practice most likely to be an unforeseeable collapse or escape, that is where the harm is caused by the unexpected act of a third party, or by an exceptional act of nature, as where a flood results from a trespasser opening sluice gates or the fracturing of a reservoir by an earthquake.[65]

NOTES: SECTION 7.2

1. *Kelsen* v. *Imperial Tobacco Co.* [1957] 2 Q.B. 334. And see *ante* p. 73f.
2. *Nicholls* v. *Ely Beet Sugar Factory* [1931] 2 Ch. 84.
3. For special circumstances where a trespasser may be prosecuted, see *ante* p. 280f.
4. *Holmes* v. *Wilson* (1839) 10 A. & E. 503.
5. *Ante* p. 174.
6. *Ante* p. 185f.
7. *Ante* p. 262f.
8. In *Simpson* v. *Weber* [1925] 41 T.L.R. 302, D.C., a creeper owner acquired an easement to grow it on his neighbour's wall (*ante* p. 204, note 63). Although he was not obliged to remove it, he was liable for allowing it to foul his neighbour's gutters.
9. *Lemmon* v. *Webb* [1895] A.C. 1, H.L., and *Davey* v. *Harrow Corporation* [1958] 1 Q.B. 60, C.A.
10. *Kynoch Ltd* v. *Rowlands* [1912] 1 Ch. 527, C.A.
11. *Esso Petroleum Co Ltd* v. *Southport Corporation* [1956] A.C. 218, H.L., *per* Lord Radcliffe, at p. 242, and Lord Tucker at p. 244.
12. *Braithwaite* v. *South Durham Steel Co Ltd* [1958] 1 W.L.R. 986.
13. *Basely* v. *Clarkson* (1682) 3 Lev. 37.
14. Law Commission (1980) Working Paper No. 78.
15. In *Letang* v. *Cooper* [1965] 1 Q.B. 232, C.A., it was held that a negligent injury to a person should be treated as negligence rather than as trespass to the person.
16. *Cope* v. *Sharpe* (No. 2) [1912] 1 K.B. 496, C.A. for the defence of necessity generally, see *ante* p. 301, but compare the position in criminal law *ante* p. 278.
17. *Harrison* v. *Duke of Rutland* [1893] 1 Q.B. 142, C.A., and see *Hickman* v. *Maissey* [1900] 1 Q.B. 752, C.A., *ante* p. 149.
18. *Halsey* v. *Esso Petroleum Co. Ltd* [1961] 1 W.L.R. 683.
19. For example, *Matania* v. *National Provincial Bank Ltd* [1936] 2 All E.R. 633, C.A., and *Andreae* v. *Selfridge & Co. Ltd* [1938] Ch. 1 C.A.
20. *Thompson-Schwab* v. *Costaki* [1956] 1 W.L.R. 335, C.A.

21. *Laws* v. *Florinplace* [1981] 1 All E.R. 659.
22. *Paine & Co. Ltd* v. *St Neots Gas and Coke Co.* [1939] 3 All E.R. 812, *per* Luxmore L.J., at p. 823.
23. *Ilford Urban District Council* v. *Beal* [1925] 1 K.B. 671.
24. *Pettey* v. *Parsons* [1914] 2 Ch. 653, C.A.
25. *Fay* v. *Prentice* (1845) 1 C.B. 828.
26. *Miller* v. *Jackson* [1977] Q.B. 966, C.A., *ante* p. 47. cf. *Bolton* v. *Stone* [1951] A.C. 850, H.L.
27. *Hooper* v. *Rodgers* [1975] Ch. 43, C.A., see *ante* p. 382.
28. *Overseas Tankship (U.K.)* v. *Miller Steamship Co. Pty, Wagon Mound* (No. 2) [1967] 1 A.C. 617, P.C., see *ante* p. 298f.
29. See *ante* p. 272f.
30. *Marshall* v. *Blackpool Corporation* [1933] A.C. 16, H.L.
31. *Attorney General* v. *P.Y.A. Quarries Ltd* [1957] 2 Q.B. 169, C.A.
32. Ibid. p. 184.
33. Ibid. p. 191.
34. *Ante* p. 101.
35. *Southport Corporation* v. *Esso Petroleum Co. Ltd* [1954] 2 Q.B. 182, C.A., *per* Denning L.J. at p. 197. The actual decision of the Court of Appeal was reversed in the House of Lords, *supra* note 11.
36. See *ante* Chapter 3, Section 3.4.
37. *National Coal Board* v. *Thorne* [1976] 1 W.L.R. 543, D.C.
38. See *ante* p. 292f.
39. *Powell* v. *Fall* (1880) 5 Q.B.D. 597.
40. *Musgrove* v. *Pandelis* [1919] 2 K.B. 43, C.A.
41. *Goldman* v. *Hargrave* [1967] 1 A.C. 645, P.C., from the High Court of Australia, and see *post* p. 357.
42. See *ante* p. 74.
43. Animals Act 1971, s. 4.
44. *Ante* p. 196.
45. *Ante* p. 292f and 297f.
46. Animals Act 1971, s. 8, overruling the rule in *Searle* v. *Wallbank* [1947] A.C. 341.
47. *Gayler and Pope Ltd* v. *B. Davies and Son Ltd* [1924] 2 K.B. 75.
48. *Wringe* v. *Cohen* [1940] 1 K.B. 229.
49. *Post* p. 356f.
50. *Rylands* v. *Fletcher* (1868) 3 L.R. H.L. 330, affirming (1866) 1 L.R. Ex 265.
51. Ibid. at p. 279.
52. *Read* v. *J. Lyons & Co Ltd* [1947] A.C. 156, H.L.
53. *Rickards* v. *Lothian* [1913] A.C. 263, Privy Council from the Supreme Court of Victoria.
54. *Collingwood* v. *Home and Colonial Stores* [1936] 3 All E.R. 200, C.A.
55. *Rylands* v. *Fletcher supra* note 50, *per* Lord Cairns L.C., at p. 338.
56. *Read* v. *J. Lyons & Co Ltd, supra* note 52, *per* Lord Macmillan at p. 172.
57. *Humphries* v. *Cousins* (1877) 2 C.P.D. 239.
58. *North western Utilities Ltd* v. *London Guarantee and Accident Co.* [1936] A.C. 108, P.C. from the Supreme Court of Alberta.
59. *Crowhurst* v. *Amersham Burial Board* (1878) 4 Ex.D. 5
60. *Attorney General* v. *Cory Brothers* [1921] 1 A.C. 521, H.L.
61. *National Telephone Co.* v. *Baker* [1893] 2 Ch. 186.
62. *Miles* v. *Forest Rock Granite Co.* (1918) 34 T.L.R. 500, C.A.
63. *Hoare and Co.* v. *McAlpine* [1923] 1 Ch. 167. There the defendants were in any event liable for nuisance.

64. *West* v. *Bristol Tramways Co.* [1908] 2 K.B. 14, C.A.
65. *Ante* p. 297.

7.3   Forms of harm on other people's land and liability for them

7.3.1   Liability for physical harm

A landowner generally has a clear right to protect his land from physical harm. Conversely he will rarely be allowed to carry out activities on his land which cause such harm across a neighbour's boundary. In trespass, there may be liability even if no harm at all is caused. A surveyor who strays on to neighbouring land when measuring a boundary will clearly be liable in trespass, although a court would normally only award nominal damages against him, unless he had intentionally ignored the landowner's request to keep off or unless he had caused harm. A court will not normally grant an injunction unless a trespasser seems likely to trespass again. At the other extreme, liability may be strict, for the very reason that there is a high risk of physical harm. Therefore, cases of strict liability, such as under the rule in *Rylands* v. *Fletcher*,[1] necessarily involve physical harm. Again, a public or a private nuisance may exist where there is only an interference with amenity, but if there is physical harm, responsibility is more likely to be recognized by the courts. In *St Helens Smelting Co.* v. *Tipping*,[2] in 1865, Mr Tipping obtained damages, where his estate of Bold Hall, near Liverpool, was being spoiled by the effects of copper smelting. The defendants argued that they were merely carrying out works which were normal and reasonable for the locality, but the House of Lords held that, as Mr Tipping's shrubs and trees were physically injured, there was liability despite the industrial nature of the area.

(a)   The nature of physical harm

For a nuisance to be treated as causing physical harm, in the words of Sir George Jessel M.R., in *Salvin* v. *North Brancepeth Coal Co*,[3] there must be harm 'visible to the ordinary person conversant with the subject matter'. Thus, if trees and shrubs are affected by fumes from a neighbouring factory, the harm must be clearly visible. As the Master of the Rolls continued: 'I do not think that this condition is satisfied by getting a scientific man to say that, by the use of scientific appliances, microscopic or otherwise, he can state that there will be in future time an injury.' Furthermore if, for example, a factory owner is to be sued successfully sued in negligence for causing physical harm, it must be shown that this was at least contributed to by his particular factory.

(b) The limits of common law control over physical harm

In some cases, a landowner may cause clear physical harm to neighbouring land, but not be answerable legally for it. Notably, as we saw in Chapter 4, Section 4.4, a landowner had an absolute right at common law to extract water percolating below his land, even if he did so with the express purpose of interfering with his neighbour's supply,[4] and caused it to dry up.[5] He would not even be liable for interfering with the water table in such a manner as to cause the collapse of buildings on adjacent land.[6] Rights to extract water have been strictly curtailed by statute, but the old freedom remains in certain circumstances,[7] including where it is necessary to prevent interference with mining, quarrying, engineering, building or other operations, or to prevent damage to works resulting from any such operations.[8] It is in just such circumstances that harm may be caused to neighbouring buildings or to other structures. Thus, in *Langbrook Properties Ltd* v. *Surrey County Council*,[9] developers on a 3-acre site at Sunbury-on-Thames were held to have no cause of action against a water authority or a highway authority which had diverted a reservoir, so as to allow for the building of the M3 motorway, and had caused subsidence by affecting the water table. However, even where a landowner is free to divert water which would otherwise percolate onto neighbouring land, he will be liable if he adds pollutive material to such water as does percolate through.[10] Also a landowner is under a duty not to increase actively the water flow onto neighbouring land. Thus it is a nuisance to divert existing water onto another person's land, for example by blocking up a stream, so that its waters unduly swell another stream on neighbouring land,[11] or by cutting drainage channels to let out onto neighbouring land floodwater which has already accumulated.[12] Once a landowner learns, or ought reasonably to know, that drainage of his land has been interfered with, he has a responsibility to keep drainage channels clear.[13]

A landowner is entitled to take precautions to guard his own land from future flooding, such as by erecting embankments, even if this later results in deeper flooding of neighbouring land.[14] On the other hand there is no duty to build barriers to protect one's own land, and if such precautions are not taken, there will be no liability if a flood passes across it to damage neighbouring land.[15] Similarly it would seem that a landowner would not be liable for fire, or a landslide, which passed right across his land onto someone else's. Water may accumulate naturally in artificial workings, such as a gravel pit or quarry. It used to be thought that, if this escaped or caused erosion on a boundary, the neighbouring landowner had no redress.[16] Similarly if cultivated land were allowed to run wild so that weeds such as thistles grew there, it was thought that there would be no liability for their spreading onto neighbouring lands.[17] It now appears likely that, provided they are in a position to safeguard against such hazards, landowners will be under a duty to do so. They even have a responsibility for hazards which arise entirely naturally, for example where a landslide results in a lake building up or a stream being diverted.[18]

Another area where there may be no liability for physical harm, is where some delicate property is damaged in circumstances where there would not normally have been any harm. In *Robinson* v. *Kilvert*,[19] Robinson rented part of a warehouse. He later sought an injunction to stop his landlord heating the cellar beneath because this was damaging some brown paper he was storing. The Court of Appeal held that there was no nuisance because the heat would not have damaged ordinary paper and was not shown to incommode work people in the warehouse.[20] Nevertheless the courts are reluctant to treat particular examples of normal uses as so sensitive that they are not protected. Thus it may be a nuisance to damage old buildings by causing heavy vibrations nearby, even if a more modern building might not have been affected.[21] Also, if nuisance is once established, damages may be recovered for harm to specially sensitive property. Thus if fumes are sufficiently bad to constitute an unreasonable interference with amenity,[22] or physical harm to ordinary plants, damages may be recovered for harm to specially sensitive plants.[23] However, before a court will award damages for physical harm in nuisance, as in negligence, it must be shown that that sort of harm was reasonably foreseeable.[24] Thus, even if it is well known that certain fumes or noises are likely to be unpleasant to neighbours and could corrode brickwork, there will be no liability for harm which they cause to plants nearby, whether sensitive or not, if no reasonably informed person could have told in advance that any plants were likely to be damaged.

7.3.2   Protection of amenity

As we have seen in Chapter 3, during the twentieth century Parliament has increasingly recognized the importance of improving the quality of life for ordinary members of the public, in particular by protecting the amenities of pleasant surroundings to live in and open places for recreation. Over the same period, the courts have taken increasing account of the amenity rights of private land owners, for example by recognizing easements of recreation for the benefit of one piece of land, over neighbouring land.[25] However, certain amenities, such as a right to a view, still can not be protected as easements,[26] but only under express restrictive covenants.[27]

If amenity is directly interfered with, an action in trespass may be available, for example against someone throwing rubbish onto neighbouring land. Generally, however, interference with amenity is less tangible. Where there is an easement providing an amenity, it may be protected by an action in nuisance. Thus, a person with an easement entitling him to walk in a park, may sue in nuisance a developer who builds on the park. Actions in nuisance may also be used to protect the rights of a landowner, or the public to such amenities as pure air and peace and quiet. However, rights such as these are not absolute. The courts will only protect them at a level which is reasonable in the circumstances. Other landowners have rights to carry on activities which are smelly and noisy, within reasonable bounds. Particularly in applying the law of nuisance, the courts have the task of balancing these conflicting rights.

(a) The public setting

The courts balance competing interests in land with little regard to the wider public interest. If a new use is popular with people nearby this does not extinguish existing rights of one or of a few who object. Thus in *Adams* v. *Ursell*,[28] in 1913, an injunction was granted to close down a fish and chip shop in Dingley, because the smell pervaded the home of a neighbouring veterinary surgeon, contaminating the butter in his larder and filling his house with vapour like a fog or mist. It made no difference if many poor people in the vicinity could be caused hardship by the closing of the shop. Similarly, if a new development amounts to a nuisance it is not a defence that the development has been given planning permission. Express statutory authority is necessary.[29]

What is unreasonable enough to amount to a nuisance varies very much with the *locality*. In *Sturges* v. *Bridgman*,[30] a doctor obtained an injunction to stop a confectioner grinding sugar in premises next to his surgery, which was in Wimpole Street, a medical enclave of London. Thessiger L.J. commented that, 'what would be a nuisance in Belgrave Square would not necessarily be so in Bermondsey'.[31] However, the character of a neighbourhood may change so that what was once a nuisance may cease to be so, for example where industry invades a rural area.[32] Conversely, what would once have been an acceptable use may become unreasonable. Cockerels crowing in the early morning at a farm on the edge of a new housing estate could be a nuisance. In *Leeman* v. *Montagu*,[33] the plaintiff likened such crowing to a crowd at a football match, and slept with cotton wool in his ears to keep the noise out. Even without a change in the neighbourhood as a whole, a new use which amounts to a nuisance may become established by time. Subject to modern statutory control,[34] a factory which has been pumping out fumes into neighbouring gardens for over 20 years may have acquired an easement to continue doing so. However, where an activity which is out of character with the neighbourhood only begins to cause annoyance once an adjacent owner starts to use his property in a manner which is affected by it, the activity is only treated as a nuisance from that time. Thus in *Sturges* v. *Bridgman*,[35] the plaintiff doctor succeeded in his action where he had only just built a new surgery, even though the confectionery business of which he complained had been in operation for 60 years. In trying the case, Jessel M.R. gave the illustration of a blacksmith's forge in the middle of a barren moor:

there is no remedy whatever, because it is a barren moor. Presently, this which is useless as a barren moor becomes available for building land by reason of the growth of a neighbouring town: is it to be said that the owner has lost the right to this barren moor, which has now become worth perhaps hundreds of pounds, by being unable to build upon it by reason of this noisy business.[36]

As Thessiger L.J. commented in the Court of Appeal, if the smith wanted to protect his rights he would have to keep a large area around his forge as a barrier, to prevent it amounting to a nuisance in the event of later development.[37] Thus changes in planning policy may turn an activity from a nuisance or into one, but only once a new policy has been carried through. The mere fact that a residential area is shown on a local plan as a proposed general industrial area, would not make general industrial activity reasonable until it had actually become established.

What is reasonable for a given locality, therefore, tends to be uncertain, because the character of the locality may change. Also, a serious addition to an activity so as to reduce the amenity of an area may be treated as a nuisance, even though the original activity was well established. On this basis, the House of Lords, in *Polsue and Alfieri Ltd* v. *Rushmer*,[38] upheld an injunction granted to a dairyman living in Fleet Street to stop new machinery being operated next door. Again, the fact that one sort of activity would be reasonable in a locality does not make a different sort of activity reasonable even if the annoyance which it generates is similar. In *Ball* v. *Ray*[39] a captain in the Lifeguards was banned from keeping horses on the ground floor of his house in Green Street, London and Mellish L.J. said, 'we are not to consider the noise of horses from that stable like the noise of a pianoforte from a neighbour's house, or the noise of a neighbour's children in their nursery, which are noises which we must reasonably expect and must to a considerable extent put up with'.[40]

Even if the fact that a particular activity may be in the interest of the general public is not a good reason for a court to refuse to treat it as nuisance, it might have been expected that it would be a good reason for only granting persons offended by it damages, rather than an injunction to stop it altogether. However, as we shall see in Chapter 8, Section 8.1, an injunction will not generally be refused simply so as to safeguard some superior public good.[41]

(b) Long-term and short-term nuisances

No right to conduct a public nuisance may be acquired by long use, but where a private nuisance is carried on for a long time a right to continue doing so may be prescripted.[42] On the other hand, activities which are only temporary, such as noisy and dirty construction work, may not be regarded as nuisances at all, provided they are carried out quickly, and at hours when they cause minimum disturbance. Thus in *Andreae* v. *Selfridge & Co.*,[43] the Court of Appeal allowed some damages in a claim by a hotel proprietor complaining of noise and dirt from a series of demolition and building operations on an island site between Wigmore Street and Somerset Street in London, but only because the works were done by Selfridge with what, Sir Wilfred Greene M.R. described as, 'a reprehensible lack of regard for the duty which it owes to its neighbours.[44] The courts tend to permit short-term annoyance on the basis that otherwise normal changes in land use would not be possible. 'The business of life could not be carried on if it were not so.'[45] What is reasonable alters over the years, as construction techniques change. Bennet J., the trial judge in *Andreae's Case*, took the view that then, in 1936, construction of steel-framed buildings with 60 feet foundations, and demolition of five or six houses at a time with pneumatic hammers was abnormal. The Court of Appeal did not agree. In contrast with the courts' indulgence to construction work, a short-term use of land which is carried out simply for its own sake will not be regarded as reasonable merely because it does not last long. Thus a circus will not be regarded as a reasonable use of land merely because it will only be there for ten days.[46] Generally planning control does not apply to users of land which do not last more than twenty-eight days,[47] but the law of nuisance is available to stop such short-term uses where they are of an anti-social nature.

(c) Sensitive and malicious parties

What is unreasonable enough to be treated as a nuisance, is generally decided objectively in accordance with 'what is reasonable according to the ordinary usages of mankind living in society, or more correctly in a particular society'.[48] No one may prevent someone else's use of their land on the grounds that they are irritated by it, unless normal people in their position would be similarly affected. Thus, the incumbent of a church failed in an action against a local authority which ran an electricity generating station nearby, the hum of which upset him when he was in his church, because, on the evidence of an expert witness, only 'a person of an unusually sensitive nature would be affected'.[49] As Lord Chancellor Selborne had said, some years before, 'a nervous or anxious or prepossessed listener hears sounds which would otherwise have passed unnoticed, and magnifies and exaggerates into some new significance, originating within himself, sounds which at other times would have been passively heard and not regarded'.[50]

Just as peculiarly sensitive persons may not be able to prevent activities which annoy them, those who carry on sensitive activities may have no protection under the law of nuisance. In *Bridlington Relay Ltd* v. *Yorkshire Electricity Board*,[51] Buckley J. refused relief to the proprietors of a large aerial who relayed television to subscribers, when reception was affected by an electricity power line. The judge expressed doubts as whether any purely recreational facilities could be protected by the law of nuisance, and stated specifically:

I do not think that it can at present be said that the ability to receive television free from occasional, even if recurrent and severe electrical interference is so important a part of an ordinary householder's enjoyment of his property that such interference should be regarded as a legal nuisance, particularly, perhaps, if such interference affects only one of the available alternative programmes.[52]

Today it probably would be considered that interference with television reception could constitute a nuisance.[53] However, other more specialized activities, even if carried out by public bodies, such as the operation of a radio telescope, might well not be protected by the law of nuisance.[54] A herb garden or a wine-tasting establishment might not be protected from slight smells which would not be regarded as objectionable by ordinary members of the public.

Although interference with the specially sensitive is not normally a nuisance, individual property owners may be able to acquire protection by covenants or by easements. For example, someone may acquire by long use a right to an exceptional degree of light from neighbouring land, such as might be needed to grow sensitive plants indoors, provided the owner of the neighbouring land is aware of the special use being developed.[55] Even a person who is only harmed because of his hypersensitivity may be protected by the law of nuisance against someone who harms him maliciously. A person who intends to harm another will be regarded as acting unreasonably even if what he did could have been reasonable had it been done with a proper motive. Thus in *Hollywood Silver Fox Farm Ltd* v. *Emmett*,[56] a builder who thought that a farm for breeding silver foxes would put off prospective purchasers of houses he was constructing nearby, sent his son to shoot on the boundary of the property during the foxes' breeding season. One fox ate its litter and others did not mate. Macnaghton J. granted the company owning the farm an injunction to prevent this malicious behaviour recurring, although had the gun simply been used to shoot rabbits, the builder would probably not have been liable in nuisance. Again, in *Christie* v. *Davey*,[57] North J. granted an injunction to stop a householder shrieking and hammering and beating trays on the party wall of his semi-detached house in retaliation for piano lessons and the playing of music by his neighbour's wife and family. The noises were made 'deliberately and maliciously for the purpose of annoying the plaintiff'. By contrast the court allowed the neighbours' music to continue.

NOTES: SECTION 7.3.

1. *Ante* p. 344.
2. *St Helens Smelting Company* v. *Tipping* (1865) 11 Ho. Lords C. 642.
3. *Salvin* v. *North Brancepeth Coal Co.* (1874) 9 L.R. Ch. App. 705, at p. 706. The case was tried originally by Sir George Jessell M.R.
4. *Mayor of Bradford* v. *Pickles* [1895] A.C. 587, and see *ante* p. 200.
5. *Chasemore* v. *Richards* (1859) 7 H. Lords C. 349.
6. *Popplewell* v. *Hodgkinson* (1869) 4 L.R. Ex. 248, see *ante* p. 199.
7. *Ante* p. 137 and p. 199.
8. Water Resources Act 1963, s. 24.
9. *Langbrook Properties Ltd* v. *Surrey County Council* [1970] 1 W.L.R. 161.
10. *Ballard* v. *Tomlinson* (1885) 29 Ch.D. 115.
11. *Thomas* v. *Gower Rural District Council* [1922] 2 K.B. 76, D.C.
12. *Whalley* v. *Lancashire and Yorkshire Railway Co.* [1884] 13 Q.B.D 131, C.A.
13. *Sedleigh-Denfield* v. *O'Callaghan* [1940] A.C. 880, H.L., *post* p. 357.
14. *Lagan Navigation Co.* v. *Lambeg Bleaching and Dyeing Co. Ltd* [1927] A.C. 226.
15. *Hudson* v. *Tabor* (1877) 2 Q.B.D. 290.
16. *Rouse* v. *Gravel Works* [1940] 1 K.B. 489, C.A.
17. *Giles* v. *Walker* (1890) 24 Q.B.D. 656, D.C.
18. *Leakey* v. *National Trust* [1980] Q.B. 485, C.A., *post* p. 357.
19. *Robinson* v. *Kilvert* (1889) 41 Ch.D. 88, C.A.
20. Had the landlord known that the warehouse was needed for specially sensitive paper when he let it, he would have been liable under the lease. In cases of independent neighbouring properties, a right to freedom from interference with some specially sensitive use may be acquired as an easement. see *post* p. 353.
21. *Hoare & Co.* v. *McAlpine* [1923] 1 Ch. 167.
22. *Cooke* v. *Forbes* (1867) 5 L.R. Eq. 166, as explained by Lindley L.J. in *Robinson* v. *Kilvert, supra,* note 19, at p. 96.
23. *McKinnon Industries Ltd* v. *Walker* [1951] 3 D.L.R. 577.
24. *Overseas Tankship (U.K.)* v. *Miller Steamship Co. Pty (The Wagon Mound* (No. 2) [1967] 1 A.C. 617, P.C., see *ante* p. 299.
25. *Re Ellenborough Park* [1956] 1 Ch. 131, C.A., *ante* p. 195 and p. 202.
26. *Phipps* v. *Pears* [1964] 1 Q.B. 76, C.A., *per* Lord Denning *obiter dicta,* at p. 83, *ante* p. 198.
27. See *Gilbert* v. *Spoor* [1982] 2 All E.R. 576, *ante* p. 210.
28. *Adams* v. *Ursell* [1913] 1 Ch. 269, and see *Kennaway* v. *Thompson* [1981] 1 Q.B. 88, C.A., *post* p. 384.
29. As in *Allen* v. *Gulf Oil Ltd* [1981] A.C. 1001, *ante* p. 19.
30. *Sturges* v. *Bridgman* (1879) Ch.D. 852.
31. Ibid. at p. 865.
32. *Salvin* v. *North Brancepeth Coal Co., supra* note 3.
33. *Leeman* v. *Montagu* [1936] 2 All E.R. 1677.
34. See *ante* p. 144.
35. *Supra* note 30.
36. *Sturges* v. *Bridgman* (1879) Ch. D. 852, *per* Jessel M.R. at p. 858 f.
37. Ibid. p. 865.
38. *Polsue and Alfieri Ltd* v. *Rushmer* [1907] A.C. 121, H.L.
39. *Ball* v. *Ray* (1873) 8 L.R. C. App. 467.
40. Ibid. p. 471.

41. See *post* p. 384.
42. See *ante* p. 265f.
43. *Andreae* v. *Selfridge & Co.* [1938] Ch. 1.
44. Ibid. at p. 11.
45. *Per* Vaughan Williams J. in *Harrison* v. *Southwark and Vauxhall Water Co.* [1891] 2 Ch. 409, at p. 413.
46. *Kinney* v. *Hove Corporation* (1950) 49 L.G.R. 696.
47. Town and Country Planning General Development Order 1977, S.I. 1977, No. 289, Sched. 1, Class IV.
48. *Sedleigh-Denfield* v. *O'Callaghan* [1940] A.C. 880, *per* Lord Wright at p. 903.
49. *Heath and others* v. *Mayor of Brighton* (1908) 98 L.T. 718.
50. *Gaunt* v. *Fynney* (1872) 8 L.R. Ch. App. 8, *per* Lord Selborne at p. 13.
51. *Bridlington Relay Ltd* v. *Yorkshire Electricity Board* [1965] Ch. 436.
52. Ibid. at p. 447.
53. This view has been taken in Canada in *Nor-Video Services Ltd* v. *Ontario Hydro* (1978) 84 D.L.R. (3d) 221.
54. *Stringer* v. *Minister of Housing and Local Government* [1970] 1 W.L.R. 1281, *ante* p. 119., shows how even planning law may have its limitations in protecting such activities.
55. *Allen* v. *Greenwood* [1980] 1 Ch. 119, see *ante* p. 204.
56. *Hollywood Silver Fox Farm Ltd* v. *Emmett* [1936] 2 K.B. 468.
57. *Christie* v. *Davey* [1893] 1 Ch. 316.

7.4   The allocation of responsibility for harm on other people's land

7.4.1   The relevance of the source of nuisance and trespass

Torts which protect land use may be committed by people who do not themselves have control of any neighbouring land. Thus, a trespasser may be a homeless squatter who takes over a house to live in, or he may be a contractor who is working on neighbouring land or on the highway and strays across a boundary to obtain access or to make a turning place for heavy machinery. A public nuisance may originate on the highway, on a river, or on the sea. Thus, owners of a tanker would be liable in public nuisance for jettisoning oil in an estuary so that it was washed up on the shore, unless the oil had to be abandoned because of a dire emergency, for example to avoid the ship breaking up.[1] By contrast, it may be that no private nuisance can arise unless it originates on private land other than that where it causes harm,[2] except that, where a nuisance is caused by one co-owner of land a fellow owner may still be able to sue him for harm caused to his own property. In *Hooper* v. *Rogers*,[3] one co-owner of a farm in Cornwall enlarged a track on a slope, so endangering, higher up the slope, the farmhouse of his co-owner, with whom he was on bad terms. The Court of Appeal approved damages which would enable the track to be restored. Similarly, if one co-owner displaces his fellow from their shared land, he may be liable for trespass.[4] He will not be liable in trespass for taking more than his share of the land, for example the whole of a shared hay crop, although he will be bound to account to his fellows for their share.[5] On the other hand a co-owner may be liable if he destroys the land itself, other than in the course of an agreed use. Thus he could be liable for removing top soil or turf from agricultural land.[6] Similarly he might be liable for transforming the physical nature of land by putting up new buildings on it without agreement.[7]

Where a tenant or other person who is entitled to be on land damages it, this may be a trespass against someone with a long-term interest. If such a person has a reversion[8] which entitles him to the future control of the land, he may have an immediate cause of action. Thus, he may sue in trespass a tenant who cuts down trees, removes turf or puts up permanent buildings without his consent.[9] He may also sue a person whose trespass could become a valid easement, such as a right of way, or whose nuisance could defeat his own rights, such as those to light,[10] if it were not challenged. Again he may sue in nuisance anyone who indirectly damages the property, for example by vibrations.[11]

7.4.2   Creators of harm

Whether harm across a boundary is created directly or indirectly, the person actually causing it will generally be responsible. A contractor may erect a building for a client so that it constitutes a trespass on neighbouring land, or causes a nuisance by interfering with a right of light to neighbouring windows, or with a private right of way. The contractor will be liable even though he does not own the land where the building is put up.[12] If the client authorizes the building he too will be regarded as responsible for the trespass or nuisance. Even if the building is later sold or let to a third party, provided they were initially responsible, the contractor and the original owner may remain liable for any harm which results. Such long-term liability could arise from flood damage caused by rubbish which had been left blocking a drainage system.[13]

7.4.3   Occupiers of land where harm originates

Where an occupier of land does not himself create or authorize a nuisance arising on his land, he may still be liable for it if he knows or ought reasonably to know of its presence and fails to take reasonable steps to remedy it. In such a situation he is under a positive duty to take precautions and is liable in negligence if he fails. However, provided the occupier does not initially authorize a nuisance started on his land, once he disposes of the land his responsibility ceases. Thus in *Attorney General* v. *Tod Heatley*,[14] Tod Heatley was discharged from liability where he was sued for allowing filth including dead animals to accumulate on a piece of wasteland in Westminster which had been his. The current owner was found liable.

(a) Naturally occurring nuisances

An occupier may become responsible for a nuisance created naturally, for example a fire started by lightning,[15] or a landslip brought about by extreme weather conditions.[16] Similar principles apply if an occupier acquires the land when it already contains a nuisance, or if the nuisance is created by some third party. In *Wilkins* v. *Leighton*,[17] Mr Wilkins had a boarding house at Boscombe. Next to it was a bank protected by a 13-feet high retaining wall. The wall collapsed because of the weight of the Leightons' house which was built above it and did not have deep enough foundations. The Leightons were not liable for the collapse, because they did not know of the defect and were not the builders or original owners. By contrast, in *Sedleigh-Denfield* v. *O'Callaghan*,[18] a nuisance was caused by a trespasser laying a drainage pipe with its mouth on the defendants' land, unprotected by a grid which was needed to keep out debris. The drain became blocked and caused flooding on Sedleigh-Denfield's land. Here the defendants were held liable because they were presumed to have knowledge of the situation through their servants who had cleared out the mouth of the pipe in the past.

Where a nuisance arises naturally, the Court of Appeal has said that the occupier is only required to do what can reasonably be expected of someone 'with his personal circumstances', including his financial resources. In the case of *Leakey* v. *National Trust*,[19] the Court of Appeal held that the National Trust was responsible for preventing damage to neighbouring property from a mound which it owned at Burrowbridge in Somerset, called Burrow Mump and which became very unstable following the very dry summer and autumn of 1976 (Fig. 7.3). In that case Megaw L.J. explained how it was necessary to take account of a landowner's personal circumstances.[20]

If a stream flows through A's land, A being a small farmer, and there is a known danger that in times of heavy rainfall, because of the configuration of A's land and the nature of the stream's course and flow, there may be an overflow, which will pass beyond A's land and damage the property of A's neighbours, perhaps much wealthier neighbours, it may require expensive works, far beyond A's means to prevent or even diminish the risk of such flooding . . . If the risk is one which can readily be overcome or lessened, for example by reasonable steps on the part of a landowner to keep the stream free from blockage by flotsam or silt carried down, he will be in breach of duty if he does nothing or does too little. But if the only remedy is substantial and expensive works, then it might well be that the landowner would have discharged his duty by saying to his neighbours, who also know of the risk and who have asked him to do something about it, *You have my permission to come onto my land and do agreed work at your expense*; or, it may be, *on the basis of a fair sharing of expense.*

This approach aims at fairness in retrospect where damage has occurred. However, if a landowner has a nuisance on his land which occurred naturally, such as a flood-prone stream or an unstable mound of earth, it makes it difficult for him to know in advance what precautions are expected of him,

Fig. 7.3 Burrow Mump, Somerset, by kind permission of Stephen Harte Esq.

unless he has the time, and incurs the expense, of asking the court for a declaration before any harm results.

(b) Nuisances caused by third parties

An occupier may also be responsible for a nuisance caused on his land by some other person. Indeed simply allowing certain persons to be on his land may make an occupier liable in nuisance. Thus in *Attorney General* v. *Stone*,[21] a district council obtained an injunction in a relator action brought by the Attorney General on behalf of the public to prevent Stone from permitting gypsies to camp on his land, in tents and vans, for a small payment, since they were there in such numbers and lived 'in such manner as to make the land unsanitary and offensive and dangerous to the health of the neighbourhood'. Again, in *Page Motors Ltd* v. *Epsom and Ewell Borough Council*,[22] a local authority was ordered to pay damages for allowing gypsies to camp on an industrial estate which they owned, because the gypsies had damaged the trade of a nearby garage business by putting off its customers with their fierce dogs and the smell of burning rubber tyres. Under the Caravan Sites Act 1968,[23] county councils have a statutory duty to provide caravan sites, and district councils to supervise them.[24] By the time the Epsom and Ewell case was heard, proper sites had been provided for the offending gypsies. However, a local authority might still be liable in nuisance, even for a statutory site, if this was in a clearly unsuitable setting. Nevertheless, an occupier will not be liable for the misbehaviour of trespassers on his land if he cannot reasonably be expected to get them off,[25] nor does he owe a duty to his neighbours to choose suitable tenants.[26]

In *P. Perl (Exporters) Ltd* v. *Camden London Borough Council*,[27] the Borough Council owned an empty flat next to another flat where Perl stored scottish sweaters. Burglars broke through an 18-inch wall from the empty flat and stole 700 sweaters. The Council's flat was not secure and it was known that trespassers had been in the building before. Nevertheless the Court of Appeal reversed the decision of the trial judge that the Council was liable for the theft. Thus it appears that, unless a property owner has some special responsibility for third parties who may come on to his premises, or unless he is aware that they are actually there and does nothing about them, he is unlikely to be liable for any harm which they may cause his neighbours, even if it was foreseeable that they might come onto his land and cause such harm.

(c) Nuisances caused by contractors

If an occupier authorizes work to be done on his land which necessarily creates a risk of nuisance, he may be liable if nuisance does result. In *Bower* v. *Peate*,[28] Peate was held liable for his independent contractor who rebuilt his house without properly underpinning that of his neighbour, as a result of which the neighbour's house was damaged. Cockburn C.J. ruled that, 'there is an obvious difference between committing work to a contractor to be executed from which, if properly done, no injurious consequences can arise, and handing over to him work to be done from which mischievous consequences will arise unless preventive measures are adopted.' Similarly in *Spicer* v. *Smee*,[29] a householder was held liable for the destruction of a neighbour's house by a fire arising from her house which she had sub-let with faulty wiring carried out by a contractor. However, it may be difficult to know in advance what work is inherently hazardous. Thus in *Salsbury* v. *Woodland*,[30] a householder employed a contractor to fell a tree in his garden. The contractor felled it onto telephone wires. These fell onto a road and Salsbury, a neighbour, was injured when he tried to pull them out of the way of an oncoming car. The householder was held not to be liable. In the words of Widgery L.J., 'the acts commissioned in the present case, if done with ordinary elementary caution by skilled men, presented no hazard to anyone at all'. Yet, it is difficult to see why the felling of a tree is significantly less risky than rewiring a house.

An occupier may be responsible for interference by a contractor with his neighbour's amenity as well as for physical damage, as where the contract necessarily involves noise and dust.[31] However, he will not be liable for harm caused by the contractor which is collateral to or separate from the work which he was instructed to do, such as injuries which were caused when a tool left on a windowsill by a contractor's workman was knocked off onto a passer-by as the window slammed.[32] Again, the occupier would probably not be liable if the contractor carried out work in a dangerous manner, which he had no reason to expect, for example if he demolished a building or a rock outcrop with explosives, where mechanical excavation would have been the normal method and would have been safe. The occupier may also escape liability if he can show that he had handed over the control of the premises completely to the contractor at the relevant time.[33]

A person who accumulates anything potentially dangerous for his own purposes and for which strict liability arises under the rule in *Rylands* v. *Fletcher*,[34] will be responsible whether he accumulated it on his own or someone's else's land. An occupier who has authorized the dangerous accumulation will also be responsible. In September 1916 there was a violent explosion at Rainham, in Essex, caused in the manufacture for the Minister of Munitions of a high explosive called picric acid. Amongst others, the works of the Belvedere Fish Guano Co were severely damaged. The House of Lords held[35] the manufacturing company, Rainham Chemical Works Ltd, strictly responsible, because they were in control of the premises and had brought in dangerous chemicals. However, they had no legal title to the land and were carrying out the processes in anticipation of having a lease assigned by the tenants who had set up the company. These were also held liable. On the other hand, provided a contractor or occupier of land has taken all reasonable care in the relevant accumulation, it seems unlikely that either will be legally responsible for any subsequent escape after they have ceased to have any control.[36]

If a person acquires land with a potential hazard which is not a nuisance, but could be harmful if it escapes, he may make himself strictly liable under the rule in *Rylands* v. *Fletcher* by continuing it. Thus if a farmer acquires land with a reservoir on it which he continues to keep filled up, he may be strictly liable should the water flood onto neighbouring land.

7.4.4. Landlords

A landlord will share liability with his tenant or be entirely responsible for a nuisance which he has created,[37] or is responsible for at the time of letting,[38] even if the tenant has covenanted to remedy any defects in the premises.[39] He will also be liable if he lets the land for a purpose, which will, with virtual certainty, amount to a nuisance. Thus in *Winter* v. *Baker*,[40] an injunction was awarded against Mr Baker who had let land at his model lodging house in King's Road, Brentwood, Essex on a weekly tenancy to a showman who drew crowds by the antics of 'iron faced ladies, the wonder of the world', a description which 'did not, as might be supposed refer to their powers of loquacity but their capacity of lifting heavy weights with their teeth', and who operated, 'an organ with 27 trumpets, which was remarkable not only for its noise but the monotony of its music'. More prosaically in *Harris* v. *James*,[41] a landlord was held to be liable for smoke from lime kilns and for dust and showers of stones from blasting where he had let land specifically for these processes. However, where there is only a possibility of harm, for example where land is let to dubious tenants, the landlord is not regarded as responsible if a nuisance does occur.[42]

A landlord may be liable for a nuisance caused by any defect which appears after letting premises if he has agreed with the tenant to be responsible for repair, or even if he has merely retained the power to carry them out. In circumstances where there is strict liability for nuisance, as where part of a building falls onto a highway, or a man-hole in a highway is defective, if the landlord has the duty or power to repair, he will be liable, even if unaware of the defect.[43] In *Attorney General* v. *Cory Bros.*[44] landlords of a tip which collapsed in the Rhondda Valley were treated as liable to the victims of the disaster, under the rule in *Rylands* v. *Fletcher*. However, they were entitled to be indemnified by their tenants who had constructed the tip negligently without proper drainage, on a steep mountain.

NOTES: SECTION 7.4.

1. *Southport Corporation* v. *Esso Petroleum Co. Ltd* [1956] A.C. 218, H.L.
2. Ibid. *per* Lord Radcliffe *obiter dicta* at p. 242, but cf. Devlin J. at p. 225.
3. *Hooper* v. *Rogers* [1975] Ch. 43, C.A.
4. *Bull* v. *Bull* [1955] 1 Q.B. 234, C.A., *per* Denning L.J. at p. 237.
5. *Jacobs* v. *Seward* (1872) L.R. 5 H.L. 464.
6. *Wilkinson* v. *Haygarth* (1864) 12 Q.B. 837.
7. *Stedman* v. *Smith* (1857) 8 E. & B. 1.
8. *Ante* p. 174.
9. *Mayfair Property Co.* v. *Johnston* [1894] 1 Ch. 508.
10. *The Metropolitan Assoc. for Improving the Dwellings of the Industrious Classes* v. *Petch* (1858) 5 C.B., N.S. 504.
11. *Shelfer* v. *City of London Electric Lighting Co.* [1895] 1 Ch. 287.
12. *Thompson* v. *Gibson* (1841) 7 M. & W. 456.
13. *Konskier* v. *Goodman Ltd* [1928] 1 K.B. 421, C.A.
14. *Attorney General* v. *Tod Heatley* [1897] 1 Ch. 560, C.A.
15. *Goldman* v. *Hargrave* [1967] 1 A.C. 645, P.C. from the High Court of Australia.
16. *Leakey* v. *National Trust* [1980] Q.B. 485, C.A.
17. *Wilkins* v. *Leighton* [1932] 2 Ch. 106.
18. *Sedleigh-Denfield* v. *O'Callaghan* [1940] A.C. 880.
19. *Leakey* v. *National Trust supra* note 16.
20. *Leakey* v. *National Trust supra* note 16, *per* Megaw L.J. at pp. 524 and 526.
21. *Attorney General* v. *Stone* (1895) 12 T.L.R. 76.
22. *Page Motors Ltd* v. *Epsom and Ewell Borough Council* (1980) 78 L.G.R. 505.
23. Caravan Sites Act 1968, s. 6.
24. Ibid. s. 7.

25. *Bromsgrove District Council* v. *Carthy* [1975] P. & C.R. 34.
26. *Smith* v. *Scott* [1973] Ch. 314.
27. *P. Perl (Exporters) Ltd* v. *Camden London Borough Council* [1983] 3 All E.R. 161.
28. *Bower* v. *Peate* (1876) 1 Q.B.D. 321.
29. *Spicer* v. *Smee* [1946] 1 All E.R. 489.
30. *Salsbury* v. *Woodland* [1970] 1 Q.B. 324, C.A.
31. *Matania* v. *National Provincial Bank Ltd* [1936] 2 All E.R. 633.
32. *Padbury* v. *Holliday and Greenwood Ltd* (1912) 28 T.L.R. 492.
33. *Gourock Ropework Co.* v. *Greenock Corporation* 1966 S.L.T. 125.
34. *Ante* p. 344.
35. *Rainham Chemical Works Ltd* v. *Belvedere Fish Guano Co* [1921] 2 A.C. 465, H.L.
36. Ibid. *per* Lord Buckmaster at p. 478.
37. *Metropolitan Properties Ltd* v. *Jones* [1939] 2 All E.R. 202.
38. *Todd* v. *Flight* (1860) 9 C.B., N.S. 377.
39. *Brew Bros. Ltd* v. *Snax (Ross) Ltd* [1970] 1 Q.B. 612, C.A.
40. *Winter* v. *Baker* (1887) 3 T.L.R. 569.
41. *Harris* v. *James* (1876) 45 L.J. Q.B. 545.
42. *Smith* v. *Scott, supra* note 26.
43. *Heap* v. *Ind. Coop and Allsopp Ltd* [1940] 2 K.B. 476, C.A.
44. *Attorney General* v. *Cory Bros.* [1921] 1 A.C. 521.

7.5.   Legal responsibility of land-use specialists

Those who are concerned professionally with the use of land usually carry out their work in accordance with contracts made in various standard forms. However, if they affect others with whom they do not have a direct contract they may still be liable in negligence or some other form of tort. As we have seen at the end of Chapter 6, Section 6.5, where a person is liable for a breach of contract he may be concurrently liable in tort, to a greater or lesser extent, for the same harm, even to another party to the contract.

7.5.1   Contracts for specialists in land use

Those whose work may affect and change the face of the landscape belong to professional bodies as diverse as the National Union of Farmers and the National Federation of Building Trades Employers. Several of such bodies, particularly those concerned with building, engineering and landscape design, have produced standard forms of contract which are normally used to regulate their work. Thus if a person intending to carry out building work employs an architect, the architect will normally agree to act under a direct contract with the client. Since 1 July 1982 this will have been in the form of the Royal Institute of British Architects' 'Architects Appointment'. If the proposed work is carried out, the architect will arrange for the appointment of a contractor who will also enter into a contract direct with the employer. A standard form for such a contract began to be used as early as the end of the nineteenth century. Since 1977 it has been known as the JCT standard form. It is produced by an informal body known as the Joint Contracts Tribunal with representatives from the Royal Institute of British Architects, which owns the copyright in the standard form, the Royal Institution of Chartered Surveyors, the Association of Consulting Engineers, organizations representing the building and engineering industries, such as the National Federation of Building Trades Employers, and bodies representing local authorities, such as the Association of District Councils. There are a number of variations of the standard form, for example to cover local authority and private work. The present form of JCT was produced in 1980 and is known as the JCT 80. A shorter alternative standard form, the ACA form of building agreement, was produced in 1982, by the Association of Consultant Architects.

Additional specialists, such as surveyors, quantity surveyors or consulting engineers, brought in by an architect, are likely to be employed as consultants directly by the client. Specialized work on a site, such as demolition, landscaping or decoration may be carried out by sub-contractors nominated separately by the employer or by the architect on his behalf. Under the JCT 80, provision is made for the architect to have contract forms for each sub-contractor signed by the sub-contractor, the employer and also the main contractor, so that all are parties to the sub-contractor's contract. However, sub-contractors may be employed directly by a head contractor who will then be answerable for them to the client. In such a case, if something goes wrong, the client may not be entitled to sue the sub-contractor directly in contract, but may often have a direct cause of action in tort that is if the sub-contractor carried out his work in a negligent manner so that it proved defective.[1]

Engineering work, such as road construction, bridge building or recontouring of land, will normally be supervised by an engineer instead of an architect, and the contract between the client and the contractor will be in the form of the ICE form of contract, the present, fifth edition, of which was drawn up in 1973. For landscape work, a landscape architect will normally agree to act under the Landscape Institute Conditions of Engagement of 1979, and the contractor will be employed under the JCLI standard form, last revised in 1981, which is produced by the Joint Council for Landscape Industries. This comprises the Landscape Institute, the Horticultural Trades Association, the British Association of Landscape Industries and the National Farmers Union.

Standard forms of contract deal with quality of work and the allocation of responsibility between the different specialists involved. These are dealt with in the next sub-section. Other vital matters also have to be provided for. It cannot be stressed too strongly that standard form contracts must be handled with as much caution as tailor-made contracts. They have been produced as a compromise between specialists with different interests who are bound to be in competition if not in conflict. In submitting tenders, each will be vying to obtain the best profit from the contract and yet to keep the cost low enough for the client to accept his tender. Therefore terms may be framed ambiguously and if something goes wrong, each specialist may try to shift the blame or the cost to the others. It has been observed that the standard form of building contract 'is like the Thirty-Nine Articles of the Church of England, an attempt to reconcile the unreconcilable. Like that document, it works very well in practice so long as it is not read.'[2] When disputes arise it has to be read. In particular there may be difficulties as to exactly what is included in the terms of the contract based on a standard form. The JCT 80 starts with five articles forming the foundation of the contract and continues with forty conditions making detailed provisions. Article 2.2 provides that, 'nothing contained in the contract Bills shall override or modify the application or interpretation of the Articles of Agreement, the Conditions or the Appendix'. Normally however, tenders are actually based on bills of quantities, showing the materials needed for a job. These often do purport to vary the contract and if it were not for Article 2.2, would be treated as taking priority over the contract form.[3] Even under a standard building contract extra terms in the bills of quantities may be given some weight if they elaborate on the standard conditions, rather than modify them.[4]

(a) *The work to be done and payment for it*

Payment for construction work may be in the form of a lump sum quantified in advance, or on a *quantum meruit*, that is a fair valuation, estimated after the work is completed. In practice, arrangements are usually more complex. The RIBA '*Architect's Appointment*', Part I, sets out the stages of work for a scheme supervised by an architect. For works which are carried out, the architect will usually charge a percentage of the construction costs together with expenses. Otherwise fees may well be agreed on a time basis. The preliminary work can be expensive.

A, *inception*, involves an initial outline of possible courses of action, advice on other specialists and determination of a brief. For example, here or in the resulting feasibility studies, the risk should be checked that the scheme might conflict with any rights of neighbouring landowners, such as a right of way or a right to light acquired by long use in the manner discussed in Chapter 5, Section 5.5. An architect will be expected to check on rights of lessees of any part of the site and on the location of boundaries.

B, *feasbility studies*, include advice on the technical feasibility of what is proposed, a rough timetable and costing, checking the planning situation and the implication of building regulations, and, if necessary, seeking outline planning consent.

C, *outline proposals*, lead to D, *scheme design*, which gives a general idea of spatial arrangements, materials and appearance and a more specific timetable and costing. This in turn leads to E, *detail design*, F and G, *production drawings, specifications of materials and bills of quantities*, and H, arranging for the scheme to be put out to *tender*. If the work is begun, J, *project planning* and K, *operations on site* involve setting up and supervising the project as it is carried out.

L, *completion* involves handing the site over to the client with general guidance on maintenance and with drawings to show where drainage and services are located.

The work of a landscape architect is summarized more tersely in the general conditions of the Landscape Institute Conditions of Engagement.

1.1 The work of a Landscape Consultant is to study the requirements of the Client and of the site. The principle on which the Conditions of Engagement operates is that the Landscape Consultant performs a continuing service for his client during the period of his engagement and is entitled to regular payment for his services. He will advise upon, and agree with his client a course of action suitable for the situation. When so required he will prepare, by means of drawings and specifications, a contract for the physical execution of the work on site. He will then act as the agent of his client in the direction and supervision of the work, and settle the financial account between the client and the contractor, acting as arbitrator if necessary in any area of dispute.

In Britain, the cost of construction work depends on a complex system of bills of quantity. These are usually prepared by specialist quantity surveyors. An architect will obtain detailed specifications of the materials needed for a job from the employer's quantity surveyor, and these will be stated in the invitation to contractors to tender for the work. The contractors use their own quantity surveyors to make their tenders competitive, for example by identifying where the client's quantities may be more than will be needed, so allowing a lower cost to be safely quoted by the contractor.

If a contractor tenders for work in accordance with a lump sum, the strict rule is that he will not receive any payment until he substantially performs the whole of the work.[5] Thus in *Sumpter* v. *Hedges*,[6] the Court of Appeal held that a builder was entitled to nothing for two houses and a stable which he had agreed to build for £565 and had left unfinished after doing work worth £333, even though the client finished the work himself and so ended up with a bargain. However, a measure of defective workmanship, such as the use of inferior materials or the omission of one coat of paint in a building may only mean that the contractor will have damages deducted from the price which he is paid.[7]

If a contractor is prevented by his employer from doing his work he can claim damages. Also, in practice, during the course of a contract, variations are constantly needed and under standard form contracts will be made in accordance with written instructions from the supervising specialist. These will entitle the contractor to extra payments. Construction contracts are normally divided into stages, so that the contractor is paid as work progresses. One of the skills he will demand of his quantity surveyor is to make estimates for earlier work higher than those for later work so that the contractor will get a larger sum earlier on. From the point of view of the client and the architect, this removes a stimulus for the work to be finished and encourages protracted claims for items of extra work in the later stages. One of an architect's functions is to certify that each stage of the work has been carried out satisfactorily. At the end of a contract, a period will be provided for after which a full check may be made for outstanding defects, such as cracks resulting from settlement. Then a final certificate will be given approving the concluding payment to the contractor.

The JCT 80, Conditions 27 and 28, make express provision for early determination of a building contract by the employer or contractor respectively as a result of the fault of the other. The contractor may withdraw if work is suspended through various events beyond the control of the parties, such as exceptionally adverse weather conditions, industrial action or loss or damage occasioned by what are known as Clause 22 perils, that is those matters in respect of which an appropriate party must provide insurance on the site.[8]

(b) Time

Closely related to the payment for a job is the time which it takes. A contract may or may not stipulate a time for its completion. Whether it does or not, it is to be decided from the surrounding circumstances whether time is of the essence. Where time is of the essence failure to complete a required act within the relevant time will entitle the other party to repudiate the contract. In *United Scientific Holdings Ltd* v. *Burnley Borough Council*,[9] the House of Lords considered a lease which provided at certain dates for increased rent if the landlords initiated a review procedure. The House held that time was not of the essence so that the procedure could still be initiated even after the specified date. However, if time is not of the essence, one party may give notice requiring that the contract be carried out within a reasonable time. If this notice is not complied with, the party serving it will then be entitled to repudiate the contract.

Standard construction contracts specify dates for each stage of the work and provide that the supervising architect or engineer may authorize extensions, in writing, in particular to allow for delay from such interruptions as bad weather or industrial action. Special provision is made in Clause 34 of the JCT 80 for the protection of fossils, antiquities and other objects of interest or value which may be met in the progress of work and cause delay. Generally, if an architect fails within twelve weeks to give a written response to a contractor's request for more time, he may be unable to certify that any deduction for delay should be made from the contractor's payment, and his client may be bound to pay for extra costs of the contractor. Standard-form contracts often provide a specific sum of *liquidated damages* for failure to complete on time. This is a genuine estimate of the damages for which a party would be liable, preassessed so as to limit any subsequent dispute. Thus, the JCT 80, Condition 24, refers to an appendix where liquidated damages may be filled in.

A major financial consideration which has to be covered in construction contracts is tax liability. Thus the JCT 80 provides special supplemental provisions dealing with Value Added Tax,[11] for example allowing for the employer to challenge this tax when it is claimed against his contractor.

(c) Insurance

Whatever the liability of a specialist to those who may be hurt in the course of his work, standard contracts allocate the ultimate responsibility to pay by requiring an appropriate party to cover the work with insurance. Thus under the JCT 80, Clause 20, the main contractor will normally be responsible for indemnifying the employer for any personal injuries which may occur on the work site and for any damage to property caused by the contractor's fault. Under Clause 21, the main contractor is required to make sure that adequate insurance is provided both for himself and for any sub-contractor. There will be circumstances where these provisions may not provide the employer with an indemnity, as where he himself is negligent. However, there would normally be an indemnity where the employer had merely been in breach of a strict statutory duty and had not been negligent as well.[12]

Where a contractor causes damage to property of a third party, perhaps across a boundary, under the standard form he is not obliged to provide an indemnity unless he is himself at fault. Thus it is vital that the employer is himself covered by insurance in such a case. In 1954 contractors erecting a new building at Buckingham Gate in London caused subsidence to neighbouring property, through pile driving which they had been instructed to carry out by the employer or his architect. The contractors were not negligent, and the Court of Appeal ruled that, under the terms of the RIBA contract which were similar to those of the JCT 80 form, they had not been responsible for insuring against the harm which occurred.[13]

It is important that materials and other property on a construction site should be insured against fire and other risks. Under the JCT 80, the risks to be guarded against are known as Clause 22 perils. These are essentially, 'fire, lightning, explosion, storm, tempest, flood, bursting or overflowing of water tanks apparatus or pipes, earthquake, aircraft and other aerial devices or articles dropped therefrom, riot and civil commotion'. There are certain exceptions, notably harm caused by radio-activity in various forms. Clause

22 contains alternative provisions to make the contractor or the employer responsible for completed work and materials at the site of new buildings. Whoever is responsible for insurance, if work is destroyed before it is handed over to the employer, the contractor may be obliged to rebuild,[14] unless he withdraws under rights given him by Clause 28. The standard provision for renovation and similar work is that the employer must insure. Difficulties may arise particularly if materials do not belong to the person who is treated as responsible for insuring them. For example they may belong to the supplier or a sub-contractor. In that case the person insuring may not have an insurable interest[15] and so may not be able to recover compensation under the policy.

(d) Disputes

The system whereby an architect certifies various stages of work carried out by a contractor, is designed to reduce disputes. If the architect approves defective work he may be liable in negligence to the employer.[16] This function is not treated as a judicial one as would an independent arbitration where there would be immunity from any action in the courts. Standard form contracts normally provide for arbitration of disputes. Thus the JCT 80, Article 5, provides for an arbitrator to be appointed by agreement of the parties or if they fail to agree by the President of the RIBA. In the event of a dispute between the employer and his architect, arbitration is provided for under the RIBA conditions of engagement, Clause 7.5. There, if the parties cannot agree an arbitrator, he is to be appointed by the President of the Institute of Arbitrators but shall normally be a chartered architect.

7.5.2 The nature of professional duty

The nature of a professional person's contractual duty may be set out expressly in a contract. Often the standard demanded under a contract consists, like that in tort, of taking reasonable care in all the circumstances, and this standard will generally be implied if no other is stipulated. However, a contract may specify or imply a different standard. Thus, if a contract requires something specific to be done it may be no defence that all reasonable care was taken to do what was agreed, if it was not in fact done. The JCT 80, Clause 2, requires a contractor to use materials and workmanship of the quality and standard specified in the contract document. By itself this suggests that the contractor would be liable if he failed to use specified materials even if they had become totally unavailable through no fault of his own. However, Clause 8.2 makes the apparently contradictory provision that all materials, goods and workmanship shall, 'so far as procurable', be as specified in the contract bills. It is not clear to what extent this entitles a contractor to use alternative materials.[17]

(a) Heightened duty and approved practice

Where reasonable care is owed whether under the general rules of negligence or under a contract what does this mean? If anyone claims to have special skills which he ought to realize he is not competent to exercise, then this itself is likely to be negligence. Thus if a landscape gardener were to design a large bridge which proved unsafe, even though he were as careful as any layman would be, he could be liable to anyone injured by the fall of the bridge because he should not have tried to do a job which required proper engineering skills. On the other hand he might reasonably erect a modest artificial bank without calling in a civil engineer. Where a person does have professional skill more will be expected of him than of a layman or even a person with more modest professional qualifications. Thus a building inspector who conscientiously checked foundations of a house erected on an unfilled gravel pit was not at fault in failing to make extra bore holes to check that the foundations were secure. He was not a civil engineer, architect or chartered surveyor and could not be expected to show the expertise of these professions.[18] In *Caminer v. Northern and London Investment Trust*,[19] the landlords of a block of flats were held not to be liable for an elm tree which dropped a branch on a passing car. Lord Normand, in the House of Lords, recognized that more knowledge would be expected of trees from a landlord of commercial property than from 'the ordinary observer of trees or even the countryman not practically concerned with their care'. However, such a landlord could not be expected to show the expertise of a professional arboriculturalist.

The standard expected of a professional person is that of 'the ordinary skilled man exercising and professing to have that special skill'.[20] He is expected to keep up with new developments in his subject but not necessarily to know of new research findings which are as yet unpublished.[21] However, if he personally is aware of information which is not generally known in his profession he will be expected to make use of it. An architect who has discovered that a form of concrete he has been using is prone to collapse, would be at fault if he went on using it, even if it was generally still regarded as safe by the remainder of his profession. If a particular practice is always followed in a certain type of work it is no defence for someone who follows it, when he knows himself that it is unsafe, or if the practice is clearly unsafe to a reasonable observer. Thus in *Manchester Corporation v. Markland*,[22] the House of Lords held that a local authority responsible for water pipes was liable for a fatal road accident caused when water from a burst pipe had frozen on the road. The authority's system of checks for burst pipes was the same as that practiced by all other water authorities,[23] but it was still, 'precarious, unreliable and unco-ordinated'. Normally, however, where a professional person can show that he was following approved practice in his field, that will be enough to prove that he was acting in a reasonably competent manner.[24] Often professionals differ over the best course to take in a particular situation. For example architects may differ strongly over the distance at which it is safe to build in relation to trees.[25] However, an architect who puts up a building which he can show many of his colleagues would regard as safe may well not be found negligent if the building develops cracks, even if other members of his profession were to claim that they would never have built so close to a tree.

(b) Contracts and negligence

We have seen in Chapter 6, Section 6.3 the restricted extent to which a contract may exclude liability for negligence. By their contracts, those involved in land use owe a duty of care in various aspects of their work. Thus an architect owes a duty at least of reasonable care as to height, design, and choice of materials for which he is responsible.[26] An engineer will owe a similar duty in designing a bridge or other structure. A professional person carrying out work on land in which he has no legal interest is normally acting under a contract which will determine his responsibility. However, the exact nature of his duties may not be fixed in the contract, in which case they may be implied from normal practice. These standards may be the same which would be required where there was no contract. Thus a landscape architect who is under a contract to design the grounds for a school owes a duty to take care for the safety of many with whom he has no contract. If he plants shrubs with highly poisonous leaves or berries he may be directly liable to any child who eats them. If he erects banks at an unsafe angle so that they collapse onto an adjacent house he may be liable to the householder. If his contract with the school authority provided that he was to take reasonable care in carrying out the work he may simultaneously be liable, both under the contract and in negligence to his employer; as, for example, if animals which he knew would be kept at the school are poisoned by the shrubs or if the banks collapse on the school itself.

One area where it used to be thought that there would be no liability in tort, but only in contract, was where a person carried out work for the owner of a site with whom he had no direct contract, and where his workmanship was defective but not such as to cause foreseeable risk to any person or other property. It has now been decided by the House of Lords in the Scottish case of *Junior Books Ltd* v. *Veitchi & Co. Ltd,*[27] that a sub-contractor in such a case may owe a direct duty to the client. There sub-contractors had laid flooring in a factory which cracked so badly within two years that it was going to require replacement.

As we saw in the case of the architect involved in *Clay* v. *Crump*, outlined at the beginning of Chapter 6, Section 6.4, a professional person responsible for supervising the construction of works will owe a duty to those with whom he has no contract, but who may be affected by the works, to see that any directions he gives are safe. However, most standard contracts leave day-to-day matters of work as the responsibility of contractors, and this may protect an architect or other person exercising professional supervision from legal proceedings by the client or by third parties. Thus in *Clayton* v. *Woodman and Son (Builders) Ltd*,[28] an architect was supervising building work at a hospital in Exeter where a gable end, previously used as a bell tower, was to be incorporated into a lift motor house. On a site visit, made after an interval of six days, the supervising architect was asked by Clayton, a bricklayer working on the roof, whether the gable could be pulled down, as it was difficult to tie in with the new work. Clayton also raised the question of whether cutting a chase in the gable would be safe. The architect refused to order the demolition of the gable as this would have involved varying his contract with the client. Later the gable fell on Clayton and injured him. The Court of Appeal ruled that responsibility for ensuring that the chase was cut safely was solely that of the building company for whom Clayton worked. The architect would only have been liable, in the words of Donovan L.J., if he had 'usurped the position of the builder' and had actually ordered the chase to be cut in an unsafe manner without proper support for the gable.

(c) Negligent advice

Landscape architects, surveyors and members of similar professions concerned with land use, run a particular risk of causing harm to others if they make inaccurate statements or give bad advice either under a contract or independently of one. We have seen in Chapter 6, Section 6.2 that the courts are somewhat restrictive in recognizing a duty of care in giving advice. However, such a duty is much more likely to be recognized where the advice is given by a professional person. If bad advice results in physical harm it is treated in essentially the same manner as a negligent act.[29] However, bad professional advice may result in many different forms of harm. A landowner seeing an inaccurately drawn survey of the neighbourhood may build a house on land which he does not own and may later be compelled to pull it down. Someone else may plant expensive trees in an unsuitable place where they promptly die, as a result of bad advice from a landscape architect. Since *Hedley Bryne and Co Ltd* v. *Heller and Partners*,[30] it has been well established that a person who gives bad advice may in certain circumstances be liable for even purely financial loss which this causes to those who rely upon it. As we have seen in Chapter 6, Section 6.2, the duty will not arise where a statement is made in a purely social or informal situation such as at a party or in a chance encounter in the street. Otherwise, anyone who claims to have expert knowledge on a particular subject may be liable for giving bad advice which he ought to foresee as likely to cause financial loss to a person who actually sustains such loss. Such a duty may be owed not only to the person given the advice, but also to any individual who it should have been contemplated was likely to be affected by it.

(d) Sharing responsibility between specialists

The type of expertise expected of professionals concerned with land use varies with their professions. A consultant planner will be expected to know more about planning law, but less about safe construction techniques than will an architect or an engineer. Generally a person asked to provide a particular design or scheme, or to give advice on a specific problem will be expected to appreciate wider difficulties which the work may throw up and of which a layman might have been oblivious. A builder who puts up a house with a perfectly proper and safe design may be liable if the property is damaged by a landslip from neighbouring land which he ought to have foreseen.[31] Often the skill required of a professional is the awareness of when it is necessary to consult another expert. If another expert is called in he will normally become directly liable for any harm which he causes. Subject to the terms of his contract with the client, the first expert who called him in may avoid liability. Thus any professional is expected to know the basic legal principles concerned with his work.[32] However, an architect or surveyor who calls in a lawyer or specialist planner on a matter of land law or planning law can normally safely rely on the advice received, unless from his own knowledge he should have realized that it was wrong. In *B.L. Holdings Ltd* v. *Robert J. Wood & Partners*[33] a firm of architects designed offices for a client who then had difficulty in leasing them because the prospective tenant believed that they required an office development permit.[34] The architects had checked with the local planning office and been told that a permit was not required. The difficulty arose because a permit was required where new office floor space exceeded 10 000 square feet. The relevant premises comprised more than that area but only if car parking and a caretaker's flat were included. The planning authority maintained that it had a discretion whether or not to take account of this additional space. The Court of Appeal held that the architects were entitled to assume that the local authority knew their job and it made no difference in the circumstances whether or not they had such a discretion. The architects were not liable.

Even where a professional may not unload liability entirely onto someone else, he may be entitled to a contribution. In *Acrecrest Ltd* v. *Hattrell & Partners*,[35] an architect designed a two-storey block of flats in Harrow. The local authority building inspector ordered certain of the foundations to be deepened because of the presence of tree roots but this was still insufficient. In an action in respect of the defective state of the building, the Court of Appeal approved an award against the local authority of 25% although the architect was made to bear 75% of the blame.

As we have seen, where several independent parties are working on a scheme, it now appears that even those who do not have a contract with the client may owe a duty to him directly to ensure that the standard of their work is reasonable.[36] As the client may now be able to sue such a party directly it may be easier to fix responsibility where it should properly lie.

7.5.3 Public authorities

Professional people working for a public authority may be personally liable for their own negligence although in practice damages will normally be paid by the authority on the basis of its vicarious liability.[37] Public authorities act under statutory duties or powers and may be protected by these from legal liability. Such protection may extend to their employees. Thus the private Act of Parliament which authorized the erection of Milford Haven Oil Refinery was held by the House of Lords to imply immunity from any claims for nuisance which could be shown to be the inevitable result of erecting any refinery on the site.[38] However, any nuisance going beyond this or any negligence in the operation of such a refinery would be actionable.

(a) Negligent exercise of statutory powers

If a public authority is given a statutory power it will normally not be liable if it chooses not to use the power at all. If it does exercise the power, but does so negligently, it normally will be liable. In December 1936 the river Debden broke through a sea wall and flooded the Suffolk marshes. The East Suffolk Rivers Catchment Board had statutory powers to mend the breach. They did so but took 178 days. The House of Lords concluded that a tenant farmer whose land was damaged during this time had no cause of action. The board had no duty to mend the breach but only a power to do so, although it could have been directed to do the work by the Minister of Agriculture. In the words of Viscount Simon, even where a body with a power sought to exercise it, it would not be liable 'for failing to render reasonable adequate and efficient service. On the other hand if the public body by its unskilful intervention created new dangers or traps it would be liable for its negligence to those who suffered thereby.'[39] More recently, in a number of cases where local authorities have actively exercised their powers under building regulations to approve buildings which were defective, they have been held liable. In 1958 one of a number of houses in a new development in Bognor Regis was built on a rubbish tip. In 1961 the house was bought by Mrs Dutton from an original owner to whom the builders had sold it. She found that the house was in a very defective state. The Court of Appeal held that she could recover damages from the local authority because its building inspector had been negligent in passing the foundations when he should have recognized the problems of the site. Had it not been for his approval the house would never have been built.[40]

In 1978 the House of Lords went further, in the case of *Anns* v. *Merton London Borough Council*.[41] Owners of a long lease on flats in Wimbledon sued the local authority for allowing the block to be erected with inadequate foundations which were shallower than shown in the developer's original approved plan. The House of Lords said, on a preliminary application, that not only was there a duty to take care in carrying out any inspection, but if the authority improperly exercised its discretion whether or not to inspect, for example by resolving not to make any inspections at all, this could probably be challenged by an application to the courts for an administrative order, even though it might not give rise to a claim in negligence.[42] As the Merton Borough surveyor appeared to have admitted, and indeed had stressed, that there must have been an inspection, the council would have owed a duty to ensure that this was carried out with reasonable care and skill. The duty would have been owed to subsequent purchasers of the property even if these knew nothing of the inspection, since those carrying it out should have contemplated that such purchasers would be adversely affected if they approved a defective or dangerous building.

A public authority may not bind itself in such a way as to prevent future exercise of its powers. Thus where a planning official without proper authorization purports to grant planning permission or to give a ruling that such permission is not needed this will not normally prevent the planning authority from later bringing enforcement proceedings.[43] However, in such a case an action may well lie against the planning authority and its employee for the negligent misstatement.

A person who complains of abuse of statutory powers may have to rely upon the special public law procedures for judicial review discussed in Chapter 8, Section 8.2, and may not seek to bypass them by bringing an ordinary action.[44] However, he may well be able to recover damages for harm suffered from the abuse. In *Davy* v. *Spelthorne Borough Council*,[45] Davy had a precast concrete works at Nutty Lane in Shepperton which he asked planning permission to continue operating for ten years. He subsequently claimed that the local planning authority had agreed that, provided he did not resist an enforcement notice, they would allow him to continue the works for three years. As a result he did not challenge the enforcement notice but later sought an injunction in the courts to stop the planning authority acting upon it and claimed damages on the grounds that he had been misled into not resisting the notice. On a preliminary point the local authority applied for the claim to be struck out because it was a matter that involved challenging the enforcement notice and should have been dealt with under a judicial review. However, although the Court of Appeal did not allow the claim for an injunction to go ahead, both that court and the House of Lords allowed Davey to proceed with his claim for damages.

(b) Nuisance in the exercise of statutory powers

Where a public body is authorized by statute to carry out some activity, unless the statute expressly provides that it will not be liable for any nuisance which results, that body will be responsible for any nuisance which it causes negligently. Indeed if it acts under a statutory power, as opposed to a statutory duty, it will be strictly liable. However, where it was carrying out a statutory duty the normal rule is that it will only be liable for any nuisance which it caused negligently. Thus in *Department of Transport* v. *North West Water Authority*,[46] the House of Lords held that the water authority was not liable for damage to a road resulting from a burst main because the pipe was being used under a statutory duty to supply water under pressure.

7.5.4 Copyright

Much information concerned with land use is protected by the law of copyright and any owner of copyright may sue anyone who infringes it by copying what he has created without his permission. Under the Copyright Act, 1956, any original written material, including written surveys or descriptions of land or a history or proposals for development, is protected from publication as *literary notes*. By Section 2 protection is for fifty years from the author's death or from the date of publication if this occurs after his death. Maps, plans, drawings and photographs are protected by Section 3, as *artistic works*, in most cases for fifty years from the author's death. Copyright in an engraving unpublished during the author's lifetime lasts for fifty years from the date of subsequent publication. Copyright in a photograph runs for fifty years from the date of publication wherever that occurs. Copyright usually belongs to the author but if material is commissioned or is produced in the course of the author's employment it generally belongs to the employer. Thus copyright of plans produced for a park by an employee of a firm of landscape architects will probably belong either to the firm or to the client. A person who would be entitled to copyright under the general law may transfer it to someone else or otherwise agree to special arrangements. Thus the RIBA Architects' Appointment provides that copyright of drawings for a scheme will remain the architect's, but the client may generally build in accordance with them provided the architect has been paid even if he is not retained to supervise the works.[47]

Buildings, including *any structure* such as an obelisk or monumental sculpture, are specially protected. However, reconstruction of a building according to the original design does not need new permission of the person owning the copyright in the building.[48] A landscape layout would not seem to be protected by copyright, although plans are, either for buildings or for landscape work. Here, it is permissible to reuse parts of a design in a subsequent work.[49] It will be a question of fact where a design is essentially a repeat of an earlier one and where it merely incorporates some earlier elements. There are special provisions to permit photographs and other reproductions of works which are open to public view, or of any piece of architecture.[50]

NOTES: SECTION 7.5

1. *Junior Books Ltd* v. *Veitchi Co. Ltd* [1983] 1 A.C. 520 *post* p. 370.
2. Parris, J. (1983) *The Standard Form of Building Contract JCT 80*, Granada, Great Britain.
3. *Sutro and Company* v. *Heilbut Symons & Company* [1917] 2 K.B. 348, C.A., comments of Scrutton L.J. at p. 360 f.
4. *English Industrial Estates Corporation* v. *George Wimpey & Co. Ltd* [1973] 1 Ll. L. R. 118, C.A.
5. Compare *Cutter* v. *Powell* (1795) 6 T.R., 320 and *Boone* v. *Eyre* (1779) 1 Bl. H. 273, note.
6. *Sumpter* v. *Hedges* [1898] 1 Q.B., 673, C.A. The law was recently reviewed in *Bolton* v. *Mahadeva* [1972] 1 W.L.R. 1009, C.A.
7. *H. Dakin & Co. Ltd* v. *Lee* [1916] 1 Q.B. 566, C.A., see too *Hoenig* v. *Isaacs* [1952] 2 All E.R. 176, C.A.
8. *Appleby* v. *Myers* (1866) 2 L.R. C.P. 651, illustrates the importance of a contractor covering himself against destruction of work which he has carried out.
9. *United Scientific Holdings Ltd* v. *Burnley Borough Council* [1978] A.C., 904, H.L.
10. JCT 80, Conditions 38.4.8.2, 39.5.8.2 and 40.7.2.2
11. *Ante* p. 98.
12. *Murfin* v. *United Steel Co. Ltd* [1957] 1 W.L.R., 104, C.A.
13. *Gold* v. *Patman & Fotheringham Ltd* [1958] 1 W.L.R. 697.
14. *Charon (Finchley) Ltd* v. *Singer Sewing Machines* (1968) 207 E.G. 140.
15. *Ante* p. 314.
16. *Sutcliffe* v. *Thackrah* [1974] A.C. 727, H.L.
17. Parris John, *supra* note 2, p. 52.
18. *Stewart* v. *East Cambridgeshire District Council* [1980] J.P.L. 171.
19. *Caminer* v. *Northern and London Investment Trust* [1951] A.C. 88, H.L.
20. *Bolam* v. *Friern Hospital Management Committee* [1957] 1 W.L.R. 582, *per* McNair J. at p. 586.
21. *Graham* v. *Co-operative Wholesale Society Ltd* [1957] 1 W.L.R. 511.
22. *Manchester Corporation* v. *Markland* [1936] A.C. 360, H.L.
23. Ibid. in the Court of Appeal under the name of *Markland* v. *Manchester Corporation* [1934] 1 K.B. 566, at p. 573.
24. *Wright* v. *Cheshire County Council* [1952] 2 All E.R. 789.
25. Clouston, B. and Stansfield, K. (eds) (1981) *Trees in Towns*, Architectural Press, London, Chap. 6.
26. *Moresk Cleaners Ltd* v. *Hicks* [1966] 2 Ll. L.R. 338. There an architect was held to be in breach of contract for leaving detailed design work to a contractor who carried it out defectively.
27. *Supra* note 1. See also *ante* p. 284.
28. *Clayton* v. *Woodman and Son (Builders) Ltd* [1962] 1 W.L.R. 585, C.A., reversing the decision of Salmon J. [1962] 2 Q.B. 533.

29. *Clay* v. *Crump* [1964] 1 Q.B. 533, *ante* p. 306.
30. *Hedley Bryne and Co Ltd* v. *Heller and Partners* [1964] A.C. 465, H.L., *ante* p. 288.
31. *Batty* v. *Metropolitan Realisations Ltd* [1978] 1 Q.B. 554, C.A.
32. *Jenkins* v. *Betham* (1855) 15 C.B. 168.
33. *B.L. Holdings Ltd* v. *Robert J. Wood & Partners* (1979) 12 Build. L. R. 1, C.A.
34. *Ante* p. 105.
35. *Acrecrest Ltd* v. *Hattrell & Partners* [1983] Q.B. 260, C.A.
36. *Junior Books Ltd* v. *Veitchi Co. Ltd*, *anti* note 1.
37. *Ante* p. 310f.
38. *Allen* v. *Gulf Oil Refinery Ltd* [1981] A.C. 1001, H.L., *ante* p. 302.
39. *East Suffolk Rivers Catchment Board* v. *Kent* [1941] A.C. 74, H.L., *per* Viscount Simon at p. 87.
40. *Dutton* v. *Bognor Regis Urban District Council* [1972] 1 Q.B. 373, *per* Stamp L.J. at p. 413.
41. *Anns* v. *Merton London Borough Council* [1978] A.C. 728, H.L.
42. Ibid. per Lord Salmon at p. 762. As to judicial reviews see *post* p. 392f.
43. *Western Fish Products Ltd* v. *Penwith D.C.* [1981] 2 All E.R. 204, C.A.
44. *O'Reilly* v. *Mackman* [1982] 2 All E.R. 1124, H.L.
45. *Davy* v. *Spelthorne Borough Council* [1983] 3 All E.R. 278, H.L.
46. *Department of Transport* v. *North West Water Authority* [1983] 3 All E.R. 273.
47. RIBA Architects' Appointment Clauses 3.15–3.18.
48. Copyright Act 1956, s. 8 (1). This would not seem to include building an identical building on a different site.
49. Ibid. s. 9 (9).
50. Ibid. s. 9 (3) and (4).

Chapter 8

LEGAL POWERS AND THEIR AVAILABILITY

The attitude of planning authorities is too often, perhaps, that the desire of a landowner to carry out some development on his land should be prevented at all costs unless he can show overwhelming reasons for being allowed to do so. It seems to me that an inspector who takes the view that perhaps the wishes of the landowner might be considered more sympathetically should be encouraged. It is at least a possible view to take, even though it may prove unpopular with local planning authorities, that a landowner should be allowed to develop his land unless there are compelling planning objections to such development. Indeed there are ministerial pronouncements to this effect . . . I might go further, perhaps, and say that, when one is dealing with questions of aesthetic value, I very much doubt whether experts are necessarily of any use at all . . . It would not, . . . really help, it seems to me, if one is dealing with pure aesthetic values, to call witnesses to say that a painting was beautiful. It would be of considerable assistance, of course, if it were relevant, to call experts to say that it was worth £50,000, but not that it was beautiful or that a piece of architecture was of high quality, and the reason for that seems to me to be this: that experts do tend to differ and for every expert that one could find who said, looking at pure aesthetics, that something was exceptionally fine one might quite easily find another expert who took exactly the opposite view.

> *Winchester City Council* v. *Secretary of State*
> *for the Environment* (1978) 36 P. & C.R. 455,
> *per* Forbes J. at pp. 467, 472 and 473

The words of Forbes J. quoted above might suggest a philistine disregard for the quality of the landscape. The outcome of the case which he was deciding was rather different. Mr Johnathan Eccles inherited from his father a house at Martyr Worthy in Hampshire, called the New House, designed after the

Second World War by Sir Albert Richardson, a distinguished architect in the classical tradition. Mr Eccles required a six-bedroom house for his own large family, but as he was concerned not to damage the New House by adding to it, he applied for planning permission to build what Forbes J. referred to as, 'a fresh house', in the grounds. When this was refused, Mr Eccles appealed to the Secretary of State, who gave permission for the fresh house on the recommendation of his inspector, following a public inquiry. The council appealed on the grounds that permission had been given for the fresh house on the basis that the New House was of such merit that it deserved preservation and yet the inspector, who had recommended this conclusion, had not allowed the council to call its own architectural witness to refute Mr Eccles' architectural judgment. Forbes J. dismissed the council's appeal and ruled that judgments on aesthetics were matters for the inspector rather than for a judge or for expert witnesses called by the council. The Department of the Environment was entitled to rely on the inspector's views that the house was of exceptional quality, particularly inside.

The case of the New House illustrates the uneasy role of the courts in supervising official decisions on land use. The courts are reluctant to enter into subjective questions with which they do not regard themselves as competent to deal. On the other hand they are prepared to adjudicate between some views over which experts disagree equally vehemently, for example over whether a particular building technique which led to an accident was foreseeably unsafe. Courts profess to be happier dealing with claims which can be quantified in terms of money. However, just as experts differ over the quality of such matters as works of art and areas of natural beauty, they differ over the price to be put on these and judges may be called on to resolve such disputes. Despite his protestations about the subjective nature of aesthetic judgments, Forbes J. robustly upheld a principle which is equally open to philosophical dispute, that the judgment of the landowner over what is aesthetically best for a piece of land should take precedence over that of the local planning authority.

Traditionally judges were seen as upholders of private rights, including property rights, against the power of the state. Today the executive and the judiciary in a democratic society are expected to act as servants of the people, but views differ over whether this primarily involves the courts backing up administrative decisions or acting as ever ready watchdogs to keep them in check. Certainly the judges were long unwilling to develop a distinct body of administrative law.[1] And today legal and political commentators have portrayed judges as an arm of the state concerned to protect only selected rights, notably those in property which are enjoyed by the socially powerful.[2] However, whether they are dealing with claims against private citizens or challenges to the decisions of public bodies, the courts necessarily are limited by the powers at their disposal.

NOTES

1. Lord Hewart, C.J. (1929) *The New Despotism*, Ernest Benn, London.
2. Griffiths, J.A. (1978) *Administrative Law and the Judges*, The Haldane Society Pritt Memorial Lecture; and (1977) *the Politics of the Judiciary*, Fontana, Glasgow.

8.1   The sanctions and remedies available from the courts

The powers of punishment available to criminal courts are one of the main features which distinguish them from civil courts.[1] However, criminal courts do have certain powers to order those convicted of criminal offences to make restitution of their victims' property,[2] or to pay them compensation.[3] Conversely, in civil cases, an award of exemplary damages may occasionally be made as a form of punishment, rather than purely for purposes of compensating an injured person.[4] The prospect of civil proceedings may in practice be more of a deterrent to anti-social behaviour than the threat of criminal prosecution. Many people would refrain from committing serious criminal offences in any event but would, for example, freely trespass on the land of others, commit nuisances which interfered with their neighbours' enjoyment of land, or take risks which might endanger their safety, were it not for the prospect of civil proceedings. Irrespective of the methods used to protect them, the existence of private property rights may do much to ensure that land is properly looked after and is not over-exploited. Those with private property rights may be expected to respect the rights of others, and they are more likely to take prompt action to protect their own property than would be any public enforcement agency, whether police, local government planning officers or health and safety inspectors. In practice, the powers of the courts which are most significant in controlling the use of land are public law remedies available against administrators, and the civil remedies evolved by the common law and by equity which are now generally available from all courts.[5]

8.1.1   Public law remedies

The public law remedies which are used to control administrative actions include the three orders of *mandamus, prohibition* and *certiorari*, which were originally introduced by the ancient common law courts as a means of controlling rival courts. The orders may now be sought on an application for judicial review to the Queen's Bench Divisional Court of the High Court. On a review the court may also grant the equitable remedy of an injunction, and a declaration, both of which are also available as remedies in private disputes. The prerogative order appropriate to control a particular administrative decision depends upon the stage which that decision has reached.

(a) Mandamus

Mandamus is an order requiring the carrying out of a public duty. For example it could be sought against the Secretary of State for the Department of the Environment if he refused to deal with a planning appeal.[6] However, this remedy will only be granted as a last resort and not where some other remedy is available, such as an administrative appeal.[7] Thus the appropriate means of handling a refusal by a local planning authority to deal at all with an application for planning permission is to appeal to the Secretary of State.[8]

(b) Prohibition and certiorari

Orders of prohibition or certiorari may be sought against any body with powers to determine questions which affect the rights of the subject and which has exceeded its jurisdiction. The courts used to insist that the power must be essentially judicial in nature,[9] but it now appears that they will act much more widely to control unfair use of public power even where this cannot be categorized as judicial,[10] provided no other adequate remedy is available.

Prohibition is used to prevent an anticipated misuse of power, for example to restrain a minister from calling in for his own decision matters reserved on the approval of outline planning permission,[11] after the reserved matters have already been authorized. *Certiorari* may be sought to bring up before the High Court and to quash an order which has already been made, for example an erroneous planning decision where there is no provision for a statutory appeal to the courts, such as a decision by the Secretary of State where he has called in for his own consideration the matters reserved on a grant of outline planning permission.[12]

8.1.2 Specific remedies

A person whose rights have been harmed by someone else normally wants to be restored to the position in which he would have been had the harm never occurred. Sometimes the courts are able to ensure precisely or nearly this result, by means of specific remedies. In other cases they can only provide the substitutionary remedy of damages, to compensate for the harm in financial terms.

(a) Possessory remedies

As we have seen, the old common law judges treated land as different from other forms of property.[13] Thus a freeholder who was dispossessed of a piece of land could seek reinstatement in his land from the courts. Under other systems of law, such as those inspired by Roman Law which were developed on the continent, remedies were normally specific. A person dispossessed of something other than land, such as animals or furniture, could obtain an order for their recovery. In such cases the English common law courts only granted damages. Today there is a single action for possession of land by anyone claiming a better title over it than that of whoever is in occupation. This is essentially the old action known as *ejectment*. It can now be obtained within seven days under special speedy procedures designed to deal with squatters whose identity is not known to the plaintiff.[14] More lengthy procedures for possession of land must be used by a landlord seeking possession from a tenant whose lease has expired.

As we saw in the introduction to this book, the Chancellor supplemented common law remedies by equitable remedies such as those of *specific recovery* whereby a person dispossessed of property other than land could recover it, provided damages would not be adequate compensation and the demands of equity were satisfied. Thus the plaintiff had to act fairly and the defendant must not be made to suffer undue hardship. The Chancellor also granted *specific performance* to enforce contracts in similar circumstances. Thus if a person agreed to sell land or some other item which was unique or in short supply and failed to transfer it he could be committed to prison for contempt until he did so. From 1830 the court was itself empowered by Parliament to execute any necessary conveyance.[15] Today the whole range of remedies is normally available from any English court.[16] However, contracts relating to land of sufficient value to be dealt with by the High Court are generally handled by the Chancery Division, since it was the Chancery Court which developed the jurisdiction for specific performance still generally applicable in such cases.

(b) Injunctions

An outstanding creation of equity was the injunction. A *mandatory injunction* is one which orders a positive act, usually to restore some harm which has taken place. A *prohibitory injunction* forbids interference with the rights of another. Injunctions may be used to control public authorities as an alternative to the prerogative remedies. Injunctions may also be used to support public controls over land use, for example to add extra weight to tree preservation orders where there appears to be a risk that these may be flouted.[17] Breach of an injunction may be punished by imprisonment for contempt of court. If there is a real prospect of a right being broken, even before any breach occurs, the courts may grant a *quia timet injunction*. If the matter is urgent an *interlocutory injunction* may be granted to stop harmful activities pending a full hearing. Before granting an interlocutory injunction, the Court must be satisfied that there is a serious issue to be tried and that 'the balance of convenience',[18] requires the situation to be frozen. The person granted an interlocutory injunction will be required to compensate the person against whom he obtained it for any loss suffered if the court eventually decides that no injunction is justified.

Since Lord Cairn's Chancery Amendment Act 1858,[19] the courts have had power to quantify the harm which an injunction would prevent and to award damages instead.[20] However, this power is used sparingly. Thus, provided nuisance has already begun, an injunction will usually be granted to stop it. In *Imperial Gas Light and Coke Co. v. Broadbent*,[21] a market gardener obtained an injunction to protect his plants from a gas retort house erected only 40 feet away which 'was very large and contained many openings from some or all of which, at several hours during day and night, noxious gases were emitted, highly injurious to his flowers, fruit and vegetables'. The Lord Chancellor, Lord Campbell, said in the House of Lords than an injunction should usually be granted in such a case as a matter of course.

Nevertheless if an interference with land is trivial, and especially if it is in the public interest not to penalize it, a court may refuse to grant an injunction. Thus in cases where courts have declared that a trespass did take place, and even recognized that it might occur again, they have sometimes refused to grant injunctions. For example, an Anglican clergyman who preached on the sands at Llandudno was technically a trespasser, but as the judge said, when asked for an injunction to stop him, that 'is a formidable legal weapon which ought to be reserved for a less trivial occasion'[22] (Fig. 8.1).

Fig. 8.1 Llandudno Beach, 1875, by kind permission of Gwynedd County Council.

In *Behrens* v. *Richards*,[23] Behrens bought an estate at St Hilary, near Marazion in Cornwall, and proceeded to enrage the inhabitants by blocking up their access to the beach with trenches, walls and banks of hyacinths. When the inhabitants broke these down, he sued them. Buckley J. acknowledged that, 'no doubt it is true that rights of property are as a general proposition entitled to protection by, if necessary, an injunction of this court'. However, the upshot of the case was that the plaintiff agreed to allow the defendants reasonable access and was awarded 40 shillings damages but no injunction. Each side paid its own costs. As the judge commented:

The existing security of tenure of land in this country is largely maintained by the fact that the owners of the land behave reasonably in the matter of its enjoyment. It would, in my judgement, be a disastrous thing not for the public only, but for the landowners also, if this court, at the caprice of the landowner, not because circumstances have altered, but merely because he was minded that it should be so, entertained every trivial application to restrain persons by injunction from using paths which, though not public highways, have in fact been used by the permission of the owners for many generations, and whose use is no injury to the owner of the land.

An injunction may be granted to prevent a trivial interference with land if this might grow into a right by the passage of time, but a court may turn a blind eye to a merely temporary interference even if it will continue for some time.[24] If an injunction is granted it may be suspended so that the defendant can finish what he is doing. Thus in *Woollerton and Wilson* v. *Richard Costain Ltd*,[25] an interlocutory injunction to stop Richard Costain Ltd trespassing in the air space of a neighbouring factory whilst constructing the general post office in Leicester was suspended until work with a crane was finished. The judge, Stamp J., stressed that the defendant had not flagrantly disregarded the plaintiff's property rights, but had made a generous offer of compensation which it had expected to be accepted.

As we have seen, the fact that a particular activity may be in the interest of the general public is not a good reason for a court to refuse to treat it as a nuisance, nor even a good reason for only granting persons offended by it damages rather than an injunction to stop it altogether.[26] In 1981 in *Kennaway* v. *Thomson*,[27] Cotswold Motor Boat Racing Club had expanded their racing on Mallam Water near Fairford in Gloucestershire. Since that time, Miss Kennaway had built a house on the lake (Fig. 8.2). Despite the considerable popularity of the racing, the Court of Appeal granted an injunction to restrain the level of racing to what it had been when the house was built. As was said nearly a century ago:

the court has always protested against the notion that it ought to allow a wrong to continue simply because the wrongdoer is able and willing to pay for the injury he may inflict. Neither has the circumstance that the wrongdoer is in some sense a public benefactor ... ever been considered a sufficient reason for refusing to protect by injunction an individual whose rights are being persistently infringed.[28]

Fig. 8.2 Mallam Water near Fairford, showing the house affected in the case of *Kennaway* v. *Thompson* [1981] 1 Q.B. 88, by kind permission of M.S.C. Lee-Brown Esq and of Wilmot & Co., Solicitors, Swindon.

However, damages may be granted in lieu of an injunction if the person seeking a remedy has acted inequitably, for example in delaying an excessive time before making any complaint.[29]

The courts are more ready to refuse injunctions which are mandatory rather than prohibitive. They are reluctant to order the removal of a building or even a lesser structure. In *Shepherd Homes Ltd* v. *Sandham*,[30] Megarry J. refused to grant an interlocutory mandatory injunction for the removal of fences on an open-plan luxury estate in Caerphilly which were erected to keep out Welsh mountain sheep and horses, but in breach of a restrictive covenant. He stressed that a mandatory injunction may be refused if it will result in a disproportionate detriment to the defendant with comparatively slight benefit to the plaintiff. This may seen surprising as the courts regard themselves as obliged to prohibit interferences with neighbouring land even where this requires a defendant to spend immense sums on improving his processes or even compels him to close down. It is said that mandatory injunctions are difficult to frame with precision and to supervise, but the same can be said of an injunction requiring a factory or a speed-boat club to keep fumes or noise to a specified level.

In *Morris* v. *Redland Brick Ltd*,[31] a brick company excavated clay pits 60 yards from the Morrises' 8-acre strawberry farm at Swanwick in Hampshire.

Part of the strawberry farm slipped into the clay pits. The Morrises obtained injunctions in the Portsmouth County Court to stop the brick company digging out more clay unless it left adequate support for their land. The brick company accepted the restriction on further excavations, but in the House of Lords a mandatory injunction to restore the already damaged land was quashed, partly on the ground that the county court judge had failed to take account of the cost of providing support. This was relevant because the defendants had acted reasonably in carrying out the work. They thought that they had left a safe margin of land. However, the cost might have been over £30 000 whereas the entire 8-acre farm was not worth more than £12 000. The conclusive point was that the mandatory injunction did not make clear what the defendant was required to do to restore adequate support.

If a person knowingly flouts a neighbour's rights, the courts will more readily order him to restore the situation even if it is very costly to do so. In *Daniel* v. *Ferguson*,[32] an interlocutory mandatory injunction was granted to demolish a building in Bayswater which the plantiff alleged interfered with his right to light. The defendant had built the walls as fast as he could using large numbers of men working day and night. By contrast in *Wrotham Park Estate Co. Ltd* v. *Parkside Homes Ltd*,[33] Brightman J. refused an injunction to demolish homes built in breach of restrictive covenants and which were now inhabited. It would be 'an unpardonable waste of much needed houses', and he 'never had a moment's doubt during the hearing of the case that such an order ought to be refused'.

8.1.3   Damages

Damages are the most common form of remedy for tort or breach of contract. They are normally intended to put the plaintiff, so far as possible, financially in the position in which he would have been had he not suffered harm, or, in the case of contract, in the position in which he would have been had the contract been carried out. Although, as we have seen, they may sometimes be awarded instead of a specific remedy such as an injunction, which the plaintiff would have preferred, in many cases, damages are the only feasible remedy. A farmer suing for the destruction of cattle by trespassers or of a barn by subsidence caused by a neighbour is probably best helped with money to buy replacements. It is physically impossible to resuscitate his cattle and impracticable to make the neighbour himself restore the barn.

(a) Compensatory damages

The assessment of damages is a complex subject, and the law of damages has been described as, 'one of the most difficult and, one might say, disorderly, parts of the law'.[34] In personal injuries cases, as where a visitor on land is injured, there are conventional tariffs of standard payments for loss of particular limbs, and principles for assessing lost earnings by multiplying the prospective loss of annual income by an appropriate number of years to produced a capital sum, which will allow suitable income for the period during which the plaintiff might have expected to earn it. There are also rather more fluid heads of damages, such as pain and suffering. Other forms of loss, for example the destruction of a building, can usually be assessed fairly readily in terms of the economic loss to the plaintiff. This may be the cost of a replacement, or if that would amount to a windfall it may be less. Thus if a building, burnt through the defendant's negligence, was going to be demolished in any event, the defendants may be expected to pay only the increased cost of clearing the site.

(b) Non-compensatory damages

Normally damages are only awarded to compensate for harm which has actually occurred. However breaches of contract and certain torts, notably trespass, including trespass to land, are actionable without evidence of harm.[35] Thus a farmer who objects to people regularly walking on his farm may sue them even though they have done no harm. He is thus able to assert his right in the courts. Disputes over who owns a piece of land or is entitled to a right of way or some other right over it may be resolved by one party suing the other in trespass.[36] Although an injunction or a declaration will generally be the most appropriate court order in such a case, an award of damages may make the point better, for example, against a trespasser who knows that he has no right to use the land. Such damages will be *nominal*, limited perhaps to £5. However, if the plaintiff was justified in bringing the action, the defendant will probably have to bear all the costs. On the other hand if the court considers that such an action should not have been brought, it will award *contemptuous* damages, which may be a mere penny, and will order the plaintiff to pay his own costs and probably those of the defendant as well.[37]

(c) Exemplary and aggravated damages

In limited circumstances, damages may be awarded in a civil action, for the anomalous purpose of punishing the defendant's tort,[38] but not for his breach of contract,[39] where compensatory damages are 'inadequate to punish him for his outrageous conduct, to mark . . . disapproval of [his] conduct and to deter him from repeating it'.[40] In particular such damages may be awarded where a public official has acted in an 'oppressive, arbitrary or unconstitutional manner', or where the wrongdoer stands to make a profit from his wrong, even after paying compensation, as where a landlord has unlawfully evicted, by strong arm methods, a tenant who had obtained a reduced rent by applying to a rent officer under the Rent Acts.[41] Often, because such behaviour causes exceptional pain and inconvenience, compensation may in any event include an element of aggravated damages in tort or for breach of contract.

8.1.4   Declarations

Where parties in a dispute wish to resolve their differences reasonably and amicably, they may be happy simply to seek a declaration of their rights from the courts. Often a declaration will be granted in addition to some other remedy, such as an injunction or damages. The Crown is deemed always to be law abiding and it is considered inappropriate that coercive remedies such as to recover land, specific performance or an injunction,[42] should be made against it. Where the Crown is in dispute with a subject, the subject will simply be granted a declaration. In any case where a declaration is sought, 'the question must be a real and not a theoretical question; the person raising it must have a real interest to raise it; he must be able to secure a proper contradictor, that is to say someone presently existing who has a true interest to oppose the declaration sought'.[43]

8.1.5   Self help

In some cases, rather than seeking a remedy from the courts, even today, a person may protect his rights by taking the law into his own hands. Thus a landowner may remove a trespasser provided he only uses reasonable force.[44] He may also remove anything which the trespasser has brought onto his land, such as a building he has erected there. However, where a person is not in possession of land, statute has long restricted his rights to eject trespassers. In recent years there has been a spate of squatters taking over empty buildings or even houses whose owners were on holiday. There is also long-standing concern over harassment by landlords of such people as ex-tenants remaining on their land after the end of their tenancies. The law in this area has been restated in Part II of the Criminal Law Act 1977. This has replaced a number of old statutes on forcible entry, some dating back to the reign of Richard II. Thus it is an offence, even for a person with a right to possession, to use or threaten violence for the purpose of securing entry to premises with the knowledge that there is someone on them who is opposed to the entry.[45] The violence may be against the property. It would include breaking down a door. However, there is an exception which does permit the use of reasonable force by or on behalf of a residential occupier of the premises who has actually been displaced. It is also an offence for a trespasser to fail to leave premises at the request of a displaced residential occupier or of persons with rights to possess the land for residential use.[46] If a person entitled to possession of land does evict a trespasser he may himself be convicted of a crime and might be sued successfully for damage for trespass to the person of the trespasser, however, as the courts would not order him to leave the property, his act of ejecting the trespasser would effectively restore his rights.

Self help may also be used by a landowner threatened by a nuisance. If a tree is technically a nuisance, because it projects over a boundary, but is not dangerous, the only remedy available to the offended neighbour is to cut it back to the boundary.[47] He need give no notice to the tree owner unless he crosses the boundary. A neighbour is entitled to abate other nuisances such as a fire or a collapsing wall or bank, by going onto the land where the danger has arisen. However, before going onto other land, notice must be given to the person responsible for it, unless he himself created the nuisance, or unless the situation is urgent because of risk to the security of lives or property.[48] If there are alternatives the nuisance must always be abated in the manner which avoids harm to third parties and otherwise causes least harm to the person responsible.[49] A member of the public may abate a public nuisance provided this is necessary to enable him to exercise his public rights. For example, he may remove a barrier blocking a public footpath if this is necessary for him to use the footpath.[50] Local authorities often have statutory powers to remove public nuisances such as obstructions to the highway[51] and may generally do so under common law in any event.

NOTES: SECTION 8.1

1. *Ante* p. 8.
2. Theft Act 1968, s. 28, as substituted by the Criminal Justice Act 1972, and s. 6 of that act.
3. Powers of Criminal Courts Act 1973, s. 35 and Magistrates' Courts Act 1980, s. 40.
4. *Post* p. 387.
5. *Ante* p. 6.
6. *R. v. Secretary of State ex parte Percy Bilton Industrial Properties* (1976) 31 P. & C.R. 154.
7. *Stepney Borough Council* v. *John Walker & Sons Ltd.* [1934] A.C. 365, H.L.
8. Town and Country Planning Act 1971, s. 37.
9. *R.* v. *Electricity Commissioners* [1924] 1 K.B. 171, C.A.
10. *R.* v. *Hillingdon London Borough Council ex parte Royco Homes Ltd* [1974] Q.B. 270, *ante* p. 124, note 75.
11. Under Town and Country Planning Act 1971, s. 35.
12. See *Turner* v. *Secretary of State for the Environment* [1973] 28 P. and C.R. 123, and also *ante* p. 116 and *post* p. 395.
13. *Ante* p. 167.
14. The Rules of the Supreme Court, Order 113 or County Court Rules, Order 26.
15. Today see Supreme Court Act 1981, s. 39.
16. Where there is a conflict, the rules of equity prevail. Supreme Court Act 1981, s. 49.

17. *Attorney General* v. *Melville Construction Co. Ltd* (1968) 20 P. & C.R. 131 and *Kent County Council* v. *Batchelor* (No. 1) (1977) 33 P. & C.R. 185, C.A.
18. *American Cyanamid Co.* v. *Ethicon Ltd* [1975] A.C. 396, H.L., at p. 408.
19. Chancery Amendment Act 1858, s. 2. See now Supreme Court Act 1981, s. 50.
20. *Slack* v. *Leeds Industrial Society* [1924] 2 Ch. 475, C.A.
21. *Imperial Gas Light and Coke Co.* v. *Broadbent* [1859] 7 Ho. Lords C. 600, at p. 609.
22. *Llandudno Urban District Council* v. *Woods* [1899] 2 Ch. 705, see *ante* p. 150, note 8.
23. *Behrens* v. *Richards* [1905] 2 Ch. 614.
24. For a temporary interference there may be no liability at all in nuisance, see *ante* p. 351f.
25. *Woollerton and Wilson* v. *Richard Costain Ltd* [1970] 1 W.L.R. 411.
26. *Miller* v. *Jackson* [1977] 1 Q.B. 966, C.A. *ante* p. 47. See also *ante* p. 350f.
27. *Kennaway* v. *Thomson* [1981] 1 Q.B. 88 C.A.
28. *Shelfer* v. *City of London Electric Lighting Co.* [1895] 1 Ch. 287. The view that this approach may be out of date has been powerfully argued in the context of pollution control by nuisance actions, by Ogus A.I. and Richardson, G.M. (1977) Economics and the environment: A study of private nuisance. *Cambridge Law Review*, 36, 284.
29. *Bracewell* v. *Appleby* [1975] 1 Ch. 408, *ante* p. 201.
30. *Shepherd Homes Ltd* v. *Sandham* [1971] Ch. 340.
31. *Morris* v. *Redland Brick Ltd* [1970] A.C. 652, H.L.
32. *Daniel* v. *Ferguson* [1891] 2 Ch. 27, C.A.
33. *Wrotham Park Estates Co. Ltd* v. *Parkside Homes Ltd* [1974] 1 W.L.R. 798.
34. Lawson, F.H. (1980) *Remedies of English Law*, 2nd edn, Butterworths, London.
35. *Ante* p. 337f.
36. *Ante* p. 75 and Chapter 5, Section 5.5.
37. Detailed rules as to costs are set out in Rules of the Supreme Court, Order 62, and County Court Rules, 1981, Order 38.
38. *Rookes* v. *Barnard* [1964] A.C. 1129, H.L.
39. *Addis* v. *Gramophone Co. Ltd* [1909] A.C. 488, H.L.
40. *Rookes* v. *Barnard, supra* note 38, *per* Lord Devlin at p. 1227.
41. See *ante,* p. 185, and *Drane* v. *Evangelou* [1978] 2 All E.R. 437.
42. Crown Proceedings Act 1947, s. 21. And see *ante* p. 86.
43. *Russian Commercial and Industrial Bank* v. *British Bank for Foreign Trade Ltd* [1921] 2 A.C. 438, *per* Lord Dunedin at p. 448.
44. *Harrison* v. *Duke of Rutland* [1893] 1 Q.B. 142, see *ante* p. 338.
45. The Criminal Law Act 1977, s. 6.
46. Ibid. s. 7.
47. *Lemmon* v. *Webb* [1894] 3 Ch. 1, C.A., affirmed [1895] A.C. 1 H.L.
48. *Earl of Lonsdale* v. *Nelson* (1823) 2 Barn. & Cress. 302, at p. 311.
49. *Lagan Navigation* v. *Lambeg Bleaching, Dyeing and Finishing Co.* [1927] A.C. 226, at pp. 247–248.
50. *Bagshaw* v. *Buxton Local Board of Health* (1875) 1 Ch.D. 220, *per* Sir George Jessel M.R. at p. 224.
51. Highways Act 1980, s. 143.

8.2   The role of the courts in controlling public bodies

In various circumstances statutes provide specifically for an appeal to the courts against particular administrative decisions. Where there is no such provision, the courts frequently exercise a supervisory function, by means of prerogative orders and other conventional remedies on a judicial review.[1] As we have seen in Chapter 7, Section 7.5.3, where a decision by a public body can not be challenged, a person who has been harmed by it may nevertheless claim damages to compensate him for that harm.

8.2.1 Statutory rights of appeal

Important statutory provisions for appeal to the courts are contained in the Town and Country Planning Act 1971, Part XII, against most planning decisions of the Department of the Environment,[2] and in the Acquisition of Land Act 1981, Part IV, for anyone desiring to question the validity or terms of a compulsory purchase order.[3] Statutory rights of appeal must usually be exercised within much stricter time limits than is required for a judicial review. In the case of planning decisions and compulsory purchase orders the time is six weeks.[4]

Statutory rights of appeal are frequently on the basis that the relevant decision shall not otherwise 'be questioned in any legal proceedings whatsoever'.[5] Such *exclusion* or *ouster clauses* do not always deter courts from considering an administrative decision. In particular where administrators purport to act under statutory powers which do not provide them with jurisdiction to act, the High Court may rule that they have not made a valid decision at all, and so quash any order which they have purported to make.[6] Nevertheless, where legislation does not purport to exclude them from reviewing a decision altogether, but does provide a restricted form of appeal, the courts will probably not intervene except through the statutory form of appeal. In *R. v. Secretary of State for the Environment ex parte Ostler*,[7] Ostler sought the remedy of *certiorari*, to quash two orders made so as to enable the construction of an inner relief road at Boston in Lincolnshire. In 1973, an order was made to acquire land for the road itself. A firm of wine merchants, who initially objected because they would lose their access, withdrew their objection because of a secret promise that they would be given a new access by widening a lane called Craythorne Lane. Two years later, the second order was made, for the widening of Craythorne Lane. Mr Ostler was a corn merchant at the corner of the lane. He objected that his business would be damaged but at the ensuing inquiry he was not allowed to raise the circumstances of the original order although he claimed that if he had known then that it would affect his premises he would have objected to it. Two or three months after the Craythorne Lane order was approved, Mr Ostler learnt of the secret agreement. It was then that he challenged both orders in the High Court. When that court proposed to go into the merits of these, the Secretary of State successfully appealed to the Court of Appeal on the grounds that the orders could only be challenged on a statutory appeal.[8] The Court of Appeal held that even if the order had been made in bad faith it was now too late to challenge it. 'It would be contrary to the pubic interest that the demolition should be held up or delayed by further evidence or enquiry.'[9]

8.2.2   Judicial review

The battery of prerogative remedies with which the High Court may control the decisions of public bodies,[10] may now be sought through a standardized procedure for judicial review introduced in 1977 on the recommendation of the Law Commission.[11] On such a review it is also possible to seek damages, injunctions and declarations.

(a)   The procedure for judicial review

The standard procedure for judicial review was introduced in 1977 by amendments to the rules of the Supreme Court.[12] Persons seeking a judicial review must first obtain leave to apply, by a preliminary application to a single Queen's Bench Division judge of the High Court. The application is *ex parte*, that is without serving proceedings on anyone else involved. The judge will only grant leave if he considers that this is justified by the applicant having a sufficient interest in the matter. If the application is more than three months after the event complained of, the court will only approve it if it considers that there is a good reason for extending the period. A preliminary application is dealt with without a hearing unless the applicant requires one. If the application is authorized it will be heard by a Divisional Court. All persons directly affected must then be served with notice of the proceedings and the court will hear anyone else who appears to it to be a proper person to be heard.

(b)   Decisions subject to review

One of the most difficult aspects of administrative law is recognizing exactly when the courts will be prepared to exercise their powers of review. Because of a reluctance to challenge the executive, judges used often to decline to review its decisions. Frequently this reluctance was rationalized by dividing decisions into judicial or quasi-judicial decisions, which the courts would review, and purely administrative decisions which they would not. This distinction was made particularly where the courts were considering an application for the remedy of *certiorari*.[13] However, the distinction is a difficult one to maintain. A court is essentially only concerned with resolving disputes in which it is impartial, but the very fact that in a dispute between administrators and members of the public, the administrators are very much involved in furthering their official ends, makes the need for independent supervision the more vital. Courts remain concerned not to interfere with matters which are properly within the discretion of an administrator, but they now generally are prepared to consider whether administrators have acted within their powers and followed appropriate procedures.

Although the courts will never challenge an Act of Parliament,[14] they will review the validity of *delegated legislation*. They did so in *Agricultural, Horticultural and Forestry Industry Training Board* v. *Aylesbury Mushrooms Ltd*.[15] The Board applied to the High Court for a ruling as to whether Aylesbury Mushrooms Ltd, were entitled to opt out of a training scheme which the Board had been set up to administer. It had been established under the Industrial Training Act 1964, by powers delegated to the Minister of Labour who was first required to consult with employers in the relevant industry, since these would be obliged to pay levies to support the scheme. Aylesbury Mushrooms were members of the Mushroom Growers' Association which was a specialist branch of the National Farmers Union. They claimed that the Association had not been consulted. The Act only required the Minister to consult those organizations appearing to him to be representative of employers. The Mushroom Growers' Association was only a small organization and if the Minister had chosen merely to consult with the National Farmers Union this would probably have been sufficient. However, the Minister actually had written separately to the Mushroom Growers' but his letter had never arrived. Therefore Donaldson J. held that the Minister had failed to carry out the consultations which he himself considered necessary and members of the Mushroom Growers' Association were not bound by the scheme.

The making of delegated legislation may involve a considerable element of discretion by an administrator. At the other extreme are acts which allow no, or virtually no, discretion and are known as *ministerial acts*. The courts will enforce a duty to carry out such an act. They may also award damages for harm which results from a breach of the duty. Thus if a local authority failed to record in a public register details of grants of planning permission which it had made, as required by the Town and Country Planning Act 1971,[16] it could be compelled to do so by the courts. If, because of such a breach of duty, someone bought land on the basis that there was no planning permission for development on neighbouring land, he might be able to recover damages for paying an inflated price.

Other administrative decisions are more clearly of a *judicial* or *quasi-judicial* nature, notably those affecting property rights, such as planning decisions and decisions to make compulsory purchase orders, both the original decisions and those made on appeal to a higher administrative body, such as the Secretary of State for the Department of the Environment, or anyone such as a planning inspector to whom the decision is delegated.[17]

Although decisions by the Secretary of State may generally only be reviewed on a statutory appeal, an application may be made for judicial review of an initial planning decision, especially where delay could be crucial.[18] However, the courts, in their discretion, may reject an application if they consider administrative appeal to the Secretary of State more appropriate.

8.2.3 Locus standi

Whether the courts are asked to intervene in an administrative decision on a statutory appeal or under their powers of judicial review, they will only act if the application is made by a person with *locus standi*, that is with some appropriate interest, or as both the Town and Country Planning Act 1971,[19] and the Acquisition of Land Act 1981,[20] put it, by 'a person aggrieved'. Exactly who has *locus standi* is another uncertain aspect of administrative law. On application for judicial review the answer may vary depending on the remedy sought. However, the general tendency today is for the courts to recognize increasingly those with more general interests in amenity. The restrictive approach was shown in *Buxton* v. *Minister of Housing and Local Government*,[21] in 1960. D. Heath & Son Ltd, a firm of mineral operators, sought planning consent to dig chalk at a site near Saffron Walden in Essex. Although the Saffron Walden Rural District Council refused permission and opposed an appeal to the Minister, when he allowed the appeal it did not wish to take the matter further. Neighbouring landowners did. It was they who applied to the High Court,[22] alleging that the Minister had improperly taken account of advice from the Minister of Agriculture which was obtained after the public inquiry on the matter was over, and that the decision was inconsistent with others on similar land nearby. Mr Buxton, who was an enthusiast in landscape gardening and ornithology, had spent considerable sums on his 250 acres adjacent to the proposed chalk pit. He also kept a herd of pedigree pigs and some breeding mares close by. Nevertheless, although he had been heard by the inspector who had in fact recommended against allowing the appeal, Salmon J. held that Mr Buxton and three other landowners had no standing to be heard. If they had no rights at common law to prevent the development, Town and Country Planning legislation gave them no new rights. Its purpose was 'to restrict development for the benefit of the public at large and not to confer new rights on any individual member of the public, whether they lived close to or far from the proposed development'.[23]

Now, as we have seen in Chapter 3, Section 3.5, in certain circumstances, interested persons have a right to be informed of impending development. They also have a right for their representations to be taken into account both at an initial planning decision and also on appeal.[24] Such individuals at any rate, now appear to have a right to appeal to the courts. Further it has been held that those who are merely allowed to speak at a public inquiry at the discretion of the inspector have similar rights. In *Turner* v. *Secretary of State*,[25] the Secretary of State called in an application to build two single-story dwellings in the grounds of Rutland Lodge, a renovated seventeenth-century mansion, in a conservation area at Petersham, because of possible detrimental impact on a famous view of Richmond Hill. After an inquiry, the Secretary of State allowed the scheme to go ahead. It was treated as reserved matters in respect of an earlier outline planning permission. Elstan Grey Turner, the Chairman of the Petersham Society, supported by other pressure groups including the National Trust and the Georgian Group had appeared at the inquiry and appealed to the High Court on the ground that the approved plan did not relate properly to the outline planning consent and should have been dealt with as a new application. Ackner J. ruled that there was no statutory provision in any event for appealing to the courts against a decision on reserved details which had been called in by the Secretary of State. However, he accepted that where there was a right of appeal to the courts for aggrieved persons these would include those who had been objectors at an inquiry. Where there is no statutory right of appeal, it now appears that groups such as residents' associations may apply to the courts for a judicial review.[26] The courts may now also be more ready to consider an application by an interested outsider for a judicial review although again there was once reluctance to do so.[27]

8.2.4   Powers of the courts

Even if a decision is subject to appeal or review, the powers of the courts are restricted. The decision may only be challenged on certain grounds. In particular findings of fact may generally not be disputed.[28] If the grounds are upheld, generally the most that a court can do is to quash the decision. It may not substitute its own, and it will often be obliged to refer the matter back to the original decision-maker with its directions on the limited point raised in the appeal.

(a)   Grounds for acting

An administrative decision may be *ultra vires*, that is outwith the powers of the persons making it, and thus invalid, because it involves an error of law. Often this is a result of the improper interpretation of a statute. The cases discussed in Chapter 3, Section 3.3, on development control, illustrate such disputes. A decision may be *ultra vires* because there was no jurisdiction to make it in the first place. For example a local planning authority would be acting outside its powers if it purported to make a tree preservation order,[29] to protect the shrubs growing in a famous herb garden. Often the error alleged will be over the rules under which a decision has been made, as where irrelevant considerations may have been taken into account in refusing an application for planning permission, or in imposing conditions on a grant of planning consent.[30] Procedural errors are also frequently challenged. These are illustrated in the next section.

Often a dispute which comes before a court over the interpretation of administrative powers is a joint matter of law and fact. For example in *Re Ripon (Highfield) Housing Order, 1939*[31] Ripon Borough Council made a compulsory purchase order which was confirmed by the Minister of Health on 20 acres of the grounds of a house called Highfield, with the intention of providing new housing. The council acted under statutory powers which did not allow land to be taken if it formed 'part of any park, garden or pleasure ground, or [was] otherwise required for the amenity or convenience of any house'.[32] The occupant of Highfield was an old lady of unsound mind but those looking after her affairs and those entitled to the property after her challenged the order. The dispute turned on whether the land to be acquired was part of a *park*. The Court of Appeal held that it was, even though the land was let for the agricultural purpose of grazing cattle. Therefore, the order was invalid. The question of what constituted a park was one of law, even although it depended upon such facts as the form of the land and the manner in which it was used.

Generally on appeal a court will not consider new evidence but will only review a decision as to the interpretation of facts established by the person making the original decision. In *Ashbridge Investments Ltd* v. *Minister of Housing and Local Government*,[33] Stalybridge Borough Council made a compulsory purchase order for slum clearance of some houses.[34] A dispute arose over whether a certain building was a *house* within the meaning of the act, as this would affect the compensation payable. The owners sought an order to quash the order on this point. When Charles J. ruled that he was entitled to hear new evidence on the matter, the Minister successfully appealed to the Court of Appeal where it was held that a court could only intervene in such a case if the Minister

has acted on no evidence; or if he has come to a conclusion to which on the evidence he could not reasonably come; or if he has given a wrong interpretation to the words of the statute; or if he has taken into consideration matters which he ought not to have taken into account, or vice versa; or has otherwise gone wrong in law.

The nearest that a court will go in challenging a policy decision by an administrator is where, in an extreme case, it will strike down a decision as *unreasonable*. This may be where evidence has been interpreted unreasonably, or where the decision itself 'is so unreasonable that no reasonable authority could ever have come to it'.[35] In practice where a court wishes to quash a decision which it regards as unreasonable, it will often do so by finding some other ground, in particular that the decision was based on irrelevant considerations. However, a court may sometimes openly strike out an administrative decision as unreasonable. In *J.A. Hall and Co. Ltd* v. *Shoreham Urban District Council*,[36] Halls were importers of sand and gravel with premises on a strip of land at Shoreham in Sussex between the main Brighton road and the estuary of the river Adur. They obtained planning permission to erect plant for making concrete and a new access to the main road, but subject to conditions that the new access should only be temporary until they constructed an ancillary road over the entire frontage of the site, at their own expense, making it available for access by occupiers of neighbouring land. Glyn Jones J. refused a declaration that the conditions were void, but the Court of Appeal held that, although in themselves these were imposed for purposes which were appropriate from a planning point of view, to improve traffic flow on the main road, they were void because they laid an unreasonable burden on Halls, in effect to create a public road at their own expense. However the Court of Appeal went on to hold that because the conditions were invalid, so was the planning permission to which they were attached.[37]

(b) Effects of judicial action

In some circumstances a court order may have a positive effect. Thus a declaration that a particular proposal does not amount to development, or a ruling to the same effect on an appeal from a decision by the Secretary of State on such an issue,[38] provides a safe basis for carrying out the relevant proposal. Again, if after a planning authority has granted outline planning permission, it rejects the reserved details on grounds which the courts rule to be inconsistent with the outline permission, the decision of the courts serves as a licence to carry out the development without the need for further permission.[39] On the other hand, as we have seen in the case of *Hall* v. *Shoreham Urban District Council*,[40] a successful appeal against the terms of a particular planning condition may result in the planning consent to which the condition was attached being quashed as well. Thus if a developer is given planning permission to carry out development subject to an invalid condition that he should build a public road, or lay out a public park, it will be risky to challenge the condition in case it results in losing the right to build at all. Normally a successful appeal against an administrative decision results in the case being referred back to the original decision-maker.[41] Sometimes it will then be decided differently, but often the conclusion will be the same.

NOTES: SECTION 8.2

1. *Ante* p. 380f.
2. *Ante* Chapter 3, Section 3.3.

3. *Ante* Chapter 5, Section 5.1.

4. Town and Country Planning Act 1971, s. 245 (1) and Acquisition of Land Act 1981, s. 23 (4).

5. Town and Country Planning Act 1971, s. 242 (1) and Acquisition of Land Act 1981, s. 25.

6. *Anisminic Ltd* v. *Foreign Compensation Commission* [1969] 2 A.C. 147, H.L.

7. *R.* v. *Secretary of State for the Environment ex parte Ostler* [1977] Q.B. 122, C.A. following *Smith* v. *East Elloe Rural District Council* [1956] A.C. 736, H.L.

8. Under Highways Act 1959, Sched. 2, Paragraphs 2 and 4, now superceded by provisions in the Highways Act 1980.

9. *R.* v. *Secretary of State for the Environment ex parte Ostler, supra* note 7, *per* Lord Denning M.R. at p. 136.

10. *Ante* p. 381.

11. Law Commission (1971) Working Paper 40.

12. Order 53 (3), substituted by Rules of the Supreme Court (Amendment No. 3) 1977, S.I. 1977, No. 1955 and further amended by Rules of the Supreme Court (Amendment No. 4) 1980, S.I. 1980, No. 2000. The procedure now has direct statutory authority under Supreme Court Act 1981, s. 31.

13. For example, *R* v. *Electricity Commissioners* [1924] 1 K.B. 171, for *certiorari* generally see *ante* p. 381.

14. *Pickin* v. *British Railways Board* [1974] A.C. 765, H.L. see *ante* p. 19.

15. *Agricultural, Horticultural and Forestry Industry Training Board* v. *Aylesbury Mushrooms Ltd.* [1972] 1 W.L.R. 190.

16. Town and Country Planning Act 1971, s. 34 (1). See *ante* p. 153.

17. Town and Country Planning Act (Determination of appeals by appointed persons) (Prescribed classes) Regulations, 1981 S.I. 1981, No. 804. See *post* p. 400.

18. *R.* v. *Hillingdon London Borough Council, ex parte Royco Homes Ltd* [1974] 1 Q.B. 721. And see *ante* p. 124.

19. Town and Country Planning Act 1971, s. 245 (1).

20. Acquisition of Land Act 1981, s. 23 (1).

21. *Buxton* v. *Minister of Housing and Local Government* [1961] 1 Q.B. 278.

22. Under Town and Country Planning Act 1959, s. 31 (1)(b); now superceded by Town and Country Planning Act 1971, s. 245 (1)(b).

23. *Supra* note 21, at p. 283.

24. Town and Country Planning Act 1971, s. 29 (2) and S.I. 1974, No. 419 Rules 7 (1) and 12 (2); and S.I. 1974, No. 420, Rules 9 (1) and 14 (1).

25. *Turner* v. *Secretary of State* (1973) 28 P. & C.R. 123.

26. *Covent Garden Community Association Ltd* v. *Greater London Council* [1981] J.P.L. 183.

27. *Gregory* v. *Camden London Borough Council* [1966] 1 W.L.R. 899.

28. *Ante* p. 49.

29. Town and Country Planning Act 1971, s. 60, and see *ante* p. 141f.

30. *Ante* Chapt. 3, Section 3.3.4.

31. *Re Ripon (Highfield) Housing Order* [1939] 3 All E.R. 548.

32. Under Housing Act 1936, ss. 74 and 75.

33. *Ashbridge Investments Ltd* v. *Minister of Housing and Local Government* [1965] 1 W.L.R. 1320.

34. Housing Act 1957, s. 43 (2).

35. *Associated Provincial Picture Houses Ltd* v. *Wednesbury Corporation* [1948] 1 Q.B. 223, C.A., *per* Lord Greene M.R. at p. 230.

36. *J.A. Hall and Co Ltd* v. *Shoreham Urban District Council* [1964] 1 W.L.R. 241, C.A.

37. See *ante* p. 124.
38. Town and Country Planning Act 1971, s. 247.
39. *Hamilton* v. *West Sussex County Council* [1958] 2 Q.B. 286, but compare *Shemara Ltd* v. *Luton Corporation* [1967] 18 P. & C.R. 520.
40. *Ante* note 36. See also *Kingsway Investments (Kent) Ltd* v. *Kent County Council* [1971] A.C. 72, *ante* p. 124.
41. See, for example, *Birmingham Corporation* v. *Minister of Housing and Local Government and Habib Ullah* [1964] 1 Q.B. 178, *ante* p. 49f.

8.3 Procedural safeguards

An important aspect of administrative law is the function of the courts in ensuring that public officials scrupulously follow correct procedures in exercising their duties where these affect the rights of the citizen, and particularly the private landowner. For many forms of administrative decision, particularly administrative appeals, procedural rules are laid down in statutory instruments. A Standing Council on Tribunals, which must be consulted on new rules for statutory tribunals, provides a consistent standard for administrative rules of procedure generally.[1] Even where statutory rules have been observed, the courts may treat a decision as being contrary to an underlying principle of natural justice, *audi alteram partem*, that a person whose rights are affected by an administrative decision is entitled to a fair hearing. In *Hambledon and Chiddingfold Parish Councils* v. *Secretary of State for the Environment*,[2] the Secretary of State granted Surrey County Council permission for a gypsy caravan site. There had been a public inquiry at which the two parish councils had opposed the scheme. After the inquiry the Secretary of State corresponded with the interested parties over the need for suitable drainage. The parish councils pointed out that the county had an alternative site where money could be saved on drainage. The county then informed the Secretary of State that this site was an additional one and not, as they had originally stated, an alternative. The parish councils were given no chance to comment on this policy change. The inquiry was held and the Secretary of State's decision was made under the Town and Country Planning (Inquiry Procedure) Rules, 1974.[3] In granting permission for the site, the Secretary of State followed his inspector's recommendation. Under the rules he was only expressly required to give objectors an opportunity to comment on new matters raised after the inquiry if he rejected the inspector's recommendations. However, when the parish councils applied to the High Court for the permission to be quashed, Ackner J. did quash it on the grounds that the rules of natural justice demanded that the parish councils be given a chance to comment on the crucial policy change.

8.3.1 The right to a fair hearing

What amounts to a fair hearing varies with different decisions. However, standardized rules are laid down for some, notably for the conduct of public inquiries dealing with appeals against the refusal of planning permission by a local planning authority,[4] and against objections to a compulsory purchase order.[5] Most planning appeals are now decided by an inspector from the departmental panel who will be the person appointed to hold the public inquiry.[6] The rules for appeals of this sort provide a typical example of procedural safeguards.[7] Thus the appellant must be notified of representations by those who have a statutory right to objection,[8] and normally given forty-two days' notice of the date, time and place of the inquiry.[9] Normally at least twenty-eight days before the hearing, the local planning authority must serve a notice setting out their reasons for objecting to the appeal and must make available for inspection maps, plans and other documents to which it intends to refer.[10] If a government department,[11] or any other local authority,[12] oppose the appeal, the appellant is entitled to require that they send a representative to give evidence at the inquiry. At the inquiry the appellant is entitled to be represented by a lawyer or anyone else he chooses,[13] to call his own witnesses and to cross examine others either himself or through his representative.[14] After the inquiry the inspector will normally make a site visit and at this the appellant is entitled to be present.[15] If the inspector proposes to take into account any new evidence in making his decision, he must allow the appellant to comment on this.[16] The appellant must be notified of the decision together with the reasons for it.[17] Similar rights are provided for other interested parties.

Although detailed statutory rules are now common, where none are laid down for a particular decision the safeguards may be much less. The person affected will, however, generally be entitled to know the case against him and to make comments on it.[18] He will not necessarily be entitled to a hearing in public or even an oral hearing of any sort where he may attend to speak on his own behalf and cross-examine his opponents either by himself or with representatives.[19] Often a person affected by an administrative decision may not wish to stand on his statutory rights in any case, but will prefer a speedy decision by written representations.[20]

8.3.2 The rule against bias

A second underlying rule of natural justice which may be enforced by the courts is known as the rule against bias and is designed to prevent bias on the part of any decision-maker. The courts are particularly concerned to disqualify a decision-maker who has any financial interest in a decision. In the Victorian case of *Dimes* v. *Grand Junction Canal Co. Proprietors*,[21] the canal company brought a successful action against Dimes who had tried to stop its operations. The decision was upheld on appeal to the Lord Chancellor, Lord Cottenham. Because Lord Cottenham owned shares in the canal company, the House of Lords set his decision aside, even though, as Lord Campbell commented no one could suppose that Lord Cottenham was 'in the remotest degree influenced by the interest that he had in this concern'. The House of Lords in any event went on to reach the same decision itself!

Under the rule against bias a decision on a planning appeal would be quashed if it was made by an inspector who himself owned shares in a company which was applying to develop the appeal site. A decision would probably also be quashed if the inspector owned land nearby, whose value might be increased or impaired if the development were carried out or not. However, an indirect financial interest may not necessarily result in a decision being quashed. It would not seem to be fatal to a decision if the person making it owns shares or other property connected with the decision, not in his own right, but merely as a trustee.[22] Apart from financial interest in a decision, bias may take many forms, and it is often difficult to tell in advance whether the courts would regard it as sufficiently serious for the decision which it affected to be quashed. In R. v. *Hendon Rural District Council ex parte Chorley*,[23] the rural district council gave permission for the Old Brewery Stables at Great Stanmore, Middlesex to be converted into a garage, petrol filling station, restaurant and tea garden with bathing pool. Mr Chorley, a barrister, who lived opposite at the Rookery, had the decision quashed by the High Court under an order of *certiorari*. The developer, a Mr Archer, had a provisional contract to buy the Old Brewery, which was being sold by a firm of estate agents whose sole member was Councillor F. H. Cross. The councillor had been present at the council meeting approving the proposal and at a subsequent meeting when a motion to rescind the permission was lost. For good measure, he was a member of the Plans and Highway Committee which recommended the scheme to the main council. The part played by the councillor at the meetings was not very active, but he was present at least, at the main council meetings. The initial decision was reached unanimously without discussion and the Divisional Court treated him as having taken part in it.

A person complaining of bias does not need to show that the decision-maker was actually affected. The courts have swung between two forms of a more objective test. The stricter of these, expressed by Devlin L.J., is that it must be possible to infer bias 'from the circumstances, not upon the basis of the impression that might reasonably be left on the minds of the party aggrieved or the public at large'.[24] On this view where, say, the chairman of a planning committee was the brother of a director of a firm applying for development consent, a decision of the committee to grant the application might be upheld, provided it was clear to the court that the chairman was unaware of his brother's involvement. On the alternative view, provided that the relationship was known to the interested parties at the time the decision was made, that might be enough to defeat it. This view stems from a well known dictum of Lord Hewart C.J., that 'it is of fundamental importance that justice should both be done and be manifestly seen to be done'.[25]

Situations may arise where a decision has to be made by a particular official who happens to have some personal interest in the matter. For reasons of necessity his decision would probably not be challenged even if the interest was a fundamental one, as where the Secretary of State for the Department of the Environment had to decide whether to confirm a compulsory purchase order on land he himself owned.[26] In certain cases statute defines where a person with a particular interest in a decision may or may not be involved in making it. Thus the Local Government Act 1972,[27] makes it an offence for any member of a local authority to take part in the consideration of or discussion by the authority on any contract, proposed contract or other matter in which he has a pecuniary interest direct or indirect. This expressly includes any interest of his spouse, provided they are living together, but not membership of or employment by any public body, nor any interest which the member has simply as a ratepayer, inhabitant of the area, or consumer of water or other goods or services provided to the general public. A decision taken in breach of these requirements would probably be quashed as contrary to the rules of natural justice, but decisions not offending the section might also be quashed, as where a councillor had a personal, rather than a financial, interest in a proposal.

Although financial or personal bias may lead to a decision being quashed, prejudice towards a particular result may be inevitable. It has been said that 'a judge who tries a theft charge may safely be assumed to be against theft'.[28] Similarly a government minister may be expected to make decisions in accordance with predetermined policies. He must conscientiously consider whether an exception should be made to a policy in any case where it is relevant, but he is then free to apply the policy. In *Franklin* v. *Minister of Town and Country Planning*,[29] the Minister, Lewis Silkin, confirmed an order designating land for Stevenage New Town. The order was challenged by objectors whose land would be affected, but the Court of Appeal and the House of Lords held that there was no breach of the rules of natural justice. Indeed the House of Lords held that the Minister was carrying out an administrative function where the rules of natural justice did not apply. However, the New Towns Act 1946, under which the order was made, did require that an inquiry be held, that the report of the inquiry, including objections, should be considered and that the Minister's mind should not be 'so foreclosed that he gave no genuine consideration to them'. Although the Minister had made clear his firm intention to build the new town at a public meeting before the inquiry, there was still no reason to doubt that he had considered the objections adequately.

NOTES: SECTION 8.3

1. Tribunals and Inquiries Act 1971, s. 1.
2. *Hambledon and Chiddingford Parish Councils* v. *Secretary of State for the Environment* (1976) J.P.L. 502.
3. S.I. 1974, No. 419.
4. S.I. 1974, Nos 419 and 420.
5. S.I. 1976, No. 746.
6. S.I. 1981, No. 804.
7. S.I. 1974, No. 420.
8. Ibid. Rule 4 (1).
9. Ibid. Rule 5.
10. Ibid. Rule 7.
11. Ibid. Rule 10.
12. Ibid. Rule 11.
13. Ibid. Rule 9 (3).
14. Ibid. Rule 12 (3).
15. Ibid. Rule 13 (3).
16. Ibid. Rule 14 (1).
17. Ibid. Rule 16 (1).
18. *Ridge* v. *Baldwin* [1964] A.C. 40, H.L.
19. *R.* v. *Housing Appeal Tribunal* [1920] 3 K.B. 334.
20. Town and Country Planning Act 1971, s. 36 (4) and Department of the Environment Circular 38/81, Para. 10.
21. *Dimes* v. *Grand Junction Canal Co. Proprietors* (1852) 3 Ho. Lords C. 759.
22. *R.* v. *Rand* (1866) 1 L.R. Q.B. 230.
23. *R.* v. *Hendon Rural District Council ex parte Chorley* [1933] 2 K.B. 696.
24. *R.* v. *Barnsley Licencing Justices* [1960] 2 Q.B. 167 C.A., at p. 187.
25. *R.* v. *Sussex Justices ex parte McCarthy* [1924] 1 K.B. 256, at p. 259, and see *Metropolitan Properties Co. (F.G.C.) Ltd* v. *Lannon* [1969] 1 Q.B. 577, C.A.
26. De Smith, S.A. and Evans, J.M. (1980) *Judicial Review of Administrative Action*, 4th edn, Stevens, London, p. 277.
27. Local Government Act 1972, s. 94 and 95.
28. *Gee* v. *Freeman* (1959) 16 D.L.R. (2d) 65, *per* Wilson J. at p. 74.
29. *Franklin* v. *Minister of Town and Country Planning* [1948] A.C. 87; H.L.

CONCLUSION: ALTERNATIVES TO THE LAW

No system of law can by itself create an attractive landscape or distribute control over land so as to satisfy everyone in society. The more that legislators try to trap elusive qualities, such as beauty or amenity, in a framework of rules, the less clear the law becomes, and the more initiative is stifled.

We have seen in this book that in England the basis of land law is still a mosaic of private rights over land and that to a large extent the law treats interests in land as financial assets of those with specific property rights. Modern public forms of control restrict and frustrate the landowner, particularly where he wants to carry out development, but it does not necessarily satisfy those members of the public who are ardently concerned to improve the quality of the environment and to provide for its enjoyment to be shared to the fullest.

(a) Amplifying the public voice

In the field of public control of land perhaps the most valuable contribution which the law can make is that of ensuring that decisions are reached openly so that all relevant issues are taken into account and that what members of the public themselves want is not ignored. Administrators and some lawyers,[1] often see public involvement in land use as a source of inconvenience and delay. However, sensible public participation may improve the quality of new schemes of development. For example at a public inquiry into the line of a proposed road diversion, where the Department of Transport provides full facilities for objectors by drawing up their alternative suggestions and advising the inquiry on the relative advantages and disadvantages of these, it has been known for the eventual result to be generally more acceptable to interested parties, for the quality of the local environment to be less drastically impaired, and even for the scheme to end up cheaper than originally proposed.

The large sums of money spent on public inquiries are intended at least to give those who are interested in the proposed development an opportunity to air their views, which will make them readier to accept the eventual decision, whatever that is. Unfortunately where objectors are not allowed to raise what they regard as key issues they may end up more frustrated than ever. Thus in *Bushell* v. *Secretary of State for the Environment*,[2] Mr Bushell and other objectors opposed to the scheme for a new motorway connection between the M42 and M40 motorways in Worcestershire, took part in a public inquiry on the scheme which lasted 100 days. When the scheme was later approved by the Secretary of State on the recommendation of his inspector the objectors applied to the High Court for it to be quashed on the grounds that neither the inquiry nor the eventual decision had complied with the rules of natural justice. At the inquiry the inspector had refused to allow the objectors to cross examine departmental witnesses so as to challenge material known as the red book which contained data on the need for the relevant connection in the first place. After the inquiry, new data was published by the Department which showed that the existing roads in the area could accommodate much more traffic than the Department had previously claimed, but this did not deflect the Secretary of State from his decision and he refused to re-open the inquiry to consider it. The objectors' reception by the courts was mixed. To start with Sir Douglas Frank Q.C., sitting as a Deputy High Court judge, dismissed their application. However, it was allowed in the Court of Appeal by Lord Denning M.R. and Shaw L.J., with Templeman L.J. dissenting. It was finally rejected by four members of the House of Lords with Lord Edmund Davies dissenting. The material was in what Lord Diplock described as a 'grey area',[3] but in the view of the House of Lords it was rightly to be regarded as a matter of policy for which the inquiry was not a proper forum for debate. It is such fundamental policy issues as whether a new road, or on a larger scale a new airport, the transformation of the Vale of Belvoir by coal mining, or a new system of atomic power stations, are required at all, which give rise to the highest popular feelings. If public inquiries do not provide a suitable forum in which to resolve such matters, the alternative of a few hours debate in Parliament is certainly inadequate. A solution can only be found in the political arena and not by the law. In the meantime the role of the press and other media and of pressure groups which are able to present their case coherently through these means may be the most important aspect of controlling such decisions on land use so that they accord with what the public themselves, as opposed to their servants, perceive as the public interest.

(b) Independent arbiters

In making controversial decisions on land use, public bodies are often bound to be prejudiced.[4] Other public bodies may seem tarred with the same brush whether they are a higher administrative tier such as the Department of the Environment dealing with planning appeals from a local planning authority,[5] or the courts themselves. One development which provides an apparently more independent element is the system of *ombudsmen*. The first of these was the *Parliamentary Commissioner* set up under the Parliamentary Commissioner Act 1967. Separate Commissioners for Local Administration were set up by the Local Government Act 1974, Part III. The commissioners functions are to investigate and report on central or local government administration and to recommend redress. They have powers to order the production of documents and to call and cross examine witnesses. However, their terms of reference are limited to matters which may not be resolved in the courts or elsewhere. The Parliamentary Commissioner can only investigate cases referred to him by a Member of Parliament, and normally a complaint to the Commissioners for Local Administration should be referred through a local councillor. Crucially the commissioners cannot force any body which they declare guilty of maladministration to make amends but can only hold it up for political action by others.

(c) Improvements in private law

To some extent, changes in private law could contribute to the conservation and improvement of the landscape. Thus, greater flexibility might be possible in creating rights for private landowners to go onto neighbouring land so as to enable them to carry out maintenance work or even new development on their own land.[6] Again greater government encouragement could be given to arrangements for holding land with the specific purpose of conserving and enhancing its amenity value for the community at large, for example by granting greater tax concessions, notably on value added tax,[7] or by widening the concept of the charitable trust,[8] so as to allow land holders, who see themselves as stewards of their land and buildings, to transfer these to charitable trusts whilst retaining some control themselves.

Perhaps an extreme example of how the law could be used to uphold amenity values in the landscape is suggested by the unsuccessful attempt in the United States of the Sierra Club of California to prevent federal government approval of a recreation complex to be developed by Walt Disney Enterprises in the Mineral King Valley, once a centre of mining but now an area of natural beauty next to the Sequoia National Park. The United States District Court allowed the Club a preliminary injunction on the basis of their 'special interest in the conservation and the sound maintenance of the national parks, game refuges and forests of the country'. Although the Federal Appeal Court and then the majority of the Supreme Court of the United States subsequently ruled that the Club did not have sufficient legal interest to maintain its claim, three members of the Supreme Court dissented, and Mr Justice Douglas suggested a federal rule which would have allowed environmental issues to be litigated before the courts in the name of the environmental object worthy of preservation,[9]

Those who hike it, fish it, hunt it, camp in it, frequent it, or visit it merely to sit in solitude and wonderment are legitimate spokesmen for it, whether they may be few or many. Those who have that intimate relation with the inanimate object about to be injured, polluted, or otherwise despoiled are its legitimate spokesman . . . [B]efore these priceless bits . . . (such as a valley, an alpine meadow, river, or a lake) are forever lost or are so transformed as to be reduced to the eventual rubble of our urban environment, the voice of the existing beneficiaries of these environmental wonders should be heard.

NOTES: CONCLUSION

1. Heap, D. (1975) The land and the development or the turmoil and the torment, *The Hamlyn Lectures 1975*, Stevens, London.
2. *Bushell* v. *Secretary of State for the Environment* [1981] A.C. 75, H.L.
3. Ibid. at p. 98.
4. For example, *Franklin* v. *Minister of Town and Country Planning* [1948] A.C. 87, H.L., *ante* p. 402.
5. *Ante* p. 399f.
6. *Ante* p. 338.
7. *Ante* p. 98.
8. *Ante* p. 188.
9. U.S. Supreme Courts Reports (1971) 31 L.Ed 2d 636, at p. 648.

SUGGESTIONS
FOR FURTHER READING

1. Original materials

Most original legal materials, that is legislation and case law may usually only be found in a law library. However, local government offices and large public libraries often do contain some.

(a) Legislation

Statutes are published individually by Her Majesty's Stationery Office (HMSO) which produces them in one or two bound annual volumes and also provides annually updated indexes. Statutes are also available in forms which are more easy to use. Thus HMSO itself publishes all statutes under headings in a loose-leaf collection called *Statutes in Force*. These are updated so that the current text contains all amendments. The law publishers, Sweet & Maxwell, provide annotated *Current Law Statutes* in a number of issues throughout the year which are bound into annual volumes. *Halsbury's Statutes* is an annotated encyclopaedia of statutes under headings, with a regular system of updating by year books containing new statutes. Alterations to previous statute law is found by means of cumulative supplements.

Statutory Instruments are published by HMSO which also produces annual bound volumes with annually updated indexes to show what instruments are currently in force. *Halsbury's Statutory Instruments* provides a selection of the main statutory instruments under subject headings with year books and cumulative supplements.

(b) Case law

English cases are reported by barristers in a number of series of reports. Before 1864, individual barristers published private collections of cases in their own names. These varied much in usefulness and accuracy. These old *nominate reports* have been gathered together in a series known as the *English Reports*.

From 1865, a comprehensive system of reporting noteworthy cases was developed by a body which became The *Incorporated Council of Law Reporting*. Their reports are known as *The Law Reports* and are revised by the judges concerned before publication. The Council also issues reports in unrevised form as *The Weekly Law Reports*, although despite this name there is often not space to publish a case until long after it has been decided. The *Weekly Law Reports* are bound into annual volumes and volume 1 includes cases which are not repeated in *The Law Reports*.

Other general series of law reports provide duplicate sources, with some cases not found elsewhere, notably *The All England Law Reports*, produced by Butterworth, the law publishers. In addition, there are series of specialized reports, such as the *Property and Compensation Reports* including many cases on planning law and compulsory purchase, especially those heard in the Lands Tribunal. The *Local Government Reports* provides a service with statutes and statutory instruments as well as cases relating to local government. Much of this material is concerned with town and country planning.

Apart from law reports, decided cases may be summarized in journals. *The Journal of Planning and Environment Law* includes summaries of planning cases in the Courts and Lands Tribunal, and also planning decisions of the Secretary of State for the Department of the Environment and other departments and ministries, and reports on local government maladministration by the Local Government Commissioners.

The English and Empire Digest is an encyclopaedia with summaries of all English cases and many from other jurisdictions, under topical headings, with annual supplements. Recent legal developments in case law may also be found through the monthly issues of *Current Law*, published by Sweet & Maxwell. These are reprinted in annual volumes with developments in the year summarized under headings. The current law citators and annual supplements also provide a system for updating case law, by citing any occasion when a previous case has been considered on appeal or in a later case, whether it has been overruled or doubted, affirmed or distinguished. The *Indexes to the Law Reports* include cases reported in various series and details of the effect of recent cases upon earlier case law.

(c) EEC sources of law

The Official Journal of the EEC containing EEC legislation has been published in English since 1973. Earlier legislation has now also been published in English. The *Official Journal* is published in two series. The 'C' Series contains information and the 'L' Series contains actual legislation. Cases decided by the European Court are officially reported in the *European Court Reports*. The European Law Centre publishes the informal *Common Market Law Reports* and these include some cases decided in national courts.

2. Secondary materials

The non-lawyers who wish to find the law on a particular subject, and often the lawyers as well, will rely mainly on secondary materials. In particular there are *encyclopaedias* and *text books*. *Halsbury's Laws* is an encyclopaedia covering the entire English law under subject headings with regular loose-leaf cumulative supplements. Sweet & Maxwell publish a series of loose-leaf encyclopaedias in their *Local Government Library* series, containing annotated statutes, statutory instruments and other materials, on such subjects as local government law in general, town and country planning, housing and highways. The same publishers produce the *Common Law Library* series consisting of substantial practitioner's books on various areas which are still dominated by case law, notably contract and tort.

The following are some specific references to practitioners' works and textbooks concerned with the areas of law dealt with in this book.

Chapter 1: The legal background

Central and local government

Byrne, T. (1981) *Local Government in Britain*, Penguin, England. Harmondsworth.
Cross, C.A. (1981) *Principles of Local Government Law*, 6th edn, Sweet & Maxwell, London.
De Smith, S.A. (1981) *Constitutional and Administrative Law*, 4th edn (eds H. Street and R. Brazier) Penguin, Harmondsworth.

The English court system

Ingman, T. (1983) *The English Legal Process*, Financial Training, London.
Walker, R.J. (1980) *Walker and Walker, The English Legal System*, 5th edn, Butterworth, London.

Legal materials

Bennion, F. (1980) *Statute Law*, Oyez, London.
Cross, R. (1976) *Statutory Interpretation*, Butterworth, London.
Cross, R. (1977) *Precedent in English Law*, 3rd edn, Clarendon Press, Oxford.

European Community law

Mathijsen, P.R.R.F. (1980) *A guide to European Community Law*, 3rd edn, Sweet & Maxwell, London.
Encyclopaedia of European Community Law, Sweet & Maxwell, London.

Chapter 2: The law and physical boundaries

See the books listed under Development Control in Chapter 3, and under Chapter 4;
Also see:
Aldridge, T.M. (1982) *Boundaries, Walls and Fences*, 5th edn, Oyez, London.

Chapter 3: Public law and the control of land use

See generally, *Encyclopaedia of Town and Country Planning Law*, Sweet & Maxwell, London.

Public Authorities

See the books listed under *Central and Local government* in Chapter 1.

Development control

Alder, J. (1979) *Development Control*, Sweet & Maxwell, London.
Grant, M. (1982) *Urban Planning Law*, Sweet & Maxwell, London.

Heap, D. (1982) *An Outline of Planning Law*, Sweet & Maxwell, London.
McAuslan, P. (1980) *The Ideologies of Planning Law*, Pergamon, Oxford.

Chapter 4: Private law and the control of land use

See generally,

Burn, E.H. (1982) *Cheshire and Burn's Modern Law of Real Property* 13th edn, Butterworth, London.
Gray, K.S. and Symes, P.D. (1981) *Real Property and Real People*, Butterworth, London.
Megarry, R.E. (1982) in *Manual of the Law of Real Property*, 6th edn, (ed. D. Hayton Stevens, London.
Riddall, J.G. (1983) *Introduction to Land Law*, 3rd edn, Butterworth, London.

Easements and profits

Jackson, P. (1978) *The Law of Easements and Profits*, Butterworth, London.

Mortgages

Fairest, P.B. (1980) *Mortgages*, 2nd edn, Sweet & Maxwell, London.

Restrictive Covenants

Newsom, G.H. (1982) *Preston and Newsom's Restrictive Covenants Affecting Freehold Land*, Sweet & Maxwell, London.

Chapter 5: Acquiring and extinguishing control of land

Acquisition by public authorities

Corfield, F.V. and Carnwath, A.J.A. (1978) *Compulsory Acquisition and Compensation*, Butterworth, London.

Private transfer of land

See here the general works listed for Chapter 4 and also:

Barnsley, D.G. and Smith, P.W. (1982) *Barnsley's Conveyancing Law and Practice*, 2nd edn, Butterworth London.
Farrand, J.T. (1980) *Contract and Conveyance*, Oyez, London.
Rowton Simpson, S. (1976) *Land Law and Registration*, University Press, Cambridge.

Chapters 6 and 7: Legal responsibility for harm in land use

Criminal law

Smith, J.C. and Hogan, B. (1983) *Criminal Law*, 5th edn, Butterworth, London.

Tort

Clerk and Lindsell on Torts (1982) 15th edn, Sweet & Maxwell, London (The
   Common Law Library).
Street, H. (1983) The Law of Torts, 7th edn, Butterworth, London.

Contract

Chitty on Contracts (1983) 25th edn, Sweet & Maxwell, London (The Common Law
   Library).
Furmston, M.P. (1981) Cheshire and Fifoot's Law of Contract, 10th edn,
   Butterworth, London.

Chapter 8: Legal powers and their availability

Craig, P.P. (1983) Administrative Law, Sweet & Maxwell, London.
Wade, H.W.R. (1983) Administrative Law, 5th edn, Clarendon Press, Oxford.
Yardley, D.C.M. (1981) Principles of Administrative Law, Butterworth, London.

TABLE OF CASES

A page number printed in square brackets thus [123], indicates that the case does not actually appear on that page, but that the note where the case does appear refers to the text on that page, e.g. Cousens *v*. Rose [201], 209 n. 37.

TABLE OF STATUTES

A page number printed in square brackets thus [123], indicates that the Act or section in question does not actually appear on that page, but that the note where the Act or section does appear refers to the text on that page, e.g. Town and Country Planning Act 1971, s.55 [95], 106 n.30

TABLE OF DELEGATED LEGISLATION

A page number printed in square brackets thus [123], indicates that the legislation does not actually appear on that page, but that the note where the legislation does appear refers to the text on that page, e.g. Church of England Ordnance (No. 18 of 1559) [56], 64 n.1.

INDEX

Page numbers in *italic* refer to main entries